BLACK JETS

BLACK JETS

The Development and Operation of America's Most Secret Warplanes

General Editor
David Donald

AIRtime Publishing Inc.
United States of America • United Kingdom

Published by AIRtime Publishing Inc.
USA: 120 East Avenue, Norwalk, CT 06851
Tel (203) 838-7979 • Fax (203) 838-7344
email: airpower@airtimepublishing.com
www.airtimepublishing.com
UK: CAB Intl. Centre, Nosworthy Way, Wallingford OX10 8DE
Tel +44 (0)1491 829230 • Fax +44 (0)1491 829334
email: airpower@btinternet.com

© 1994, 1997 Aerospace Publishing Ltd.
© 1999, 2000, 2001, 2002, 2003 AIRtime Publishing Inc.
Photos and illustrations are copyright of their respective owners

ISBN 1-880588-67-6

Editors
  David Donald and Robert Hewson

Contributing Authors
  Bill Sweetman, additional material by
          David Donald and Brad Elward (B-2)
  Robert F. Dorr, additional material by
          David Donald, Jon Lake and Warren Thompson (F-117)
  Paul F. Crickmore (A-12, YF-12 and SR-71)
  Chris Pocock (U-2)
  James C. Goodall and Nora D. Goodall (Appendix A)
  David Donald (Appendix B)

  Additional material by David Donald and Rob Hewson

Artists
  Mike Badrocke, Chris Davey, Keith Fretwell, Mark Rolfe, Mark Styling

Jacket Design
  Zaur Eylanbekov

Controller
  Linda Deangelis

Publisher
  Mel Williams

PRINTED IN SINGAPORE

To order more copies of this book or any of our other titles call toll free within the United States 1 800 359-3003, or visit our website at: *www.airtimepublishing.com*

Other books by AIRtime Publishing include:
  United States Military Aviation Directory
  Carrier Aviation Air Power Directory
  Superfighters The Next Generation of Combat Aircraft
  Phantom: Spirit in the Skies Updated and Expanded Edition
  Tupolev Bombers
  Russian Military Aviation Directory (Fall/Autumn 2003)

Retail distribution via:

Direct from Publisher
AIRtime Publishing Inc.
PO Box 5074, Westport, CT 06881, USA
Tel (203) 838-7979 • Fax (203) 838-7344
Toll-free 1 800 359-3003

USA & Canada
Specialty Press Inc.
39966 Grand Avenue, North Branch
MN 55056
Tel (651) 277-1400 • Fax (651) 277-1203
Toll-free 1 800 895-4585

UK & Europe
Midland Counties Publications
4 Watling Drive
Hinckley LE10 3EY
Tel 01455 233 747 • Fax 01455 233 737

INTRODUCTION

This unique book is based on four highly detailed reports first published during the 1990s in World Air Power Journal and Wings of Fame. These profiled the development, service history and technical aspects of the F-117, B-2, U-2 and SR-71 programmes. In the preparation this special volume, much new information has been added including system, weapon and aircraft upgrades, plus combat reports from Operations Allied Force, Enduring Freedom and Iraqi Freedom. Additionally, two appendices covering the Lockheed D-21 drone and preserved aircraft have been incorporated, as well as a host of new photos and artwork. For ease of reference, a comprehensive index is provided.

BLACK JETS

CONTENTS

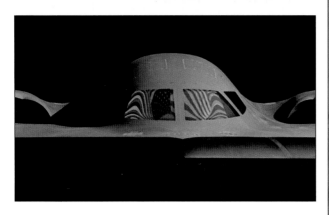

The B-2 is the ultimate symbol of the United States' supremacy as a military and technological superpower. An aircraft like no other, it was conceived with a single mission in mind: to range unseen into the Soviet Union's Arctic hinterland and destroy the ballistic missiles of the Strategic Rocket Forces before they could be launched at the USA. That mission was reason enough to pour immense sums of money into building the 'Stealth Bomber' – the ultimate monument to the Cold War. Now the USAF has to find new missions for its tiny B-2 force which has been cut back in numbers from 132 to just 21, but is still expected to meet a whole new range of tactical and strategic roles. This task may prove almost as complex as developing and building the B-2 in the first place.

I t would have been cold in southern Missouri on 17 December 1993 if you were not standing in the middle of a windswept airfield, under a ragged and spattering sky. Kansas City, with its blues, barbecue and heating, seemed a long way off.

That was when the B-2 arrived, dropping through a rent in the clouds. Those who had never seen a B-2 in the air before forgot how cold they were, because a B-2 in flight is a strange and mystifying sight that changes from second to second. Head-on, it is barely visible at the other end of the airfield, a charcoal-pencil stroke across your vision. From the side, a flying saucer from a 1950s movie, its wings invisible. Overhead, a manta ray executed in black by Picasso.

The bomber landed, the first of its type to join the 509th Bomb Wing at Whiteman AFB, close to the bustling metropolis of Knob Noster, and was handed over in a brief ceremony. Defense Secretary Les Aspin, who had just tendered his resignation, was not present. Air Force Secretary Sheila Widnall was there, but answered few questions. The date at which the B-2 would become operational was still classified. Somehow, a grey cloud seemed to surround the B-2, even when the sun was shining.

Now, as the bomber finally nears a full operational capability with the 509th, more of its extraordinary story can be put together. It is a tale of determination and innovation that defies most comparisons.

The technology that would make the B-2 possible originated in the mid-1970s, from two unrelated developments. After the successful use of remotely piloted vehicles (RPVs) in Vietnam, USAF and industry researchers were looking at smaller, less complex mini-RPVs. In the process, a Teledyne Ryan mini-RPV had been flown against both US and foreign radars at Eglin AFB, and proved very difficult to detect.

Lockheed and Northrop were the two greatest American rivals in the quest for stealth. A wise official decision to keep both company's R&D efforts alive meant that Lockheed built the Have Blue/F-117 for the USAF, but Northrop 'won' the B-2.

B-2 Spirit

The 'Stealth Bomber'

B-2 Spirit: The 'Stealth Bomber'

Above: In April 1988, after years of secrecy, the US DoD unveiled an artist's impression of the ATB, and announced that the aircraft would henceforth be known as the B-2. Many had correctly speculated that the ATB would be a flying wing design and the single public drawing of the ATB was a very close representation of the real aircraft – far less confusing than the first official image of the F-117. Secretary of the Air Force Edward C. Aldridge said that, "the first flight of the B-2... will represent a dramatic leap forward in technology and the achievement of a major milestone in our nation's strategic modernisation programme." By then, the first flight had been rescheduled several times from 1987 to late 1988, but the USAF still planed to acquire 132 B-2s at a total estimated cost (in FY81 dollars) of $36.6 billion.

Above right: AV-1014, 89-0129/Spirit of Georgia was delivered to the 393rd Bomb Squadron in November 1995 as one of the last Block 10 standard aircraft to be handed over. It has now been upgraded to Block 20 standard. A three-phase programme of airframe improvements and weapons integration (Blocks 10, 20 and 30) is now underway to expand the B-2's warfighting capability far beyond the SIOP role originally planned for it.

Opposite page, bottom right: Although many have pointed to similarities between the B-2 and Northrop's earlier flying wings, there is little linking the two. Quite apart from its technical sophistication, the B-2 flys and handles in a way never achieved by the ill-fated YB-49.

The Pentagon's scientific consulting group, the Defense Science Board, had meanwhile completed its annual Summer Study for 1974. With fresh experience of Vietnam and the 1973 air battles over the Middle East, the DSB concluded that conventional aircraft would face severe challenges surviving against the type of robust, networked air defence system which the Soviet Union was developing.

In the early autumn, the Pentagon's deputy director for research and engineering, Malcolm Currie, brought a request to a group at Wright-Patterson AFB which supported the Defense Advanced Research Projects Agency (DARPA), and which had links to the USAF scientists who had been researching the subject of radar cross-section (RCS) for decades: could they build a manned aircraft with a signature as low as the tiny mini-RPV?

Despite a great deal of work on RCS reduction in the 1950s and 1960s – including the testing and operational use of stealthy drones and reconnaissance aircraft, and the use of RCS-reduction technology on the Hound Dog missile – the smallest RCS achieved for a real aircraft was still too large for the aircraft to survive by stealth alone. On the Hound Dog, stealth bought time as the missile bored in on the SAM sites it was intended to destroy. On the Teledyne Ryan AQM-91 Firefly drone, it was combined with high altitude, and on the SR-71 it was combined with altitude and speed.

Project Harvey

Late in 1974, DARPA contacted the main US manufacturers of fighters and other military aircraft, to determine which of them might be interested in bidding on the study. It was codenamed Harvey, in an ironic reference to the 6-ft (1.8-m) invisible rabbit which haunted James Stewart in the film of the same name. It was a low-profile project, but not particularly secret, because nobody knew whether or not it would even be important. In January 1975, DARPA awarded small contracts to McDonnell Douglas and Northrop, calling for designs for a low-RCS manned aircraft. Neither weapons nor sensors need be carried and at that stage there was no guarantee that there would be money to take the project further.

At Northrop's Aircraft Division, the DARPA proposal arrived two months after John Cashen joined the Division. Cashen had been a phenomenologist at Hughes, tasked with defining what targets looked like to the company's radar and infra-red sensors, and had come to Northrop in 1973 to work on lasers.

Cashen had gathered a solid background in signatures through his work at Hughes, including the work that had been done on SRAM and other missiles. A forceful personality, not reticent about putting his views forward, Cashen became the leader and spokesman for the more junior electromagnetics experts on the team. "I was well aware that RCS was not dependent on size, area or volume," he says. RCS "is local. If you deal with each local phenomenon, you can make a very large object very small on radar."

Headed by Cashen, and using the RCS-prediction equations that had been developed at universities in the 1950s and 1960s, the Northrop group started to work on the DARPA requirement.

They were joined by Irv Waaland, a veteran hands-on designer who had come to Northrop from Grumman barely a year earlier. The work started with "a lot of systems analysis," Waaland recalls. "While the RCS people were estimating how low they could get, we did systems analysis to determine what kind of reductions would be required to impact the air defences."

Northrop's goal was to develop a low-altitude attack aircraft, and the analysts concluded that it was most important to reduce its RCS from the nose and tail. Detecting a low-flying aircraft from the side is difficult (because look-down radars rely on the Doppler effect caused by the target's movement relative to the radar and to the ground beneath it); and, because it is less easy to shoot down an aircraft in a tail-chase, the tail-on signature was less important than the nose.

The 'Northrop approach' and XST

It has often been stated that Northrop's approach to stealth relied on advancing computer technology, but Cashen tells a different story. "If we'd had a computer (that could predict RCS) we'd have used it," he says. "We were not able to synthesise RCS, we couldn't get a complete answer. It was better to use experience and the tools that we had, and do it experimentally. We ended up using a shaping solution that, in general, ended up working when we tested it."

Lockheed's Skunk Works had not been asked to compete in the Harvey project, but found out about the project and entered the fray using its own funds. The Lockheed and Northrop companies both outperformed their competition, and in September 1975 they were awarded contracts to design a stealth demonstrator – known as the Experimental Survivable Testbed, or XST. Each company would build a full-scale RCS model for a 'pole-off' at the USAF's RCS range at Holloman AFB in New Mexico.

Northrop had two problems. First, the Northrop XST had been designed on the assumption that the nose-on RCS was more important than the rear aspect. Its planview shape was a diamond with more sweep on the leading edges than the trailing edges. From the rear, it sustained its low RCS as long as the radar was no more than 35° off the tail, but beyond that, the radar would be at right angles to the trailing edge.

Unfortunately, the DARPA requirement treated RCS by quadrants: the rear quadrant extended to 45° either side of the tail, taking in the Northrop design's RCS 'spikes'. Waaland could not solve the problem by stretching the tail and increasing the sweep angle, because the diamond-shaped aircraft would become uncontrollable. Lockheed, however, had made the jump to a swept wing with a deeply notched trailing edge, and could handle the problem.

Northrop's other shortcoming was radar absorbent material (RAM). Northrop was unaware of Lockheed's long background of work on RAM, including the sophisticated high-temperature plastic used in the SR-71's leading edges. In June 1975, the USAF convened a secret Radar Camouflage Symposium at Wright-Patterson, where the Skunk Works' Kelly Johnson revealed the decade-old secret of the SR-71's stealth technology, but it was too late to catch up in time to compete in XST.

Lockheed also proved bolder in designing its XST. Northrop's design had curved wing surfaces; Lockheed built its entire shape from flat plates. Northrop used a top-mounted inlet with a serpentine duct and a mesh screen; Lockheed adopted inlet grilles. There was disappointment but little surprise when Lockheed was selected to build XST in March 1976, under the codename Have Blue, which ultimately evolved into the F-117 (see *World Air Power Journal* Volume 19).

DARPA and the USAF wanted a second source of stealth technology, but did not want to focus attention on the secret magic of stealth by holding another open competition. In December 1976, DARPA approached Northrop about an agency project called Assault Breaker. Its goal was to stop a Soviet tank attack in Central Europe with preci-

B-2 Spirit: The 'Stealth Bomber'

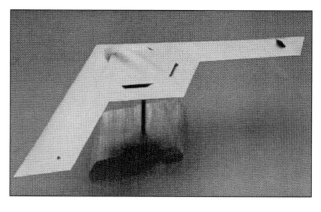

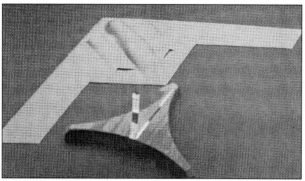

sion-guided weapons. It depended on an airborne radar to track the tanks and the incoming missiles – but how would a radar-carrying craft survive within line-of-sight of its targets? The answer was what DARPA called Battlefield Surveillance Aircraft – Experimental (BSAX). DARPA planned to award this programme to Northrop, both to keep Northrop's stealth technology moving and to avoid the risk of distracting Lockheed from Have Blue.

BSAX was considerably more difficult than Have Blue. A stealth aircraft has been described as a very inefficient antenna that flies; but a radar antenna has to be an efficient reflector. The radar-range equation was also at work: a radar signal that is strong enough to detect a target can itself be intercepted at a much greater distance.

Although Have Blue was an attack aircraft, intended to make a straight run for its target and to spend as little time in a defended area as possible, BSAX would have to loiter over the battlefield for hours, during which it would be illuminated by many radars from different directions. Unlike Have Blue, which was more detectable from the side than from the front and rear, BSAX would have to be the first 'all-aspect stealth' design.

Part of the solution was in hand at Hughes, which was already working on low probability of intercept (LPI) technology, the radar world's equivalent of stealth, and designing low-RCS antennas.

The pace quickens

As Northrop started to design BSAX, the Ford administration packed its bags in Washington. The incoming Carter team, including Defense Secretary Harold Brown and Under-Secretary William Perry (who would become Secretary from 1993 until 1996), was heavy with engineers and academics. Perry himself had built up his own company to manufacture electronics for the Pentagon and intelligence agencies. One of Perry's first actions on stealth was to appoint Air Force scientist Paul Kaminski "to serve as his technical conscience," as Kaminski puts it. "Was it real or not?" Kaminski's report was positive. The next step was more difficult. Assuming that Have Blue worked, how should stealth be used?

Some high-level discussions followed in the spring of 1977, involving Perry, General Al Slay – the chief of USAF research and development, and General Robert Bond, a rising Air Force star who later died while flying a MiG from the Nellis ranges. The support group included two majors, Ken Staton and Joe Ralston: today, the latter is vice-chairman of the Joint Staff.

At a conference in 1990, Ralston remarked that one option studied by the group was whether stealth research should be shut down, the programmes stopped and the data locked away, because the potential of stealth was so explosive. Stealth did not discriminate between US and Soviet radars, and the Soviet Union was showing a disconcerting tendency to develop new generations of weapons on a shorter cycle than the US, and to field them more quickly once developed. But Perry, as Kaminski recalls, "thought it was better to run fast than to behave like an ostrich."

The study group looked at how stealth could be applied to any type of conflict, ranging from counter-insurgency operations through regional and European conventional conflict to nuclear deterrence. Large-scale conventional warfare and nuclear attack were seen as the missions where stealth provided the greatest military advantage.

Stealthy bomber studies

Next, the Pentagon group examined what kind of operational stealth aircraft could and should be developed first. The debate closed in on two concepts. The 'A airplane' was a scaled-up Have Blue, with the fewest possible changes to its shape, and off-the-shelf systems. It was designed to be fielded quickly with minimum risk and to be built as a 'silver bullet' system for attacks on a few crucial targets. The 'B airplane' was much larger, around the size of the 45-ton FB-111 bomber, with a two-member crew, and would be more expensive but more flexible.

There was some enthusiasm for a larger aircraft within the USAF, particularly after the new administration cancelled the B-1 in June 1977. "We had much less confidence that we could pull that design off," says Ralston. "There were some tough decisions that had to be made by a small group of people." One critical issue was whether or not a single pilot could perform the mission envisaged for the smaller aircraft. "We flew a simulator and found one person could do it."

During 1977, the USAF decided to focus on the A design first, but continued to fund Lockheed's studies of the larger 'B airplane'. After the cancellation of the B-1, the design started to grow in size and performance, until it was capable of both conventional and nuclear missions.

These decisions had little impact on Northrop, which was preoccupied with BSAX. The design matured as an awkward-looking aircraft designed rather like a 'Huey' helicopter, around a huge box with open sides. The concept was to concentrate all the radar reflectivity into one 'spike' at right angles to the body, and to manoeuvre the aircraft so that the 'spikes' never dwelt on a hostile radar.

Northrop put the first BSAX models on the pole in the summer of 1977. "It was a disaster," says Waaland, who

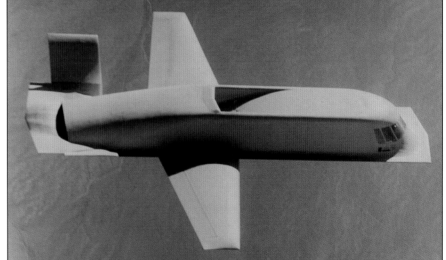

Above and top: Northrop's BSAX design, Tacit Blue (above), was not successful but did make a contribution to the ATB design, which was proceeding in parallel. The B-2 seen here is AV-4, pictured during flight no. 80 on 2 May 1995.

Left: The jet-powered Northrop YB-49 was developed from the piston-engined XB-35 that first flew in June 1946. The YB-49 took to the air in October 1947. The two YB-49s had very unpredictable handling characteristics and one crashed in June 1949 after back-flipping into a high-speed spin.

was quickly summoned to rescue the programme. DARPA's Ken Perko, worried that Northrop might not now be able to make BSAX work, quietly invited their rivals at Lockheed to study the concept also.

B-2 Spirit: The 'Stealth Bomber'

It was Fred Oshira, one of Cashen's electromagneticists, who saved Northrop's face. With the BSAX problems constantly in his mind, Oshira had taken to carrying a piece of modelling clay at all times – even when he took his family to Disneyland. Sitting on a bench, watching his children on the teacup ride, Oshira moulded the clay into a new shape, with a rounded top and flat sloped sides that flared down and outward into a knife-edge.

It worked like a charm, flowing the radar energy around the body rather than scattering it like a mirror. Northrop had not only found a way to remain stealthy from any direction, but had significantly expanded the range of radar

frequencies that stealth technology could defeat. Northrop's philosophy was also inherently compatible with curvature, promising greater aerodynamic efficiency. Again, better computers helped, "but we didn't design the aircraft on the computer," says Waaland. "Computers allowed us to look at parts of the aircraft in two dimensions. We could blend them together but we didn't have an integrated model."

Northrop's BSAX emerges

With the major RCS problem solved, the BSAX design came together in the second half of 1977. It had a bluff-nosed, bulky body to accommodate the radar. The engines were buried at the rear behind a flush dorsal inlet, with no screens or grilles. It had an unswept wing, which used a Clark Y airfoil section that had not been seen since the 1930s – the advantage was that the lower surface was flat. Pitch and yaw were controlled by a fly-by-wire system driving two all-moving V-tails. Worried about how the ends of the angled tail would appear on radar, the designers curved the tips of the V-tails towards the horizon. It was a final, organic touch to the design, which acquired the nickname 'Whale'. DARPA awarded the company a contract for a single prototype in April 1978, under the codename Tacit Blue.

By the end of that year, there were several stealth programmes under development. Have Blue was flying. Its operational derivative, the F-117, was the subject of a development contract late in 1978. Lockheed was working on the still-classified Senior Prom air-launched cruise missile – and a stealthy nuclear bomber.

Even though the Carter administration had cancelled the B-1 only months before, it was increasingly committed to developing a new bomber. US nuclear deterrence relied on a 'triad' of systems – bombers, ICBMs and submarine-launched missiles – which supported one another, because it was almost impossible for an adversary to attack them all at the same time.

In the late 1970s, however, CIA analysis identified an emerging 'window of vulnerability'. More accurate Soviet ICBMs would destroy more US ICBMs on the ground. This would mean that the bombers would be attacking an almost intact and fully operational Soviet air-defence system, and this system itself was being strengthened. Cities and other targets were being ringed with high-power radars and new missiles. The new long-range MiG-31 interceptor was designed to push the air battle hundreds of miles further from the targets, over the Arctic, so that the vulnerable B-52s could be engaged before they were within cruise-missile range of their objectives.

Stealth bomber go-ahead

By 1979, the Carter administration had secretly authorised the start a stealth bomber programme. The requirement had become more demanding, and the Lockheed design had evolved to meet it. It acquired curvature on the wings, and rounded edges rather than sharply defined facets – although its surfaces were curved in one dimension rather than two, and the shape still retained flat surfaces. But because the USAF was looking at a stealth bomber which could penetrate for hundreds of miles into an undamaged Soviet air defence system, Northrop's all-aspect, wide-bandwidth stealth technology began to look promising.

Northrop was not known as a builder of large aircraft, and its last bomber programme (the B-35/B-49) had almost destroyed it, so it took some high-level persuasion from the Air Force before the company would even begin a small-scale bomber study.

Northrop's analysis of the threat showed a weakness: the Soviet air defences were being bolstered against low-level penetrators and cruise missiles, but remained thinner at high altitudes. The designers concluded that they needed a bomber capable of U-2-like altitudes, with a planform shape that generated the smallest possible number of RCS 'spikes'. High altitude meant a large wing area and span.

It was natural for Northrop to look at a flying wing design: not only did it recall Northrop's most famous product, the XB-35/YB-49 of the late 1940s, but the wing had been the subject of numerous studies in the 1970s.

In the summer of 1979, designer Hal Markarian produced a sketch that is recognisably an ancestor of the B-2 in the arrangement of its basic components and the philosophy that drove them. Each feature was determined by a different sub-set of the mission requirements. It was a flying wing, because there is nothing quite as stealthy as a flat plate viewed edge-on, and the wing is the closest

approach to such a shape. Payload and range set a lower limit to the wing span. The leading-edge sweep angle was determined by the desired high subsonic cruising speed and by the need to locate the aerodynamic centre close to the centre of gravity: given that the wing extends to the front of the vehicle, it must be swept back to place the centre of lift where it needs to be.

The length of the centrebody section was determined by depth: it had to be deep enough to accommodate a normal cockpit and the weapon bays, and this meant that it had to be a minimum length to avoid excessive drag at high subsonic speeds. Outboard of the centrebody section, the chord was set by the need to integrate the engines and their low-observable inlet and exhaust systems into the wing. The inlets and exhaust were set well aft and well forward of the wing edges, the better to shield them from radar.

Although the chord close to the centreline had to be long, the planform area of a flying wing sets its weight and drag. As a result, the design had a long, deep centre-section, married to slender outer wings. With just eight ruler-straight edges, it presented only four main-lobe reflections.

In August 1979, Northrop presented Perry with two designs: Markarian's flying-wing design with parallel edges, using the shaping techniques developed on Tacit Blue, and a diamond-shaped aircraft similar to its Have Blue. Perry asked for a further study to flesh out the flying wing design. The maximum cost was $2 million, because a $2 million project did not have to be reported to Congress.

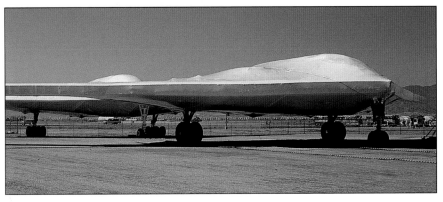

Left and below: These strange shapes are the two little-known static ground test airframes, built for the B-2 programme. Note the completely non-standard undercarriage on one of the airframes. Both 'iron birds' are seen in storage at Plant 42, in March 1994.

B-2 Spirit: The 'Stealth Bomber'

Above and opposite page: The B-2's first flight took it from Palmdale to Edwards AFB. It had originally been planned to make the journey on 15 July but a fault in the aircraft's heat exchanger (which uses fuel to cool accessory drive oil) forced the flight's postponement.

Landing the B-2 requires virtually no back pressure on the stick. When its 172-ft (52.4-m) wing enters ground effect (at approximately half a span's distance from the ground) sink rate decreases almost automatically. In the words of one pilot, "think about flaring – and you're down."

The team was joined by Dick Scherrer, who had joined Northrop from Lockheed. Scherrer, Waaland and aerodynamicist Hans Grellman started to work out the design details. They developed a $14 million, 11-month proposal (with a $2 million contract price), including wind-tunnel and RCS tests, and Northrop received a contract for the Advanced Strategic Penetration Aircraft (ASPA) in January 1980. "There was one condition," Waaland recalls. "We were advised at the highest levels that we were an insurance policy. We were told not to start lobbying."

The ATB emerges

A steady stream of visitors from Wright-Patterson, Strategic Air Command and the Pentagon passed through Northrop's offices. Northrop learned from them that the USAF and SAC were pushing for more weapons capacity and more flexibility, and responded by making the bomber's centre-section deeper, increasing its weight and reducing its U-2-like cruising altitude.

When the USAF issued a request for proposals for development and production of the Advanced Technology Bomber (ATB) in September 1980, there was little doubt that Northrop had advanced from an insurance policy to at least equal standing. Lockheed had already teamed with Rockwell for the bomber competition, and Northrop's leaders realised that they would have to find a partner as well. Jones asked for a meeting with Boeing's chairman, Thornton 'T.' Wilson. With one company chief on either side of a long table, flanked by their subordinates, Jones told Wilson about the ATB competition and invited Boeing to join Northrop. It was one of the most valuable contests in history, but Wilson had heard next to nothing about it. Waaland recalls that Wilson accepted Jones's offer, turned to the Boeing executive next to him and said, "Don't ever let me be in this position again."

Senior Ice and Senior Peg

The Northrop proposal, codenamed Senior Ice, was submitted in December. "It was one of the best proposal efforts I'd been on," says Waaland, "and we ended up feeling pretty buoyant. It was part exhaustion, part fatigue and part euphoria." By the early spring "we had indications that we had buried the competition."

Lockheed's Senior Peg design is still classified, making a comparison impossible. In his autobiography, Skunk Works leader Ben Rich claimed that the Lockheed design was more stealthy and that Northrop prevailed because of a small edge in aerodynamic performance and because it was a larger aircraft. Cashen disputes that claim. "We had a hell of an aircraft, it's as simple as that. We beat them on the pole, we beat them in the air, we beat them on everything."

As the engineers prepared their final proposals, President Jimmy Carter and the Congressional Democrats were defeated by Ronald Reagan in the November 1980 election. Under Carter, several options for renewing the bomber force had been studied. One option was to bring the ATB into service as soon as possible; another was to delay the ATB and concentrate on a more stealthy development of the B-1; and at one point, Strategic Air Command favoured a plan that would have produced an interim bomber by radically modifying its existing FB-111As.

Reagan's defence secretary, Caspar Weinberger, decided on the most expensive option: a full-speed-ahead programme to build 100 B-1s in the mid-1980s, followed by 132 stealth bombers.

Northrop was awarded the ATB contract in October 1981, covering full-scale development, preparations for production and the manufacture of six flying aircraft and two static-test airframes. Including options for the production of 127 more bombers (one of the prototypes would not be operational), the contract was worth $36.6 billion in 1981 dollars. The Pentagon wanted to keep the award secret –

announcing, for legal reasons, nothing more than the award of a 'study' to Northrop – but Northrop chairman Tom Jones pointed out that securities law required disclosure of contracts that would materially affect the company's business. A 12-line statement was issued – the last that would be heard of the programme, officially, until 1988. The programme was codenamed Senior CJ in tribute to Connie Jo Kelly, the indispensable and hard-working secretary to the stealth programme office in the Pentagon.

Although Northrop had a contract to build the new bomber, its design was not frozen, and, in fact, it would change dramatically in the first year of the programme.

Planning for operations

In 1980, in the Pentagon, Paul Kaminski had decided to invest one per cent of the stealth budget in counter-stealth studies. The Red Team was divided in two. One group worked with full knowledge of stealth; the other worked from public sources. The effort led to major changes in the bomber design.

The most important lesson was that a stealth aircraft was not invisible. It could and would be detected if its operators did not use tactics that exploited its stealth. The Red Team underscored the importance of planning routes so that the stealth aircraft would show its least visible side to known radars. This led to the development of the first automated mission planning system for the F-117A. Constantly updated with the location of hostile radars, the system devised the stealthiest routes to any chosen target. (Pilots nicknamed it 'Elvira', after late-night TV's Mistress of the Dark.) A similar system would be developed to support the ATB.

More significantly, the Red Team suggested that, within the new bomber's service life, the Soviet Union might build large ground-based radars that could overpower stealth technology at a useful range. The USAF decided to design the bomber so that it could bypass those radars on the deck, using terrain to protect itself.

The design that Northrop had submitted for the ATB competition in 1980 was very similar to Hal Markarian's first sketches, with the exception that it was noticeably deeper at the centre-section: in response to Strategic Air Command's indications that they wanted a multi-mission bomber, the aircraft had grown heavier, with larger weapons bays. This had been accomplished within the original planform at the expense of some altitude performance.

ATB changes

When the Red Team's low-altitude requirement was added to the specification, Northrop initially offered a revised ATB that would fly at Mach 0.55 at low altitude (about the same as the B-52). However, as the competition entered its final stages, it became clear that the bomber would have enough power (because of its low drag) to reach Mach 0.8. Northrop adjusted its final offer to reflect this, while cautioning the USAF that it had not had time to fully model the aeroelastic effects of the higher loads and more rigid structure. Designers expected that some local stiffening would be required, along with changes to the environmental control system (ECS) to deal with friction heating encountered at high speed and low level.

The issue turned out to be more complex. The designers developed a new computer model that took account of external air loads, the internal structure and the control laws. This showed that the control surfaces – all of which were on the relatively flexible outer wings, apart from a gust-alleviation flap on the extreme tail – were located ahead of the primary longitudinal bending mode line, which curved across the centrebody. In low-altitude turbulence, these controls would tend to excite bending in the structure as they attempted to counter gust-induced pitch movements. Stiffening the structure would add at least 10,000 lb (4500 kg) to the empty weight.

Above: AV-2 is seen here on flight no. 53, coasting out over Moro Bay, California. Close by is Half Moon Bay where, in 1949, radar operators were amazed that they could not track Northrop's YB-49 until it was "right on top of them."

Top: Early in the flight test programme, aircraft were fitted with a 300-ft (91.4-m) trailing wire/ cone to provide reliable static air pressure reference (undisturbed by the aircraft shape) for airspeed, altitude and the air data system.

Instead, the bomber was redesigned. The outer wings became shorter and thinner, and carried only two control segments instead of three. The outboard centrebody sections were extended backwards, creating the characteristic 'double-W' trailing edge, and the exhausts were changed to a V-shape. Two elevon sections were added to each side of the centrebody, placing them on a stiffer part of the structure, and further aft for greater effectiveness.

At the same time, the RCS group at Northrop produced a different type of radar absorbent structure for the leading edge of the wing, which could provide the required absorption with less depth. This meant that the wing spar and cockpit could be moved forward. The inlets had originally been designed so that part of the duct passed through the spar, with a stream-wise vane to help conceal the compressor face from the engine. With the spar moved forward, it was possible to move the entire duct behind the spar and simplify the structural design.

The revised aircraft would not only be lighter but would have a better ride at low altitude, so it was possible to eliminate an isolated, palletised cockpit which had been incorporated in the original design.

Low-altitude performance was only one area in which the USAF and Northrop raised their sights as the design evolved. The customer was well aware that the B-2 would be the last new bomber for a long time. With strong support from those members of Congress who were permitted to know about stealth, and encouragement from a hawkish administration, the USAF wrote the toughest set of requirements ever seen. "In the requirements stage, money was no object," one engineer recalls.

Demands of the strategic mission

The ATB design assumed that the bombers would have to penetrate Soviet territory after a successful first strike by Soviet missiles had destroyed the US ICBM force. This meant that they would have fully operational threat radars all around them: hence, the requirement for a very low RCS in all bandwidths and from all directions. Moreover, the bomber's crew would have to be able to detect and avoid threats that had not been predicted.

The bomber was intended to be fully autonomous and able to attack almost any target, ranging from deeply buried bunkers – using high-yield thermonuclear weapons such as the multi-megaton B53 bomb – to mobile, protected missile launchers. Its radar would have to combine LPI with long range and high resolution.

Since the bombers and submarines might be the only surviving element of the US nuclear strike force, the ATB was designed to be recovered and reconstituted. After their first nuclear mission, the bombers would return to the US and land at dispersal airfields (the ATB can operate from any airfield that can handle a Boeing 727), where they could be rearmed and launched on a second strike.

No previous bomber, including the B-1, had been designed to meet such a requirement. It meant not only that the bomber needed a high level of reliability and redundancy, but that every part of the aircraft had to be radiation-hardened to an unprecedented degree, to survive the blasts of radiation from its own nuclear bombs and from Soviet nuclear air-defence warheads. Even mundane components like the TACAN receiver had to be specially designed. "About the only thing that was not rad-hardened was the anti-skid system," Waaland recalled.

When it came to deciding how to meet these requirements, the Air Force and civilian engineers worked closely together – but in a management system which, programme participants recall, did not allow them to see the cost impacts of their decisions. "There was a lack of cost information to the engineers," Waaland remarks. "If engineers are left unchecked, they will always go for the best solution." One example was as simple as the radio: from the early stages of the programme, it was decided that the ATB should have an advanced anti-jam radio. "After we put it in," says Waaland, "we had nobody to talk to, because apart from the B-2 the programme had been cancelled."

Moreover, there are features of the aircraft that apparently have not been discussed at all. "From the beginning, it was the Advanced Technology Bomber," one insider notes, "not just the stealth bomber. That's where the money is, not in the stealth. There are certain special technologies that cost a fortune."

The bomber described

In 1984, with its redesign complete, the bomber passed an unusual second preliminary design review. The challenge was to build it. This was to prove more difficult than expected, and as always the devil was in the details.

Bombers present a unique design challenge because of their combination of transport-like size and fighter-like intricacy, and the B-2 is an elegant, densely packed aircraft.

The centrebody is little longer than the fuselage of an F-15 but is as deep as a B-52 fuselage, accommodating two large weapon bays, one each side of the centreline. Each bay contains either a Boeing-developed Advanced Rotary Launcher (ARL) capable of carrying eight 1000-kg (2,204-lb) class weapons, or, alternatively, two Bomb Rack Assembly (BRA) units for carrying smaller conventional weapons.

The centrebody accommodates the crew compartment, reached through a ventral hatch. The B-2's cockpit windows are so large that they make the aircraft look smaller than it is. They are large for the same reason that the cockpit windows of a DC-10 are large: a cockpit window has to provide the pilot with a given angular field of view, and the further the window is from the pilot's seat, the bigger it has to be. Comparing the location of the ejection-seat hatches with the width of the dorsal hump shows how wide and high the latter is. Even so, fighter pilots transitioning to the B-2 sometimes feel "that they are trapped in a dumpster" because of the restricted field of view. The nose-down view is limited.

Stealthy features

The engines, outboard of the weapon bays, are buried completely within the wing. The S-shaped inlet ducts curve down to the engines, which are accessible from below the aircraft. Curvature conceals the compressor faces from direct line-of-sight illumination by radar, and RAM on the duct walls suppresses any radar energy which could bounce off the duct walls to reach the engines. Ahead of each inlet is a jagged slit-like auxiliary inlet which removes the turbulent boundary layer, and provides cool air which is mixed into the exhaust to reduce the bomber's infra-red signature. The bizarre, modern-sculpture shape of the inlets results from the combination of the straight-edge planform alignments with the curvature of the surfaces.

The exhaust ducts are curved in profile. They flatten out to wide slits and open into overwing trenches. As in the case of the F-117, the exhaust system exploits the Coanda effect (the phenomenon that causes spilt water to follow the curved side of a glass rather than falling straight down) to direct the thrust aft while concealing the nozzle openings from a direct rear view.

The B-2's aerodynamic characteristics are unique. Compared with a wing-body design of the same weight, the B-2 has much more span and wing area, so the lift coefficient (a measure of how much lift must be produced

Above: AV-2 joined the flight test programme when it departed Palmdale for the first time on 19 October 1989. It was flown by Northrop pilot Leroy Schroeder and Lt Col John Small of the (then) 6520th Test Squadron. The first flight of the second B-2 was nearly aborted by high winds which were gusting outside the aircraft's limits. As a result the crew elected to depart on runway 25, to avoid an excessive tailwind component, but had to make a snappy right turn on departure to avoid downtown Palmdale. Rising crosswinds at Edwards AFB forced the crew to land ahead of their scheduled time, after 67 minutes in the air. AV-2 was instrumented for load testing and was originally the only one of the six-strong test fleet that was not scheduled to be returned to active service at Whiteman AFB.

The B-2 was rolled out during the transition from the Reagan to the Bush administration, and began flying when the first deep cuts in the US military budget were being initiated, in the early 1990s. F-117 procurement had been cut almost in half, rail-basing plans for the MX missile (MGM-118) force were slashed, the small ICBM programme was cancelled (as ultimately was the rail-based MX) and the B-2 had to compete for funds with other high-spenders such as the ATF and SDI.

Top and above: Tanking trials for the B-2 were not restricted to specialist refuelling units, although for the sake of convenience locally-based units (such as the 22nd Air Refueling Wing at nearby March AFB) were used to support missions from Edwards AFB. Here B-2s are seen tanking from a 22nd ARW Extender on two separate occasions – including a rare glimpse of two B-2s in the air together. The compact size of the B-2 always comes as a surprise when viewed alongside most other aircraft. It is even more impressive when one remembers that the B-2 can carry as many bombs as a 'Big Belly'-modified B-52D.

by each square foot of wing) does not have to be as high. While conventional aircraft have complex flaps to raise the lift coefficient for take-off and landing, the B-2 needs none, and lifts off at a conservative speed of just 140 kt (160 mph; 258 km/h).

Another effect of the big wing is that the B-2 operates over a smaller angle of attack range than a conventional aircraft and flies in a fairly flat, constant attitude regardless of speed and weight. A sophisticated fuel-management system is used for zero-drag trim. The net result is that the B-2 is very efficient, even though the lift distribution was not what it would be in an ideal flying wing.

The B-2 is lighter than the B-1, but has a far better warload and range performance. It can carry about as much and as far as the B-52, which is 59 tons heavier.

The B-2's weight is a curious subject. Early fact sheets gave the maximum take-off weight as 375,000 lb (170500 kg). Later, this number was reduced to 336,500 lb (152600 kg), and other documents place the aircraft "in the 350,000-lb (158730-kg) class." The most probable explanation for this discrepancy is that the bomber's structural life is based on the lowest figure, reflecting a take-off with full fuel but no weapons. Since a full load has relatively little effect on the bomber's flying qualities, a B-2 will probably never fly with a full load except in combat, which represents a tiny percentage of its lifetime sorties.

Its aerodynamic efficiency is close to that of the Lockheed U-2, a very specialised aircraft with a much smaller design envelope. The B-2's altitude performance is another interesting question: with its great span and wing area, the B-2 is certainly capable of exceeding the nominal 50,000-ft (15000-m) ceiling cited in official statements. The only real question is by how much.

In most respects, the B-2 is close to neutrally stable. If it had conventional controls, any disturbance would tend to push the aircraft on to a new flightpath. It would not diverge further from its original path unless it was disturbed again, but it would require an action by the pilot to resume its former attitude and speed. However, it is rendered stable by a quadruplex fly-by-wire (FBW) system. The flight control computer (FCC) units were developed by General Electric, which provided the hardware for the F/A-18 and Tacit Blue. (This GE unit is now part of Lockheed Martin.)

Control system and surfaces

The FBW system drives nine very large control surfaces which occupy the entire trailing edge, apart from the area behind the engines. The outermost pair of surfaces is split horizontally and operates symmetrically as speedbrakes, and asymmetrically as rudders. The flattened, pointed tail of the centrebody – known as the gust load alleviation system (GLAS) or simply the 'beavertail' – is primarily used to counter pitch movements caused by vertical gusts at low level. The remaining six surfaces are elevons for pitch and roll control, although the outermost pair functions purely as ailerons at low speed.

The absence of a vertical fin is one of the B-2's unique features. B-2 designer Irv Waaland describes a conventional aircraft without a vertical fin as "like an arrow without feathers." The flying wing is different, because it is short from front to rear and has no features to generate destabilising side forces. "The all-wing design is neutrally stable directionally," Waaland says: "all you need is adequate control." Northrop's first designs had small, inward-canted vertical control surfaces on the centrebody, immediately outboard of the exhausts. Alternative approaches were evaluated, including a combination of small outboard verticals and reaction controls, before Northrop settled on the brake-rudder surfaces.

The brake-rudders are the primary means of yaw control, but because of the boundary layer over the wing, the surfaces are ineffective until they have moved about 5° from their trail position. The B-2 normally flies with the rudders at 'five and five' – that is, slightly displaced so that any movement takes it immediately into a responsive zone. This is not compatible with stealth, so the rudders are closed when the cockpit master mode switch is in its 'go to war' position. Instead (according to a 1991 technical paper, although this area is now classified), the B-2 uses differential engine thrust for stealthy directional control.

The flight control system presented its own challenges. Because the B-2 is short, the elevons have a short moment arm in pitch, and must be large to provide adequate power. Being on the wing trailing edge, they are not mass-balanced, so the loads at the hinge line are high. On the other hand, the designers had also elected to use the controls to counter gust loads in low-level flight, so the controls had to be able to move very quickly.

To meet these conflicting requirements, Moog and Lear Astronics developed a unique actuation system. The B-2 is fitted with eight actuator remote terminals (ARTs) spread out along the wing span, which receive their instructions from the GE flight control computers over a quadruplex digital bus. The ARTs issue analog commands to the actuators and control all the necessary feedback loops, saving complexity and weight in the wiring between the FCCs and the actuators. The entire system runs at 4,000 psi (27580 kPa) to reduce the size and weight of the actuators.

The Rosemount air data system is also new, but proved less troublesome than the air data system on the F-117. (For one agonising period in the F-117's development, the team was working with several air-data systems, none of which had yet been made to work.) The B-2's system is based on a circular heated port which can measure both normal (static pressure) and pitot pressure. There are five groups of four ports, each arranged on a common pressure line. The system compares pressures at upper and lower ports to determine Alpha, and left and right to determine sideslip.

Aerodynamic design

The B-2 aerodynamic design was primarily based on computational fluid dynamics (CFD), according to aerodynamicist Hans Grellmann, although CFD for whole-airframe design was in its infancy when the programme started. "We had to make do with tools that were never designed to do the job," he says. A transonic wing analysis code was adapted to define the entire wing. CFD could not directly account for engine flows, so the aerodynamics team subtracted the engine flow from their calculations, leaving only the spilling airflow. CFD was also used to investigate important handling areas such as inflight refuelling and behaviour in ground effect. "We relied on CFD, and used the wind tunnel to tell us that our codes were valid," says Grellmann. Several models – all produced by numerically controlled machines, driven from the same computer database which was used in the production of the full-size aircraft – were used for more than 24,000 hours of total tunnel time. The 'workhorse' was a sting-mounted force and moment model with working primary and BLC inlets.

Detail design challenges included the need to push the thickness of the centre-section to the limit of flow separation,

to accommodate a body depth equal to that of the B-52 in the bomber's 69-ft (21-m) overall length. The aircraft was also to have conventional pitch and stalling characteristics, even though Cashen's stealth group wanted the leading edge to be as sharp as possible. The wing section itself is a modified NASA laminar-flow profile, chosen because it can combine the camber demanded by cruise aerodynamics with a sharp leading edge. The high degree of twist and drastic leading-edge camber variation which are visible on the B-2 evolved as a complex compromise between aerodynamics and stealth.

All-new engine

Northrop selected a new engine from General Electric in the early stages of the ASPA contest. It was based on the F101-X, a fighter engine derived from the B-1's powerplant that later became the F110. Compared with the F101, the F101-X had a smaller low-pressure spool, scaled up from that of the F404, which reduced the bypass ratio from 2:1 to 0.87:1. The F101-X was attractive for two reasons. Although a higher-bypass-ratio engine would be more

Above and top: In these two views the 5,000 sq ft (464.4 m²) wing area of the B-2 can be compared to that of a KC-135E and a KC-10A. The B-2 has a wing span of exactly 172 ft (52.43 m) which, co-incidentally, is the same as that of the XB-35/YB-49. The B-2 was originally designed with a pair of split flaps located under the aft centre fuselage. Tunnel tests indicated that they would probably not be needed, so the actuators were removed and the flaps were bolted shut on AV-1. Vestiges of the flaps remain on later aircraft.

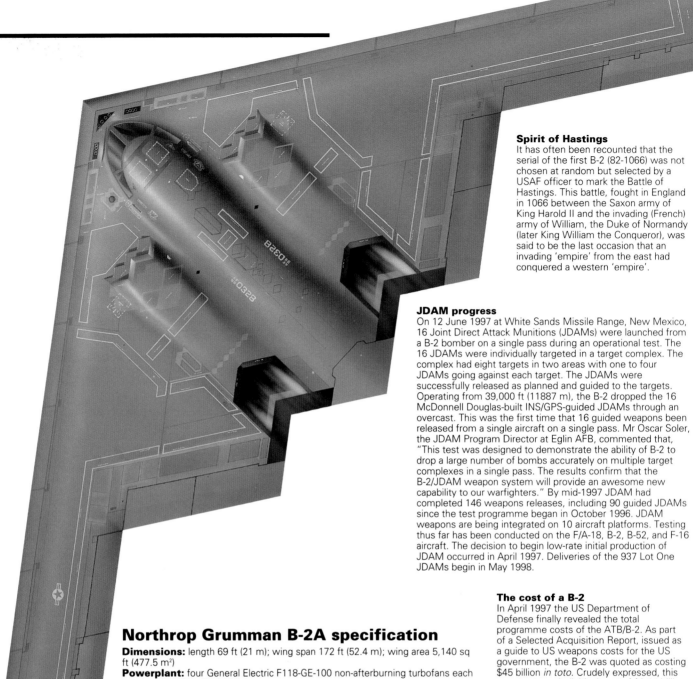

Spirit of Hastings
It has often been recounted that the serial of the first B-2 (82-1066) was not chosen at random but selected by a USAF officer to mark the Battle of Hastings. This battle, fought in England in 1066 between the Saxon army of King Harold II and the invading (French) army of William, the Duke of Normandy (later King William the Conqueror), was said to be the last occasion that an invading 'empire' from the east had conquered a western 'empire'.

JDAM progress
On 12 June 1997 at White Sands Missile Range, New Mexico, 16 Joint Direct Attack Munitions (JDAMs) were launched from a B-2 bomber on a single pass during an operational test. The 16 JDAMs were individually targeted in a target complex. The complex had eight targets in two areas with one to four JDAMs going against each target. The JDAMs were successfully released as planned and guided to the targets. Operating from 39,000 ft (11887 m), the B-2 dropped the 16 McDonnell Douglas-built INS/GPS-guided JDAMs through an overcast. This was the first time that 16 guided weapons been released from a single aircraft on a single pass. Mr Oscar Soler, the JDAM Program Director at Eglin AFB, commented that, "This test was designed to demonstrate the ability of B-2 to drop a large number of bombs accurately on multiple target complexes in a single pass. The results confirm that the B-2/JDAM weapon system will provide an awesome new capability to our warfighters." By mid-1997 JDAM had completed 146 weapons releases, including 90 guided JDAMs since the test programme began in October 1996. JDAM weapons are being integrated on 10 aircraft platforms. Testing thus far has been conducted on the F/A-18, B-2, B-52, and F-16 aircraft. The decision to begin low-rate initial production of JDAM occurred in April 1997. Deliveries of the 937 Lot One JDAMs begin in May 1998.

The cost of a B-2
In April 1997 the US Department of Defense finally revealed the total programme costs of the ATB/B-2. As part of a Selected Acquisition Report, issued as a guide to US weapons costs for the US government, the B-2 was quoted as costing $45 billion *in toto*. Crudely expressed, this equates to an individual cost of $2.14 billion per aircraft, which is twice what most previous public estimates had been. The USAF would never express individual aircraft costs in such terms, preferring instead more nebulous calculations such as 'flyaway cost' or 'then-year dollar price'.

Northrop Grumman B-2A specification
Dimensions: length 69 ft (21 m); wing span 172 ft (52.4 m); wing area 5,140 sq ft (477.5 m²)
Powerplant: four General Electric F118-GE-100 non-afterburning turbofans each rated at 19,000 lb (84.5 kN) thrust
Weights: operational empty 153,700 lb (69705 kg); normal take-off 336,500 lb (152607 kg); maximum take-off 375,000 lb (170070 kg)
Fuel and load: internal fuel capacity 180,000 lb (81635 kg); maximum weapon load 50,000 lb (22700 kg)
Performance: cruising speed Mach 0.85/485 kt/900 km/h at 36,000 ft (10972 m); speed at sea level Mach 0.8/530 kt/980 km/h; service ceiling above 50,000 ft (15240 m); range, unrefuelled with 8 SRAM and 8 B83 (37,300-lb/16919-kg) warload, 4,410 nm (8167 km; 5,075 miles) with a 1,000-nm (1852-km; 1,151-mile) low-altitude segment, or 6,300 nm (11667 km; 7,250 miles) at high level

Penetrating weapons
Lessons learned during the war against Iraq provided fresh impetus for research into weapons designed to destroy hardened or underground targets. Such research had been underway in the USA and UK since the 1980s, but at a leisurely pace. The realisation that many potential 'threat nations' such as Iran, Libya and North Korea were investing huge sums in developing large underground weapons manufacturing and operational facilities (in some cases for so-called Weapons of Mass Destruction/WMD), changed all that. By 1995, as part of its Advanced Concept Demonstration (ACTD) programme, the US had begun tests of 2,000-lb GBU-24 LGBs with BLU-109 penetrating warheads and new 'smart' fuses against earthmounded bunkers at the White Sands Missile range. Phase II of this testing (planned for 1998) calls for a weapon that can penetrate up to 6 m (19.6 ft) of hardened concrete. Such weapons are primarily intended for targets believed to be storing chemical or biological weapons. As such, they must be capable of destroying CW/BW agents without releasing them into the atmosphere. An air-droppable environmental sensor to detect agents in the air (before and after the attack) is also part of the potential package.

Northrop Grumman B-2A

The only aircraft which have ever looked remotely like
the B-2 were flown in the 1940s, when designers in the
United States, Britain and Germany were pursuing the
idea of an all-wing aircraft, or flying wing. As its name
suggests, the all-wing aircraft has neither fuselage nor
tail, but carries all its payload, fuel and components
inside the wing. Even those distant ancestors did not
share the single dominating, most bizarre feature of the
B-2's shape. Viewed from directly above or below, the
B-2's boomerang-like shape comprises 12 ruler-straight
lines. The leading edges, the long sides of the
boomerang, run straight from the extreme nose to the
extreme tips of the wing. The wingtips are not parallel
with the airflow, like those on most normal aircraft, but
are cut off at a near-right angle to the leading edges.
Apart from the tips, the outer wings have no taper:
again, this is completely unlike any normal aircraft. The
inner trailing edges form a jagged shape, jutting
rearward toward the centreline. A closer inspection
shows that the edges form two groups of six exactly
parallel lines. Look at the B-2 from any point in the
horizontal plane, however, and the shape changes. In
front, rear or side view, the bomber has virtually no
straight lines and no hard edges. The top and bottom
surfaces are both continuous, three-dimensional curved
surfaces. Even the overwing air inlets, which look
jagged from a distance, can be seen at close range to be
made up of many curved segments. There are even very
few curves of constant radius; rather, the surfaces
change radius continuously, as though they were
produced from segments of a spiral. The shape has no
abrupt distinctions between body and wing; a dorsal
hump with the cockpit in front rises smoothly from the
top surface, but the underside swells gradually from the
outermost trailing-edge kink to the centreline.
Combined with the things that the eye expects to see,
but which are not there – engine pods, a fuselage, a
vertical fin and a stabiliser – the effect is to make the
B-2 look like something organic rather than a machine.

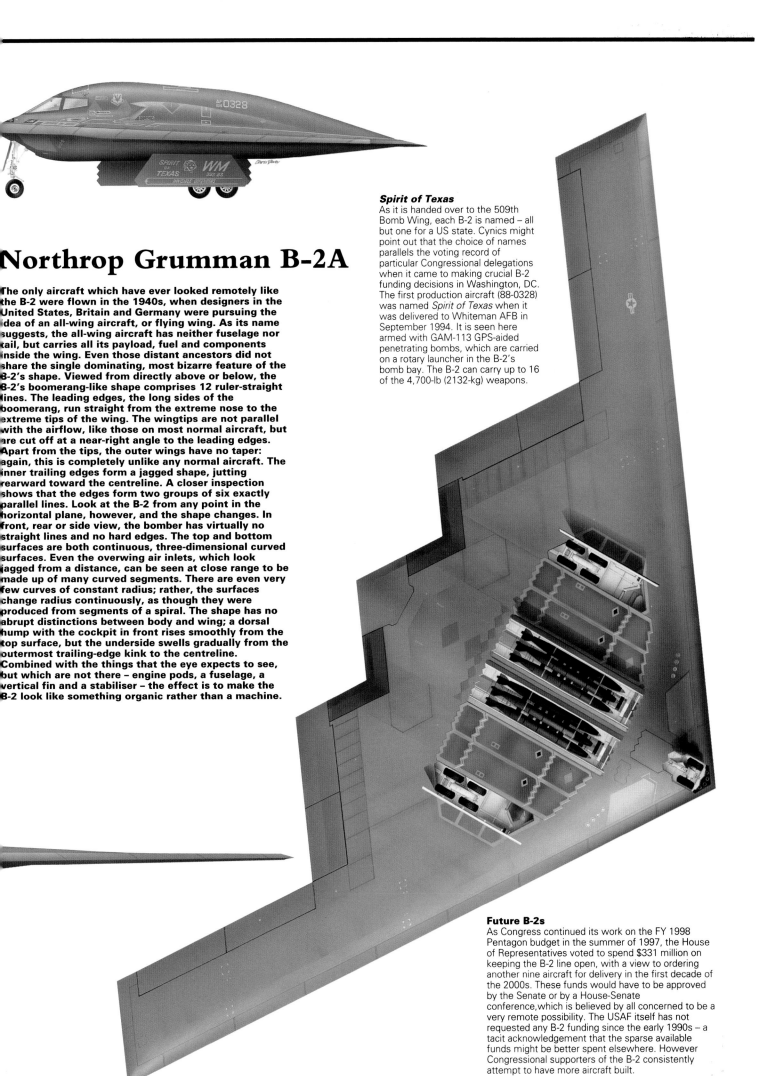

Spirit of Texas
As it is handed over to the 509th
Bomb Wing, each B-2 is named – all
but one for a US state. Cynics might
point out that the choice of names
parallels the voting record of
particular Congressional delegations
when it came to making crucial B-2
funding decisions in Washington, DC.
The first production aircraft (88-0328)
was named *Spirit of Texas* when it
was delivered to Whiteman AFB in
September 1994. It is seen here
armed with GAM-113 GPS-aided
penetrating bombs, which are carried
on a rotary launcher in the B-2's
bomb bay. The B-2 can carry up to 16
of the 4,700-lb (2132-kg) weapons.

Future B-2s
As Congress continued its work on the FY 1998
Pentagon budget in the summer of 1997, the House
of Representatives voted to spend $331 million on
keeping the B-2 line open, with a view to ordering
another nine aircraft for delivery in the first decade of
the 2000s. These funds would have to be approved
by the Senate or by a House-Senate
conference,which is believed by all concerned to be a
very remote possibility. The USAF itself has not
requested any B-2 funding since the early 1990s – a
tacit acknowledgement that the sparse available
funds might be better spent elsewhere. However
Congressional supporters of the B-2 consistently
attempt to have more aircraft built.

efficient, it would need a bigger exhaust and inlet system that would add to the bomber's weight, and it would lose thrust more rapidly with altitude.

The definitive B-2 engine was originally referred to as F101-F29, but was officially designated F118-GE-100. Compared with the F110, it has a redesigned, higher-airflow fan that provides more non-afterburning power. Its high-altitude potential is indicated by the fact that it has been retrofitted to the Lockheed U-2S.

Inlet design was difficult. The completely flush inlet used on Tacit Blue had worked adequately, but had experienced starting problems (at one point, the flight test crew borrowed a C-130 to generate airspeed over the inlet of the 'Whale') and Northrop was looking for better pressure recovery and efficiency on the bomber. However, the last place to put an efficient inlet is on top of the wing.

Supercritical wing

Although the B-2 is subsonic, its thick supercritical wing sections accelerate the air to supersonic speeds over the wing. The inlet region resembles two supercritical wing sections in series. The first is the area behind the leading edge, where the airflow accelerates to supersonic speed and is then recompressed to subsonic speed before being swallowed by the main inlet and the auxiliary boundary-layer/IR suppression scoop. The second supercritical section comprises the region from the inlet lip to the exhaust exit, where the flow is accelerated and recompressed once again. In cruising flight, the inlet is spilling air (as most inlets do) and the interaction with the flow over the wing translates all the way to the wingtip. Because of this, it was impossible to predict or test the B-2's aerodynamic performance without taking the propulsion system into account.

In the early days of the programme, Northrop built a full-scale replica of the inlet, complete with two engines,

and tested it on the ground. Only one serious problem turned up: a certain amount of flow separation in the tightly curved duct, leading to a loss of power at low speeds. The solution was to add retractable auxiliary inlet scoops above the wing.

Structural elements

Structurally, the B-2 consists of six major assemblies. The centre wing assembly, built by Boeing, contains the weapon bays and the avionics bays above and behind them. In front of this is the crew station assembly, produced by Northrop in California. On either side are the two very complex intermediate wing assemblies, which house the inlets, exhausts, engine bays and main landing gear bays. (The company responsible for them at the start of the programme – Vought – has since been acquired by Northrop Grumman.) The outer wings are produced by Boeing, which is also responsible for the weapon launchers and landing gear.

The components of the B-2 actually built by Northrop are only a small proportion of the total weight – the cockpit and the entire perimeter of the aircraft, comprising the leading edges, wingtips, control surfaces and fixed trailing-edge structure. For Northrop, this makes good business sense. Much of the value of a contract resides in the design, the integration (which includes the cockpit) and the use of company-proprietary technology, such as the radar-absorbent edges of a stealth aircraft.

Inside the centre and intermediate wing sections are two very large titanium carry-through box (CTB) structures, one behind the cockpit and the other one aft of the engine bay. Otherwise, the primary structural material is carbon-fibre/epoxy composite, which is used for most of the skin and the spars of the outer wing. The B-2 includes many of the largest carbon-fibre parts ever made, including centre-section skins that are more than 1 in (2.5 cm) thick, and spars and skins more than 70 ft (21 m) long, and is still by far the largest aircraft ever built primarily from composites.

One of the most important reasons for choosing the new material had to do with stealth. Carbon-fibre is less dense than metal, so carbon-fibre skins are thicker than metal skins of the same strength, and composite parts can be assembled by 'co-curing' them: autoclaving them together, so that the parts bond together with a strength equal to that of the original material. Most of the stiffeners are co-cured to the skins. The thick, fastener-free skins produced by this method are smoother than riveted metal skins, and will stay that way in service – a characteristic that was critical to Northrop's 'seamless' stealth design technique. Large skin panels reduced the number of joints, which were possible sources of unwanted radar reflections. The result was a durable and relatively simple structural design: the question was whether anyone could draw it, let alone build it.

Building the B-2

Northrop's stealth design philosophy, with its continuous flowing curves, had worked on the hand-built Tacit Blue prototype, but a large mass-produced bomber was a different matter. Most aircraft are built from the inside out, starting with spars, ribs and frames. They are all parts which are defined in two dimensions, and are assembled into the complete structure. Any deviances from the design accumulate into small errors in fit and surface finish, which are fixed during final assembly; and errors are usually larger on large aircraft.

The B-2 could not be built this way. The major skin components had to fit almost perfectly, so that there would be no gaps or steps even when the aircraft was pummelled and bent by turbulence. The classic methods of ensuring that parts conformed to the design shape were inadequate, being basically designed for single-curvature surfaces.

Since stealth was a critical aspect of the design, and would have to be demonstrated by the first B-2s, the first aircraft off the line would have to be exactly the same in every external detail as all the others; that is to say, it would be built on hard tooling. This tooling would have to be

As the combat assets of SAC and TAC were merged into Air Combat Command, plans for the B-2 entered a state of flux. From a proposed total of 132, by late 1991/early 1992 a force of 75 B-2s was looking unlikely and as few as 15 aircraft seemed more like the truth. It was the then-Chairman of the House Armed Services Committee, Les Aspin, who coined the phrase 'silver bullet' force for such a tiny number of B-2s. Deep splits arose between factions in the USAF and the DoD as to whether some aircraft were better than none at all, and quite what the value of a single B-2 might be when compared to existing assets. Major General Stephen Croker, the architect of ACC (and a Vietnam MiG-killer), said, "[there will be a] serious practical problem day-to-day to use 15 aircraft for a long period. You could get a job done with 15 airplanes, 10 of which you have access to, five of which you used on any given day, but it would take an awful lot of days." Croker oversaw SAC's SR-71 operations, and said, "those eight aircraft cost me more in operations and support for a year than 3½ B-52 wings."

installed and aligned to unprecedented standards of accuracy before the first bomber was built.

The answer was twofold. First, the B-2 would be defined and built from the outside in. Instead of being made of flexible sheets fastened to substructure, the skin panels would be laid up in precise female moulds. Second, to make sure that everything would fit, the entire aircraft would be designed on computers.

As the company renovated the massive Ford automobile plant at Pico Rivera, where much of the B-2 was to be built, it did so according to a new concept: computer integrated manufacturing (CIM). At Pico Rivera, the image of

computer-aided design became the reality. The external shape of the new bomber was defined on a computer database, not in terms of sections and stations, but in its totality; the database could define the precise three-dimensional co-ordinates of any point on the skin. The database was housed on banks of tape drives and managed by a Cray supercomputer. Connected to the database were more than 400 computer work-stations at Pico Rivera; the database was shared with major sub-contractors Boeing and Vought, and their own engineers. As detail design proceeded, the engineers could work from the outside in; as the design of each part was completed, it was added to the database. The computer system grew to define the shape and location of every component of the B-2, down to the smallest fastener.

New approaches, new materials

Quite early in the programme, the database took over from the first 'engineering fixture' produced to support the B-2 design, so that the aircraft became the first to be created without a true mock-up. Computer-aided design is standard practice now, but it was far from being so in 1983, and the Northrop team found itself breaking new ground. Even with CIM, the internal plumbing and wiring of AV-1, the first aircraft, proved to be a voracious consumer of manhours.

Materials were another problem area. The skin had to be made thicker and heavier than predicted, because its stealth characteristics might be compromised if it buckled under loads. Other requirements compounded the problem, Waaland said later: "We entered the programme with what we thought was a full range of validated materials, both low-observable and non-low-observable. We were required to validate our materials for nuclear flash and dust, long-life ultra-violet exposure, rain, supportability, producibility and a lot of other concerns. The bottom line is that nothing that we started with survived."

Before the first B-2 was completed, Northrop and its team-mates tested more than 900 materials. Where the chosen approach seemed risky, the customer demanded extensive demonstrations: for example, three complete 15-m (49-ft) composite wing skin panels were built in 1982-83 before the USAF was satisfied that the material would be durable, that there would be no problems with

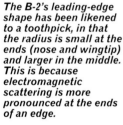

lightning and that the promised 3.2-ton weight saving would be achieved. Only then could Northrop and Boeing cease working on a back-up aluminium-alloy design.

In many cases, new materials not only cost money to develop, but were more expensive in production as well. Like other manufacturers, Northrop had to switch from early epoxy resins to new formulations which offered better through-the-skin toughness and resisted delamination better. Around the engines, epoxies gave way to new heat-tolerant bismaleimide and polyimide resins. Many of these materials and processes have or will become standard on later programmes.

The third principal driver behind the design, along with aerodynamics and structures, was stealth technology. The concept of 'balanced observables' is essential to understanding the design of the B-2. In the ideal 'balanced' aircraft, its detection range in any spectrum – radar, IR, visual or acoustic – will be much the same.

The demands of 'stealth'

On a stealth aircraft, routine things can become difficult. Because access panels have to be treated so carefully, it is best to eliminate as many of them as possible. This involves careful design. On the B-2, one panel usually gives access to several systems; other sub-systems, such as the avionics, are installed so that they can be reached through existing apertures such as the crew boarding hatch, weapons bay and landing gear bay. The B-2 is also unusual in that it has no drain holes. Instead, drain paths lead to collectors that can be emptied on the ground.

RCS reduction is the most critical element of stealth, because radar provides the defender with the most information at the longest range. Denys Overholser, one of the key

players in the Lockheed Have Blue design, lists the four most important factors in RCS reduction as "shape, shape, shape and materials." Shape is by far the biggest factor in reducing RCS, but special radar-absorbent material (RAM) is necessary to mop up residual scattering from the shaped surfaces and to suppress reflections from features such as inlets, which cannot be totally stealthy in their basic design. RAM is applied to an existing structure and adds to its weight without increasing its strength; radar-absorbing structure (RAS) involves building these materials into load-bearing structure. Most of the B-2 is covered by multi-layer sprayed-on elastomeric coatings that maintain a uniform conductivity at the surface. RAM is used selectively in areas such as control-surface gaps, doors and other apertures, and inside the inlet ducts.

The principles of RAM

RAM consists of an active element – a material such as carbonyl iron particles, which transform radar energy into heat – embedded in a dielectric plastic matrix. It is usually formulated and applied so that the small reflection from the front face of the absorber is cancelled by a residual reflection from the structure beneath it. The basic technique is to make the total pathway of energy within the RAM equal to half a wavelength, so that the residual reflection is exactly out of phase with the front-face reflection. The RAM can be much thinner than the nominal wavelength of the radar and still achieve cancellation, because the wavelength inside the material is much shorter than it is in free space.

Solid RAM coatings cover a frequency range of about 20:1. This is enough to address air-to-air and surface-to-air missile radars (from the L-band up to the Ku-band) but

more elaborate schemes are used to cover the full radar spectrum, which includes VHF radars with wavelengths of almost 2 m (6.5 ft).

Although the leading edges of the B-2 cannot be described in detail, a wide-band radar-absorbent structure (RAS), used on the edges of a stealth aircraft, has been compared to a stereo system, with a 'tweeter' and a 'woofer'. The 'tweeter' is a high-frequency ferromagnetic absorber, applied over a resistive layer that reflects higher frequencies but allows low-frequency signals to pass through. Beneath this resistive layer is the low-frequency 'woofer': a glass-fibre honeycomb core, treated from front to back with a steadily increasing amount of resistant material. Behind this is a sharp-edged, wedge-section reflective surface. What little energy reaches this surface will be attenuated once again before it escapes from the absorber.

Suppressing the IR signature

After radar, infra-red systems have the greatest potential range of any sensor. There are many types of infra-red sensor in service, and their different capabilities are sometimes confused. At a range of a few miles, a small IR sensor can receive enough energy to produce a TV-type image of the target, but this capability diminishes quickly with range.

Longer-range IR sensors, such as the infra-red search and track systems (IRSTS) fitted to fighters and the homing heads of IR-guided missiles, do not usually detect the IR emissions from the aircraft itself, but instead detect the radiation from the hot gas and water vapour emitted by its engines. The stealth designer's first task is therefore to deal with the exhausts.

The B-2's exhausts are built into the top of the wing. The primary nozzles are well ahead of the trailing edge, and lead into a pair of soft-lipped trenches, which flare outward. The engines are fitted with flow mixers to blend the cold bypass air with the hot core stream, and cold boundary layer which is swallowed by the secondary inlets is injected into the exhaust stream to cool it further. The exhausts are wide and flat, so the perimeter of the plume is longer than the perimeter of a round exhaust stream, and mixing takes place more quickly. Finally, the interaction between the exhaust stream and the airflow over the aircraft, at each angled side of the exhaust 'trench', creates a vortex which further promotes mixing.

At shorter ranges, IR systems detect radiation from the aircraft's skin. This is produced in two ways: from reflected sunlight and skin friction. IR-absorbent paints are widely used; containing compounds such as zinc sulfide, they work exactly like paints with visual colours, absorbing energy in a certain waveband. In this case, they absorb IR radiation from sunlight.

Heat generated by skin friction cannot be affected by an absorbing paint, but coatings have been developed which change the 'emissivity' of the surface – that is, the efficiency

with which it converts heat into IR radiation. Only certain bands of IR radiation travel efficiently through the atmosphere, so if the aircraft is coated with a substance that can shift energy into a different band, an IR detector may not be able to see it. IR emissions can also be reduced by slowing down or climbing into thinner air – both of which a B-2, with its modest wing loading, can do.

The most conspicuous element of the visual signature is not part of the aircraft, but its contrail, which can be suppressed by changing altitude. In 1995, NASA released

On 14 July 1994, during flight no. 36, AV-6 staged this unique formation with a pair of Lockheed F-117s. The orange diamond on the B-2's spine is a temporary test antenna (for TACAN or GPS, etc.). Another temporary test fit, the trailing wire rig, is seen here on AV-1 (above).

B-2 Spirit: The 'Stealth Bomber'

In October 1996 General Richard Hawley, Commander of Air Combat Command, stated that, "the B-2 is almost as revolutionary as the concept of flight itself. And true to its revolutionary capabilities, the B-2 is opening up new frontiers in the planning and execution of our national military strategy…it's an aircraft for all seasons – a true renaissance in aerial achievement." USAF air power theory proposes that the B-2 combines four characteristics never before combined in one aircraft: intercontinental range, large payload, precision weaponry and stealth technology. As the denial of foreign bases to US forces becomes increasingly likely, the B-2 is intended to stage from its home at Whiteman AFB, or from secure forward locations such as Guam in the Pacific Ocean or Diego Garcia in the Indian Ocean, from where it can strike virtually any target on the globe. The key to this capability will be the new range of precision-guided weapons now being fielded for the B-2. However, not one of the weapons currently earmarked for the B-2 yet has sufficient stand-off range to ensure that the B-2 will not come within lethal range of enemy air defences – so its stealthy credentials must be unassailable.

details of a LIDAR (light detection and ranging) system, being tested on an F/A-18, which would allow pilots to see their own contrails and change altitude to reduce them. The agency was later asked to stop talking about it in public, suggesting that a similar system may be used on stealth aircraft.

Suppressing the visible

Contrails can be made less visible by injecting chemicals into the exhaust that break the water into droplets which are smaller than the wavelength of visible light. In the 1960s, the USAF tested a system that injected chloro-flouro-sulfonic acid (CSA) into the exhaust stream on B-47 and B-52 bombers. CSA is toxic and corrosive and was abandoned in favour of a new, classified system that is in use on the B-2 and F-117. (One alternative in the open literature is an alcohol/surfactant mixture.)

Because the B-2's underside is a dark grey, people tend to think that it is intended to fight only at night. This is unlikely, because the B-2 was designed to bomb the Soviet Union, and the direct route from the central US to Central Russia lies smack across the Arctic Circle, where it is daylight 24 hours a day for a large part of the year.

Altitude is critical to visual signature. An airliner at its cruising height always appears brightly lit against the sky, regardless of whether it is finished in American's bare metal or United's formal grey. This is because both the aircraft and the sky above it are illuminated by light that is scattered by dust and moisture in the air. There is not much of either in the thin air above the aircraft, and lots of both below it.

The higher the aircraft flies, the more light is scattered onto its underside and the darker the sky behind it. The B-2's undersides are dark because it cruises at altitudes as high as 50,000 ft (15240 m), where a dark grey blends into the sky. It would not be surprising if the B-2 had an upward-facing light sensor that would instruct the pilot to increase or reduce altitude slightly to match the changing luminance of the sky.

Again, the goal is not to be invisible, but to be so hard to detect that no reliable and affordable detection scheme can be found. The sharpest fighter pilot has a hard time seeing another aircraft more than 5 nm (5.75 miles; 9.2 km) away, in the absence of a contrail or a 'cue'. The B-2 is likely to be at least 2 miles (3.2 km) away from any loitering fighter in the vertical plane alone – which also reduces the chance that it will be back-lit against the horizon.

The Red Team studied, built and tested acoustic detection devices, and determined that they did not present a threat to high-altitude aircraft. Even the quietest places on earth have too much background noise to permit high-flying aircraft to be detected. Finally, there is one signature that exceeds the range of radar, and provides even better identi-

One of the great benefits of Edwards AFB as a base for testing is the wide diversity of terrain and climatic conditions that are just a short flight away. Though situated in the Mojave desert, Edwards is within 30 minutes flying time of the Pacific Ocean. The Sierra Nevada mountains and more rugged terrain are also close at hand to the flat dry lake bed at Muroc – which is not always dry and does receive some rainfall. Nearby Mt Whitney is the highest point in the 'lower 48'. This is an early view of AV-3 seen during B-2 test flight no. 8 on 22 November 1991.

fication: emissions from the aircraft's own systems. Stealth has been a major influence on the design, manufacture and cost of the B-2's mission avionics, which are designed to detect, identify and locate virtually any large surface target with no outside help, under any weather conditions – something which no other aircraft can do.

The mission crew and mission systems

The system is managed by the B-2's two-member crew. Both are rated pilots: the pilot occupies the left seat, and the mission commander sits on the right and has primary responsibility for navigation and weapon delivery. Behind the crew station is an area which is shared by avionics racks and space for a third crew station.

The cockpit is designed so that either crew member can perform the complete mission. Each pilot has four 6-in (15-cm) square, full-colour cathode ray tube (CRT) cockpit displays arranged in a T shape: they can display flight information, sensor inputs or systems data on command. Each pilot also has a data entry panel to his right, and a set of throttles to his left. (The throttles, like the flight controls, are linked electronically to the engines.) There is also a set of 'master mode switches' which configure the displays and computers for pre-flight, take-off, cruise and landing.

The space for a third seat, well behind the pilots' seats, was retained in case the workload proved too great. As it was, more than 6,000 hours of manned simulation had been carried out before the B-2 was unveiled, convincing SAC that two pilots would be enough.

The primary functions of the mission avionics are navigation, target detection and self-defence. The navigation sub-system (NSS) initially combined two units, either of which is capable of navigating the aircraft on its own but

which are most accurate and reliable when they work together. One of them is an inertial measurement unit (IMU) from Kearfott, and the other is a Northrop NAS-26 astro-inertial unit (AIU). Northrop pioneered this technology in the early 1950s, when it developed the Snark long-range cruise missile.

The astro-inertial system developed for the Snark was based on a stabilised electro-optical telescope, capable of locking on to a pre-selected star even in cloudy daylight. A version of this system was used on the A-12 and SR-71, and an improved descendant is fitted to the B-2, with an observation port to the left of the windshield.

The Block 20 upgrade to the B-2 includes a global positioning system (GPS) receiver, with a specially developed low-observable antenna. GPS equals or surpasses the accuracy of the AIU, and will replace it in routine operations, although the AIU will remain in use as an unjammable backup.

LPI radar for the B-2

The B-2's APQ-181 radar (known as the radar subsystem or RSS) is developed by the Radar Systems Group of GM-Hughes Electronics. In the early days of the programme, B-2 critics often complained that the bomber would have no way of finding its targets at long stand-off ranges without betraying its presence by radar emissions. This argument was a measure of the effectiveness of the security which protected the development of low-probability-of-intercept (LPI) radar technology over many years. By the time the B-2 development programme started, in 1981, Hughes and Northrop had been actively developing LPI airborne radar for more than three years, under the Tacit Blue programme.

Northrop Grumman B-2A Spirit 393rd Bomb Squadron 509th Bomb Wing Whiteman AFB, Missouri

RAM coating

In addition to the shape of the aircraft, a key component of the RCS-reduction techniques is the use of special coatings which absorb radar energy and transmit it around the surface. The application of such materials requires attention to minute detail, and the materials themselves suffer from adverse climatic conditions. In mid-1997 the USAF admitted to the General Accounting Office that the B-2 could not be effectively deployed away from Whiteman and maintain full operational effectiveness due to the difficulties in maintaining the RAM coating at full specification. Specialised facilities would be required to maintain the stealthy properties of the aircraft, and the work required to bring a B-2 to full wartime status was considerably greater than had at first been expected. Improvements to the RAM and the methods by which it is applied were actively pursued to reduce the down-time needed between missions, reduce the associated costs and render the aircraft truly deployable to airfields without recourse to building specialised facilities. In the event, the USAF recognised that specialised hangars would be needed, and procured deployable facilities. The first were installed at Diego Garcia, and were used operationally for the first time in Operation Iraqi Freedom in March/April 2003.

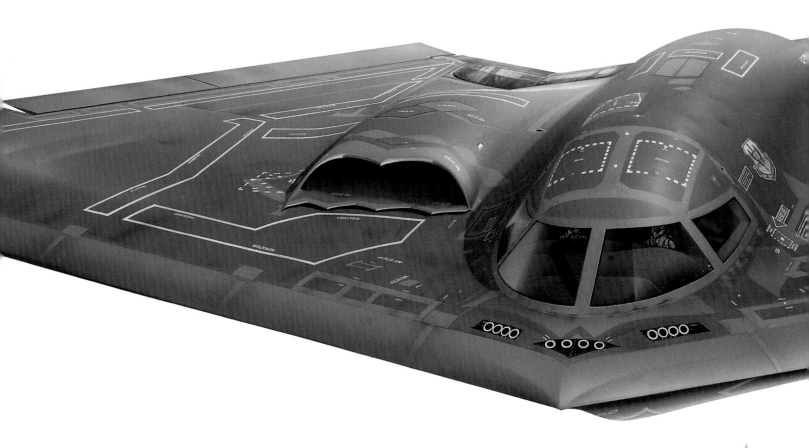

On 1 February 1997 two B-2 bomber pilots emerged from the Whiteman AFB B-2 simulator complex from what Armstrong Laboratory officials hailed as the longest simulator flight in USAF history. Major Steve Moulton and Captain Jeff Long completed the record-setting B-2 simulator flight, called Vigilant Spirit II, in 44.4 hours. Two cassette recorders were attached to each pilot by a series of nine wires to report brain electrical activity, heart rate, head movement and eye-blinking. The purpose behind the analysis was to determine how fatigue impacts pilots' abilities to perform their mission and return safely. Pilots can usually make it to their targets, but it is the return trip, through possibly a second sunrise and sunset, that is considered to be the most hazardous. These tests help pilots learn to recognise and adapt to fatigue, and diminish its consequences. Reducing the impact of fatigue can be done by teaching crews how to take 'power naps'. Naps lasting 20 to 30 minutes or three to four hours are much easier to wake from than deeper stages of sleep. Sleep, dietary strategies and seat exercises play a key role in the success of the long missions. Each crew member was allowed to sleep in a prone position (each carried a sleeping bag and pillow) and use a chemical toilet. This was the 509th Bomb Wing's third endurance simulator flight. Captain Tony Monetti and Major Chris Inman flew the first on 7 October 1996, lasting 34 hours; and Captains Scott Vander Hamm and Scott Hughes flew the second on 11 November, lasting 38 hours. The techniques derived from these tests were put to operational use during Operation Enduring Freedom, when missions from Whiteman to Afghanistan reached 44 hours, terminating (for the crew at least) at Diego Garcia in the British Indian Ocean Territories.

B83 nuclear bomb

In the strategic role the primary weapon of the B-2 is the B83, a megaton-class weapon with variable yields. It is cleared for carriage by a variety of aircraft, including tactical aircraft such as the F-16, F/A-18 and F-15E, but its high yield make it more applicable for carriage by the B-1B and B-2. It was developed as a cheaper alternative to the B77, development of which was cancelled in 1978. The B83 emerged with similar characteristics, and was the first strategic yield weapon designed for low-level laydown deliveries, replacing the B28, B43 and B53 weapons. Safety and versatility were the keywords in the bomb's development. It can be used from as low as 150 ft (46 m) and has a fully-variable fusing and yield, this being programmed by the crew in flight. The bomb uses very safe explosive initiators, which will not ignite even under extremes of temperature (such as may be caused in an aircraft fire) or if inadvertently dropped. The security code number system is highly complex and if, after a certain number of attempts the correct sequence has not been entered, a self-destruct mechanism is triggered, disabling key components without damaging the integrity of the radioactive material. The B83 was primarily targeted against hardened military targets such as ICBM silos, underground facilities and nuclear weapons storage facilities.

Defining the B-2 shape

The B-2's shape is the result of adding a new factor – observability – to the considerations which normally determine the general configuration of an aircraft, such as aerodynamics and the integration of the aircraft's major components. Northrop's low-RCS design philosophy, developed and tested on Tacit Blue, was quite straightforward but resulted in a very unusual-looking aircraft, because it rested on two fundamental principles that drove different parts of the aircraft in opposite directions. The RCS of a conventional aircraft, which is a random irregular shape from an electromagnetic viewpoint, varies sharply with the aspect angle – that is, the radar's bearing from the aircraft. Whenever a radar illuminates the aircraft, most of its energy bounces off the surface like light from a mirror. The energy may well be reflected again from another part of the aircraft (bouncing off the body to the wing, for example). Some of the energy, too, will creep along the skin like St Elmo's fire, and will be scattered whenever it reaches a gap or a change in conductivity. A basic principle behind low-RCS design is that a flat plate has both the largest and smallest RCS of any simple shape. If the plate is normal to the radar beam, its RCS is enormous; but if it is rotated away from the beam in one dimension, its RCS is far smaller, and if it is rotated in two dimensions (rotated and canted) its RCS is minute. In the F-117, Lockheed's designers produced a shape composed entirely of flat plates, aligned so that they were, at almost all times, angled away from the radar beam in two dimensions. Most radar sources that matter are now located in a narrow band of elevations around the aircraft. However, this led to a secondary problem: creeping waves over the surface tended to be scattered from the sharp edges of the shape. Unable to model these effects fully, Lockheed beat them into insignificance by 'candy-coating' the entire aircraft with RAM. Cashen's electromagneticists saw that the same results – ensuring that every part of the surface was angled away from the radar in two dimensions – could also be achieved if the surface was curved. Indeed, if the entire skin of the aircraft comprised one surface, with curving contours of constantly changing radius and direction, there might be no edges or creases at all, avoiding any 'hot spots' in the RCS. This was the first basic principle of the B-2's shape.

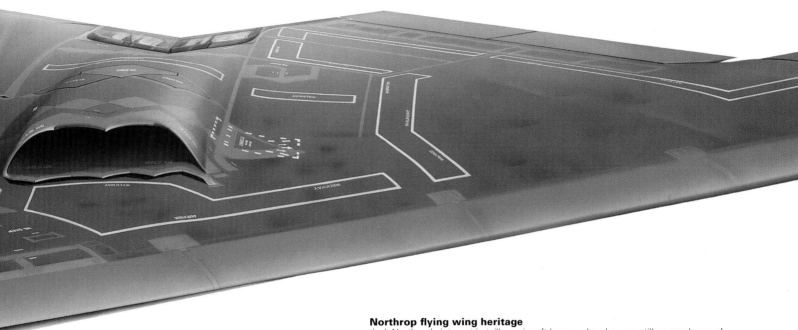

Controlling the RCS

The second element of the bomber's configuration was common to the F-117. While most of the surfaces could be concealed from radar by making them sloped or curved, the upper and lower surfaces of the aircraft would have to meet at some point. Wing and tail surfaces would also have distinct edges. How should this 'waterline' around the aircraft be handled? The edges and body sides could be treated with RAM, but not well enough to match the surfaces. Instead, the designers on both Lockheed and Northrop teams realised that while the residual reflection from the edges could not be eliminated, it could be controlled, exploiting the fact that the strongest reflection was at right angles to the edge. The design was laid out so that all the edges were grouped along a small number of alignments. The RCS would peak when the radar was normal to one of these edges – but this would happen only transiently, as the aircraft moved relative to the radar and its bearing changed. Since there is scattering both from the edge of the aircraft that faces the radar and from the edge that faces away from it, the smallest practical number of 'spikes' is four. This can be produced from a pure diamond shape or – since a diamond will not fly very well – from a shape in which all edges conform to two alignments, as on the B-2. In a later refinement, both Lockheed and Northrop designers realised that the problem of combining stealth with doors and other apertures could be eased if they conformed to the same alignments as the wing and body edges. If necessary, door edges could be serrated so that the edges were angled while the aperture itself was rectangular. The breakthrough that got Northrop out of trouble on Tacit Blue in 1977 was the shaping technique that combined the sharp edges with the curved surfaces: a gradual flare to the knife-edge, still very visible on the lower surfaces of the B-2, combined with continuous curvature to make the energy flow around the aircraft. It is this combination of smoothly curved, seamless surfaces with jagged edges that makes the bomber's appearance so distinctive. Other aspects of low-RCS design had been clear from the first Harvey studies in 1975. Conventional engine installations and external weapons were dominant RCS contributors and would have to be eliminated. Tail surfaces were not impossible to deal with, but required careful design and had to be minimised in size and number.

Northrop flying wing heritage

Jack Northrop's interest in tailless aircraft began when he was still an employee of Loughhead (before it became the Lockheed Aircraft Company), between 1919 and 1927. Northrop began working on his own design in the late 1920s and his Experimental No. 1 model flew in 1929. This aircraft did have a tail, but was a stepping stone to bigger and better things. The first true 'flying wing' was the unsuccessful N-1M which flew in July 1940. The N-1M's performance was very poor and the aircraft was reluctant to climb on take-off, let alone fly. With some changes to the aerofoil design its performance improved, and the N-1M itself survived and can be found today in the US National Air and Space Museum's collection.

The roots of the subsequent great Northrop flying wing bombers lay in the dark days of World War II when it looked as if Hitler's armies might overrun Britain, leaving the United States with a transatlantic war to fight. Preliminary requirements for a 'super bomber' that could make the round trip from the USA to Germany, carrying a 10,000-lb (4536-kg) bombload, resulted in several competing designs including Northrop's piston-powered B-35. The B-35 had the same 172-ft (52.42-m) wingspan as today's B-2 and weighed 100 tons. To build such an unprecedented aircraft was considered to be too great a technological leap, so Northrop first built the scaled-down N-9M (one-third the size of the B-35) to prove the concept. Though unpredictable in handling and at times downright uncontrollable, the N-9M proved that a flying wing could be built and flown. However, so great were the delays in the test and development programme that, by the time the B-35 was ready to fly, the war was virtually over. As a result, all contracts were cancelled, leaving only two XB-35 experimental prototypes and 13 YB-35 service development aircraft to be built. Powered by four 3,000-hp (2238-kW) Pratt & Whitney Wasp Major R-4360-17 engines, the XB-35 first flew on 25 June 1946. Flying was such a mechanical nightmare that the two XB-35 aircraft spent a grand total of 36 hours in the air.

The B-35 was already obsolete with the coming of the jet age, however, and USAF attention instead turned to building a jet-powered, eight-engined flying wing, the B-49. The B-49 simply swapped the new engines into the airframes of nine YB-35s and production proceeded smoothly and quickly. Fitted with eight General Electric TG-180/Allison J35 axial turbojets, the first YB-49 flew from Northrop's Hawthorne factory on 21 October 1947. The YB-49 encountered some minor problems such as its lack of fuel baffles, which left fuel sloshing back and forth through the large span-wise tanks, More serious was the loss of the stabilising effect of the piston-engines, prop-shafts and props, which led to wing fences being incorporated on the jet flying wings. Most importantly, the YB-49 soon proved to be deficient in range, load-carrying ability and overall performance, and was essentially unable to carry out its intended mission as a long-range nuclear bomber. The seal was set on the story when aircraft No. 2 crashed on 5 June 1948, wildly out of control after having entered a tail slide during stall testing, killing test pilot Glen Edwards. The place of the B-49 was soon taken by Boeing's B-47, and all flying wing contracts were cancelled.

Above: In November 1994 the Planes of Fame Museum at Chino, California restored one of the original Northrop N-9MBs to airworthy condition. The following February the N-9MB flew to Edwards where it sat alongside AV-6 for the 50th anniversary of its first flight – and just 100 yd from where its hangars of 50 years ago had stood. At least one B-2 pilot, Bruce Hinds, got to fly the N-9M.

Top: AV-4 is seen here in November 1993, in formation with one of the test force's F-16B chase planes, before all the F-16s adopted a red and white 'high-vis' scheme. The F-16s accompanied the B-2 as a 'visual augmentor' because, in many circumstances, they were easier for other traffic to see than the B-2 itself.

Right: AV-3 seen hooked up to a KC-135E at dusk during its flight no. 57, on 10 June 1993.

The basic principle of LPI is to emit the least amount of energy required to detect and track the target, while manipulating the signal to make it difficult for an adversary to detect it among all the electronic burps, honks and squeals that pollute the high-tech battlefield. LPI techniques include the adaptive management of power (the radar gradually increases its power until it can see a target, and then holds its power level or reduces it as the range declines), the use of very-low-sidelobe antennas, and constant variations in frequency and waveform.

The APQ-181 has two 265-kg (584-lb) electronically scanned antennas built into the lower leading edge of the wing, one on each side. Each radar antenna has its own power supply, transmitter/receiver and signal processing unit, and the two chains are cross-connected so that the radar can continue to perform even if part of one chain fails. The radar operates in the Ku-band (12-18 GHz), which is a higher frequency and shorter wavelength than the X-band (around 10 GHz) where most airborne radars operate. Ku-band radars suffer from more atmospheric absorption than X-band, and are less suitable for large-area searches because, all other things being equal, they require more power and more time to scan a given volume. However, they have inherently higher resolution than X-band radars, and, for a given antenna size, a Ku-band radar will have smaller and weaker sidelobes that will dissipate more quickly.

APQ-181 modes

Among the most important of the radar's 20 modes are a synthetic aperture radar (SAR) mode, and terrain following and terrain avoidance (TF/TA). The latter modes provide data to dual TF/TA processors which interface with the flight control system. The radar has a ground moving target indication (GMTI) mode to detect vehicles on the ground,

and an LPI air-to-air mode which may be used during inflight refuelling, as well as more conventional long-range mapping and weather modes.

Radar development proved difficult and expensive. The first experimental radar antenna in the programme flatly refused to transmit a coherent beam. The problem caused near-panic in the programme office, but it was soon realised that it was due to leakage among the ports in the electronically scanned antenna: the antenna had not been built to sufficiently tight tolerances. Each antenna included more than 400 precision-machined parts with a total of 600,000 high-tolerance features. Among those parts were 85 'phasor plates', machined from a solid slab of magnesium in a cutting process during which the machine head moves 6.4 km (3.7 miles). Using conventional machining, each plate would take 25 hours of cutting work – which meant that one machine working regular hours would take two years to build this single part for one aircraft. Hughes addressed the problem by introducing the emerging technology of high-speed machining, with cutter heads rotating at 25,000-75,000 rpm. This reduced the machining time to 4.5 hours for each of the plates, making the manufacture of the antenna practicable – if still not exactly cheap.

ZSR-62 and -63: the mystery DMS

The third main element of the B-2 mission avionics is the defensive management sub-system (DMS). Details of the DMS, which includes components from Lockheed Martin, Raytheon and Honeywell, are largely classified. However, its most important element appears to be the Lockheed Martin (formerly Loral, and before that, IBM) APR-50, which has also been identified by the internal designation ZSR-63.

The ZSR-63 replaced an earlier Northrop-developed system called ZSR-62, which was abandoned after encountering development problems. As far as is known, this was the only major sub-system to be scrapped during development, a measure of the difficulty of the DMS task. All details of the problems with the ZSR-62 remain secret.

The APR-50 is designed to detect, classify, identify and locate hostile systems that emit radio-frequency energy. Although the B-2's mission can be pre-planned to present

the aircraft's least detectable aspects to known threats, there is always the risk that some radars have been moved or have not been detected before the mission. The APR-50 – which has been compared to the electronic surveillance measures capability of a dedicated electronic warfare aircraft such as the EA-6B – provides the B-2 crew with real-time updates. It consists of an automated signal-processing and analysis system, linked to receiver antennas distributed across the airframe.

In combat, the B-2's information management system and cockpit displays should be able to 'fuse' data from many sources. Radar imagery, for example, will be superimposed on maps of the target area, acquired by satellite and stored onboard the B-2. The physical and electronic characteristics of known threats can also be stored and fused. If an SA-5 radar is detected, the system can display its location, its predicted area of coverage and the bomber's projected track on the CRT; the crew can determine instantly whether a course change is necessary.

Above: AV-4 seen during flight no. 194 on 28 February 1997 in the pattern for Vandenburg AFB. The white marks on the leading edges are for icing tests – the tests were long since finished but the markings were never removed. Note the drag rudders open to 45° for approach and the drooped gust alleviation surface on the tail.

Top: AV-6 is seen here on a rare humid day over Edwards in March 1994 with a strong laminal condensation flow building up as the aircraft approaches its critical Mach number.

Much of the avionics system is based on 13 common avionics control unit (ACU) processors (built by a former Unisys unit which is now part of Lockheed Martin), which carry out several functions which, in earlier systems, were performed by special-purpose computers: TF/TA, navigation, defensive systems and stores management are all carried out by ACUs. Designed to stringent requirements for radiation-hardening and vibration tolerance (some of them are installed in the aft centrebody, between the engine exhausts), the ACUs can be expanded to handle more complex processing tasks through new software.

The navigation and radar systems have been tested on a Boeing C-135, known as the flight-test avionics laboratory (FTAL), which made its first flight in January 1987. The FTAL was needed because many radar modes cannot be adequately tested on a static test rig and some (such as SAR) cannot be demonstrated at all except in the air.

Programme history

In 1997, more than 15 years after the B-2 was designed, it is interesting to ask how many other combat aircraft in service have multi-mode LPI radars; how many incorporate what can almost be classed as a signals intelligence system; how many use differential thrust for control; how many are primarily built from composite materials. The answer to these and many other questions is a Big Fat Zero. Little wonder, then, that the B-2 development was not easy.

In mid-1997, the initial B-2 flight-test programme is drawing to a close, eight years after the bomber's first flight, and the first fully operational aircraft is ready for delivery to the USAF. Quite clearly, there have been some delays in the programme, along with the cost overruns that inevitably accompany such delays. Pervasive secrecy has made it extremely difficult to put together the entire story of the programme. Even what follows is a preliminary account of a story that remains very sensitive, for reasons of politics and national security.

When the B-2 programme started, in October 1981, the first aircraft was planned to fly around the end of 1987. By that time, a concurrent production programme would be

under way, with the rate increasing as the 'learning curve' took effect. The bomber would attain an initial operating capability (IOC) in 1991 or 1992; around then, the production rate would attain a peak of 30 aircraft per year.

A common factor in almost any project that runs late is excessive optimism at the outset, and the B-2 was no exception. In a 1996 interview, Dr Paul Kaminski noted that hopes for stealth were high when the B-2 started. "The success of the F-117 had set up expectations. It was a given that we could achieve everything that we could do on the F-117, while eliminating all its deficiencies and limitations. But it wasn't just like falling off a log."

B-2 versus B-1

From the start, the B-2 was affected by the progress of the B-1B programme. In fact, work on the B-2 was quite slow for the first year, because the B-1B was 'ramping up' so quickly and absorbing most of the available money. Most of that time was taken up with the wing redesign; by extensive penetration studies, to validate the basic principles of the design; and by a lengthy study of the two-versus-three-crew issue.

However, the target first-flight and IOC dates did not change during 1983, despite the fact that the wing redesign had put the programme about a year behind where it was expected to be. The reason was in large measure political. Rockwell, teamed with Lockheed, was still actively promoting a follow-on B-1, and there was some concern that delays in the B-2 programme, acknowledged so early in its life, would make an improved B-1 more attractive.

The USAF was concerned about technical risks, and set up a 'risk closure' programme in which large-scale tests (such as the full-scale inlet rig) were used in an attempt to identify and solve problems before they could manifest themselves on the full-size aircraft. Designer Irv Waaland calls it "the world's most complete R&D programme. There was a belief that nothing should go untested." This philosophy has been sustained throughout the programme. To this day, it ensures that what is delivered to the user actually works, but it does not foster rapid progress.

Security was a larger-than-expected factor in the cost of the programme. Have Blue and Tacit Blue had been developed in strict secrecy, but they were smaller programmes. They were developed by small, hand-picked teams, and as few people as possible were told that they existed. The companies did not need to hire new people to build the aircraft, and many components were bought from third-party suppliers who did not need to know to purpose to which their products were put.

On those programmes, "we protected the perimeters," says Waaland. "We researched people, investigated and did background checks, but information within the programme was free-flowing. On the B-2, we introduced total accountability for everything." At any time, the USAF expected to be able to ask the location of any document in the programme. "It really added costs and reduced productivity."

Secrecy, on the B-2, "had many non-beneficial aspects," Kaminski says now. The classification level meant that the most stringent regulations had to be put into effect over thousands of sub-contractors. Tens of thousands of newly hired people had to be security vetted and tested for drug use (this in Los Angeles, in the early 1980s). The vetting system was swamped, and many employees spent weeks in limbo, on the payroll but unable to work. Overall, secrecy added 10-15 per cent to the cost of the programme.

Together with the technical challenges in every area – manufacturing, controls, avionics – these measures drove up costs and caused delay. However, since no schedule had been published, and since the project was shrouded in secrecy, public criticism was muted – at least for a time.

Out of the black and into the flak

The B-2 emerged from the black on 22 November 1988, when AV-1 (82-1066) was unveiled at Palmdale. Invited guests were allowed to view only the front of the bomber, and no pictures of the planview were released – a security measure that failed to deter *Aviation Week*'s Mike Dornheim, who flew a photographer over the roll-out site, above the minimum altitude set by the FAA, and secured clear shots of the planview shape and exhaust nozzles.

By this time, the programme was drawing more criticism from the media and from politicians. The fact that the production and service-entry schedule was still secret tended to heighten speculation that there were serious problems with the B-2. In fact, the programme was running 18-24 months behind the original schedule, and AV-1 was far from ready to fly: many internal parts had not been installed when it rolled out.

There were understandable reasons behind the delays: the B-2 had undergone a major redesign, it was breaking ground in many areas, and the programme philosophy favoured completeness over schedule. These were all secret, so the public and the media were left to draw their own conclusions as the winter of 1988 turned into the summer of 1989 and AV-1 remained firmly on the ground. Scepticism about the management of Air Force programmes in general, and bombers in particular, had been fostered by intractable problems with the B-1B's defensive avionics system. Ironically, the root of these problems was that crucial tests had not been performed before the design was committed to production, in direct contrast to the cause of the B-2 delays. Nevertheless, Congress became reluctant to commit the B-2 to production until flight tests were well advanced. Representative Les Aspin, the Wisconsin Democrat who chaired the House Armed Services Committee, used his committee to block full-rate production.

Under the original plan, B-2 production should have picked up pace in the FY88-89 budgets. B-2s could be delivered 60 months after being ordered, putting large-scale deliveries and full operational capability in 1994-95. But

The 509th BW at Whiteman AFB, MO gained Initial Operational Capability (IOC) on 1 April 1997. The granting of IOC enables the B-2 to be included in any contingency plans for combat operations on a limited basis. On 19 and 20 March the type performed one of its longest non-stop Global Power missions to date when 92-0700 flew from Whiteman AFB across the Atlantic Ocean before heading for the Vieques Range off Puerto Rico to deliver live conventional weapons. The 30-hour mission involved four inflight refuellings, including one by a KC-135R of the 100th ARW from RAF Mildenhall which rendezvoused near the Azores.

On 11 June 1995 B-2 88-0329/Spirit of Missouri (AV-1008) made the type's first appearance outside the USA, with a 1-hour 20-minute visit to the Paris air show. The aircraft was flown by Brigadier General Ronald Marcotte, commander of the 509th BW, and Major Jim Smith, who acted as mission commander.

The B-2 dropped out of the grey skies over Le Bourget right on schedule, at 10:00 a.m., and made several figure of eight circuits around the airfield, including steeply banked turns, before landing to steal the show at the 41st Paris Salon. The Paris appearance was part of an 11-hour 30-minute Global Power training mission from Whiteman AFB to the Vliehors bombing range in the Netherlands, where the B-2 simulated the dropping of 16 Mk 84 bombs before arriving at the show. The B-2 remained on the ground under heavy guard, with its engines running.

The GBU-31 JDAM (Joint Direct Attack Munition) is a 2,000-lb Mk 84 bomb body (with an optional BLU-109 hardened target penetrating warhead) fitted with a laser-ring gyro, GPS receivers and actuated fins along the body. JDAM was built to a requirement that demanded a CEP of 13 m (42.6 ft), but has demonstrated a CEP of 9 m (29.5 ft). The first JDAM was dropped from a B-2 on 28 February 1997. From a release point of 40,000 ft (12192 m) – at Mach 0.8, with an impact angle of 60° – JDAM can travel up to 13 miles (21 km) to the target.

Congress refused to appropriate the money. The start of production was, first, delayed to take account of the late start of flight-testing; then, it was further postponed so that more flight tests, including the first stage of observables testing, could be completed before production could begin. Preparations for production were well under way, and more than 40,000 people were working on the B-2 programme. Suspending production would have had a catastrophic impact; workers would have been lost, together with their hard-earned knowledge, and many sub-contractors would have had to find other business. Instead, the programme was stretched out, so that the USAF would buy only two or three B-2s per year until the start of full-rate production was authorised.

The maiden flight, and storm clouds

On 17 July 1989 AV-1 made its 2-hour 20-minute first flight from Palmdale to Edwards AFB. Pilots were Bruce Hinds, chief test pilot for the Northrop B-2 Division, and Colonel Richard Couch, commander of the B-2 Combined Test Force at Edwards AFB.

The mass media, which had largely ignored the B-2 during its years of secret development, were overwhelmingly negative in their coverage of the bomber in 1989 and 1990. Influential outlets such as Newsweek and the high-

rated TV magazine 60 Minutes ran damning anti-B-2 diatribes, long on hyperbole, short on evidence and entirely free of balance. Flying-wing critics from the 1940s emerged from holes in the woodwork and were reverently quoted in major newspapers. Northrop employees alleged that there were safety-of-flight problems with the bomber. They were also widely quoted, and the media seldom explained clearly that they were allied with attorneys bringing actions under the Civil War-era False Claims Act, under which the whistle-blowers and their lawyers stood to make fortunes if claims were upheld or settled.

In June 1990, the Air Force held a B-2 media briefing at Palmdale, and described the B-2 and its planned missions in unprecedented detail. The Wall Street Journal's reporter summed up the USAF's entire case in one word: "tendentious". In the same report, he quoted Congressman John Kasich, an opponent of the B-2, as saying that the B-2 would "bankrupt America". Considering that the programme's peak annual cost at the time was one per cent of the defence budget, that statement could (and should) have been called something more than tendentious.

The case for the B-2 was not helped by the fact that the apparent progress with the programme was slow. By June 1990, AV-1 had flown only 16 times, for some 67 hours. There had been one mechanical problem – cracking in the aircraft mounted accessory drive (AMAD) casings – but it had been anticipated as a result of earlier tests and was solved fairly quickly. AV-2 (82-1067) was still in final assembly, and would not fly until 19 October 1990. On its maiden flight AV-2 followed AV-1's original route, flying from Palmdale to Edwards also.

Although the programme was behind the original schedule, it was not out of control; the USAF was doing what it could to mitigate the impact of Congress's changes to the programme. By mid-1989, it was clear that the B-2 could not be declared fully operational for many years, because there would not be enough aircraft available to form a squadron. Congress had authorised procurement of only 11 flying B-2s – six development aircraft and five production aircraft, the last of which would not be delivered until late 1994. Long-lead items for five more B-2s had been authorised, but these aircraft would not be ready until 1995.

Congress had blocked full-rate production until the B-2 passed its critical RCS tests, but AV-1 would not be ready to perform them until late 1990 and they would not be complete until the summer of 1991. Since it took five years from go-ahead to build a B-2, full-rate deliveries could not start until 1996, even if everything went perfectly.

Accordingly, the B-2 programme office, in 1989, defined a test programme that would finish in June 1997. The last items to be completed would be the final radar modes, because some of them (such as TF/TA) could not start their testing until other parts of the system, such as the navigation and flight control systems, had been fully validated.

The long gap between AV-1 and AV-2 reflected Northrop's concentration of its efforts on getting AV-1 in the air, to validate the bomber's flight performance and to prepare for the RCS tests, because until that could be done there would be no go-ahead for production. The company was reluctant to increase its workforce to build the development aircraft, and then end up with more people than were needed for low-rate production, so work on AV-2 and subsequent aircraft slowed down.

But the USAF, still under heavy fire from the media and Congress, was justifiably concerned about what might happen if it were revealed that the new bomber was still seven to eight years away from a full operational capability

– even though the bulk of the delay could be attributed directly to Les Aspin and the House Armed Services Committee. The IOC date for the bomber remained secret.

Affirming its LO credentials

AV-1 went into a lay-up period in the late summer of 1990, and resumed flying in November to carry out initial RCS measurements. Details of the process are still classified, but the tests were carried out incrementally, with components being adjusted and individual 'hot spots' being treated between flights until the desired RCS was attained.

Some of the tests involved flights against ground-based radars, while other tests were performed on the ground, with radars that moved on tracks to image parts of the aircraft. For air-to-air measurements – the only opportunity to examine the aircraft with its wheels up, its engines running and with no interference from the ground – Northrop used a NTA-3B Skywarrior bomber modified by Metratek to carry its Model 100 AIRSAR radar, in a bizarre frying-pan-shaped radome on the rear fuselage.

There were two significant differences between the B-2 and the F-117, the only stealth aircraft to have passed through full-scale development before it. First, it was much bigger, and it was too large to test on an RCS range at anything like full scale. The largest B-2 model that could be

To many, the prospect of the B-2 carrying loads of dumb bombs is alarming, but these weapons (including CBUs and mines) are still included in its notional warloads. AV-4 is seen here conducting conventional bomb drops with a full load of 500-lb Mk 82 bombs in August 1995 (above left) and then, in March 1997, with 750-lb M117 bombs. The B-2 can carry 80 Mk 82s or 36 M117s. The Vietnam-era M117 is an anachronism and quite why such a vintage weapon has been qualified for use with the B-2 is a mystery.

The first bomb to be tested by a B-2 was a 2,000-lb Mk 84, which was dropped from AV-4 on 12 September 1992. The Mk 84 forms the core of the GAM-84 (GPS-Aided Munition), part of the family of GAM bombs now in development for the B-2 and other aircraft. By January 1997 B-2s had reached limited operational capability with the GAM-84, which is essentially a Mk 84 bomb centrebody with a new tail section. The tail kit, which can be bolted on to any existing bomb, contains two GPS antennas and steerable fins with a MIL-STD 1760 interface for the B-2. A grooved 'tie-on' sleeve is also fitted to the nose of the bomb, which keeps it aerodynamically stable while guiding.

B-2 Spirit: The 'Stealth Bomber'

Far right: The 12-ft (3.65-m) long B83 thermonuclear bomb is one of the two nuclear weapons cleared for use on the B-2. In its original role as a hunter of mobile missiles, silos and command posts, the B-2 would have used the B83 as its primary weapon. The B83 was specifically designed for such a role, and was the first US nuclear bomb intended for 'laydown' deliveries. The bomb is dropped at high speed and low level (as little as 150-ft/45.7 m) and slowed by a parachute. Fusing can be set for air burst, ground burst or delayed action. The B83 was intended to replace the earlier B28, B43 and B53 weapons and over 1,000 were originally expected to be built. With the implementation of the START treaty this number was cut back, and approximately 650 B83s are estimated to be in the current US inventory. AV-4 is seen here during B83 tests over the Vandenburg ranges in November 1994.

The GAM-113 hardened target penetrator bomb is a new weapon specifically developed for the B-2. The 4,700-lb GAM-113 – which is similar to the GBU-28 'Deep Throat' LGB used in the final stages of Desert Storm – mates the BLU-113 penetrating warhead with a GPS guidance system. A B-2 can carry up to 16 GAM-113s, which are designed to destroy deeply buried targets. AV-4 made the first GAM-113 drop on 21 March 1997.

tested was about one-third of full size, whereas Lockheed had tested the F-117 at 70 per cent scale. The B-2 was also designed for stealth across a wider range of aspects and frequencies than the F-117; in particular, its leading edges were required to attenuate VHF frequencies – used by the Soviet 'Tall King' early warning radar – more efficiently than those of the F-117. These differences were at the root of the problems encountered in RCS testing. Higher-than-predicted reflections were found very early on, and by the summer it was clear that simple adjustments were not enough. The media and Congress panicked, and Air Force Secretary Donald Rice issued elaborate statements to quell the crowd without betraying any significant information.

Behind the scenes, the Pentagon's Defense Science Board reviewed the problems. Although details are classified, most observers believe that the problems were encountered in the VHF realm, where stealth is hardest to achieve, and that they were attributable to problems such as gaps, surface discontinuities and creeping waves, which are very difficult to model or predict and which cannot be adequately tested on a scale model.

An early conclusion was that the problems could be solved by changing coatings and edge materials; there was no need to alter the basic structure of the aircraft, so that any solution to the problem could be retrofittable, and B-2 production could be continued. The DSB also noted that, with the break-up of the Soviet Union, it might make sense to relax the RCS specification in some respects, to reflect threats that the bomber was likely to face, rather than to spend far more money to meet the original requirement.

It was announced in early 1993 that Northrop, Boeing and Lockheed had developed a set of RCS improvements that would be applied to the last B-2s off the line and retrofitted to earlier aircraft. This fix was described as the least costly and risky of three options which had been studied.

More B-2s in the air

Meanwhile, the remaining test aircraft had joined the programme. AV-3 (82-1068), first flown on 18 June 1991, was the first radar and navigation test aircraft. AV-4 (82-1069) and AV-5 (82-1070), designated for avionics and weapons testing, followed on 17 April and 5 October 1992, respectively. The last development aircraft, AV-6 (82-1071), flew on 2 February 1993. The NKC-135A avionics testbed resumed flying in 1992 to support tests of the TF/TA radar modes. In early 1993, AV-1 was placed in storage – with its incomplete avionics suite and non-standard instrumentation, it could no longer contribute to the programme.

The first production B-2, AV-1007 (88-0328), was delivered to Whiteman AFB, Missouri, in December 1993.

By then, however, it was clear that – barring a miracle – Whiteman would be the only operational B-2 base, because the programme had been scaled back to near extinction.

By 1990, with the Soviet Union on the verge of breaking up, the Democratic Congress was pressing the Bush administration for cuts in defence expenditures – the so-called peace dividend. The B-2 was a prime target, but the larger concern was that several large aircraft programmes – the B-2, the Navy's A-12 attack aircraft, the Advanced Tactical Fighter and the C-17 transport – were expected to be in full-rate production by the mid-1990s, and they could not all be supported by lower budgets.

A temporary compromise was announced in April 1990, when Defense Secretary Richard Cheney unveiled the results of the Pentagon's Major Aircraft Review (MAR).

The MAR kept all the Pentagon's aircraft projects alive, but sharply reduced production numbers in the mid-1990s. Under the MAR, the total planned B-2 buy was cut from 132 to 75, and the production rate was cut drastically; instead of a steady increase to a maximum of 33 aircraft in the final year, the rate would reach a plateau of 12 aircraft a year in the mid-1990s. Then-year programme cost would decline from $75.4 billion (having increased since late 1988 due to the delay in production) to $61.1 billion.

A 19 per cent cost saving as a result of a 43 per cent cut in output may seem asymmetric, but it has to be remembered that the non-recurring costs of the programme were unaffected by the cutback (most of them had been spent) and savings were further offset by the lower and less efficient production rate.

Ironically, one of the programmes preserved by the MAR, largely at the B-2's expense, was the Navy's A-12.

Cheney and Congress were equally unaware that the A-12 was in grave trouble, because the Navy was concealing the problems that had resulted from the arrogance and ineptitude of the service's top commanders and civilian leaders. Nine months later, the programme was dead.

Production freeze

Neither did the MAR satisfy Congressional foes of the B-2. In October 1991, Congress froze production at 16 aircraft, in the aftermath of the summer's failed military coup in the Soviet Union, the irreversible rupture of the Warsaw Pact, and the bad news from the RCS tests. In an attempt to turn the apparently inevitable halting of the programme into a political asset in an election year, President Bush announced in January 1992 that the administration would seek funds for only five more B-2s, bringing production to 21 including the six test aircraft. The cutback

Left: The B61-11 bomb is now the other arrow in the B-2's nuclear quiver. The B61-11 is a modification of the existing B61-7 bomb, specially altered for a specific task – destroying underground targets. The USAF already had a nuclear weapon tasked with this job, the 9-MT B53. However, the B53 is an old weapon, one which weighs 8,800 lb (3992 kg) and is 4 ft 2 in (1.28 m) in diameter. The B53 is so large it can only be carried by the B-52, but it has been retained in the inventory as it was the only US weapon capable of destroying a buried target. In 1987, Sandia National Laboratories proposed a penetrator modification of the B61, but approval for the actual B61-11 version was not given until August 1995. Drop tests were first made by the F-16, B-1B and the B-2, followed, in July 1997, by the B-52. The B61-11 is a rugged weapon, designed for high-speed 'laydown' deliveries, though most tests (to date) have been made at altitude. Exact release parameters are classified, but Donald McCoy, the programme manager, was quoted in Aviation Week as saying, "this one will skip. If you get it too shallow, it'll go in and come back out."

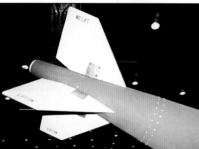

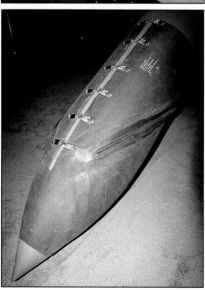

The GATS/GAM system is a B-2-specific family of bombs, intended to give the aircraft an immediate PGM capability. The most important of these bombs is the GAM-113 (above). GAM-113 final testing was conducted in early 1997, at the China Lake Naval Weapons Center. Like all GAM bombs, the GAM-113 uses an easily attachable tail unit, with GPS receivers and steerable fins (above left). To the nose of the bomb (left) is strapped a grooved aerodynamic 'jacket' that keeps the bomb falling at a constant angle. These two elements have also been fitted to the Mk 84 bomb (below) to produce the GAM-84. The first GAM-84 drop tests were conducted in June 1995, with live tests in October 1996.

Northrop Grumman B-2A Spirit

1 Retractable ILS antenna
2 Starboard navigation light, not used operationally
3 Split drag rudder/airbrake with aileron function
4 Drag rudder rotary actuators
5 Outboard elevon
6 Elevon hydraulic actuators
7 Inboard elevons
8 Starboard integral fuel tankage, total capacity approximately 130,000 lb
9 Starboard main undercarriage, stowed position
10 Intake suction relief doors
11 Starboard engine bays
12 Rotating inflight-refuelling receptacle
13 Cockpit rear pressure bulkhead
14 Structural cut-out, provision for third crew member ejection seat
15 Engine-driven auxiliary equipment gearbox
16 Starboard engine combined air intake
17 Avionics equipment racks
18 Two-crew flight deck
19 Cockpit roof escape hatches, port and starboard
20 Pilot's Aces II ejection seat
21 Mission commander's ejection seat
22 Conventional stick and rudder flight controls, quadruplex digital flight control system
23 Instrument panel with multi-function full-colour CRT displays
24 Instrument panel shroud
25 Starboard AN/APQ-181 Low Probability of Intercept (LPI) electronically scanned multi-function J-band radar unit
26 Airflow data sensors, above and below
27 Nosewheel leg door
28 Twin-wheel nose undercarriage, aft retracting
29 Taxiing lights
30 Crew door mounted boarding ladder
31 Port AN/APQ-181 radar unit
32 Astro navigation sensor port
33 Cockpit hatch emergency release
34 Weapons bay retractable spoiler panels
35 Port weapons bay outer door
36 Environmental control system equipment bay, port and starboard
37 Hydraulic equipment bay
38 Boundary layer splitter
39 Boundary layer secondary intake duct to air systems and APU

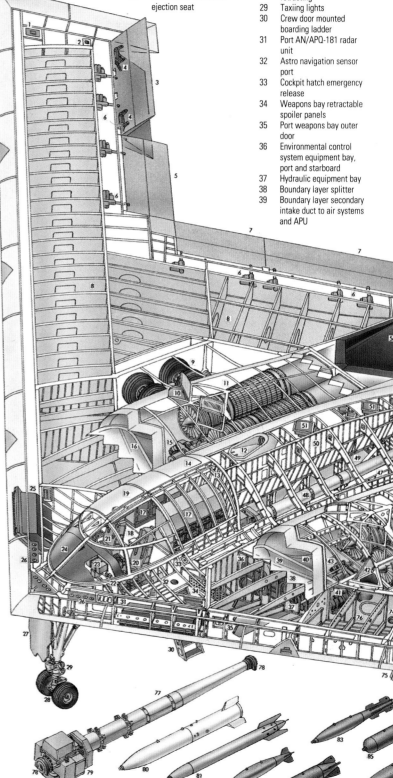

The B-2 cockpit is built around a nine-screen EFIS system, all with colour MFDs. Primary flight systems have been supplied by Rockwell-Collins. All relevant information – for onboard systems, navigation or attack – can be displayed to either pilot. However, the mission commander's seat (to starboard) has the majority of data entry panels within easier reach. The cockpit systems reportedly have a three-phased setting, to ease mission workload. Systems can be set for: 'take-off' (upload mission data from the mission planning system, set take-off control settings for the FCS and display relevant checklists); 'go to war' (assume stealthy control inputs, emissions controlled and weapons ready); and 'landing' (reactivate some controls and display final checklists).

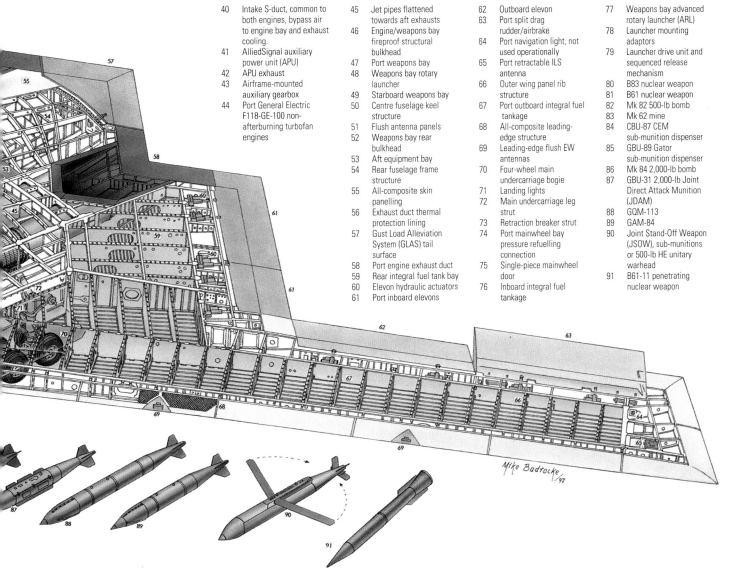

40 Intake S-duct, common to both engines, bypass air to engine bay and exhaust cooling.
41 AlliedSignal auxiliary power unit (APU)
42 APU exhaust
43 Airframe-mounted auxiliary gearbox
44 Port General Electric F118-GE-100 non-afterburning turbofan engines

45 Jet pipes flattened towards aft exhausts
46 Engine/weapons bay fireproof structural bulkhead
47 Port weapons bay
48 Weapons bay rotary launcher
49 Starboard weapons bay
50 Centre fuselage keel structure
51 Flush antenna panels
52 Weapons bay rear bulkhead
53 Aft equipment bay
54 Rear fuselage frame structure
55 All-composite skin panelling
56 Exhaust duct thermal protection lining
57 Gust Load Alleviation System (GLAS) tail surface
58 Port engine exhaust duct
59 Rear integral fuel tank bay
60 Elevon hydraulic actuators
61 Port inboard elevons

62 Outboard elevon
63 Port split drag rudder/airbrake
64 Port navigation light, not used operationally
65 Port retractable ILS antenna
66 Outer wing panel rib structure
67 Port outboard integral fuel tankage
68 All-composite leading-edge structure
69 Leading-edge flush EW antennas
70 Four-wheel main undercarriage bogie
71 Landing lights
72 Main undercarriage leg strut
73 Retraction breaker strut
74 Port mainwheel bay pressure refuelling connection
75 Single-piece mainwheel door
76 Inboard integral fuel tankage

77 Weapons bay advanced rotary launcher (ARL)
78 Launcher mounting adaptors
79 Launcher drive unit and sequenced release mechanism
80 B83 nuclear weapon
81 B61 nuclear weapon
82 Mk 82 500-lb bomb
83 Mk 62 mine
84 CBU-87 CEM sub-munition dispenser
85 GBU-89 Gator sub-munition dispenser
86 Mk 84 2,000-lb bomb
87 GBU-31 2,000-lb Joint Direct Attack Munition (JDAM)
88 GQM-113
89 GAM-84
90 Joint Stand-Off Weapon (JSOW), sub-munitions or 500-lb HE unitary warhead
91 B61-11 penetrating nuclear weapon

Mike Badrocke /97

hardly likely to authorise an increase in the number of B-2s; this was confirmed by the appointment of Les Aspin as Secretary of Defense. As the former chair of the House Armed Services Committee, Aspin had been instrumental in delaying and cutting back the B-2 programme.

Hopes rise and fall

Hopes that more B-2s might be produced rose in November 1994, when the Republican party unexpectedly seized control of the House and Senate. In May 1995, the House added $500 million to the FY96 defence budget to start producing two more B-2s, and Northrop Grumman (Northrop had acquired Grumman in 1994) offered to build 20 more B-2s at a flyaway cost of $566 million each.

The logic behind the proposal was solid. The 1993 Bottom-Up Review of the US military posture had confirmed the need for long-range bombers, because of their ability to bring heavy firepower to bear anywhere in the world at short notice, and supported the retention of the B-52H, B-1 and B-2. Building more B-2s, at a slow rate, would keep the force effective, despite attrition, and in the longer term provide a replacement for the B-52.

The action was supported by the Senate, but opposed by the administration and the Air Force, and the money was earmarked instead to bring AV-1 to operational status and to fund other improvements.

The administration's opposition to the B-2 is political. The cutbacks in production have driven the 'then-year unit programme cost' of the B-2 above $2 billion. This number is based on dividing the total cost of the programme by the

During March 1996 AV-5 was detached to Eielson AFB, in Alaska, for Exercise Frozen Spirit 96 – an extreme climatic test. AV-5 was the dedicated climatic test aircraft and had already spent two months during 1994 in Eglin AFB's climatic test chamber. Frozen Spirit was a follow-up exercise described by one participant as "a graduation exercise for the final configuration." For this deployment the aircraft was christened Fire and Ice by the B-2 CTF and wore special artwork on the nosewheel door. Several of the CTF B-2s received unofficial names other than their assigned Spirit of... titles. Fire and Ice received the most publicity of any of them, but only on the strict understanding that the artwork would be removed before its return to the 509th BW. Note the Aurora Borealis in the uppermost picture.

was one of a group of post-Cold War changes to the US strategic forces, which included a fundamental restructuring of the US Air Force. In June 1992, Strategic Air Command ceased to exist, and the USAF's heavy bombers were reassigned to the newly formed Air Combat Command (ACC).

The last significant event of 1992, for the B-2 programme, was the Presidential election. The incoming Democratic administration, accompanied by a new and largely liberal influx of Representatives and Senators, was

number of aircraft built, and is a fiscal fiction – for example, you could never have saved $2 billion by cancelling one B-2, nor does an additional B-2 cost $2 billion. However, braying politicians and know-nothing columnists have now lodged the number in the public mind, to the point where few people will advocate building more B-2s.

Generally, too, the Clinton administration has been content to defer major military modernisation costs until after 2000, keeping the current budgets balanced and leaving later administrations to pay the bills, a pattern which is also visible in fighter modernisation.

The B-2 and the USAF

The USAF's opposition to more B-2s is pragmatic: the service considers that the money would be better spent elsewhere. The B-2 is a valuable aircraft, but it is not cheap to acquire or to operate, and the USAF's tactical forces have already been substantially cut back. The demise of SAC has not favoured the B-2; while ACC has not ignored bomber modernisation, the new command is inevitably dominated by fighter pilots, who are reluctant to see more fighter wings shut down in order to fund small numbers of bombers.

Another argument with some merit is that the B-52H, armed with JASSM, will be useful until 2015-2020, and that by that time a replacement long-range aircraft may be very different from the B-2. A future bomber might not need the same payload as the B-2, particularly with today's smaller, more accurate weapons. Unrefuelled range could be traded off against tanker support: there is no need for a 1,000-nm (1,148-mile; 1847-km) penetration of hostile territory if the Soviet Union is not the target. A new bomber would take advantage of the more modern stealth technology developed for the F-22 and Joint Strike Fighter, and it would certainly use less costly avionics. Despite the development bill, it might be cheaper in the long run than more B-2s. The USAF's Scientific Advisory Board, in its

1996 New World Vistas study, postulated an even more radical solution for long-range attack: a large global-range aircraft that would combine the roles of transport and strike, carrying uninhabited combat air vehicles (UCAVs) into the battle area.

Return to flight test

While this debate drew to a close, testing proceeded on a deliberate, complex schedule, with aircraft being grounded periodically so that they could be upgraded with new hardware and software for the next series of flights. Avionics hardware and software paced the schedule, but the programme office noted in late 1996 that development had broadly followed the schedule laid down in 1989. While not every radar and DMS mode was available for testing on time, many of the modes were not dependent on others, so

This photograph shows AV-2 engaged in 'splash' tests on a wet runway at Edwards. For these tests the runways were flooded by fire trucks – though in the desert heat the water would evaporate after only 30 to 45 minutes. Crews were concerned mainly with testing the brakes, steering and anti-skid mechanisms under these conditions. Water ingestion via the engine inlets is not a problem for the B-2.

Above and left: Initial terrain-following (TF) certification flights were undertaken by AV-4 in September 1996. Low-level penetration is still considered to be an important potential element of the B-2's mission profile and the aircraft will ultimately be cleared to TF down to a height of 500 ft (152 m) in Block 30 aircraft. Block 20 standard B-2s are cleared to fly manual terrain-avoidance profiles down to 600 ft (182 m).

Above and top: B-2s have no obvious surfaces on which to carry their serials, tailcodes and assigned names. Instead, they have set a unique trend in carrying this information on their main gear doors.

Below: This view of an operational B-2 (88-0330/ Spirit of California) shows the airflow baffles that drop down in front of the weapons bays to ensure clean separation of bombs.

another part of the test programme could be brought forward to use the aircraft and other resources. As a result, some modes were delivered ahead of schedule and the entire programme remained on track.

Apart from the RCS problem and the anticipated detail headaches with radar performance, only two substantial problems emerged during flight testing: structural cracking in the aft decks, and problems with the radomes. A new aft deck material (unspecified, but possibly based on carbon-carbon composites) was developed for retrofit to the aircraft and incorporated from the 14th aircraft. The original plastic radomes were found to absorb water, degrading the performance of the radar, and have been replaced by a honeycomb material.

The flight-test programme was planned to comprise 2,359 'test point hours'; throughout the programme, the Combined Test Force at Edwards AFB accomplished an

average of 65 hours on test for every 100 hours the aircraft flew, so the aircraft would fly a total of 4,000 hours in the programme. Productivity was increased by inflight refuelling, which helped raise the average length of a test sortie to six hours, and by the time the programme drew to a close, each test aircraft was averaging six sorties per month.

The basic B-2 test programme was due to be completed by 1 July 1997. It has been a long, drawn-out effort, but, as we have seen, the bulk of the delays and many of the associated increases in the programme's cost are directly attributable to decisions taken on Capitol Hill.

The aircraft itself works much as it was initially designed to do. The major exception has been the RCS shortfall, but the modifications to correct this problem do not affect the basic structure or the systems. On the other hand, the B-2 has already acquired a unique multi-target near-precision conventional strike capability, using existing sensors and inexpensive weapons. Most of the charges levelled at the aircraft by its critics in the late 1980s have proved to be groundless.

It now seems unlikely, nonetheless, that any more B-2s will be built. The cost of doing so increases day by day, as suppliers wind up their production lines and as experienced workers move to other jobs. However, the Palmdale plant remains busy, because a good deal of work is still to be done on the 21-aircraft programme.

The B-2 blocks

Because of the production delays imposed by Congress, it was clear that more than three years would elapse between the delivery of the first production aircraft, AV-1007, and the completion of flight testing. The USAF and Northrop accordingly laid out a three-stage plan that synchronised deliveries, flight-testing and the working-up of the operational wing at Whiteman.

The plan defined three B-2 configurations or blocks. To ease entry into service, two principles were adopted: the operational unit would always have at least eight aircraft in a common configuration and there would never be more than two versions in the field at the same time.

The first 10 production B-2s – AV-1007 through AV-1016 – were delivered as Block 10 aircraft between December 1993 and the end of 1995. The Block 10's primary role was as a trainer for pilots and maintenance crews. It did not operate at full flight loads (being limited to a maximum take-off weight of 305,000 lb/138300 kg), had no terrain-following or precision-weapons capability and had a limited capability in the DMS.

Three new Block 20 aircraft (1017-1019) were delivered in 1996, the last arriving in August. Starting in mid-1996, the five newest Block 10s (1012-1016) went through a 12-16-week modification programme to bring them up to Block 20 status.

With the arrival of the fifth modified aircraft in May 1997, the 509th had eight Block 20s on strength. The B-2 had been declared operational for conventional strike missions in January 1997, and – after passing standard

nuclear certification tests – the 509th attained initial operating capability (IOC) in April 1997.

The Block 20 is described as "contributing to the integrated air campaign" because it is armed with GATS/GAM (see weapons section). It operates up to a peacetime take-off weight of 336,500 lb (152600 kg). It is cleared for manual terrain following down to 600 ft (182 m), and the DMS is operational in Bands 1-3. The Block 20 also introduces an improved environmental control system.

Block 30: the ultimate B-2

By the end of 1997, the Block 20s will be joined by the first four fully operational Block 30 aircraft, comprising AV-1020 and 1021, the only new-production Block 30s; AV-1002 (formerly AV-2, the structures test aircraft); and AV-1008, the second Block 10. The scale of the Block 30 modifications can be gauged from the fact that the first modifications take two years; even later, when Block 20s are upgraded, the bombers will be on the ground for a year.

The Block 30 modification includes the removal and replacement of all the aircraft's edges, including the leading edges and control surfaces, in order to meet RCS requirements. The leading edges, visibly segmented on the Block 20, will be joined into an electrically continuous structure. Aircraft prior to AV-1014 receive the new aft deck structure.

All the surface coatings on the B-2, including absorbent and conductive layers, are removed and replaced with improved materials. After having a great deal of difficulty in finding an environmentally safe stripping medium that would remove the coatings without damaging the composite skins, Northrop Grumman developed a technique to 'depaint' the B-2 using crystallised wheat starch and high-pressure air.

The modification includes some rewiring, particularly for the test aircraft. New weapons include JDAM, and the Bomb Rack Assembly units are being used for the first time, allowing the B-2 to carry CBU-87s, mines or other small stores.

Avionics software and hardware changes include automatic TF/TA down to 200 ft (60 m) and the installation of a Milstar satellite communications terminal. DMS reaches its full capability with the addition of Band 4, allowing crews to replan their missions in flight when an unexpected threat is detected.

Another change, introduced in two phases in Blocks 20 and 30, is the integration of the B-2 with the Air Force Mission Support System (AFMSS). This replaces the Strategic Mission Development and Planning System (SMDPS), which was originally developed for the B-2. The SMDPS was designed for nuclear warfighting, and was never intended to be installed outside the B-2's main operating bases. The switch to the transportable AFMSS will allow

the B-2 to sustain operations from bases around the world, and makes it easier to integrate the B-2 with other USAF operations.

Stealth performance parameters are, naturally, classified. However, the Block 30 aircraft, with the final signature modifications, should have an RCS that is at least two to three orders of magnitude less than the kind of conventional target which radars are designed to detect. The effect is to reduce the radar's range by a factor of four to eight. The radars are less effective, and their areas of coverage no longer overlap; with mission planning and the DMS, the

Above: 90-0332/Spirit of Washington was the 11th B-2 and the fifth production aircraft.

Top: B-2 89-0129/Spirit of Georgia approaches a KC-135 over New Mexico. With a full warload, the B-2 has a maximum unrefuelled range of 6,300 nm (11660 km; 7,245 miles).

bomber can weave between them. It is worth noting that the F-117, with a not-dissimilar RCS to the B-2 and much less real-time data on hostile radars, was able to raid Baghdad and survive even though the Iraqi defence forces had good reason to guess when and where the fighters would attack.

Still stealthy after all those years?

Claimed 'detections' of B-2s making air show appearances should be taken with more than a pinch of salt. The F-117 is equipped with means to increase its RCS at will, for two good reasons: to ensure that civilian ATC can see the aircraft in a 'skin paint' mode, and to prevent any unauthorised radar operator from acquiring real RCS data. The B-2 indubitably has the same capability, and uses it routinely. As for British Aerospace's much-touted imaging of a B-2 at a few kilometres' range at Farnborough: how often will a defender see the top of a B-2, and how useful is it to see an aircraft at 3 miles (5 km) when it flies 9 miles (15 km) high – or more – and can deliver a conventional bomb from 13 nm (15 miles; 24 km)?

Five more Block 30s, modified from Block 10s and flight-test aircraft, will be delivered during 1998: by the late summer, therefore, the bomber should be declared fully operational. Eight more Block 30s will arrive during 1999, and the last four in 2000. On present plans, the first phase of the B-2 programme will be completed in June 2001, when the first prototype, AV-1, joins the 509th as a fully operational Block 30.

In the hands of the 509th BW

The 509th is mainly dedicated to missions which are of high importance and which only the B-2 can perform. If, for example, the US decided to destroy a chemical weapons factory in Libya without the B-2, the US government would have to secure landing and overflight permission from one or more NATO allies, either for the attack force (if F-117s were used) or the support force (if B-52s delivered the attack). In either case, the preparations would send a strong signal that an operation was under way. The B-2 can perform the mission, non-stop and unsupported, from Missouri, with one refuelling outbound, and can either recover to a secure base such as Diego Garcia or return with another refuelling direct to Whiteman.

Training and tactics development are focused on such special, B-2-unique missions. "Gulf War-type operations, where we deploy into a situation and perform like everyone else, are not in the plan now, but we will become deployable," remarks Lieutenant Colonel Jim Whitney of the 394th Combat Training Squadron.

The 509th is highly selective. Out of 60-70 pilots with the necessary paper qualifications to fly the B-2, 20 were selected for interview. After an interview and a check ride in the Hughes Weapon System Trainer, seven were chosen.

The trainees are mid-level captains with 1,000 hours in bombers or 600 hours in fighters, and ample tanking experience. Roughly one-third come from B-1s, one-third from B-52s and one-third from fighters – mostly F-15s or F-117s. As well as experience and piloting skills, the 509th is looking for people with leadership potential – "people who can be trusted to fly an expensive asset" – and individuals with initiative.

Flying the B-2

Training starts with 178 hours of academics, followed by 60 hours in the cockpit procedures trainer – a fairly basic replica of the B-2 cockpit. The next step is 40 hours of 'real time' practice in the mission trainer, another fixed-base system that "teaches pilots to be navigators."

The student then moves on to the Hughes-Link Division Weapon System Trainer (WST), an extremely sophisticated full-motion simulator that doubles as a mission rehearsal system, with access to a global database of targets and threats. Block 20 training required 15 WST flights; the Block 30 takes 19 rides, most of the increase being due to the later version's TF/TA capability. (From the pilot's viewpoint, the Block 10 to Block 20 change has been much more significant than Block 20 to 30.) After seven WST rides, the pilot takes his first flight in the B-2, and is ready for a check ride by the ninth sortie.

This process, known as initial qualification training (IQT), takes six months. After passing IQT, the pilot typically flies two sorties per month on the B-2, interspersed with four to six flights on the unit's charcoal-grey T-38 companion trainers. Like other specialised USAF units, the 509th uses the T-38s to maintain hands-on flying skills and to keep the pilots accustomed to making quick decisions.

The pilot will typically fly for about a year before upgrading to mission commander. The B-2 has a crew of two: the pilot, and the mission commander who combines the roles of pilot and weapon system operator and is additionally responsible for targeting and weapon release. As was done on the FB-111, the 509th tries to match pilots and mission commanders according to personality and compatible working methods, and to keep crews together over the long term.

Pilots describe the B-2 as a pleasant, undemanding aircraft to fly, a factor which helps to keep the workload reasonable. As in any fly-by-wire aircraft, leaving the stick in the centre position means that the aircraft will hold its

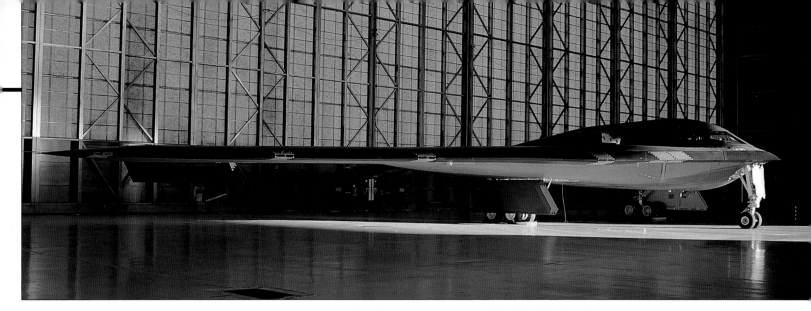

current attitude. The B-2 is not a fighter: its flying-wing design limits it to a relatively small Alpha range, its long wing span precludes a rapid roll rate, and it does not have the thrust for high-*g* manoeuvring or rapid acceleration. But it is more responsive than most large aircraft, because the control system is powerful and the airframe is stiff. Its low drag means it out-accelerates most aircraft of its size, and the fighter-type engines respond quickly to throttle inputs. The verdict, according to one operational pilot: B-52 pilots think the B-2 is manoeuvrable and B-1 pilots less so. As for fighter pilots: "It's still a Mack truck to them."

Good handling qualities

Before the B-2 flew, many critics expected the aircraft to be only marginally stable. Even on the first flight, however, observers noted the B-2's almost unnatural steadiness on final approach, with absolutely no visible wing rock or 'hunting' in Alpha. The speedbrakes are left open 45° up and down on the approach, increasing drag and placing the engines in a more responsive thrust range.

One of the bomber's quirks is apparent on landing: the broad centrebody generates a powerful ground cushion, so landings are no-flare, carrier-style affairs. One pilot notes, "If you do try to flare, the airplane says, 'You want to fly, let's go fly.' It's obvious when you see someone do that on one of their first landings." Another pilot observes that "you don't need the flight engineer barking out the radar altitude so that you don't pancake the airplane." On the other hand, the 509th pilots have noticed a tendency towards 'firm' landings on the part of pilots making their first T-38 approaches after a series of B-2 flights.

The flight control system normally keeps the B-2 at zero Beta (that is to say, with no sideslip or crab) and a constant Alpha, selected by the pilot. At low level and high speeds, the constant-Alpha law tends to counteract wind gusts immediately: an upward gust increases the aircraft's Alpha, and so the FCS commands the aircraft to pitch down. At the same time, the abrupt Alpha increase is detected by the gust-alleviation laws in the FCS, which signals the elevons and beavertail to apply more nose-up trim on the outer wings and less on the centreline. This reduces the peak bending moment. The ride quality is not quite as good as that of the B-1 – there is no substitute for very high wing loading – but is much better than a B-52's.

Low-level training was temporarily suspended in early 1997 because of the risk of birdstrikes. Crews do not expect the B-2 to be susceptible to catastrophic damage (of the kind that caused the loss of one B-1). Most vital systems are buried deeply behind the leading edges and front spars, and even the largest bird will have been slowed down by a few authoritative ricochets before it can reach the engines. However, the B-2 force cannot afford to have an aircraft down for extensive repairs, because it would disrupt the training schedule.

The entire B-2 inflight refuelling envelope was cleared in a single flight, a first-time achievement for a brand-new aircraft. This is not to say that refuelling is always easy. The KC-10 is not much of a problem, with its size and a very

long boom, but the KC-135 represents a unique situation. The B-2's refuelling slipway is located well aft, and, unlike most conventional aircraft, is behind much of the wing. The entire aircraft must be driven through two 'downbursts' – one of the engines, and one of the wing – to reach a contact position. Once the B-2 is in position, it is well inside the KC-135's 'bubble' and the two aircraft interact strongly: any movement of one aircraft tends to affect the other. "Once you're inside the tanker's envelope, the B-2 tends to slide forward on you because you're so clean."

Flying the B-2 is a great deal more than stick-and-rudder skills, because of the bomber's complex systems. "If an individual likes computer games, it suits them very well," says one pilot. "You can fly for a long time and never touch the stick or throttles. The automation frees up a lot of brainpower for other tasks." The challenge is teaching the pilot where to find the information he needs to accomplish the mission. Pilots who have grown up with computer games sometimes forget that the B-2 was designed in the early 1980s. One pilot calls this the "shock,

Above and top: AV-4 is seen here hiding in a hangar at Edwards AFB in 1993 (top). All five of the developmental aircraft will now be returned to active service, the last joining the 509th BW by June 2000. 89-0127/Spirit of Kansas (above) – the sixth production aircraft – was delivered to Whiteman AFB in February 1995.

As part of its ongoing B-2 upgrade programme, Northrop Grumman developed an environmentally friendly paint-stripping system for the aircraft that uses wheat starch.

denial and acceptance" syndrome. "When you start, you're always behind the system. Once you've trained, you can be waiting for the system and saying, 'Come on, I'm burning nanoseconds here'."

A GATS/GAM attack is one of the most difficult tasks on the B-2. The pilot has to fly an indirect path to the target, while the mission commander searches for the target and a secondary reference point on the SAR scope. F-15E and B-1 people find it easy, apparently, but others find radar signal interpretation (RSI) difficult. The APQ-181 is good, but performance does vary with obscurants and the size of the targets. "We start with big buildings in the

middle of nowhere, and move on to more difficult targets." GATS/GAM is "not a problem with the processors on the airplane, but with the grey matter in the pilot's head."

One unique aspect of the 509th's operations, directly related to its 'sniper squadron' role, is that some of its missions may be extremely long. The worst case is a non-stop mission halfway around the world and back, using an indirect route to avoid violating airspace. So far, the longest real mission flown by a B-2 has been 30 hours, but crews have flown mission rehearsals for up to 44.5 hours in the WST.

The simulations are as realistic as the WST can make them, including equipment failures and threats, and if the real mission would start at 02.00, the simulation does so as well. Pilots have experimented with different kinds of bedding and food; the B-2 cockpit is just large enough for a roll-up mattress and can accommodate a chemical toilet and a few personal items. Crews on the simulator rides are heavily instrumented, including an eye-blink-rate sensor attached to the oxygen mask, and their performance in air-to-air refuelling and weapon delivery is carefully monitored. So far, tests have shown that a combination of pre-flight rest and 'power napping' during the tedious parts of the flight should make it possible to fly missions of more than 50 hours without degrading the crew's performance over the target.

B-2 at Whiteman AFB

Whiteman was selected as the first home for the B-2 in 1986; it had not hosted large aircraft since the 1960s, when a B-47 wing gave way to Minuteman missiles. The base has been largely rebuilt to accommodate the new aircraft, including a row of individual docks for each bomber. Each dock opens at both ends (so that engines can be started under cover), has underfloor plumbing for fuel and fluids, and includes comprehensive test equipment and a fire-suppression system.

The B-2 maintenance crews typically compare themselves to the 'Maytag repairman', referring to a long-running advertising campaign for Maytag dishwashers, featuring the repairman whose phone never rings. The B-2 does require a fair amount of scheduled maintenance, because of its complexity, but it seldom breaks – a result of the rigorous specifications, long development and meticulous testing.

The main area where maintenance lessons are still being learned is in RCS maintenance. The normal flexing of the airframe, gust loads and vibration all affect the surface of the aircraft, and physically small discontinuities may sharply increase the RCS. The USAF and the contractors are working on maintenance materials (such as tapes and caulking compounds) and on new diagnostic tools which will allow RCS to be measured on the flight-line.

B-2: past, present and future

What the B-2 does not have, as yet, is a name. In accordance with USAF tradition, the official name of 'Spirit' is never heard around the aircraft. The name 'Bat' has been suggested (it fits neatly with the one-syllable 'Buff' and 'Bone') but has not caught on. Neither has 'Voron' – Russian for raven, and the callsign for B-2 flight tests. Meanwhile, crews call it simply 'the jet' and there is no doubt at Whiteman as to what that means.

The B-2 is an extremely complex and technologically advanced aircraft that has emerged from a long, controversial development programme. It has suffered – and still suffers – from being at the mercy of decisions made by people who do not understand its capabilities.

Myths and misconceptions about the B-2 are everywhere, and will be destroyed only gradually; as Mark Twain remarked, "a lie can be half way around the world before the truth has got its boots on."

The B-2's builders and operators are confident that the fully operational aircraft will be stealthy enough to perform its mission: to deliver 16 near-precision, hard-target weapons per sortie, anywhere in the world, with no support except tankers. There is nothing else in the world that even comes close to this capability, nor will there be for decades – the B-2's capabilities will be unique when most of us have retired.

It still seems puzzling and incongruous that, while there is no money for more B-2s, the Pentagon is pushing hard for a Joint Strike Fighter which will not be much more survivable than a B-2, at best; carries one-eighth of its

weapon load; has one-fifth of its unrefuelled range; relies on the availability of overseas bases; and will not be available for another decade. Are numbers everything?

More than half a century ago, the US Army Air Corps wanted to buy a new bomber. It was large, sophisticated and the most expensive combat aircraft in the world.

Critics in Congress and the other branches of the military argued that economic times were tight and that the United States was not about to become embroiled in any conflicts where the big bomber's unique assets – range and survivability – would be necessary. A cheaper warplane, based on an existing airframe to save money, would be adequate.

The Air Corps lost its fight and received only a small test squadron of the big bombers. Most of the money earmarked for bombers went to buy hundreds of the less expensive aircraft.

The cheaper bomber was the Douglas B-18A Bolo, a derivative of the DC-2 airliner. In the Air Force Museum, a plaque in front of an immaculate B-18 sums up its front-line combat career: "Several of these aircraft were destroyed by the Japanese on 7 December 1941."

The big, costly bomber that the nation could not afford was, of course, the Boeing B-17 Flying Fortress.

Bill Sweetman

Although this photograph is perhaps the result of a quiet afternoon at the Edwards photo section, it does have some small message to give about the B-2's effectiveness when compared to other, conventional, aircraft. According to USAF figures, the B-2's unique combination of abilities would allow just two aircraft to carry out the same mission as 32 'dumb bomb droppers' (F-16s) and obviate the need for their associated escorts (16 F-15s), SEAD support (EF-111s and EA-6Bs) and tanker support (15 KC-135s). To put a more precise figure on matters, other USAF figures state that a strike by two C-ALCM-armed B-52Hs, with 32 missiles, costs $92.8 million (in FY97 dollars, a C-ALCM costs $2.9 million). The same mission could be accomplished by a single B-2, armed with just 16 JDAMs (only FY97 $27,000 each), for a total weapons cost of $432,000. JDAM has a CEP of less than 20 ft (6.09 m) compared to 30-45 ft (9.1-13.7 m) for a cruise missile. JDAM's warhead is also twice as heavy as a conventionally armed cruise missile.

Continued production of B-2s remained a possibility in 1997, a further nine aircraft being suggested for delivery early next century. The follow-on batch would have a much cheaper unit price than the initial 21 aircraft.

Weapons of the B-2: Past, present and future

B83
The B-2 was originally designed for nuclear strike, and its principal weapon in this role would be the B83 nuclear bomb. The B83 is the newest type of strategic nuclear bomb developed for the USAF, and was designed by the Department of Energy's Lawrence Livermore Nuclear Laboratory in California. It has a selectable yield of 1-2 MT (megatons), and is the first production bomb to be designed for 'laydown' delivery against hard, irregular targets. In such a delivery, the bomb is delay-fused so that the bomber can escape to a safe distance before the explosion. In contrast to airburst or contact fusing, however, this means that the bomb must survive the initial impact with the ground, and land without bouncing or rolling.

B61-11
The B-2 can also carry the B61-11 penetrating nuclear weapon, a newly developed bomb which has been produced by Sandia National Laboratory by modifying older B61s. The weapon has a needle-nosed casing packed with depleted uranium and no parachute, and is designed to bury itself up to 50 ft (15 m) into the ground before exploding. Sandia has also studied a gliding B61, but this has not yet been tested.

AGM-131A SRAM II (Short-Range Attack Missile)
The B-2 was also designed to use the Boeing AGM-131A SRAM II missile. SRAM II was a direct replacement for the original Boeing AGM-69 SRAM, which was designed in the 1960s. It consisted of a 200-kT warhead, a rocket motor and a Litton laser-gyro inertial navigation system. The SRAM II was due to enter service in 1993, but its development was terminated as part of the nuclear weapons cutbacks ordered by President Bush in September 1991.

AGM-137A TSSAM (Tri-Service Stand-off Attack Missile)
Another weapon intended for the B-2 was the Northrop AGM-137A TSSAM, a stealthy missile with a 250-nm (287-mile; 462-km) range, an 800-lb (360-kg) hard-target penetrator warhead and an autonomous precision guidance system. After a series of problems and cost overruns, however, TSSAM was cancelled in 1994.

GATS/GAM (GPS-Aided Targeting System/GPS-Aided Munition)
The demise of TSSAM left the B-2 in a paradoxical situation: the world's most sophisticated military aircraft, with an extremely accurate targeting system, was without any kind of precision weapon. This gap has been filled by a new class of weapon, which approaches the precision of a laser-guided bomb but is much less expensive and fully autonomous. The concept was simple: fit an inertial measurement unit in a bomb tail with moving fins, and, just before release, programme the weapon with the flightpath that the aircraft's weapon control system predicts that it will follow to the target. The guidance system will then take out random errors (such as those caused as the bomb wobbles through the aircraft's flow field) and unpredictable factors, such as changes in wind speed and direction. A number of companies, including Northrop, worked under USAF contracts in the later 1980s to develop this class of weapon.

After the Gulf War, in which coalition aircraft were forced to bomb from unexpectedly high altitudes, this concept was refined, with the addition of a global positioning system (GPS) receiver, and became the basis of a high-priority, large-scale programme: the Joint Direct Attack Munition (JDAM). Because this weapon would not be available until late in the decade, however, Northrop Grumman proposed a quick-reaction programme to build a small number of similar weapons for the B-2 force and to integrate a GPS receiver on the aircraft. This system is known as GPS Aided Targeting System/GPS Aided Munition. GATS is designed to reduce the target location error (TLE) of the B-2's bombing systems. Although the B-2's radar is capable of very high resolution, it includes inherent errors – such as INS error, uncertainty in the relative altitude of the target and the bomber, and Doppler error – which prevent the system from computing the exact distance from the aircraft to the target. This remaining zone of uncertainty is the TLE.

GATS uses GPS to correct for inertial error. In a GATS attack, the bomber makes a dog-leg approach to the target, taking several radar shots at the target and another fixed point from positions at least 30° apart. This changes the relationship among the components of TLE, allowing system software to estimate Doppler and altitude errors. The result is that GATS/GAM meets a circular error probability (CEP) requirement of 20 ft (6 m) (at least half the weapons will fall within 6 m of the target), compared with a 40 ft (13 m) CEP requirement for the standard JDAM. All 16 weapons can be released against different targets in a single pass. Alternatively, multiple weapons can be aimed at one target: the weapon is manoeuvrable enough to allow several weapons launched in sequence to strike the same target from their different release points.

The gliding bomb, a 2,000-lb Mk 84 bomb with a readily installed tail-kit, has a significant stand-off range. From a 40,000-ft (12195-m), Mach 0.8 release, the weapon can glide more than 13 nm (15 miles; 24 km) downrange, or 8 nm (8 miles; 15 km) downrange and crossrange, and hit its target at a 60° impact angle with undiminished accuracy. An all-up demonstration of GATS/GAM took place in October 1996. Three B-2s launched from Whiteman and dropped 16 live GAMs on 16 semi-trailers located on the Nellis AFB range. The leading aircraft dropped eight weapons, the rest being shared with the other two. All the targets were hit, and the third bomber used its radar to perform bomb damage assessment, imaging wreckage and the bomb craters.

JDAM (Joint Direct Attack Munition)/GBU-31
GATS will work with JDAM (Joint Direct Attack Munition) in exactly the same way as with GAM. McDonnell Douglas was selected to develop and produce JDAM in October 1995, and the weapon should achieve early operational capability on the B-2 Block 30 in July 1997. Its significance for the B-2 is that it can be used with the BLU-109 hard-target munition, allowing the B-2 to attack deeply buried or fortified targets. The Pentagon plans to acquire 87,000 JDAM guidance kits. The overall aim is to provide enough JDAMs to meet the needs of any future conflict without resorting to heavy unguided weapons. JDAM comprises a new tail with movable fins, containing a Honeywell ring-laser-gyro inertial measurement unit, a Lockheed Martin (Loral) computer, a Rockwell Collins GPS receiver and an HR Textron actuator

system. The weapon is powered by a thermal battery. Mated to a 2,000-lb warhead, either a Mk 84 blast/fragmentation type or a BLU-109, the weapon is designated GBU-31. From the outset, JDAM has been designed to be mated with a nose-mounted seeker for greater accuracy. Under current plans, a demonstration/validation programme for the seeker will start in 2002, which implies serious study of cost and performance issues from 2000 onwards. Another possibility is an extended-range JDAM with folding wings. Also under study is a 500-lb inertially guided weapon, of which the B-2 could carry and launch 76.

BLU-113/GAM-113
As JDAM enters service, it appears likely that the now-redundant GAM tail-kits will be mated with the BLU-113 hard-target penetrator. The 4,695-lb (2130-kg) BLU-113 warhead was originally developed in a quick-reaction programme during Desert Storm, in a thinly veiled attempt to 'decapitate' the Iraqi command by killing Saddam Hussein and his principal commanders. The first bombs were modified from Navy-surplus 203-mm gun barrels, fitted with nose and tail caps and mated to Texas Instruments Paveway III laser-guidance kits. In this form, the bomb was designated GBU-28. Since the retirement of the F-111F, it has been carried on the F-15E, and the USAF has acquired at least 100 new munitions from National Forge. A GAM-equipped version of the weapon, designated GAM-113, was test-dropped from a B-2 in early 1997: the bomber can carry eight GAM-113s, four on each rotary launcher.

The USAF is looking at other improvements to the BLU-113, including a hard target smart fuse (HTSF) which can count the layers in an underground structure (as the bomb passes through a void, its deceleration rate changes) and can be programmed to detonate at a certain level. A variant of the weapon with a tungsten-loaded explosive charge, weighing around 3200 kg (7,055 lb), could be used to increase the weapon's mass-to-diameter ratio and hence its penetration depth.

'Big BLU'
Before leaving the subject of deep-penetration weapons, it might be appropriate to mention the ultimate hard-target weapon, proposed by Lockheed Martin and known as 'Big BLU'. This would be a 10000-kg (22,045-lb) class bomb with a high-density nose section (filled with depleted uranium or a similarly dense material) and a GPS/inertial guidance system. In early 1997, 'Big BLU' was a candidate for Advanced Concept Technology Demonstrator funds, which would support the building of a small number of weapons for test and contingency operational use.

JASSM (Joint Air-to-Surface Stand-off Missile)
The USAF firmly plans to equip the B-2 with the JASSM, which is being developed as a less costly substitute for TSSAM. Lockheed Martin and McDonnell Douglas are competing to develop JASSM, and the USAF expects to announce a winner in the summer of 1998. The weapon is due to enter service in 2001, on the B-52. JASSM will be a 1000-kg (2,204-lb) class weapon with a 350-400-kg (771-881-lb) hard-target warhead, an autonomous precision guidance system (most likely, a GPS/INS mid-course system with an imaging infra-red terminal seeker) and a Teledyne J402 engine. The range is classified, but will be more than 250 km (155 miles). The B-2 will carry up to 16 JASSMs on its rotary launchers.

JASSM is the subject of some controversy, because the US Navy is campaigning to have the weapon cancelled in favour of its own SLAM-ER Plus. However, the USAF counters that the SLAM derivative will not fit on its bombers – a fundamental requirement for JASSM – and will probably cost more than JASSM, which is being developed under new procurement practices and is expected to cost at most $700,000 per round.

AGM-154 JSOW (Joint Stand-Off Weapon)
In early 1997, a contract was being negotiated to integrate the B-2 with the Texas Instruments AGM-154 JSOW. In its basic AGM-154A version (the only model to which the USAF is committed), JSOW is a GPS/inertial-guided gliding dispenser with a range of 75 km (46 miles) from the B-2's operating altitude, carrying a payload of Combined Effects Bomblets. It was originally developed for the US Navy as a defence-suppression weapon, because the CEBs are effective against targets such as missile sites. The B-2 can carry 16 JSOWs.

Other weapons
The Bomb Rack Assembly units can carry smaller weapons, including up to 80 225-kg (496-lb) Mk 82 bombs or 36 450-kg (992-lb) class Tactical Munitions Dispenser (TMD) weapons. The TMD is a USAF-standard weapon which can be loaded with CEBs or mines, and also forms the basis of the Textron Defense Systems Sensor Fuzed Weapon, which dispenses 40 IR-fused anti-armour weapons over the battlefield. Lockheed Martin is developing a Wind Corrected TMD with a simple inertial guidance system, which will allow weapons such as the SFW to be released at high altitude. So far, the WC-TMD is not slated for integration with the B-2, but it would pose no serious technical problems.

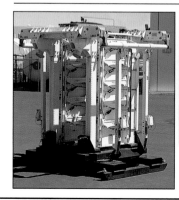

Above and left: The B-2 carries the majority of its weapons on a rotary launcher (above). Smaller bombs are dropped from the bomb rack assembly.

B-2 Production and Deliveries

Development

Construction number	Air Vehicle	Serial	First flight	Delivered as Block 30
1001	AV-1	82-1066	17/7/1989	6/2000
1002	AV-2	82-1067	19/10/1990	8/1997
1003	AV-3	82-1068	18/6/1991	10/1999
1004	AV-4	82-1069	17/4/1992	2/2000
1005	AV-5	82-1070	5/10/1992	7/1999
1006	AV-6	82-1071	2/2/1993	1/1998

Production

Construction number	Air Vehicle	Serial	Name	Delivered	Block	Upgraded/delivered Block 20	Block 30
1007	AV-7	88-0328	*Spirit of Texas*	9/1994	10		9/1998
1008	AV-8	88-0329	*Spirit of Missouri*	12/1993	10		11/1997
1009	AV-9	88-0330	*Spirit of California*	8/1994	10		6/1998
1010	AV-10	88-0331	*Spirit of South Carolina*	12/1994	10		4/1998
1011	AV-11	88-0332	*Spirit of Washington*	10/1994	10		1/1999
1012	AV-12	89-0127	*Spirit of Kansas*	2/1995	10	9/96	12/1998
1013	AV-13	89-0128	*Spirit of Nebraska*	6/1995	10	7/96	3/1999
1014	AV-14	89-0129	*Spirit of Georgia*	11/1995	10	5/97	4/1999
1015	AV-15	90-0040	*Spirit of Hawaii*	1/1996	10	3/97	7/1999
1016	AV-16	90-0041	*Spirit of Alaska*	12/1995	10	11/96	8/1999
1017	AV-17	92-0700	*Spirit of Oklahoma*	7/1996	20		11/1999
1018	AV-18	93-1085	*Spirit of Florida*	6/1996	20		1/2000
1019	AV-19	93-1086	*Spirit of Kitty Hawk*	8/1996	20		4/2000
1020	AV-20	93-1087	*Spirit of*	10/1997	30		
1021	AV-21	93-1088	*Spirit of*	12/1997	30		

The first production
B-2 to be delivered:
AV-8 (88-0329)

The second production
B-2 to be delivered:
AV-9 (88-0330)

The third production
B-2 to be delivered:
AV-7 (88-0328)

The fourth production
B-2 to be delivered:
AV-11 (88-0332)

The fifth production
B-2 to be delivered:
AV-10 (88-0331)

The sixth production
B-2 to be delivered:
AV-12 (89-0127)

The seventh production
B-2 to be delivered:
AV-13 (89-0128)

The eighth production
B-2 to be delivered:
AV-14 (89-0129)

The ninth production
B-2 to be delivered:
AV-16 (90-0041)

The 10th production
B-2 to be delivered:
AV-15 (90-0040)

The 13th production
B-2 to be delivered:
AV-19 (93-1086)

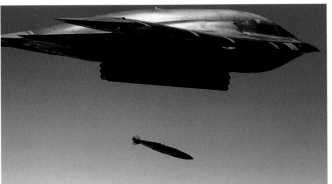
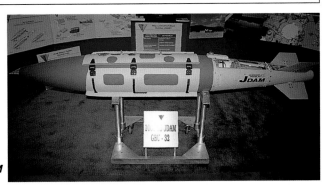

Left: On 15 June 1995 the first GAM bomb drop (a GAM-84) was made by a B-2 over the China Lake ranges. The test was a 'long-range' drop, made 45,000 ft (13716 m) 'uprange' of the target.

Right: The GBU-31 JDAM (which, like GAM-84, is based on a 2,000-lb Mk 84 bomb) will be the second PGM to be B-2 qualified.

B-2 Spirit

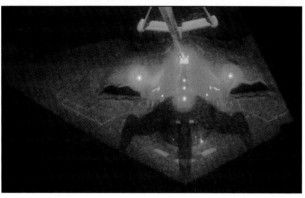

Coming of age

Deliveries of Block 30 aircraft began in the latter half of 1997 and within three years the B-2 had emerged as a pivotal player in America's conventional arsenal. It flew its first combat missions during 1999 as part of Operation Allied Force over the Balkans. The bomber proved it could merge delivery of precision-guided weapons with a stealthy platform, transforming the way Air Force planners viewed strategic and tactical air power. Rather than absolute numbers of bombers in the air, the emphasis shifted to the number of targets a single aircraft could hit.

As previously described, concurrent with the procurement reductions seen in the early 1990s there was a shift in the B-2's role from that of strategic nuclear bomber to strategic conventional bomber. The aircraft initially was delivered with a basic conventional capability limited to free-fall Mk 84 iron bombs. However, in its newest configuration it can deliver near-precision GPS-guided munitions, CBUs, 750-lb (340-kg) M117 iron bombs and Mk 62 mines, while incorporation of new systems has allowed delivery of state-of-the-art weapons like the GBU-31 JDAM, AGM-154 JSOW and the 4,700-lb (2132-kg) GBU-37 GPS-guided penetrator. Only through such programme modifications has the bomber's full conventional capability been realised.

Allied Force air operations over Yugoslavia and Kosovo demonstrated the bomber's contribution in the conventional arena beyond planners' wildest dreams. Six of the aircraft flew 49 combat missions from the continental United States against Balkan targets and although they undertook less than one percent of total NATO sorties, they delivered almost 11 percent of the bomb tonnage. Brigadier General Leroy Barnidge, Jr, commander of the 509th BW, indicated in a briefing given to the Air Force Association in late 1999 that the performance of the bomber and the JDAM, both

separately and as a system, had far exceeded expectations. This held true, according to Barnidge, despite adverse weather conditions.

Making its combat debut during Allied Force helped defeat two enemies: the Serbian air defence system, which many analysts claimed rivalled or surpassed that of Iraq during the 1991 Persian Gulf War, and the bomber's critics in the United States. The latter doubted the bomber would ever be used in combat, or that it would not perform as advertised if called to battle. Over the course of the 78-day air campaign the six bombers dropped 1.35 million tons of munitions and, of the 53 air tasking orders issued during the conflict, they participated in 34 – flying both single and two-ship missions that averaged 29 flight hours each.

The B-2 carried 16 2,000-lb JDAMs and, in many instances, targeted 16 quality designated mean points of impact (DMPIs). Approximately 652 JDAMs were dropped by the bombers, along with four 4,700-lb GBU-37/B 'bunker-busters'. Of the total JDAMs expended, 609 were GBU-31/1 Mk 84-series weapons typically used against service targets. Another 43 were GBU-31/3 BLU-109-series weapons used against hardened targets.

Reports suggest the JDAMs performed superbly with only two failures experienced. It is also reported that B-2 crews placed 90 percent of their bombs within 10 metres of their designated targets, which included Serbian air defence systems, command and control sites, runways, bridges, factories and communications systems. On one particular mission a single bomber attacked and destroyed two airfields. Photo-reconnaissance graphically showed the effects of what a B-2 could achieve in a single pass, with individual JDAMs aimed at key points on the airfield, such as runway and taxiway intersections, the control tower and hangars.

According to sources, the stealth bombers took off from Whiteman AFB about 14 hours ahead of in-theatre aircraft, carefully scripting their times of arrival and departure into and out of assigned strike areas. In many instances bombers launched together and, although they proceeded against different targets, flew in pairs over the Atlantic for mutual support. Each transatlantic flight necessitated two in-flight refuellings.

Once near the war zone, crews relied on the B-2's synthetic aperture radar to develop an accurate picture of the target area and check and confirm intelligence photos. Once crews were satisfied, GPS co-ordinates previously fed into the JDAMs were refined using the bomber's GPS-Aided Targeting System (GATS). Sources suggest this allowed mission commanders to select elevation as well as longitudinal and latitudinal co-ordinates.

hours, so US-based crews could 're-fly' critical portions of actual missions at will, using the simulator.

Equally impressive was the stealth bomber's reliability. Of the nine operational examples at Whiteman, eight were committed to combat missions, and six were available at any given time. In sharp contrast to mission-capable rates from the mid-1990s, the B-2 was able to sustain a score of 60 percent (taking into account low-observables maintenance) and about 75 percent throughout Operation Allied Force overall. All missions started on time and only one was aborted due to an in-flight mechanical problem. In addition, one aircraft was recalled due to severe weather over the target area that also caused cancellation of most other air operations for the night, and one strike was recalled when the target was denied en route.

Despite the generally good results achieved by the B-2 over Serbia, it was not all good news. On the morning of 8 May the Chinese Embassy in Belgrade was attacked by three bombs, widely attributed to a B-2. NATO admitted the mistake and stated that it had intended to attack legitimate military targets such as the MUP Special Police HQ, the hotel from which the infamous paramilitary leader Arkan operated and other key buildings. A report in the *Los Angeles Times* a week later postulated that the error in targeting came as a

92-0700* Spirit of Oklahoma *was the first of the three Block 20 aircraft to be built as such, and was delivered to the Air Force in July 1996. It joined the Block 30 upgrade programme, emerging in its new guise in November 1999.

89-0128* Spirit of Nebraska *was one of five aircraft which have served the 509th Bomb Wing in all three configurations. It was delivered as a Block 10 in June 1995, was redelivered as a Block 20 in July 1996, and emerged from Block 30 modification in March 1999. Note the deployed airflow baffles forward of the bomb bay.

Some Allied Force reporters commented on the presence of EA-6B Prowlers, the Navy's sophisticated electronic jamming aircraft, often flying in support of B-2 missions and suggested the bomber was less effective than claimed. However, Barnidge cautioned that 'non-organic' electronic support had not been needed and had not been factored into the bombing missions because the B-2 is capable of self-support. The claim was that the Prowlers had been used for added security simply because they were available. What is significant is that Allied Force operations served to validate the concept that lone B-2s can effectively launch from the USA against targets thousands of miles away.

To the surprise of critics, B-2 crews faired better physically on the long missions than expected. Despite the duration, they were well-rested and ready for the accelerated pace of operations when the crucial time came. Of 54 operational pilots, 51 flew combat missions, with some undertaking two, and one even flew three sorties. Fatigue was reduced through unconventional means. Crews often took power naps on beach chairs set up behind the mission commander's station, or snacked on hot foods. Barnidge insists that all crews got at least three days rest between missions, and pilots flying the next day's mission often preflighted the bombers. Interestingly, crew training continued throughout the entire conflict. By running simulator missions based on actual threat data accumulated from the sorties flown, pilots could get a true feel for what they might encounter. Flight times over hostile zones were limited, in some cases to less than two

B-2 Spirit

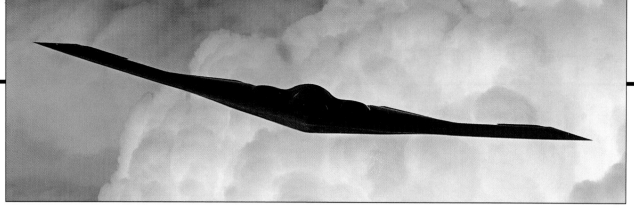

Right: From head-on the B-2 presents a very slender shape, although it is the careful blending of curved surfaces and straight edges, along with the application of RAM, which renders the aircraft invisible to radars.

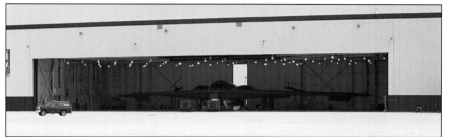

The individual hangar docks at Whiteman contain all the equipment necessary to support the requirements of the B-2, including pipes for fuel and other fluids plumbed into the floor. The rear doors open to allow the engines to be started with the aircraft still in the barn.

Continuation and conversion training for the B-2 force is undertaken by the 394th Combat Training Squadron, known as the 'Panthers'. This unit was established in November 1996, and was allocated Northrop T-38A Talons. These aircraft are used for a variety of check rides, and for providing additional flight time for B-2 crews. Pilots coming to the B-2 programme are already highly proficient, but they are required to maintain various qualifications, which may not always be possible due to the limited amount of B-2 flying time available. Much use is made of the B-2 simulator for initial conversion and continuation, and for rehearsing operational sorties.

result of the intelligence maps being wrong, despite the fact that the intended targets were clearly marked on tourist maps and in the Belgrade phone directory. If this was indeed the case, the performance of the B-2, its crew and its weapons were not at fault.

Phased evolution

Besides the initial six full-scale development (FSD) aircraft, B-2s have been delivered to the Air Force in all three Block configurations: 10, 20 and 30. Although Block 30 deliveries did not begin until 7 August 1997, when serial 93-1087 (AV-20) reached the wing, conversion of all of the bombers to Block 30 standard began in July 1995. The modifications were undertaken at the contractor's Palmdale Site 4.

Block 30 meets the requirements originally laid down by the Air Force. Block 10 aircraft, sometimes referred to as the Basic B-2, possessed only a limited combat capability (delivery of gravity nuclear or Mk 84 conventional bombs) and, as previously discussed, subsequently served solely in the training role. They could not launch any of the more complex, conventional precision-guided weapons. Block 20 represented an interim improvement because they could field some GPS-guided munitions and were tested at low altitudes with Mk 82, Mk 84, M117 and CBU-87/-87B combined effects munitions (CEMs). This Block also introduced the first defensive avionics to the fleet, providing coverage in three of the four frequency bands offered by the AN/ZSR-63 defensive system. These give crews accurate and timely information about the location of potential threats. The first Block 20 aircraft (serial 93-1085/AV-18) was delivered on 15 May 1996, having been used for Block 20 operational testing at Edwards AFB between March and May 1996.

Perhaps one of the greatest misconceptions about the stealth bomber relates to the effectiveness of its low-observables technology in adverse weather. During the early 1990s, many reports referred to the B-2's supposed inability to endure rain and extreme climatic conditions. However, they overlooked the fact that original Block 10 aircraft were not intended as full, low-observables platforms and had no combat signature. Instead, they were an attempt to field a base-level operational bomber quickly. Block 20 bombers have served as

an interim solution, offering an improved low-observables signature but did not have full rain-erosion coatings nor the combat low-observables signature planned for Block 30 bombers.

As testing of many of the systems was being conducted concurrent with production, many of the planned modifications were still under development when new bombers were rolled out. It is worth noting, however, that B-2s flying in support of Allied Force suffered little or no degradation of their low-observables signature as a result of inclement weather.

Also related to the adverse-weather issue has been criticism about certain TF/TA radar modes. A Government Accounting Office report issued in the mid-1990s contended various TF modes could not adequately distinguish rain from terrain and thus reported they were not functional in wet weather conditions. This reflects a basic misunderstanding of the bomber's TF system. As with the B-1B (and the F-111 when it was in service), the TF mode reflects a default 'fly-up' condition any time there is a possible disparity between severe weather and terrain. However, this does not render the TF mode inoperable.

Weapons of the war and beyond

Tried and tested in Operation Allied Force, the JDAM is now the B-2's primary weapon. Built by Boeing, the JDAM employs a guidance kit used to convert dumb bombs into highly accurate, GPS-guided smart bombs. Essentially, the kit consists of a new tail section housing a GPS-aided Inertial Navigation System (INS).

The 2,000-lb Mk 84 JDAM was carried exclusively by the stealth bomber for missions over the Balkans, and development of a similar 500-lb Mk 82 class weapon is now well advanced. The smaller munition will enable the aircraft to carry a higher number in its bay, thereby allowing more targets to be hit during a single mission. During tests conducted in early 1998, a bomber from the 393rd BS dropped four GBU-31 JDAMs on three targets at the White Sands Missile Range. This was to evaluate the concept of targeting two weapons against a single aim point. With less than a second of separation, the second bomb followed the first into the same hole, a feat never before accomplished with a launch-and-leave weapon. The GAM, which was originally developed as an interim solution until the JDAM could be 'married' with Block 30-configured aircraft, also played a part in Allied Force. Four were dropped during the conflict to good effect.

On 11 January 2000, members of the Whiteman B-2 Test Team began evaluating the JSOW, stressing the bomber's unique targeting option capabilities. Three tests were performed, the first of which demonstrated the weapon's ability to overfly pre-programmed waypoints. The second, conducted on 19 January, validated a manual inflight delivery selection, while the third, carried out six days later, demonstrated the weapon's ability to utilise the GATS to refine target location and update target co-ordinates in real time. All three trials were successful, with bomb fragments spread across the entire intended target area each time.

The JSOW is an area-type weapon considered by some to work best when complementing the JDAM. Offering an increased stand-off range of 40 nm (74 km) when dropped from high altitude, and 15 nm (28 km) when launched from low altitude, it is an all-weather, day and night weapon. The additional stand-off range is important because it means the bomber's radio frequency, electro-optical, infra-red and

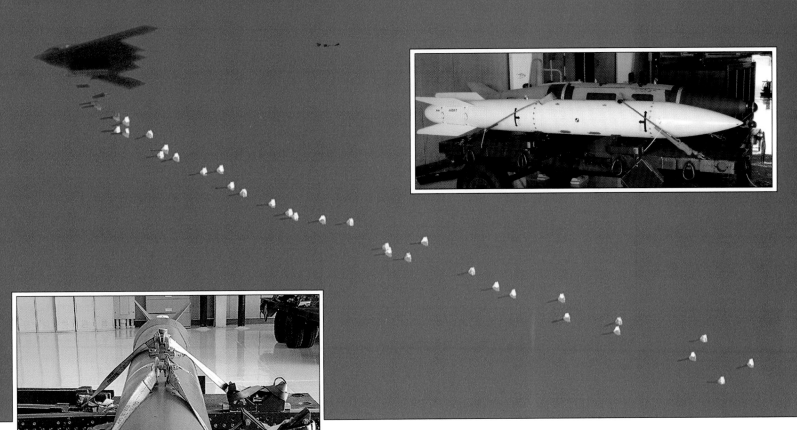

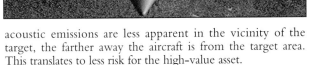

jam-resistant Link-16, referred to as the Joint Tactical Information Distribution System (JTIDS), is a true force multiplier that provides aircrews with a near-real time picture of the battlefield. Aircraft using JTIDS can exchange targeting and threat information, thereby permitting all JTIDS-linked assets to 'see' the developing battle space.

Related to this is the capability to transmit re-targeting and mission profile data while the bomber is en route to its target area, referred to as flex-targeting. Currently, crews can perform this task via secure voice communication and limited mission planning modifications but the latter involves a significant effort on the part of the crew. Transmission of data via satellite communications will allow entire mission plans to be modified and mission information to be forwarded to the

acoustic emissions are less apparent in the vicinity of the target, the farther away the aircraft is from the target area. This translates to less risk for the high-value asset.

Two variants of the JSOW have been developed for the stealth bomber. The AGM-154 dispenses 145 BLU-87 CEM bomblets for use against soft targets like airfields and SAM sites, whereas the AGM-154D dispenses BLU-108 anti-armour submunitions and can be used to attack mobile armoured forces. Plans call for the Air Force to acquire up to 3,000 AGM-154As and 3,100 AGM-154Bs.

Future upgrades

A number of enhancements to the B-2 have been discussed in recent years. Continuing modification of the baseline Block 30, most proposals focus on enhancing connectivity and mission planning responsiveness, integrating new precision-guided munitions and increasing the number of sorties that can be generated. For the entire fleet this would bring the addition of a line-of-sight (LOS) data link for aircraft-to-aircraft and aircraft-to-command data transfer. The

Above: A B-2 displays its conventional capabilities with a drop of 500-lb (227-kg) ballute-retarded bombs during a Capstone firepower demonstration on the Nellis ranges in Nevada.

Above, inset: The standard B61-7 nuclear weapon is a possible B-2 load, although the larger B83 or penetration B61-11 are more likely weapons should the Spirit have to fly the unthinkable nuclear mission. Behind the B61 is a GBU-31 2,000-lb JDAM, a weapon widely used by the B-2.

Far left: The 4,800-lb (2177-kg) 'Deep Throat' bunker-busting weapon was first used in Desert Storm when two laser-guided weapons were dropped by F-111Fs in an attempt to kill the Iraqi leadership. The bomb was then mated with a GPS guidance suite to produce the GAM-113, which was then refined to create the GBU-37 as part of the JDAM family.

Left: Another Capstone demonstration shows the B-2 dropping 'slick' Mk 82s. It is unlikely B-2s would be used to any great extent in unguided bombing attacks, although the ability to carry up to 80 Mk 82s allows the bomber to produce a dramatic 'carpet' effect if required. This capability was employed in Operation Iraqi Freedom, in attacks on the Medina division of the Republican Guard.

Along similar lines, the Air Force and Northrop Grumman have proposed the integration of an advanced extremely high-frequency (EHF) satellite communications system to ensure survivable communications for the command and control of nuclear forces. The contractor is also looking at a new radio, the Airborne Integrated Terminal, which will permit satellite voice and data communications.

Upgrades are also being explored in relation to the analog engine controller, while the jet undergoes routine maintenance and subsequent upgrades. Consideration is being given to the installation of a digital system that officials think will improve the bomber's performance and increase its reliability, supportability and maintainability. Without future funding, the Air Force will be forced to begin grounding the jets in mid-2008.

From a munitions perspective, one idea being explored is the integration of the Wind Corrected Munitions Dispenser (WCMD), although this has not yet been funded. The WCMD provides an all-weather capability to attack large target areas, such as troop concentrations, non-hardened vehicle staging areas and massed armour. It gives crews the opportunity to steer the dispenser to a selected aim point, thereby eliminating or substantially reducing ballistics-induced errors, mil dispersion and wind. The estimated footprint of the sensor-fused WCMD is approximately 1,500 x 750 ft (457 x 152 m). Its employment will require integration of a MIL-STD 1760 interface on the bomb rack assembly and other software changes to the operational flight programme.

Smaller, smarter bombs

The most important and revolutionary weapons proposals, however, stem from the advances being made with miniaturised munitions. Work is now underway to adapt JDAM and other technologies for the purpose of creating longer-range, smaller and even more accurate weapons in the 500-lb (227-kg) and 250-lb (113-kg) classes. These are referred to as Small Diameter Bombs (SDBs). The importance of such advances is three-fold. Longer range means less risk, while increased accuracy means assured destruction with minimised collateral damage. As indicated earlier, the third benefit is that more can be carried because of their small size. This translates to more kills per sortie. Another possibility, already partially funded, is the proposed EGBU-28 heavy penetrator common weapon designed to replace the GBU-37 series. This would be developed for use both by the stealth bomber and the F-15E Strike Eagle, and be available with both laser and GPS guidance.

On 11 March 2003 the USAF tested a new weapon, which is believed to be earmarked for carriage by the B-2. Known as the Massive Ordnance Air Blast, or the 'Mother Of All Bombs', the MOAB is a streamlined weapon with short wings and pop-out lattice fins, and is based on the shape of the SDB, but massively enlarged to 21,500 lb (9752 kg). The

bomber's navigation systems without the crew having to recalculate the data. The improvements proposed will unquestionably enhance the aircraft's flexibility because theatre commanders will be able to use the bombers on an 'on-call' basis, in much the same way forward air control – airborne (FAC-A) – operations were conducted during Operation Allied Force, or even on an alert basis. During operations in Afghanistan and over Iraq, B-1 bombers were employed in the 'on-call' role, and it is likely that the B-2 may be employed similarly in the future.

Part of the Link-16 programme involves installation of new 10-in (25.4-cm) displays. The B-2's cockpit currently features a 6 x 6-in (15.2 x 15.2-cm) multi-purpose display unit (MDU) that uses a combination of 'raster' and 'stroke' presentation methods to overlay data on another image. As such, it is not capable of supporting the enhanced radar modes and offers only limited situational awareness. The 10-in displays are high-resolution, active-matrix liquid-crystal displays (AMLCDs) that utilise individually addressable pixels. The result is a higher resolution and a far more accurate display of radar-processed images. The AMLCDs also allow more accurate cursor placement for navigation and targeting modes.

MOAB has been developed to replace the 15,000-lb (6804-kg) BLU-82 weapon currently in use by the Special Operations Command. Like the BLU-82, MOAB can be delivered by being rolled off the back ramp of an MC-130 special operations Hercules. The 11 March test at Eglin AFB, Florida, was conducted by an MC-130. However, at 30 ft (9.1 m) length and 40.5 in (1.03 m) diameter, the weapon is sized to fit into the B-2's bomb bay. It employs GPS/INS guidance and the wings provide a healthy stand-off glide range. The weapon detonates above ground, providing a massive blast effect and overpressure across a wide area. It can be used against entrenched ground forces and tunnel complexes, or can clear wide swathes through minefields.

In parallel to MOAB, the USAF is also working on an even larger weapon for the B-2, known as 'Big BLU'. This weighs in at around 30,000 lb (13608 kg) and has a penetrating warhead. It is being designed for use against underground targets that are outside the reach of even the 4,800-lb GBU-37 JDAM 'bunker-buster'.

Other weapons-related items under consideration include the universal release rack (URR) and the purchase of additional rotary launcher assemblies (RLA). The latter will significantly reduce nuclear-mission generation time and permit support of conventional and nuclear operations without having to dual task the RLAs. The URR provides a single rack so that both RLA and BRA weapons can be employed without the launcher assemblies needing to be switched. Currently, B-2A RLAs must be changed and a rack inserted if the mission calls for CBUs rather than JDAMs to be carried. Adaptation of a URR would allow faster turn times for aircraft employing different weapons. Moreover, this would alleviate the need for additional RLA units.

The most recent upgrades relate to the B-2A's computers and low-observables signature. State-of-the-art processors will be needed to keep pace with increasing demands on the overall system. Similarly, as threats continue to evolve and proliferate, advanced concepts will have to be explored to ensure the B-2A's low-observables signature remains proportionate.

Based on current mission profiles and data accumulated from the initial developmental test and evaluation phases, the B-2A's service life is now put at approximately 40,000 hours. The control surface attachment points on the outer wing and the areas around the deck have been subjected to vibro-acoustic stress and have been identified as the first areas that will fail. The Aircraft Structural Integrity Program (ASIP), which analyses the point at which it is more economical to replace the aircraft than continue with structural modifications, forecasts an attrition rate of one B-2A every 10 years, based on statistics derived from the B-52 programme. This means that by 2027 the B-2A fleet size is likely to have fallen below the required 19 operational aircraft. According to a 1999 Air Force White Paper on long-range bombers, a new-generation aircraft will be needed to fill the void at that time. Whether 'new' means the B-2 production line will be reopened or a new aircraft will be developed, has not been revealed.

To war again – OEF and OIF

In the meantime, the B-2 has continued its role at the tip of the USAF's spear and has seen action in two further conflicts – Enduring Freedom and Iraqi Freedom. In the first conflict, the US-led invasion of Afghanistan in response to the 11 September 2001 terrorist attacks, B-2s flew only a handful of missions (believed to be six), but they have gone into the history books as the longest bombing missions ever flown.

Operation Enduring Freedom opened on the night of 7/8 October 2001 with an air assault against Afghanistan. This

When the US and UK shaped up to attack Iraq in 2003 it seemed inevitable that the B-2 would be in the vanguard of the attack. The large-scale 'Day One' onslaught expected by many failed to materialise: instead, planners opted for a measured application of airpower in the hope of forcing Iraqi compliance with coalition demands. This campaign itself was preceded by a one-off leadership attack involving TLAMs and F-117s.

Three B-2s taxi at Diego Garcia on 21 March 2003, the second full day of Operation Iraqi Freedom. B-2s were involved in key attacks on leadership and command targets, and were involved in the heaviest attacks of the war on Baghdad on the night of 27/28 March. B-2s flew 47 sorties during the war, of which 28 involved inflight 'flex' retargeting of weapons.

B-2 Spirit

A British territory in the Indian Ocean, the island of Diego Garcia has played host to US bombers during several Middle East campaigns. In 2001 it was used as a refuelling and crew-change stop for B-2s attacking Afghanistan from Whiteman. During Operation Iraqi Freedom in 2003 the base played host to four B-2s deployed to the 40th Aerospace Expeditionary Wing, operating alongside B-52s from the 2nd BW. Here one of the stealth bombers gets airborne for the haul to Iraq which, at around 15 hours flying time, was considered a 'short' hop for the B-2.

Despite 12 years of an arms embargo and steady degradation by coalition forces during Northern and Southern Watch missions, the Iraqi air defences continued to present a real threat to US, UK and Australian aircraft during Operation Iraqi Freedom. This was especially true around Baghdad, where Iraqi forces moved their missile launchers into residential areas, and also attempted to use GPS jammers. B-2s continued to operate unhindered, carrying out attacks against strategic targets. Among these was the dropping of two GBU-37s against a communications tower on the night of 27/28 March. On the following night the B-2 was integrated into a complex strike which simultaneously involved B-1Bs and B-52Hs.

impoverished nation, stricken by decades of civil war and a repressive Taliban regime, offered few of the strategic infrastructure targets that are the 'meat and drink' of the B-2. However, a limited command and control structure, plus a few airfields and some air defence sites, were deemed valuable enough to warrant B-2 strikes.

For the first three nights of the war the 509th Bomb Wing launched two B-2 missions against Afghanistan. All originated from the home base at Whiteman. The route from Whiteman to Afghanistan remains unknown, but the aircraft recovered at Diego Garcia (British Indian Ocean Territory) after the attack. In each case this Whiteman-Afghanistan-Diego Garcia leg lasted over 40 hours, and in one case topped 44 hours. When the aircraft reached the Indian Ocean island base, they spent around an hour on the ground with engines running, during which a fresh crew took over the aircraft. They then took off for a 30-hour flight back to Whiteman. In these

remarkable missions the aircraft's engines were running continuously for more than three days! Weapons employed included 2,000-lb JDAMs, and 4,800-lb GBU-37s.

Due to a time-critical 'pop-up' target of opportunity it was the F-117, rather than the B-2, which led off the USAF's air campaign against Iraq when Operation Iraqi Freedom was launched on 19/20 March 2003. Instead of the carefully planned air assault against command and control centres, and air defence nodes, the air war kicked off with two F-117s and around 40 cruise missiles attacking a leadership target. This 'false start' is believed to have brought forward the start of the campaign proper, which involved the B-2 from the first day.

At the time of writing little detailed information has been released about the B-2's role in the war, but it can be assumed that it was used against a wide range of strategic targets, including those in downtown Baghdad. In at least one operation the activities of all three bomber types – B-1B,

B-2 Spirit: The 'Stealth Bomber'

B-52H and B-2A – were integrated into a single mission, with closely planned times-on-target. B-2s operated from both the home base at Whiteman and Diego Garcia, the first time that the B-2 had launched on a combat sortie from a forward-deployed base. Another B-2 'first' was the first B-2 combat mission by a female pilot, undertaken by Captain Jennifer Wilson on 1 April. Four B-2s were deployed to Diego Garcia for operation by the 393rd Expeditionary Bomb Squadron, 40th Aerospace Expeditionary Wing. However, it is possible that the B-2 force was in a state of flux, with aircraft rotating in and out of Whiteman and Diego Garcia between missions.

Need for a long-range bomber

What the B-2 has clearly demonstrated in three conflicts is that there is a significant role for a long-range, CONUS-based heavy bomber within today's operational force. As the drive towards weapons miniaturisation continues, there is little doubt the stealth bomber will continue to evolve as a first-day-of-the-war platform. However, as an extremely complex and technologically advanced aircraft that has emerged from a long and controversial development programme, it remains at the mercy of decisions made by people who do not fully understand its capabilities. Although less so than before, perhaps, myths and misconceptions abound and will be destroyed only gradually. As Mark Twain once remarked: "a lie can be half way around the world before the truth has got its boots on".

It is worth remembering that more than half a century ago, the US Army Air Corps wanted to buy a new bomber. It was large, sophisticated and the most expensive combat aircraft in the world. Critics in Congress and branches of the military argued that economic times were tight and that the United States was not about to become embroiled in any conflicts where the big bomber's unique assets – range and survivability – would be necessary. A cheaper warplane based on an existing airframe would be adequate. The Air Corps lost its fight and received only a small test squadron of the big bombers. Most of the money earmarked for bombers went to buy hundreds of the less expensive aircraft.

The cheaper bomber was the Douglas B-18A Bolo, a derivative of the DC-2 airliner. In the Air Force Museum a plaque in front of an immaculate B-18 sums up its front-line combat career: "Several of these aircraft were destroyed by the Japanese on 7 December 1941". The big and costly bomber that the nation supposedly could not afford was, of course, the B-17 Flying Fortress.

From the outset the B-2's builders and operators have held the belief that fully operational aircraft would be stealthy enough to perform the mission: to deliver 16 near-precision, hard-target weapons per sortie, anywhere in the world, supported only by tankers. That view has been validated. No other system in the world comes close to offering this capability, nor will it for years.

Bill Sweetman;
additional material by David Donald and Brad Elward

Above: A crew chief applies an Iraqi Freedom ('OIF') mission mark to Spirit of Arizona, after its return to Whiteman from a mission. The mark is placed alongside those indicating previous missions during Operation Allied Force ('OAF').

Above left: The old and the new: with first flights separated by nearly four decades, the B-2 and B-52 operated alongside each other from Diego Garcia during Iraqi Freedom.

Spirit of Missouri (88-0329) – the first production B-2 – lands back at Whiteman AFB on 25 March 2003 after a mission to Iraq. The round trip from Missouri was about 34 hours.

B-2 Operators

B-2 Combined Test Force (CTF), Edwards AFB

The B-2 Combined Test Force (CTF) was a joint Northrop-USAF (later Northrop Grumman) effort that brought together employees of the manufacturer and Air Force personnel to test the B-2 bomber. This industry/military team was created in part to reduce duplication in the work performed by the manufacturer and the Air Force. Unlike other such efforts, the B-2 CTF began in the 'black' world during the Reagan years (1981-89) and was not publicly acknowledged in its early existence. Historians at Edwards say that the B-2 CTF began in July 1983 without a formal name. At that time, plans for the ATB/B-2 were still at an early stage and all relevant information was SAR (Special Access Required) classified. The B-2 CTF first appears on organisation charts in July 1988, two years before the first B-2 arrived at Edwards. The B-2 CTF adopted a badge which was in use before the CTF was formally established.

The CTF brought together four parties. They were the civilian contractors such as Northrop Grumman plus other companies involved in B-2 operations, the Air Force Operational Test and Evaluation Center (AFOTEC), Air Combat Command, and Air Force Materiel Command. AFOTEC is an independent test agency responsible for testing new systems under realistic conditions to determine their operational effectiveness in the field.

The CTF was located at a purpose-built facility on 'South Base' (now renamed the Birk Flight Test Facility), site of the original Muroc Army Airfield and (subsequently) Edwards AFB, chosen because it is isolated, easy to keep secure, and has access to the main runway. The facility has its own communications, security, administration, and other support operations, styled to handle the SAR nature of all of the B-2 programme in the past, and some of it today. This is in contrast to the B-1B and B-52 test operation located on 'contractor's row' on 'Main Base' where most test aircraft have been located since the early 1960s. Each CTF at Edwards has evolved somewhat differently, including those on the C-17 and F-22. In the case of the B-2 CTF, the military commander was 'dual-hatted', serving also as commander of the 412th Test Group, parent unit of the 420th Flight Test Squadron.

First flight of the number one B-2A (82-1066 c/n 1001), known as AV-1 or Air Vehicle One, took place at Palmdale,

California on 17 July 1989, and was flown by Northrop's Bruce Hinds and Colonel Richard S. Couch. Both men became early, key figures in the B-2 CTF at Edwards. The second ship flew on 19 October 1990. Test flying to evaluate low observables (LO), or stealth, technology began on 30 October 1990.

B-2s are frequently identified by one- and two-digit 'air vehicle' numbers (AV-1 to AV-20), with the final ship presumably dubbed AV-21. Northrop c/ns, however, are four-digit numbers (1001 through 1020), with the final aircraft expected to be 1021; c/ns 998 through 1000 were assigned to three non-flying airframes, namely the static test vehicle, the durability test vehicle, and the 'iron bird' or static avionics vehicle, respectively.

Flight tests of the B-2 were expanded in late 1992 to include testing of the bomber's navigational accuracy and radar capability. The extended flights put the B-2 on a 3,100-mile (4990-km) 'box route' encompassing California, New Mexico, North Dakota, Washington, and Arizona. By the time the no. 5 B-2, ship AV-5 (82-1070), was delivered on 5 October 1992, the B-2 CTF was growing and prospering. Weapons tests began. The B-2 logged its 1,000th flight hour in February 1993. By then, six aircraft had taken part in 217 developmental sorties (with the no. 1 B-2 going into temporary storage soon afterward).

At one time or another, the B-2 CTF operated seven B-2 airframes plus two Stratotankers (see 412th TW entry), with the eighth and subsequent B-2s going directly to the operational wing at Whiteman AFB, Missouri. At one point, the B-2 CTF numbered nearly 2,000 civilians and military people, and many of them used ingenuity to

create unofficial emblems to celebrate their work. Typically, employing used computer graphics, elements within the B-2 CTF transformed an official emblem into an unofficial one, with a personalised message for a particular office or branch. CTF data handlers, for instance, processed telemetry data and turned it into the findings that engineers used to analyse the tests – and came up with an emblem showing a computer reel on the CTF predator logo. Other such special projects logos were designed but never used, illustrating the old flight test truism that the first thing done in a programme is to design the logo.

A 'Frozen Spirit' motif was designed for AV-5's deployment to Eielson AFB, Alaska, in March 1997, where the B-2 CTF operated in snow, demonstrated snow removal and anti-icing. AV-5, nicknamed Fire and Ice, had been the climatic test aircraft and was 'stuffed' into the climatic test hangar at Eglin AFB, Florida for over two months in 1994.

Both the manufacturer and the service concluded that the joint effort had finished the EMD (Engineering and Manufacturing Development) phase of B-2 testing and evaluation, so the B-2 CTF lost most of its contractor personnel by 30 June 1997. Northrop Grumman, which once had hundreds of employees in the CTF and had 440 as recently as the start of 1997, had laid off all but 43 men and women by 30 June 1997.

At the peak days of B-2 testing, pilots and engineers of the CTF had up to 10 bombers at their disposal, including three deployed from the wing in Missouri and five assigned to Edwards. To mark the expiration of the EMD contract and the 'skeletonising' of Northrop Grumman's role in the CTF,

members were issued with a brass medallion commemorating the final flight in the EMD programme. On one side, the medallion is "dedicated to [the] B-2 test team, 1985-97." On the other is a notation commemorating the final EMD flight (no. 217) on 25 June 1997 by Colonel Mike Walker and Major Jay Schwindt in aircraft AV-3, a five-hour sortie. As of 1 July 1997, the much-reduced B-2 CTF was down to two aircraft: AV-3 (82-1068) and AV-5 (82-1070 c/n 1005), the latter being scheduled to be named Spirit of Ohio and moved to Whiteman AFB. The military component of the B-2 CTF was expected to be greatly reduced by 31 December 1997, when the 412th Test Group and 420th Flight Test Squadron were scheduled to go out of existence. On that date, the amount of SAR needed for the programme was to be reduced and the test force moved to 'Main Base'. In greatly reduced form and without an EMD contract, the CTF is expected to remain in existence throughout 1998 with one B-2 aircraft.

US Air Force Materiel Command

412th Test Wing

The 412th TW (tailcode 'ED', derived from Edwards) is the flying component of the Air Force Flight Test Center (AFFTC). The wing acquired its designation on 1 October 1992

through a renumbering of the former 6510th TW. (Four-digit numbers reflect 'provisional' status, and the '6' prefix was assigned to Air Force Systems Command (AFSC) and subsequently adopted by AFMC.) Under the 6510th designation, the wing dates to March 1978. The current designation was chosen to carry on the lineage and honours

of the 412th Fighter Group, which flew Bell P-59 Airacomets and Lockheed P-80 Shooting Stars at Muroc, California (the future Edwards AFB) during World War II

The wing is responsible for virtually all aircraft tested at Edwards by the USAF. The wing is the parent for the 412th Test Group, which is concerned only with the B-2.

The 412th had a total of nine aircraft assigned during its B-2 test operations (seven B-2s and two C-135s) and has also,

on occasion, flown a B-2 borrowed from Whiteman. Some of the bombers had nicknames in test operations that are different from the names applied in operational service. The aircraft assigned to the wing were:

NC-135A 60-0377 c/n 18152, Nasty Stuff a.k.a. Miss Piggy, the 'hog-nosed' B-2 radar and avionics developmental flight testbed;
C-135C 61-2669 c/n 18245, apparently used for parts;
B-2A 82-1066 c/n 1001 AV-1, Fatal Beauty;
B-2A 82-1067 c/n 1002 AV-2 (no nickname), the aerodynamic test ship;
B-2A 82-1068 c/n 1003 AV-3, Shady Lady/The Ghost, the low observables and systems operations test ship, subsequently the Block 30 test ship;
B-2A 82-1069 c/n 1004 AV-4, Deadly Attraction/Christine, the performance and weapons development ship, equipped with external cameras for stores release tests;
B-2A 82-1070 c/n 1005 AV-5, Fire and Ice, the environmental capabilities test

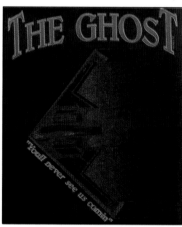

ship; evaluated at Eglin AFB, Florida and Eielson AFB, Alaska, the only test B-2 with nose art;
B-2A 82-1071 c/n 1006 AV-6, *Black Widow*, the 'easy maintenance'

demonstrator; the first ship to drop a bomb; **B-2A 88-0328 c/n 1007 AV-7**, the first production aircraft employed in the test programme for electromagnetic testing.

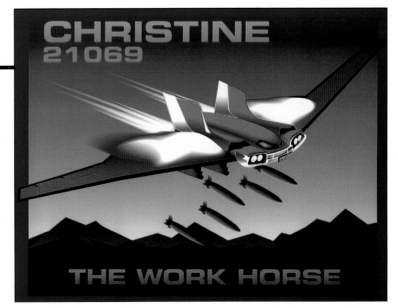

412th Test Group

The 412th TG at Edwards was formed in 1992 at the B-2 'South Base' facility to carry out B-2 tests as the military component of the B-2 Combined Test Force. The

commander of the group is also the military commander of the B-2 CTF. The group is scheduled to be deactivated on 31 December 1997, at which time bomber operations at Edwards will be merged into a single unit.

420th Flight Test Squadron

The 420th FLTS received its current designation on 2 October 1992, succeeding the 6520th Test Squadron. The squadron has the flying personnel (pilots and engineers) who carry out B-2 flight tests. The 420th FLTS is scheduled to be

deactivated on 31 December 1997, at which time B-2 flight personnel will shift to a different location on base to merge with, and assume the name of, the 419th FLTS, which currently handles B-1B and B-52H testing.

Air Combat Command

31st Test and Evaluation Squadron

The 31st TES is the Air Combat Command (ACC) test unit at Edwards AFB. It serves as ACC's 'window' to the B-2 world while the bomber is being tested at Edwards, which is an Air Force Materiel Command (AFMC) base. Most of the squadron's pilots are not Test Pilot School graduates, and their missions have more of an operational flavour than the earlier developmental missions intended to collect engineering quality data to evaluate the B-2 design.

The 31st TES was reactivated on 1 July 1986, taking over the functions of the 4200nd TES and bearing the lineage and honours of the 31st Bombardment Squadron, which dates to 1917. The squadron's emblem is a triangular skull emblem, which is linked to its origins as a bomb unit. From its reactivation, the squadron was a component of Strategic Air Command until ACC came into existence on 1 June 1992. The squadron provided flying personnel for B-2 test work beginning

in 1990. Squadron pilots have flown B-2s belonging to the 412th Test Group of the Air Force Flight Test Center (AFFTC) and, on occasion, B-2s on loan from Whiteman Air Force Base, Missouri.

509th Bomb Wing

The 509th Bomb Wing (tailcode 'WM') became operational on 1 April 1993 at Whiteman, preparing to operate the B-2. The USAF had announced in 1989 that the first B-2 operational unit would be stationed at Whiteman, then an inactive airfield 45 miles (72 km) from Kansas City, and that the unit would be the 351st Bomb Wing (by renaming an LGM-30F Minuteman II ICBM establishment). For reasons of tradition, however, there was strong sentiment to revive the 509th designation. The decision was reached in 1990 to pass the 509th flag to the first (and as it turned out, the only) B-2 wing at Whiteman. The wing's initial cadre came from Detachment 509, 351st Missile Wing, which had been the tenant at Whiteman AFB and was inactivated on that date.

To give an honoured name to its first operator of the 'Stealth Bomber', the US Air Force decided to carry on the identity of the 509th Composite Group, which was activated in secrecy on 17 December 1944 to organise, equip and train for atomic warfare. The 509th operated Martin-built 'Silver Plate' Boeing B-29s equipped to carry the first atomic bombs, and carried out the 1945 strikes on Hiroshima ('Little Boy' 6 August), and Nagasaki ('Fat Man', 9 August). In July 1946, the group was redesignated 509th Bombardment Group (Very Heavy), a change putting it in line with the terminology of the SAC, formed in March of that year. The 509th pioneered air-to-air refuelling in 1948 when it began flying Boeing KB-29M tankers in addition to its specially-modified B-29 bombers.

The group was redesignated 509th Bombardment Group (Medium) in July 1948, a step which reflected a changing view of the size of bombers as bigger aircraft began to join the inventory. The group converted from the B-29 to the B-50 shortly thereafter.

The USAF shifted from the combat group

to the combat wing as its principal establishment in 1952. Thus, although the 509th group was inactivated on 16 June 1952, the 509th Bombardment Wing (Medium) continued operations. The wing subsequently operated a variety of aircraft under 'medium' and 'heavy' designations before moving to Pease AFB, New Hampshire on 1 July 1958. As a B-52 operator, the wing deployed aircraft and crews to combat operations in Southeast Asia in 1968-69. In 1970, the 509th converted to the SRAM-equipped General Dynamics FB-111A, which it flew at Pease for almost two decades. When Pease was selected for closure and the FB-111A slated for retirement, the 509th Bombardment Wing (Medium) was inactivated in 1988.

The 509th, while inactive, moved to Whiteman on 30 September 1990 without personnel or equipment. By the time the 509th was resurrected at Whiteman to fly the B-2, the USAF had replaced the term 'Bombardment' with 'Bomb' in the designations of its units (squadrons and groups) and establishments (wings). The service had also (in mid-1992) restored the

combat group as part of its command structure while retaining the wing as its principal establishment. These changes having taken place while it was inactive, the wing began at Whiteman with the 509th Operations Group (OG) as part of its structure. The wing's flying units are the 393rd Bomb Squadron and the 394th Combat Training Squadron (CTS).

The 509th took over a base that had not handled large aircraft for three decades and all base facilities – buildings, hangars, taxiways, runways – had to be completely renovated and rebuilt. The first assigned aircraft, a Northrop T-38A Talon with a B-2-style paint scheme, joined the wing on 20 July 1993. Ten months after coming into existence, the 509th received its first B-2 bomber, AV-7 (88-0329) *Spirit of Missouri*, on 17 December 1993. A 509th B-2 participated in Exercise Red Flag at Nellis AFB, Nevada for the first time on 24 January 1995, dropping two Mk 84 bombs in a 7.5-hour mission. The 509th has since become a regular participant in Red Flag and other exercises throughout 1995. In May 1997, a B-2 crew from Whiteman flew the longest B-2 mission yet – a 30-hour round-trip to the Mildenhall Air Fete.

On 10 May 1996, the B-2 fleet was grounded for eight days while tailpipe clamps were inspected for cracks. The stand-down was ordered after mechanics at Whiteman discovered cracks in one aircraft's clamps; each bomber has eight of these titanium clamps. During the eight-day

period, 25 of 72 tailpipe clamps inspected were found to be faulty and were replaced. B-2 operations resumed on 18 May 1996.

In July 1996, the 509th announced that it had received the first 17 GAM-84 bombs for the B-2. Northrop Grumman and Hughes Aircraft Co. reportedly delivered 128 GAMs to Whiteman by the end of 1996. The bombs are considered an interim step for the B-2, providing precision-attack capability until the JDAM is fielded later in this decade.

On 1 January 1997, the USAF determined that B-2s at Whiteman had reached a 'limited' capability for delivering conventional weapons. On 1 April 1997, the USAF declared the 509th and its B-2s ready to take on nuclear and conventional combat missions. On that date, six B-2 Spirits (of 13 at the base at the time) became part of the SIOP (Single Integrated Operations Plan), the Pentagon's nuclear-warfighting plan. Two more B-2s were scheduled to be added to the SIOP on 1 January 1998.

Unfortunately, just days after the announcement of nuclear readiness, the Air Force had to ground its B-2 fleet. On 8 April 1997, the bombers were removed from flying status after an engine-shaft assembly broke during flight. An investigation revealed that the housing of the shaft assembly had nearly undetectable cracks that caused the shaft to turn in a slightly elliptical pattern rather than a circle. The bombers returned to flying status in mid-April.

393rd Bomb Squadron 'Tigers'

The 393rd Heavy Bombardment Squadron, under the command of Colonel Paul W. Tibbets, actually carried out the two atomic raids on Japan in 1945. The 393rd BS 'Tigers' ('WM' tailcode) was reactivated on 27 August 1993 as the first operational B-2 Spirit flying squadron of the 509th Bomb Wing. In addition to flying personnel, the squadron has support personnel, crew chiefs, maintainers, weaponeers, and other personnel. The 393rd is the USAF's principal B-2 combat formation and could be supplemented by personnel from the 394th CTS (below) in wartime.

394th Combat Training Squadron (CTS) 'Panthers'

The 394th CTS 'Panthers' (using the wing's 'WM' tailcode) was activated on 6 November 1996 as the second B-2 flying unit at Whiteman AFB, charged with both training and combat readiness. The 394th began as the 4th Aero Squadron in May 1917. At the time, the 4th was the fourth squadron in the group and chose the four-pointed star as its emblem. The new squadron patch has added the current squadron mascot, the panther, to its design. The 394th replaces a Formal Training Unit that had provided some aspects of B-2 type training. Its mission of training combat-ready pilots has three distinct phases, known as Initial Qualification (IQ), Mission Ready Status (MRS) and Continuation Training.

The 394th, staffed with instructor pilots, is available to train and fight. CTS pilots can support the 393rd Bomb Squadron (to

which its trainees transfer when qualified in the B-2) with personnel as needed for contingency operations. The squadron's 51 people include T-38 and B-2 instructor pilots and students, weapons system trainer personnel, schedulers and other squadron staff members. The unique requirements of the squadron require support from other outside agencies to augment its academic and flight-line support requirements. USAF officials say the squadron operates 12 Northrop T-38A Talons, maintenance for which is handled by Lockheed. The USAF inventory lists 10 T-38As, however, namely 62-3690, 64-13206, 65-10324, 65-10418/10419, 66-8402, 67-14826, 67-14845, 67-14920 and 68-8179. An additional aircraft identified by other sources, 65-10361, may be a replacement for one of the 10, or may be the 11th.
Robert F. Dorr

Lockheed F-117
The Black Jet

An extraordinary shape, revolutionary radar-defeating features and a top secret, yet highly glamorous development have combined with a star appearance in Desert Storm to make the Lockheed F-117 the best-known warplane in the world. Able to penetrate hostile airspace without being seen by radars or infra-red sensors, the F-117 can then use its sophisticated target acquisition and designation system to score strikes against vital targets with pinpoint accuracy.

The first flying aircraft to validate the revolutionary concept of facetting was the second Have Blue experimental machine, which was completed with full stealth coatings and no excrescences. Results from the Have Blue programme left Lockheed and the US Air Force in no doubt as to whether to build a full-scale operational warplane.

At 2:51 a.m. on 17 January 1991, an F-117 dropped the first bomb of the Gulf War, a laser-guided GBU-27 which destroyed half of the Iraqi air defence center at Nukayb. A second F-117 blew away the other half. Ten more F-117s, the rest of the coalition's first wave, headed downtown to Baghdad. Thirteen minutes earlier, a daring raid – known in American parlance as Objective Oklahoma – by US Army Apache helicopters had unleashed Hellfire missiles to take down a segment of Iraq's air defence radars at pivotal location, opening a passageway for coalition warplanes to attack Saddam Hussein's forces without being detected early, en route. By then, the 12-aircraft first wave of F-117s was already 50 miles (80 km) beyond Oklahoma. The US Air Force insists that this first wave of F-117s reached Baghdad while Saddam's radars were still up and running, and without being detected.

Major Jerry Leatherman was in F-117 number 85-0816, one of those first 10 over Baghdad. Leatherman's job, like that of another F-117 pilot ahead of him, was to bomb the Baghdad International Telephone Exchange, known to the F-117 pilots as the AT & T building because its real Arabic name was unwieldy. Leatherman followed the night eastward at 480 kt (551 mph; 886 km/h). He skirted the capital to attack from the north, seeing city lights, neon signs and the snake-like Tigris River winding through the city. Sixty SAM sites and 3,000 anti-aircraft guns encircled Baghdad on this night, almost all of them shooting as he overflew. Only later would Leatherman learn that, panicked, they were shooting 'blind' and not at him.

Stealth attack

At exactly 3:00 a.m., H-Hour, the F-117 in front of Leatherman hit the AT & T building with a GBU-27. On Leatherman's scope, the target abruptly glowed, hotter than adjacent office towers and the nearby, tulip-shaped Iraqi Martyrs Monument. Leatherman pickled one minute later, splitting the crosshairs on his display and blowing out the upper four floors of the building. Leatherman peeled away to the west, for the safety of the desert, and turned for home, switching on heavy metal music from Def Leppard on his Walkman. Behind him, Captain Marcel Kerdavid swooped down through a sky alive with fire and pickled a

GBU-27 through the Al Khark communications tower, to blow the 370-ft (112-m) spire in half at its mid-point.

"My biggest fear was that I would survive," said Major Mike Mahar, pilot of an F-117 in the second wave assaulting Baghdad. "'They're all dead,' I told myself. 'All the guys who went in ahead of me have been shot down. If I live through tonight, I'll be the only F-117 pilot who survived. Everybody will ask why.'

"Twenty minutes away from Saddam Hussein's presidential retreat at Abu Ghurayb, I saw what looked like red-orange explosions from bombs filling the landscape ahead. But we didn't have any aircraft up there. I know, now, I was looking at muzzle flashes from anti-aircraft guns."

The sky around Mahar seemed to be full of fire. Flak detonated above and below him, buffeting the F-117. "No one had ever seen such a nocturnal display of pyrotechnics," he remembers. "With no spatial reference, it was impossible to tell how far some of it was from my aeroplane. But it seemed very close."

There are those who believe Major Mike Mahar (today a lieutenant colonel) will be chief of staff of the United States

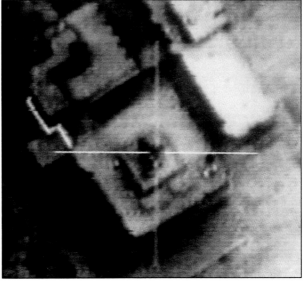

Perhaps the most memorable images of the 1991 Gulf War were those taken from infrared sensors used to guide laser weapons. This remarkable still comes from an F-117's DLIR turret, with the cross-hairs firmly aligned over an air shaft on the roof of a building in downtown Baghdad. Moments after this, the bomb is seen entering the building, and the ensuing blast is seen erupting out of the side windows.

Above: F-117s make their way to Saudi Arabia during the Desert Shield build-up, supported by KC-10 tankers. In the war which followed, the F-117s usually flew to the Iraqi border with the tankers, which waited at the border until the Nighthawks returned from their secretive forays into hostile airspace.

right way. Today, we know that no Iraqi bullet ever touched it – Mahar and everyone else who took the 'Black Jet' into combat did survive.

Two years earlier in Panama, the F-117 had been introduced to combat the wrong way. It was an uncharacteristic hiccough in a story that has been mostly smooth and seamless. On balance, very little has gone wrong in the design, development, and operational and combat employment of the mystery aircraft from the Lockheed Advanced Development Company's 'Skunk Works', headed by Ben R. Rich.

'Black' project

Rich's motto is "make things black and skunky," meaning secretly and smartly. His patron saint is Clarence L. ('Kelly') Johnson. Johnson, who died in 1990, founded the 'Skunk Works' at Burbank, California, in 1943, and was the moving force behind its products from the XP-80 Shooting Star to the SR-71 Blackbird. The nickname was originally 'Skonk Works' from a foul-smelling whiskey still in Al Capp's 'Li'l Abner' comic strip. Lockheed engineer Irv Culver, who worked with Johnson on the XP-80, thought the place smelled like the moonshine beverage, Kickapoo Joy Juice, created in the cartoon from old shoes, skunks and high-octane rubbing alcohol. Culver thought up the name because of the reek from a plastics factory across the street. The 'Skunk Works' has since relocated to a less odiferous setting and today employs 4,500 people working at Palmdale, 35 miles (56 km) west of Edwards Air Force Base in the California high desert.

The 'Skunk Works' was very much like the 4450th Tactical Group created at Groom Lake, Nevada, on 15 October 1979 under Colonel Robert A. Jackson. The cover story was that the group was formed to test A-7 avionics. In fact, the Vought A-7D, the US Air Force's version of the Navy Corsair II, was leaving the active-duty inventory (although some years of Air National Guard service lay ahead) and represented an available, credible airframe which a test/trials unit might usefully and realistically use. Pilots were told not to give out the cover story, not to say anything. The real purpose of the A-7D at first was simply to keep the men flying while their actual aircraft evolved. Later, the A-7D would be useful for cover purposes, for flying time and as a chase aircraft, known to the 4450th as a 'companion' aircraft to the new flying machine taking shape.

The real purpose of the 4450th TG was to bring into the world a new kind of warplane, so revolutionary that not

Air Force by 2010. He seems easygoing, devoid of fear. "But that first night over Baghdad, the sky itself seemed to be on fire as I turned south-east toward my target, a biological weapons bunker at Salman Pak. Another F-117 banked toward Saddam's retreat.

"I needed to get my mind away from that firestorm outside the aeroplane. I reached for a switch located on a console to my left and electrically lowered the seat of my F-117 as far as it would go. I hunkered down. I peered straight into my instrument panel and my multi-functional display. To distract myself, I muttered a song I'd often enjoyed with my children: 'Heigh-ho, heigh-ho, it's off to work we go...'

"I reached my aiming point, illuminated the target with my laser designator – we don't talk a lot about the details of that – and went down in a dive, looking into the crosshairs of my display. I dropped a laser-guided bomb [GBU-27] and banked to get out of there.

"A quick movement above my F-117 caught my attention. I looked up to see a missile streak past my canopy and explode in a brilliant flash of yellow. My aircraft shook and faltered.

"I thought, 'Maybe I won't have to explain surviving, after all...'"

The F-117 had now been introduced to combat the

The 37th TFW (Provisional) was established at King Khalid Air Base, Khamis Mushait, to control all F-117 operations in Desert Storm. Despite the high-tech nature of their charges, the 37th ground crew kept alive the traditions of wartime humour.

The cockpit of the F-117 is perhaps the most sought-after seat in the Air Force. However, the acceptance process is rigorous, and candidates must show the right mix of attitude, ability and experience.

even its existence was admitted. Both the 'Skunk Works' and the 4450th TG, which owned no aeroplanes for its first years of existence, were small, tightly integrated, relaxed and very secret.

History

Starting with the U-2 in the 1950s and continuing with the SR-71 Blackbird in the 1960s, Lockheed's 'Skunk Works' embarked on a concerted effort to become the industry authority on foiling radar. The company was first to become deeply involved with what is known today as 'stealth' or very low observables (VLO) techniques.

Recognising the company's quiet way of accumulating expertise, the Defense Advanced Research Projects Agency (DARPA) found a place for Lockheed in a generously-funded, scientific review of LO principles. Almost nothing has been disclosed about this study, which was codenamed Harvey after the invisible rabbit of a James Stewart film.

Today's 'Black Jet' owes its origins to a subsequent study, a 1974 DARPA investigation into making fighters less detectable by radar. This time, it was more than just theory. And this time, for reasons unclear, Lockheed was not at first invited to participate. To appeal the snub, 'Skunk Works' boss Ben Rich obtained CIA permission to discuss the SR-71's low-observables characteristics. With its blended wing/fuselage join and small frontal profile, the SR-71 and its Oxcart civilian counterpart properly deserved to be called the world's first stealth aircraft; Rich was promptly invited to join the DARPA study.

Soon afterward, the programme took on a status like no other in history. It became SAR (Special Access Required) and, not merely top secret, it was compartmentalised. People working in some 'compartments' had no idea what others were doing. Only a handful were 'read in' on the whole story. Later, the term 'black programme' came into vogue to describe this kind of undertaking, which was also kept secret from all but a few Congressmen. The US Air Force, which took over from DARPA, would not even acknowledge that the programme existed.

XST programme

In August 1975, Lockheed and Northrop were invited to develop and test an aircraft known as the Experimental Survivable Testbed (XST). Years later, still in the shadows and groping, an inquisitive press picked up the term and reported that it meant Experimental Stealth Testbed. This was the first of many speculations which were to prove wrong.

Both manufacturers designed small, single-seat aircraft. Northrop's XST air vehicle used a combination of rounded and angular surfaces to achieve its lowered radar cross-section. Some have referred to Northrop's design as 'Shamu' because it resembled the famous orca whale at San Diego's Sea World.

Lockheed mathematician Bill Schroeder developed a computer programme called Echo 1 that made it possible to predict the radar signature of an aircraft shaped with flat panels, or facets. This in turn led to design of a pole mode called 'the hopeless diamond', which helped Lockheed win the Have Blue stealth demonstration programme in April 1976.

Have Blue

Schroeder's research led to an aircraft concept in which individual surfaces and edges were orientated to reflect incoming radar energy into narrow beams aimed away from the radar detector. In addition to shaping, the external surface of the aircraft then being designed was to be covered with radar-absorbent material (RAM). In time, the aircraft would have canopy windows with special coatings to make the panels appear as metallic surfaces to radar.

Despite the capabilities of radar-predicting computers, there is no substitute for live testing to find radar 'hot-spots'. Pole-mounted models on outside ranges provide the best means of measuring radar cross-sections, and there have been many tests throughout the Have Blue/Senior Trend programme. Shown here is a quarter-scale model of an F-117, mounted on a pole at Lockheed's own Helendale facility in the Mojave Desert.

Have Blue testing – an early small-scale model is tested for radar cross-section in Lockheed's anechoic chamber (right) at Rye Canyon, while above a full-scale model is tested on the White Sands Ratscat Backscatter Range in New Mexico.

Lockheed built two Have Blue sub-scale proof-of-concept demonstrator aircraft, completed at Burbank within months. Have Blue was a subsonic, single-place aircraft so ugly that it was disturbing to look at, powered by two 2,950-lb (13.12-kN) thrust General Electric J85-GE-4A engines. The engines came from the government after being removed from a North American T-2B Buckeye trainer.

The sharp-nosed, bent-tail Have Blue aircraft was 47 ft 3 in (14.62 m) in length, 7 ft 6.25 in (2.33 m) high, and had a wing span of 22 ft 6 in (56.97 m) and a wing area of 386 sq ft (36 m²). The unorthodox Have Blue configuration was designed to provide a highly manoeuvrable fighter aircraft with, as they were now called, VLO characteristics. The shape of the aircraft evolved from VLO and controllability considerations. This resulted in a relaxed static stability (RSS) aircraft which necessitated a quadruply-redundant, fly-by-wire (FBW) flight control system to provide handling qualities throughout the flight envelope.

The meaning of RSS, and the remarkable instability of this aircraft and of the production warplane which followed, are highlighted in a Lockheed document: "Since this was the first aeroplane designed by electrical engineers, it is not surprising that a number of aerodynamic sins were committed. The unaugmented airframe exhibits just about every mode of unstable behaviour possible for an aircraft: longitudinal and directional instability, pitch up, pitch down, dihedral reversal, and various other cross-axis couplings. The only thing it doesn't do is tip back on its tail when it is parked."

Aerodynamic configuration

As for the aeroplane's flight surface, the wing planform was a modified delta with a dramatic sweep of 72.5°. There were no flaps, speed brakes or high lift devices. The structure was aluminium alloy with steel and titanium utilised in the hot areas. The control surfaces were elevons, located inboard on the wings, and two all-moveable fins at the wingroot that were swept back and canted inboard. A side stick controller (taken from an F-16) and conventional rudder pedals operated the control surfaces through a Lear-Sei-

gler FBW command and stability augmentation system without mechanical backup, also taken from an F-16. Elevon nose-down pitch control was augmented by a large, two-position flap called the 'platypus', which was deflected downward automatically whenever 12° angle of attack was exceeded. The unique aerodynamic configuration and complex flight control system necessitated a sophisticated and highly accurate flight test instrumentation system, and as a result a long boom was added to the nose. This carried pitot static pressure sources, angle of attack and side split vanes, and an accelerometer.

Have Blue was longer than many fighters but otherwise extremely small. Gross weight of this bizarre new aircraft ranged from 9,200 to 12,500 lb (4173 to 5669 kg). Even for an aircraft with no payload, this made it a true bantamweight. Perhaps logically, Have Blue's landing gear came from a Northrop F-5 Freedom Fighter, the only lightweight fighter then in service.

Stealth is everything

Have Blue was like nothing that had ever flown. Restrictions imposed on its designers by VLO requirements – that is, by the goal of attaining stealth – were unprecedented. "Stealth was not just part of this story," said Rich later. "It was everything."

These constraints demanded new approaches to assuring engine performance. Each inlet duct was equipped with a flat, RCS-treated grid whose porosity was sized for the cruise condition. Air flow was augmented at take-off with blow-in doors mounted on the upper fuselage surface. There was concern that the inlet grids would impair operation of the J85 engines (this was similar to a problem that later arose with the production aircraft), but these worries proved unfounded. In fact, the grids had a beneficial side effect: they helped straighten the vortex-disturbed inlet airflow from the highly swept wing leading edges, especially at high angles of attack.

Design of the exhaust system for the J85 engines, like everything else, was driven by VLO requirements. To prevent radar energy from penetrating to the turbine face, the tailpipe was transitioned from a round duct to a 17-to-1 flattened slot convergent nozzle. The trailing edge of each nozzle was terminated on a 54° scarf angle to correspond to the airframe aft closure. Vanes which were interposed and angled in the slot exit helped straighten the exhaust flow back to the longitudinal axis, although some thrust vector 'toe-in' remained. Sufficient bypass air was passed over the tailpipe to cool the aft fuselage structure.

A one-third scale RCS model of the Have Blue aircraft was tested in December 1975 at the Grey Butte Microwave Measurement facility. A smaller model was tried out in the Lockheed anechoic chamber. A second series of one-third scale model tests was conducted at Grey Butte in January 1976, confirming that minor changes in configuration had brought about considerable RCS improvement. Subsequently, a full-scale RCS model was constructed and used at the Ratscat Backscatter Measurement Range at White Sands to further develop Have Blue's VLO characteristics.

Initial engine runs were accomplished on Have Blue on 4 November 1977 at the Lockheed Burbank facility. To maintain security, the aircraft was parked between two semi tractor-trailers over which a camouflage net had been drawn. The runs were performed at night after the airport was closed. A local resident telephoned to complain about the noise, but Have Blue's secret remained intact.

The Have Blue aircraft, known as HB 1001, was taken to remote, concealed Groom Lake on a C-5A Galaxy on 16 November 1977. This was the first time a C-5A had operated from Burbank, and morning traffic was congested as people strained to see the giant transport.

At Groom Lake, engine thrust runs were performed and four low- and high-speed taxi tests conducted. During the third taxi test, a problem developed that would become a

nuisance throughout the programme: overheated brakes caused the wheel fuse plugs to melt. These tests verified the working of the drag chute and, following the fourth taxi test, HB 1001 was cleared to fly.

Lockheed test pilot Bill Park made the first flight not in January or February 1978, as widely reported, but on 1 December 1977, just 20 months from contract award. This first ship was not intended to be flown against radars but

A rare inflight photograph of HB 1002 shows the aircraft's extraordinary shape, highlighting the dramatic sweepback angle of the leading edge. Noteworthy are the facetted elevons, moving platypus tail surface and retractable blade aerial under the starboard leading edge.

The completed HB 1002 awaits a ground test prior to its first flight. This aircraft had the full-up stealth treatment, lacking the nose probe of the first aircraft and being fully covered with radar absorbent material. Construction was largely of aluminium.

Lockheed XST #1
Have Blue HB 1001

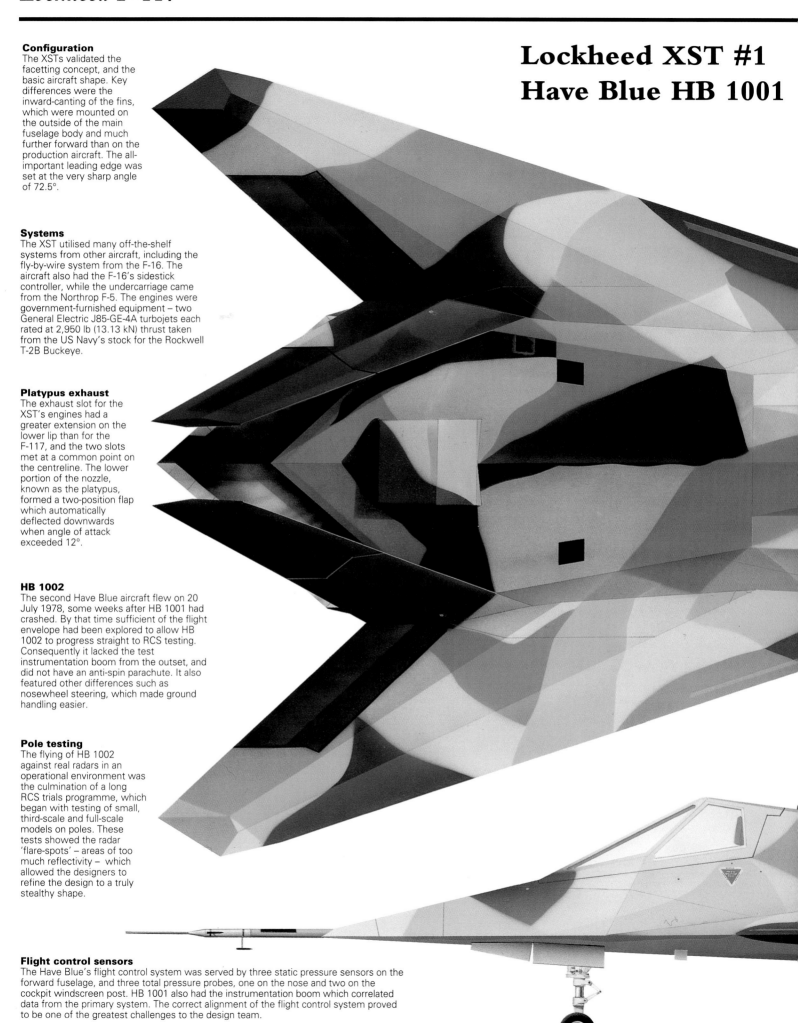

Configuration
The XSTs validated the facetting concept, and the basic aircraft shape. Key differences were the inward-canting of the fins, which were mounted on the outside of the main fuselage body and much further forward than on the production aircraft. The all-important leading edge was set at the very sharp angle of 72.5°.

Systems
The XST utilised many off-the-shelf systems from other aircraft, including the fly-by-wire system from the F-16. The aircraft also had the F-16's sidestick controller, while the undercarriage came from the Northrop F-5. The engines were government-furnished equipment – two General Electric J85-GE-4A turbojets each rated at 2,950 lb (13.13 kN) thrust taken from the US Navy's stock for the Rockwell T-2B Buckeye.

Platypus exhaust
The exhaust slot for the XST's engines had a greater extension on the lower lip than for the F-117, and the two slots met at a common point on the centreline. The lower portion of the nozzle, known as the platypus, formed a two-position flap which automatically deflected downwards when angle of attack exceeded 12°.

HB 1002
The second Have Blue aircraft flew on 20 July 1978, some weeks after HB 1001 had crashed. By that time sufficient of the flight envelope had been explored to allow HB 1002 to progress straight to RCS testing. Consequently it lacked the test instrumentation boom from the outset, and did not have an anti-spin parachute. It also featured other differences such as nosewheel steering, which made ground handling easier.

Pole testing
The flying of HB 1002 against real radars in an operational environment was the culmination of a long RCS trials programme, which began with testing of small, third-scale and full-scale models on poles. These tests showed the radar 'flare-spots' – areas of too much reflectivity – which allowed the designers to refine the design to a truly stealthy shape.

Flight control sensors
The Have Blue's flight control system was served by three static pressure sensors on the forward fuselage, and three total pressure probes, one on the nose and two on the cockpit windscreen post. HB 1001 also had the instrumentation boom which correlated data from the primary system. The correct alignment of the flight control system proved to be one of the greatest challenges to the design team.

This three-view depicts the first of the two Have Blue experimental test-ships, which paved the way for the design of a full-scale tactical stealth fighter. The aircraft was first flown by Lockheed test pilot Bill Park on 1 December 1977, and was intended purely as an aerodynamic test vehicle. It wore this strange scheme to hide its unique facetted surface, although the second Have Blue was finished in an all-over grey. HB 1001 also differed by having a decidedly non-stealthy nose instrumentation boom, whereas HB 1002 had a more refined nose sensor group for feeding the flight control system. HB 1002 was the aircraft involved in all the low-observables tests. Both aircraft crashed during the flight test programme, HB 1001 being lost on 4 May 1978 after 36 flights when a high sink rate and low landing speed resulted in damage to the undercarriage while landing at Groom Lake. Park took the aircraft to altitude and ejected, but was badly injured in the process. HB 1002 was lost in early 1980 when an engine fire forced Ken Dyson to eject.

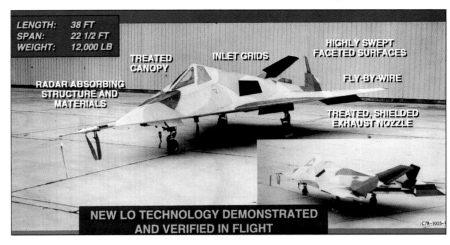

LENGTH: 38 FT
SPAN: 22 1/2 FT
WEIGHT: 12,000 LB

TREATED CANOPY
RADAR ABSORBING STRUCTURE AND MATERIALS
INLET GRIDS
HIGHLY SWEPT FACETED SURFACES
FLY-BY-WIRE
TREATED, SHIELDED EXHAUST NOZZLE

NEW LO TECHNOLOGY DEMONSTRATED AND VERIFIED IN FLIGHT

This is how Lockheed revealed the Have Blue design to the world, two photographs showing the aerodynamic test vehicle HB 1001 outside the Groom Lake test facility. HB 1001 arrived at the remote Nevada site inside the hold of a C-5 Galaxy on 16 November 1977, was reassembled, ground-tested and then flown on 1 December. Funding for the entire XST programme, one of the most important in military aviation history, totalled just $43 million, of which $10.4 million was put up by Lockheed with the remainder coming from DARPA and the US Air Force.

Handling idiosyncracies

The XST's handling was largely as predicted, but there were some notable discrepancies. The aircraft was found to be directionally unstable above Mach 0.65, but an increase in the yaw gain in the FCS software solved the problem. Heating in the platypus area caused an asymmetry of the airframe which induced a side-force. The FCS would correct this with ruddervator inputs, resulting in the aircraft crabbing. This was solved by the substitution of a side-slip angle detector in place of a lateral accelerometer for feeding the directional stability augmentation system. Finally, an asymmetric thrust situation caused roll and yaw towards the good engine rather than away from it, and the roll moment was surprisingly greater than the yaw.

Lockheed F-117

was to demonstrate loads/flutter, performance, handling qualities, and stability and control.

HB 1001 accomplished 36 flights over the next five months, and expanded the flight envelope to pave the way for RCS testing to be carried out by the second aircraft, HB 1002. The concept of a warplane capable of defeating an enemy's air defence radar was now alive and flying, but HB 1001 never saw it.

Loss of XST-1

On 4 May 1978 during HB 1001's 36th test flight, Bill Park attempted to make a landing at just a few miles per hour less than optimum setdown speed, a grim reminder of the XST's difficult handling qualities and general instability. One of the Have Blue's main landing gears hit the runway too hard, and the impact caused it to move into a half-extended, half-retracted configuration. Park made several attempts to free the jammed gear by pounding the other main wheel on the runway. As his fuel supply waned, he was ordered to make a climb to 10,000 ft (3048 m) and bail out, leaving the aircraft to its fate.

In the process of blowing the canopy and ejecting, Park hit his head and was knocked unconscious. He was still unconscious when his chute lowered him to the ground, and sustained back injuries severe enough to dictate an early retirement from flying. Park stayed on at Lockheed as director of flight operations.

HB 1002 flew on 20 July 1978, not in March or April as widely reported, apparently piloted by Lieutenant Colonel Norman 'Ken' Dyson. Like its predecessor, the No. 2 Have Blue resembled the operational warplane which was to follow. It differed from the first ship in having a 'real' air speed system fed by flush pitot static ports on the upper and lower surfaces of the nose and by three total pressure probes (thus, it required no nose boom), and did not have an anti-spin chute installed. It also incorporated nosewheel steering and was adorned with the coatings and materials needed for VLO work. Following early airspeed-calibration flights, HB 1002 made 52 flights in the next 12 months and completed the low observables testing. Final testing against mock air defence radars was in progress in July 1979 when the second XST ship was lost in a mishap.

The demise of HB 1002

One of HB 1002's hydraulic fluid line welds cracked, spraying fluid on the hot section of an engine. The fluid caught fire and flames became intense. With a fire on board that could not be extinguished and with no hydraulic power, Lieutenant Colonel Dyson was told to abandon the aircraft. He ejected safely (and later, as a civilian, became Rockwell's test pilot on the X-31A project) but the second Have Blue ship was a total loss. As they had done with the first ship, workers hauled the wreckage to a remote spot in the desert and buried it deep beneath Nevada's sagebrush and mesquite.

Even though both aircraft were lost, the Have Blue flying effort was deemed a success. The US Air Force moved quickly to the next step, a stealth fighter engineering full-scale development (FSD) contract on 16 November 1978. The original order was for 20 (five FSD and 15 production) aircraft. The effort to produce an operational fighter was codenamed Senior Trend. The aircraft had no other name.

This programme remained hidden beneath a blanket of

security rivalling the Manhattan Project, the top-secret programme during World War II under which Brigadier General Leslie Groves (architect of the Pentagon building) sequestered a small army of scientists in the remote New Mexico village of Los Alamos to design and build the first atomic bomb. Like that programme, this one moved quickly. Lockheed met wind-tunnel, pole model, and wooden mock-up milestones in record time.

Playing politics

In 1980, Presidential candidates Jimmy Carter and Ronald Reagan accused each other of risking national security by talking too much about a mysterious thing called stealth. Both talked too much about both talking too much. In fact, press leaks about a future stealth bomber forced incumbent Carter and Defense Secretary Harold Brown to acknowledge that an unnamed secret aircraft (Have Blue) had been tested. Nothing was disclosed about Senior Trend or the future bomber project. A promise to rearm America (using unprecedented public debt to pay for it) planted Reagan in the White House the following year. The new chief executive's emphasis on a military build-up went hand-in-hand with a love of secrecy which fit well with the stealth effort. Once Reagan was sworn in, no one was in any mood to disclose anything further about phantom warplanes flying in Nevada.

The separate effort aimed at developing a stealth bomber took on its own momentum and (as we know today) led to Northrop reviving its flying wing designs of the late 1940s. Early in the Reagan years, a budget item associated with this project was listed in Congressional documents under the word Aurora. The word was never intended to disguise anything: it was merely inter-office shorthand never meant to appear on a budgeting document. It referred to a component of what, in later years, became the Northrop B-2 Spirit stealth bomber. The word Aurora never did, then or later, refer to any other aircraft or 'black' programmes and, contrary to widespread rumour, no aircraft named Aurora has ever been conceived, designed, built or flown.

To set the record straight, there was one other air-breathing stealth vehicle developed during the Reagan years. It was not named Aurora, and it was unmanned. A prototype made a few test flights, crashed, and was broken up, carried to a remote stretch of desert, and buried in a deep hole. Contrary to the legend created by a misguided model-maker and others, there was never a 'black' programme for an aircraft named Aurora and there was never a 'black' reconnaissance aircraft known as the Northrop TR-3 Manta. The only manned warplanes developed in these secret programmes were the Lockheed stealth fighter and the Northrop flying-wing bomber, the future B-2 which during this era was designated Senior C. J.

Flight testing of the Lockheed's Senior Trend aircraft was preceded by a series of flights in the Calspan (Cornell Aero Labs) Lockheed NT-33 aircraft where suitability of PA (power approach) flight control laws was checked. The variable-stability NT-33 – which even then, a decade before its retirement, was the oldest aircraft in Air Force inventory – was employed primarily to simulate aircraft response to a pilot control input; with minor exceptions, it had no capability to simulate the actual performance of the subject aircraft.

First flight

Lockheed test pilot Hal Farley made the first flight of the Senior Trend aircraft on 18 June 1981, less than 31 months after go-ahead for the project. The first aircraft was serial number 79-10780, usually referred to as ship 780; it was painted light grey initially, and subsequently in disruptive camouflage (like the Have Blue) to conceal its contours and facets, and blur its general configuration, from the eyes of prying Soviet satellites. This apparently proved ineffective and the aircraft was again painted light grey, which had been the intended production colour.

Ship 780 had its V-shaped vertical fins canted exactly opposite from the inverted V-shape of the Have Blue ships, but of smaller size than later appeared on the second and subsequent aircraft. Contrary to reports, flight testing was done not at night but during daylight at Groom Lake.

It appears that the first aircraft to contain a full avionics

Photographed on the Groom Lake ramp, Aircraft 780 prepares for an early test flight. Of note are the doors covering the refuelling receptacle and brake chute, the notches on the control surfaces, wide platypus exhaust and the polygonal aerofoil section of the vertical fins.

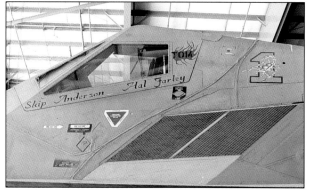

system was 79-10781, a.k.a. ship 781, which flew on 18 December 1981. VLO requirements shaped the design and development of the aircraft, while other features, particularly avionics, had to be 'made to fit' once the needs of stealth were satisfied. The result was to be an aircraft in need of avionics improvements almost from its first day of service.

The Baja Scorpions

The US Air Force had decided there would be no prototypes. The first five aircraft, the FSD vehicles, were to carry out the flight test programme. Owing to their desert home, these test aircraft were designated 'Scorpion' 1 through 5. The name comes from the decision by the Lockheed-USAF team to adopt the Baja Scorpion as its symbol after a terrifying incident in which one of the creatures – more successful than any Soviet spy – penetrated to the very heart of the 'black' programme by showing up on a desk in the team's office area. This deadly member of the *Arachnida* class, with its pincers, nipper and poisonous sting, which also kills by sucking body juices its prey, is nothing to fool with. But once they survived the office mishap without being injected with lethal venom, pilots and maintainers got their zoology mixed up and began referring to the scorpion as a 'cockroach'. Because of the ungainly shape of the aircraft, the Lockheed stealth fighter is still referred to, today, by many who fly and work on it, as the 'Cockroach'. Many

other names which appeared in the press, for example 'Wobbly Goblin', have never been used in real life at all.

The 'Scorpion' full-scale development airframes contributed to design changes that were implemented even as succeeding aircraft were rolling down the production line. From mid-1981 through early 1982, four FSD Senior Trend aircraft (ships 781 through 784) were successfully flown at Groom Lake.

MiG neighbours at Groom Lake

Groom Lake was, throughout those early days of Have Blue and Senior Trend, the most secret military airfield in the United States. In addition to the five FSD Senior Trend aircraft, Groom Lake was home of the 4477th Tactical Group 'Red Hats', equipped with Soviet aircraft as part of several compartmentalised programmes, among them Have Doughnut (for exploitation of the MiG-17), Have Drill (MiG-19), and Have Rivet (MiG-21), plus programmes for the MiG-23 and Su-7, the names of which remain undisclosed. Like Senior Trend, these were 'black' programmes, hidden from press, public and most legislators. Some reports also say that a Northrop stealth prototype flew at Groom Lake, possibly the company's XST vehicle, although (since the XST probably was never built) it was more likely a scaled-down prototype for what became the Advanced Technology Bomber (ATB), later the B-2.

Security at Groom Lake was incredible. Aircraft were kept indoors during the known overflight times of Soviet reconnaissance satellites. Weapons, including surface-to-air missiles, were available to use against any intruder who broke widely-published rules and flew within visual range of the base. There was no town adjacent to the airfield – people came and went by air – but anyone for miles around who asked questions about the Senior Trend or 'Scorpion' aircraft (still not, so far, designated F-117) was hustled into an interrogation with federal officers and, as one put it, "frightened half to death." The federal officers, themselves, did not know what was going on at Groom Lake. One of them thought the Air Force was developing a time machine.

Early in the hush-hush programme, Lockheed was pro-

Stealth on a stick: F-117s have been mounted on poles several times, but usually on a remote range for RCS testing. After a productive test career, Aircraft 780 now takes pride of place in an impressive display of pole-mounted aircraft at Nellis AFB near the Red Flag headquarters at the southern end of the base.

ceeding with the original grey paint scheme when the USAF ordered all Senior Trend aircraft painted black. This appears to have bothered no one, since the 'Skunk Works' believes in Ben Rich's version of the Golden Rule: "He who has the gold sets the rules."

For the first few years of the programme, pilots had no simulator. They trained on a no-motion, no-feedback cockpit procedures trainer (CPT) at Lockheed's Burbank facility. No two-seat model of the Senior Trend warplane was originally planned, nor was one ever built, although, even after a simulator came on line, there was a proposal to construct a two-seater using a damaged airframe, much as had been done with the Oxcart. In due course, a visual-feedback 'dynamic' simulator was installed at the Tonopah, Nevada, operating base.

The Senior Trend aircraft were built at Burbank. The wings were then removed and the aircraft crated for transport to their base (the ultra-secret Groom Lake at first, later Tonopah), where they were assembled by both Lockheed and USAF technicians. In transit, the aircraft was covered by curtains and a deceptive over-frame to hide its true shape.

On 20 April 1982, in preparation to fly the first produc-tion Senior Trend, company test pilot Robert L. Riede-nauer lined up for take-off at Groom Lake. Unknown to him or anyone else, flight-control wires had been plugged incorrectly into actuators: coded in reverse so that pitch was yaw, and vice versa. Riedenauer advanced the throttles, released the brakes and rotated for take-off. The aircraft rotated as planned but, immediately after lift-off and just after its main landing gear cleared the runway, it went berserk. Instead of its nose pitching gently upward, it yawed horizontally then pitched up violently. Loss of control was instantaneous. The aircraft hit the runway inverted, going backwards.

The 'lost' F-117

Riedenauer was seriously injured and had to retire from flying. The first production Senior Trend aircraft was dam-aged beyond repair and, since it had crashed prior to deliv-ery, was not accepted by the US Air Force. Although it fell between the final FSD ship (79-10784, alias 'Scorpion 5') and the machine which took its place as the first production craft (80-10785), Riedenauer's ship was never assigned a serial number. This was the aircraft Lockheed proposed to rebuild as a two-seater, an offer that was not accepted. Parts

Aircraft 784 ('Scorpion 5') was the last of the FSD aircraft. Here it is seen dropping a GBU-27A/B Paveway III laser-guided bomb during weapon separation trials. The large red fairings under the wing, and a small fairing under the nose, house TV cameras to record the weapon falling from the bay. Freefall weapons are believed to drop straight from inside the bay, as to extend the weapon trapeze would severely affect radar cross-section.

Lockheed F-117

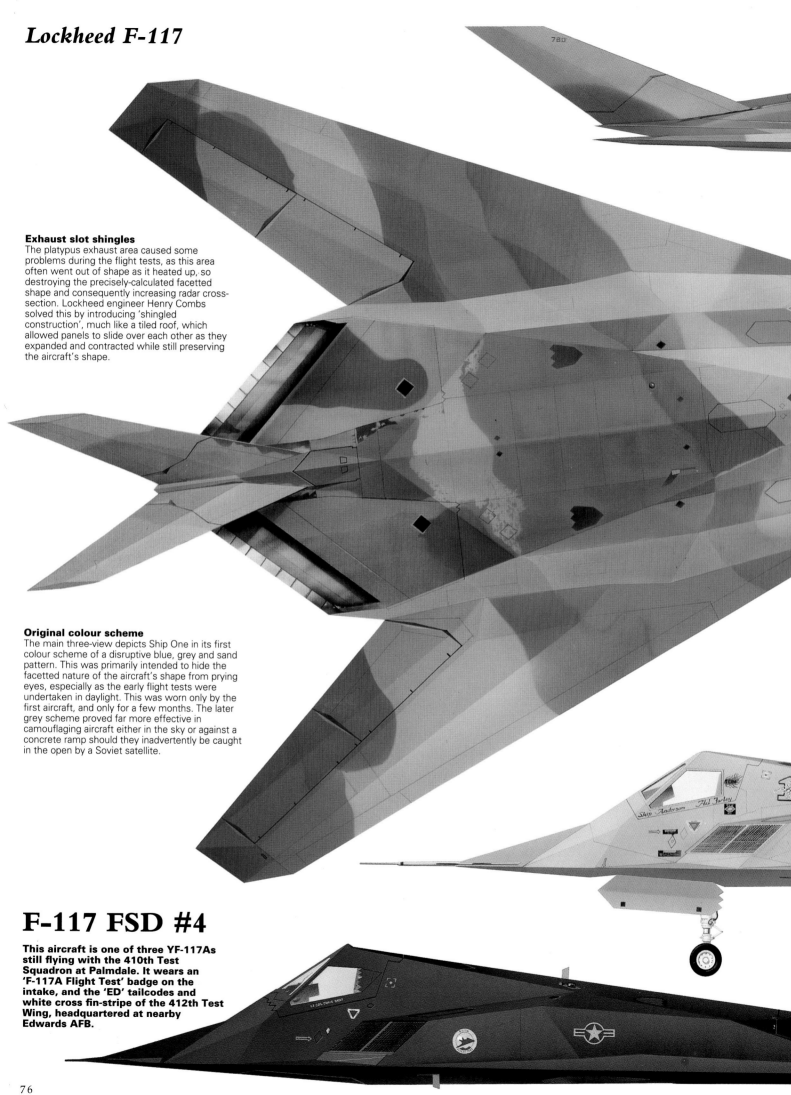

Exhaust slot shingles
The platypus exhaust area caused some problems during the flight tests, as this area often went out of shape as it heated up, so destroying the precisely-calculated facetted shape and consequently increasing radar cross-section. Lockheed engineer Henry Combs solved this by introducing 'shingled construction', much like a tiled roof, which allowed panels to slide over each other as they expanded and contracted while still preserving the aircraft's shape.

Original colour scheme
The main three-view depicts Ship One in its first colour scheme of a disruptive blue, grey and sand pattern. This was primarily intended to hide the facetted nature of the aircraft's shape from prying eyes, especially as the early flight tests were undertaken in daylight. This was worn only by the first aircraft, and only for a few months. The later grey scheme proved far more effective in camouflaging aircraft either in the sky or against a concrete ramp should they inadvertently be caught in the open by a Soviet satellite.

F-117 FSD #4

This aircraft is one of three YF-117As still flying with the 410th Test Squadron at Palmdale. It wears an 'F-117A Flight Test' badge on the intake, and the 'ED' tailcodes and white cross fin-stripe of the 412th Test Wing, headquartered at nearby Edwards AFB.

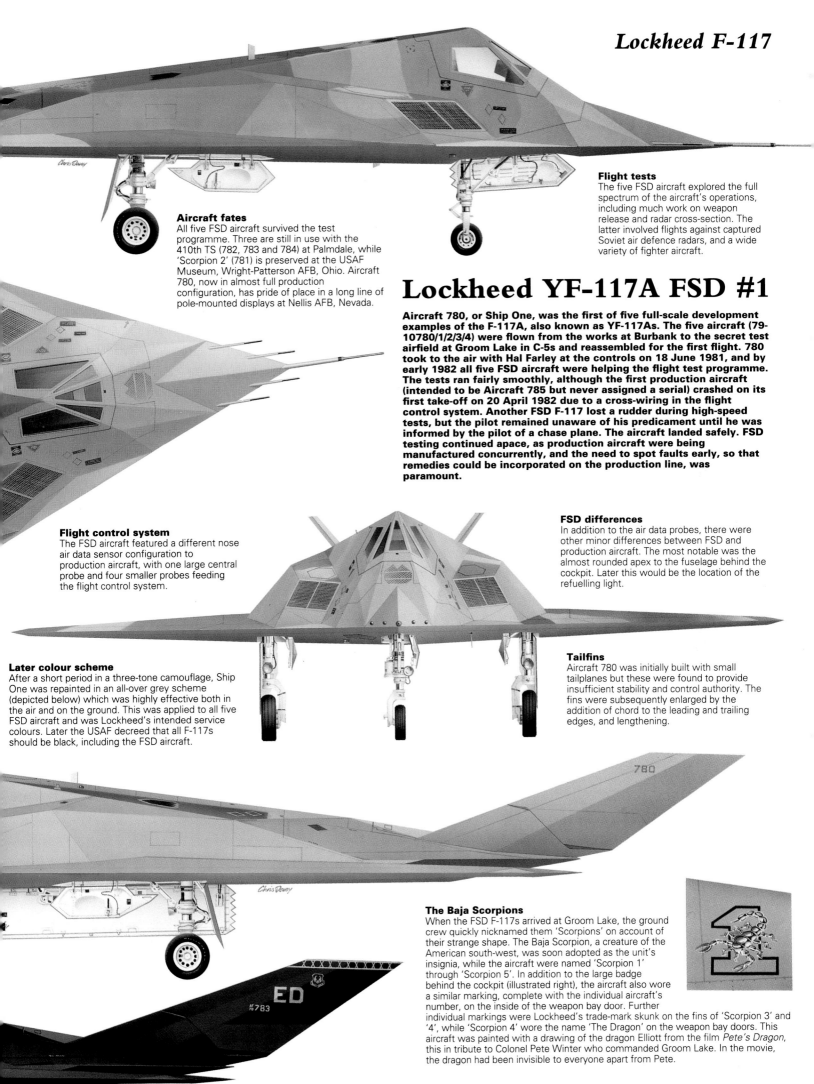

Flight tests
The five FSD aircraft explored the full spectrum of the aircraft's operations, including much work on weapon release and radar cross-section. The latter involved flights against captured Soviet air defence radars, and a wide variety of fighter aircraft.

Aircraft fates
All five FSD aircraft survived the test programme. Three are still in use with the 410th TS (782, 783 and 784) at Palmdale, while 'Scorpion 2' (781) is preserved at the USAF Museum, Wright-Patterson AFB, Ohio. Aircraft 780, now in almost full production configuration, has pride of place in a long line of pole-mounted displays at Nellis AFB, Nevada.

Lockheed YF-117A FSD #1

Aircraft 780, or Ship One, was the first of five full-scale development examples of the F-117A, also known as YF-117As. The five aircraft (79-10780/1/2/3/4) were flown from the works at Burbank to the secret test airfield at Groom Lake in C-5s and reassembled for the first flight. 780 took to the air with Hal Farley at the controls on 18 June 1981, and by early 1982 all five FSD aircraft were helping the flight test programme. The tests ran fairly smoothly, although the first production aircraft (intended to be Aircraft 785 but never assigned a serial) crashed on its first take-off on 20 April 1982 due to a cross-wiring in the flight control system. Another FSD F-117 lost a rudder during high-speed tests, but the pilot remained unaware of his predicament until he was informed by the pilot of a chase plane. The aircraft landed safely. FSD testing continued apace, as production aircraft were being manufactured concurrently, and the need to spot faults early, so that remedies could be incorporated on the production line, was paramount.

Flight control system
The FSD aircraft featured a different nose air data sensor configuration to production aircraft, with one large central probe and four smaller probes feeding the flight control system.

FSD differences
In addition to the air data probes, there were other minor differences between FSD and production aircraft. The most notable was the almost rounded apex to the fuselage behind the cockpit. Later this would be the location of the refuelling light.

Later colour scheme
After a short period in a three-tone camouflage, Ship One was repainted in an all-over grey scheme (depicted below) which was highly effective both in the air and on the ground. This was applied to all five FSD aircraft and was Lockheed's intended service colours. Later the USAF decreed that all F-117s should be black, including the FSD aircraft.

Tailfins
Aircraft 780 was initially built with small tailplanes but these were found to provide insufficient stability and control authority. The fins were subsequently enlarged by the addition of chord to the leading and trailing edges, and lengthening.

The Baja Scorpions
When the FSD F-117s arrived at Groom Lake, the ground crew quickly nicknamed them 'Scorpions' on account of their strange shape. The Baja Scorpion, a creature of the American south-west, was soon adopted as the unit's insignia, while the aircraft were named 'Scorpion 1' through 'Scorpion 5'. In addition to the large badge behind the cockpit (illustrated right), the aircraft also wore a similar marking, complete with the individual aircraft's number, on the inside of the weapon bay door. Further individual markings were Lockheed's trade-mark skunk on the fins of 'Scorpion 3' and '4', while 'Scorpion 4' wore the name 'The Dragon' on the weapon bay doors. This aircraft was painted with a drawing of the dragon Elliott from the film *Pete's Dragon*, this in tribute to Colonel Pete Winter who commanded Groom Lake. In the movie, the dragon had been invisible to everyone apart from Pete.

Aircraft 783 is still used by the 410th Test Squadron for trials work. Here the aircraft demonstrates the braking parachute, and the large suck-in auxiliary air intakes. Testing by the 410th TS of new brakes may lead to the deletion of the brake chute altogether.

of the aircraft were later used in a mock-up.

In May 1982, Colonel James S. Allen assumed command of the 4450th Tactical Group. Soon afterward, it was time to move. Groom Lake was the ideal location for a 'black' programme, but it lacked facilities for an operational unit. Additionally, at Groom Lake people on one secret project often caught glimpses of another, taking in more than they were supposed to see. Among black-world specialists this was tolerable, but an operational unit would bring in too many people with too many questions.

Move to TTR

The 4450th TG relocated to the Tonopah Test Range (TTR) airfield 140 miles (225 km) north-west of Las Vegas. The site was little known. Airmen had trained in P-39 Airacobras at Tonopah early in World War II, and Airacobra pilots shared a taxiway which encircled the field with automobiles; at traffic lights, pursuit ships had the right of way over Chevrolets. Later in the war, Tonopah was a B-24 Liberator training base. The TTR airfield has almost nothing in common with the wartime Tonopah base, which was at a different location, but the military tradition in the sparsely-populated Tonopah area is deeply rooted.

The Tonopah range lies astride the north-western corner of the Nellis complex and, throughout the Cold War, had been used for drop-tests of nuclear weapon 'shapes'. The nearest town, Tonopah itself, was 32 miles (51 km) north-west of the TTR airfield. At the field, a new control tower and other new facilities were soon joined by guard posts, revetments and security fences.

Some of the security features at the base seemed to come out of a science fiction film. As with any good security arrangement, this one existed in layers, with some people having a little knowledge of what was going on, and very few knowing all. Barbed wire appeared atop double-row fences, like those at a penitentiary. Badges were colour-coded, to indicate how deep into the layers an individual was allowed to go. Those in the inner sanctum reached the

most secure areas of the base only by gaining entry with number codes and palm prints. A special unit of security personnel was heavily armed and ready to repel an assault on the base by protesters or terrorists, if the need arose.

The cloak of secrecy hanging over the Senior Trend stealth fighter was so tight that even some visitors to the TTR airfield never learned what was going on there. One pilot, who travelled to Tonopah but was not selected for the programme, was flown there in a 'Huey' helicopter with one side of the aircraft blacked out: no windows of any kind. The flight path of the UH-1N was arranged to keep the window side of the aircraft facing away from the Tonopah airfield at all times.

Colonel Allen subsequently became the first commander to fly the Senior Trend aircraft, taking delivery of the first aircraft (counting Riedenauer's, the second production example) on 23 August 1982. This turnover appears to have taken place at Groom Lake, although by 1983 the move to Tonopah was virtually complete. At the latter airfield, a handful of Senior Trend aircraft were flying regularly. At Tonopah, initial operating capability (IOC) in Senior Trend was attained on 28 October 1983 with the delivery of aircraft 82-0799. It appears the term IOC was defined rather loosely, with less than a squadron on hand at the time.

Stealth commuters

Security dictated that only people working on Senior Trend be housed at Tonopah. There was no provision for families. Pilots were housed with their families at Nellis AFB, 190 miles (305 km) away. They commuted by air to work on Monday and returned home on Friday, an unusual transport job handled by Boeing 727s belonging to civil contractor Key Airlines. The 4450th TG also flew a Mitsubishi MU-2 turboprop aircraft to carry small groups between Tonopah and Nellis. The security force at the base operated UH-1N helicopters.

As the 4450th TG took shape, its support elements were

given short nicknames which concealed their purpose. The group itself was usually called the A-Unit. The 1880th Communications Squadron became C-Unit, Detachment 8 of the 25th Air Weather Squadron was D-Unit, and the 4450th Combat Support Group was E-Unit. The 4450th Test Squadron (which had been established on 11 June 1981) was the I-Unit. The term P-Unit was used to refer to the A-7D flying detachment, which at this point, like group HQ, remained at Nellis. Detachment 1 of the group, at Tonopah, was the Q-Unit.

Nellis 'SLUFs'

The Vought A-7Ds of P-Unit remained at Nellis and the detachment was by 1987 commanded by a pilot who was not checked out in the Senior Trend aircraft. The underlying concept was that even in a secure area, even among comrades with 'compartmented' clearances – even, for example, in the hangars at Tonopah (for the aircraft were never kept outdoors) – the men of Senior Trend never allowed their small talk, or even their shop talk, to become an outlet for terms that described their secret. "Over the Coke machine or in the cockpit, the word stealth was never mentioned," says one. A pilot was not allowed to tell his family about the 'bandit number', a secret identity awarded to each man who had flown the Senior Trend. On papers which required an entry for 'aircraft type', such as the Form 5 which listed flying hours, pilots jotted down 117, a meaningless number. No one has revealed when the US Air Force adopted this figure and made it the designation for the Senior Trend aircraft, which was never called the F-19 (as widely reported).

Senior Trend also was never known as the RF-19 or AR-19, despite reports; in fact, the aircraft had no designation for years. Nor does the F-117 appellation have any connection with the Pentagon's system for numbering fighter types, which back in 1962 jumped from F-111 to F-1.

When the 'Black Jet' was revealed in later years, all kinds

Final assembly of Aircraft 780 at the Burbank factory is shown just after the wings have been mated to the central fuselage structure. Engine systems, nose and flight control surfaces will be added next.

of nonsensical explanations for the F-117 designation were proffered by aviation editors. Although, as already explained, the designation has no connection of any kind with fighter numbers that stopped at F-111, the rumour persists (fed, in one instance, by an air traffic controller, quoted in Aviation Week & Space Technology) that 'Red Hat' Soviet MiGs concealed their real identity by using as radio callsigns terms such as F-112, F-113, and so on. This preposterous bit of fancy has absolutely no basis in truth.

As for the 'gap' in the designation system caused by the missing F-19 designation, the hoopla about its absence

A pair of Palmdale-based FSD F-117As displays the large one-piece bomb bay doors. The leading and trailing edges of the doors (and of virtually every other door or excrescence on the aircraft) has a sawtooth pattern to trap or disperse radar energy. Presenting a sharp-lined opening perpendicular to the source of radar energy would reflect a massive 'flare-spot' back to the radar.

Lockheed F-117

would make sense only if the Department of Defense properly followed its own system for designating aircraft, which it does not. It has been reported that an F-19 was skipped (F-18 to F-20) to give the Northrop F-20 Tigershark a nice, even number. It is indisputable that the absence of a real F-19 enabled the US Air Force to deny that any F-19 existed. None of this has anything to do with the F-117 story, and never did.

Operational planning

Even as they became operational, while the existence of their aircraft remained a dark secret, the 4450th TG commander and others made plans for how their warplane would be used. The stealth fighter had always been seen by American warfighters as a 'silver bullet'. Only a few existed, and they would be used against high-value assets (HVAs), the Pentagon's term for an enemy's leadership structure and for his central nodes of communication and transportation. A warfighting plan known as Downshift 02 provided for deployment of Senior Trend aircraft to Europe for 'decapitation' strikes against leadership targets such as the Soviet premier's dacha.

Washington intelligence agencies heaped upon the 4450th TG reams of briefings, satellite photos, and maps to use the group's handful of very secret warplanes to lop off the heads of any foreign adversary. Downshift 02 and other warfighting plans envisioned the secret warplanes operating without large support packages of electronic jammers,

'Wild Weasel' and other aircraft, and involved conventional munitions.

Senior Trend was considered for use in Operation Urgent Fury, the United States' combined arms invasion of Grenada in October 1983, but the 4450th TG was deemed not ready, and the F-117 not needed. When other trouble spots flared up – Beirut, the Bekaa Valley – Colonel Allen's F-117 pilots expected to be tapped. It was not until 1984 that they were reaching IOC with a second squadron, and there were more years of seclusion ahead.

F-117 description

With its clandestine stealth fighter becoming operational, the US Air Force now had a warplane which was settled into service and beginning to mature. A 'walk-around check' of the wedge-shaped, V-tailed 'Black Jet' – still performed indoors, to foil reconnaissance satellites – revealed an aircraft indisputably based upon the earlier Have Blue platforms, but different from anything else in the military's arsenal. In contrast to the Have Blue configuration, the production aircraft had a more dramatically notched leading edge and rudders which were canted outward. The aircraft was about 60 per larger than the Have Blues.

The F-117 has a modified delta planform with small wings mated to a broad lifting body, with leading edge sweep of 67.5° (or just slightly less than its Have Blue precursors). The aircraft comes close to being a flying wing with this highly-swept shape, very small vertical fins, and no horizontal tail. Stealth, or VLO, dictated every aspect of the F-117 and is the reason why the modified delta, which offers no aerodynamic advantages, was chosen. Its shape makes the aircraft not merely unstable, as been noted repeatedly, but potentially a troublemaker in the airfield pattern. Early in the test programme, the F-117 was tested with outboard leading-edge slats to reduce its landing approach speed, but it was deemed that the reduction in speed was not significant enough to warrant installing the slats on the entire fleet, and the aircraft retains its high approach speed of around 138 mph (222 km/h).

The aircraft employs RAM on external surfaces and chisel-edge, angular features which contribute to reduced RCS. These facets reduce RCS by scattering radar returns back in multiple directions, but their sharp angles prevent the F-117 from being either aerodynamic or aesthetic. Use of radar-absorbent materials makes the aircraft dim to a radar, while the facets cause it to 'glitter' irregularly as its aspect angle varies.

As one of many features which contribute to stealth, the F-117 has three or four retractable antennas, radio aerials that pop in and out of the airstream when needed. The

largest, a retractable blade antenna, is on the back of the aircraft on the starboard side of the refuelling receptacle. The stealth qualities of the aircraft are enhanced by engine exhaust nozzles located atop the fuselage along the wing-root just ahead of the tail surfaces. The exhaust bleeds over the aft fuselage to screen the heat emissions from detection below.

It is worth noting that stealth does not refer only to eluding radar detection. To quote Lockheed, "The F-117A employs a variety of design features to significantly reduce aircraft signature. There are seven different types of observable signatures of concern: radar, infra-red, visual, contrails, engine smoke, acoustics and electromagnetic emissions. The three signature characteristics providing the greatest potential for exploitation by threat systems are radar, infra-red, and electromagnetic emissions. The F-117 is designed to minimise these signatures."

In the cockpit

Pilot of the F-117 sits on a McDonnell Douglas ACES 2 ejection seat in a small cockpit which features a windshield arrangement with a separate panel in front and two different-sized windows on each side. The pilot has a conventional HUD (head-up display) for basic flight information and infra-red imagery, with an up-front control panel beneath it for radio and display mode selections. On the main panel, two MFDs (multi-function displays) flank a large monochrome CRT and IRADS (infra-red acquisition and detection system) video screen. The MFDs can present the pilot with a variety of imagery, mission data and diagnostic information. Between the HUD and the display screens is a console embracing small warning lights which come on to indicate which, if any, part of the aircraft has 'gone dirty' and lost its radar-evading LO properties. Four protruding spikes on the aircraft's nose are air data probes for air speed and altitude sensing. The F-117 has quadruply-redundant fly-by-wire flight controls.

To reduce development risks and maintain security, the F-117 was created, in part, as a hybrid of components from other aircraft types. The cockpit included dials, lights and switches which date to the analog features of the century series of fighters. Many of the cockpit systems are derived from the FA-18 Hornet, including stick grip, throttles, engine instruments, fuel gauge and HUD. The F-117 has at least one minor component from each of a dozen aircraft

types including the P-2 Neptune, F-104 Starfighter, T-33 Shooting Star, C-130 Hercules and SR-71 Blackbird. The sensor display is provided by Texas Instruments and borrows heavily from the OV-10D Bronco and P-3C Orion programmes.

Avionics

The F-117's original avionics architecture was a real-time processing system employing three Delco M326F computers from the F-16 Fighting Falcon interconnected with a dual redundant MIL-STD-1553 databus. These computers interfaced with the displays, controls, Honeywell SPN-GEANS INS (inertial navigation system, originally developed for the B-52 Stratofortress's Offensive Avionics System upgrade programme), automatic pilot, stores management system, and sensor systems. The aircraft computer system was administered by a weapons delivery computer which serviced and updated cockpit displays, performed weapons delivery ballistics projections, interfaced to the various sensor systems, and controlled the data distribution. The navigation control computer performed all navigation and control functions including the inertial measurement unit, the control display unit, navigation steering, flight director steering, position update, attitude heading reference system integration, and the TACAN (tactical aid to navigation) and ILS (instrument landing system) interface. The third computer provided control and data processing for an additional sensor system and was used as a back-up computer if one of the other two should fail. A data transfer module interface unit was provided to load pre-flight mission data via a data transfer module from the missing data planning system. At the root of all this was the concept that the avionics system would drive the cueing of the sensor to the target via a precision navigation system, thus providing updated target information for accurate weapons release. Development of the F-117's avionics was very much a second cousin to the prime goal of achieving stealth capability, and at every turn in the design of the aircraft VLO came first. The avionics system was always adequate at best, went through an early upgrade effort beginning in the mid-1980s, and is receiving attention today as the subject of a more ambitious upgrade programme.

As the F-117 was conceived, its ability to carry out a precision bombing relied upon accurate target information and the effective working of the onboard inertial system.

The 4450th Tactical Group moved to Tonopah Test Range airfield in 1982, and the F-117 force built up slowly from just two or three aircraft. This is one of the early aircraft, seen during the 'Tonopah Years' when the aircraft flew without tailcodes and almost exclusively at night.

Inside the F-117

Left and right: Tw[o] shots of the standard F-117 cockpit prior to th[e] final OCIP improvements wh[ich] add a moving map display and replac[e] the Texas Instruments displ[ay] with Honeywell colour units. Underneath the HUD is a large screen for displa[ying] infra-red imagery, beneath which is [a] main comms pane[l]. Either side of the screen is an MFD [for] aircraft systems. Beneath the right MFD is a radar altimeter and attitude instruments, and [to] the right of this ar[e] the engine instruments. Belo[w] the left MFD is th[e] weapons control panel, with standa[rd] flight instruments [to] the left. The left-s[ide] console has aircra[ft] system controls, while the right-si[de] console has the nav/comms contro[l] panel. The two si[de] handles on the se[at] initiate the ejectio[n] sequence.

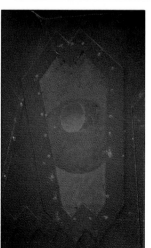

Details of the FLIR (above) and DLIR (left) turrets show the infra-red sensors and boresighted lasers. The turrets are often swivelled round when not in use so that the sensor windows are protected. The fine mesh acts like a flat surface when illuminated by radar.

Lockheed F-117

1 Air data sensors
2 Nose avionics equipment compartment
3 Air data computer
4 Starboard side downward-looking infra-red (DLIR)
5 Screened sensor aperture
6 Forward-looking infra-red (FLIR), to be replaced by Texas Instruments IRADS sensors in third phase update
7 Cockpit front pressure bulkhead
8 Nosewheel bay
9 Forward-retracting nosewheel
10 Canopy emergency release
11 Position light
12 Cockpit pressure enclosure
13 McDonnell-Douglas ACES II 'zero-zero' ejection seat
14 Instrument panel shroud, central infra-red video monitor and dual head-down multi-function CRT displays
15 Head-up display
16 Windscreen panels, gold film coated
17 Upward-hinging one-piece cockpit canopy

18 Apex-mounted refuelling floodlight
19 Starboard air intake
20 Flush HF aerials
21 Rotating flight-refuelling receptacle
22 Avionics equipment bay
23 Retractable ILS antenna
24 Retractable VHF COMM antenna
25 Port engine air intake
26 Intake screening
27 Intake lip spring-loaded secondary (cooling) air intake
28 Weapons bay doors, open
29 Retractable spoilers

30 Port weapons bay
31 Intake suction relief door aperture
32 Airframe-mounted accessory equipment gearbox
33 Engine bay bulkhead
34 Compressor intake
35 Engine fuel system equipment

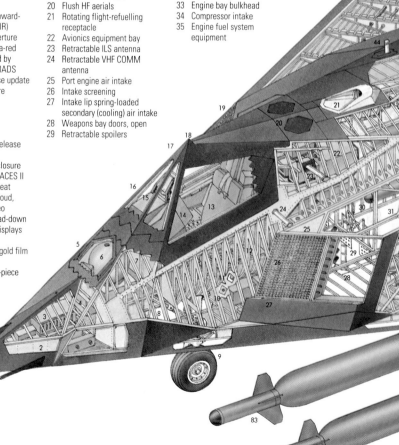

82

The engine intakes are covered with a grille to shield the compressor face from radar. The mesh has to be fine enough to reflect radar, yet wide enough to still allow the free passage of air for the engines.

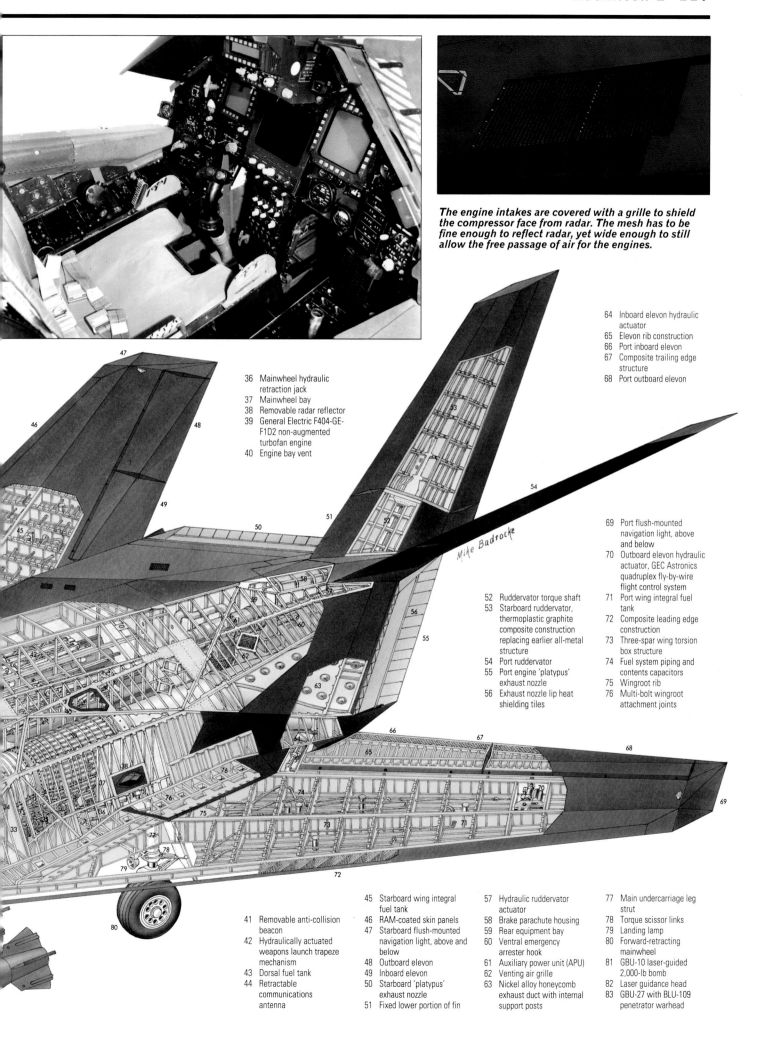

64 Inboard elevon hydraulic actuator
65 Elevon rib construction
66 Port inboard elevon
67 Composite trailing edge structure
68 Port outboard elevon

36 Mainwheel hydraulic retraction jack
37 Mainwheel bay
38 Removable radar reflector
39 General Electric F404-GE-F1D2 non-augmented turbofan engine
40 Engine bay vent

69 Port flush-mounted navigation light, above and below
70 Outboard elevon hydraulic actuator, GEC Astronics quadruplex fly-by-wire flight control system
71 Port wing integral fuel tank
72 Composite leading edge construction
73 Three-spar wing torsion box structure
74 Fuel system piping and contents capacitors
75 Wingroot rib
76 Multi-bolt wingroot attachment joints

52 Ruddervator torque shaft
53 Starboard ruddervator, thermoplastic graphite composite construction replacing earlier all-metal structure
54 Port ruddervator
55 Port engine 'platypus' exhaust nozzle
56 Exhaust nozzle lip heat shielding tiles

Mike Badrocke

41 Removable anti-collision beacon
42 Hydraulically actuated weapons launch trapeze mechanism
43 Dorsal fuel tank
44 Retractable communications antenna

45 Starboard wing integral fuel tank
46 RAM-coated skin panels
47 Starboard flush-mounted navigation light, above and below
48 Outboard elevon
49 Inboard elevon
50 Starboard 'platypus' exhaust nozzle
51 Fixed lower portion of fin

57 Hydraulic ruddervator actuator
58 Brake parachute housing
59 Rear equipment bay
60 Ventral emergency arrester hook
61 Auxiliary power unit (APU)
62 Venting air grille
63 Nickel alloy honeycomb exhaust duct with internal support posts

77 Main undercarriage leg strut
78 Torque scissor links
79 Landing lamp
80 Forward-retracting mainwheel
81 GBU-10 laser-guided 2,000-lb bomb
82 Laser guidance head
83 GBU-27 with BLU-109 penetrator warhead

Lockheed F-117

Tonopah Test Range had little more than an airstrip in the desert for supporting the missile trials before the 4450th arrived. 1982-83 saw a massive building programme to support the F-117s, including a sizeable runway and taxiway, complete wing headquarters and operations facilities, a large ramp space with individual barns for each of the F-117s and a housing/base complex some 7 miles (11 km) from the airfield site.

Target information was not always readily available, even to a great nation with enormous technical resources, and given the value of the F-117 no mission was likely to be launched without it. Given the information and an inertial system performing well enough to find the target at night looking only through a small IR window, the F-117's computer system cued the infra-red (IR) system to the target. Everything had to come together: the target had to be within the field of view of the IR system, the pilot had to

see it on his sensor display, and the pilot had to refine the aiming, designate the target, and act to release a weapon, which would occur through the stores management system.

The Texas Instruments IRADS was an off-the-shelf, single turret system adapted to a twin turret configuration due to the VLO external contour requirements. Since there was a need to see from just above the horizon to well behind the aircraft, a FLIR (forward-looking infra-red) turret and DLIR (downward-looking infra-red) were deemed neces-

An F-117 refuels from a 9th Strategic Reconnaissance Wing KC-135Q at night. During the 'black' years of F-117 operations, the 9th SRW provided virtually all of the tanker support, as the unit was very experienced in highly classified missions from its normal day-to-day work with the Lockheed SR-71. When the SR-71 passed from service, the 9th continued in its secret work supporting the F-117s.

Hidden away in the remote Cactus Flats, Tonopah Test Range was an excellent location for a classified programme. Security was without precedent for an operational unit of this size, with a layered approach keeping out all but fully-authorised personnel. Cherokee jeeps and armed assault rifles were the order of the day, and the highly-trained guards had authorisation to use them. The security measures paid dividends – the F-117 remained a total secret for five years before the Pentagon finally released details.

sary. Because of the mounting arrangement in the aircraft, the DLIR is inverted relative to the FLIR and thus required the video to be inverted electronically when displayed to the pilot. Although this meant alignment and calibration problems, any turret may be mounted in either position. Both FLIR and DLIR have proven to need screens to maintain their VLO signature and to prevent damage from acoustical effects.

Beginning in 1984, a WSCS (weapon system computer sub-system) upgrade was begun to replace the merely satisfactory (at best) M326D computers. The AP-102 MIL-STD-1750A computer package developed by IBM was chosen. This was developed from the computer installed by Rockwell in the space shuttle orbiter vehicle. Three AP-102 computers were used, each controlling a dual redundant MIL-STD-1553 bus, one set of each being a spare. The WSCS upgrade effort also gave the F-117 the capability to drop two bombs at once, where in the past the aircraft had been restricted to releasing from one of its two bays at a time. This required changes to cockpit controls, bomb bay doors and hydraulics.

Two aircraft were modified for testing during the WSCS upgrade programme. The first, 'Scorpion 3' or FSD-3 (79-10782), was modified for the computer change only and did not receive the full weapon bay upgrade. As such, it was precluded from performing dual bay bomb drops. A second aircraft, 'Scorpion 5' or FSD-5 (79-10784), later joined the test force with all capabilities. This aircraft required a significant lay-up to install the bomb bay modifications and to relocate its instrumentation package (see section on bombs, below) from the bay to a fuel tank area. Seventy-five sorties were flown in connection with the WSCS programme.

F-117 bomb

The F-117's primary weapon is the laser-guided bomb (LGB), part of the 'smart' family of ordnance known to the USAF as precision-guided munitions (PGMs).

The F-117 has a slender, centre-hinged bomb bay with two weapon-bearing hoists, or trapezes, which lift weapons up into the bay. Because the F-117 is directionally unstable over large parts of its operational envelope, it is of interest that opening the weapon bay makes the aircraft more unstable than it is already. In lieu of conventional bomb

racks such as those on the B-52, which would be inconsistent with design constraints (which required the bay to be sandwiched between the engines), the trapezes offer the most efficient way for armourers to load up the 'Black Jet'. The hoists can be lowered below the fuselage silhouette to release a bomb. The bay is too confined and too short for the GBU-24 series of bombs used by other fighter-bombers.

Trapeze drops

The requirement for weapons to be dropped with the trapeze down resulted from early concerns about possible damage to the aircraft and bay doors from fin-equipped bombs, but lowering the trapeze spoiled the F-117's VLO characteristics. Although initial certification of the F-117 with various types of ordnance was accomplished with trapeze-down launches, later efforts by Lockheed's aerodynamics department found that adequate clearance could be maintained with the trapeze up.

The F-117 is fully capable of level, loft, dive, dive toss, and LADD (low-altitude drogue delivery) weapon release manoeuvres, but usually uses straight and level overfly delivery. When weapons delivery work was carried out (by the 4450th TG during the 'black' days), early tests were restricted by the need for one of the two bomb bays to carry instrumentation. Progress was further impeded by

Civilian contractor Key Air was employed to ferry personnel from their quarters at Nellis AFB to the remote Tonopah base, using a fleet of Boeing 727s crewed by security-cleared pilots. Key Air also supported other facilities, such as Groom Lake, Palmdale and Burbank. Today this activity continues, using the Boeing 737s and ex-USAF CT-43s of EG&G Special Projects, a civilian company which undertakes 'Janet' flights on behalf of the government from Las Vegas-McCarran International into Groom Lake and other facilities hidden in the Nellis ranges.

each aircraft exhibiting its own personality due to equipment installation tolerances. BDU-33 training shapes were used in lieu of actual bombs for weapon baseline testing, and the difference between simulated and real bombs became one of several factors which caused delays. During the developmental period, the F-117 dropped 500-lb (227-kg) Mk 82 bombs. These drops caused Lockheed's Richard Silz to recommend, "Always do accuracy testing with the weapons fully combat-configured with all fuses, wires and lanyards." The BDU-50, a training version of the Mk 82,

could not be used because the weapon cannot be configured exactly like a real Mk 82.

On most missions, the F-117 carries one or two thin-skinned GBU-10 series bombs, which are in general use among USAF strike aircraft, or more thickly encased GBU-27 series bombs, which are unique to the 'Black Jet' and were developed from the wrongly-sized GBU-24. Both GBU-10 and GBU-27 employ distinctive canards and tail fins.

These bombs rated at 2,000 lb (907 kg) employ either the Mk 84 explosive warhead employed throughout the USAF's inventory, or the BLU-109B (Lockheed designation I-2000) deep-penetrating warhead designed specifically for the F-117.

The GBU-10, as employed on the F-117, combines either Mk 84 or BLU-109B warhead with a Vietnam-era Paveway II guidance kit. (The generic term Paveway comes from the acronym PAVE (precision avionics vectoring equipment), while the GBU designation means guided bomb unit.) The version employing a BLU-109B warhead is designated GBU-10I. The relatively thin casing of the GBU-10 is intended for enhanced blast effect.

Paveway III

The GBU-27, unique to the F-117 (but based on the GBU-24 in general use, but with the canards on the front clipped and the rear fins based on the Paveway II, rather than Paveway III, configuration) came with the 1984 WSCS upgrade effort and employs the more recent-technology Paveway III guidance kit. The version using a Mk 84 warhead is designated GBU-27/B; the version equipped with BLU-109B warhead is designated GBU-27A/B. The bomb is designed to be dropped from medium altitude, although its shorter wings (as compared with the GBU-24 series) degrade some of its stand-off capability.

When the GBU-27 series was being developed, there was concern whether the bombs would separate cleanly from inside the F-117's bomb bay. The bomb was nearly as long as the bay itself. As already noted, one problem was that a trapeze lowered to guarantee hazard-free release would give the 'Black Jet' a non-stealthy face to enemy radars. The changes which came with the WSCS upgrade, including changes to the twin bays, trapezes and doors, resolved this and made it possible to drop the GBU-27 with the trapeze up. The F-117 bay also has four perforated baffle plates which deploy ahead of, and flank, the bomb being released, apparently both to interrupt air flow and to minimise the unstealthy effect.

The GBU-27 offers two guidance modes, each optimised to achieve the best penetration angle for horizontally or vertically orientated targets. For a horizontal target such as a bunker, the GBU-27 flies a commanded pitch down after release to strike the target in an attitude as nearly vertical as possible. The trajectory for a vertical target such as a high-rise building is essentially the ballistic path. In early development trials, on the second occasion when a Senior Trend aircraft dropped a GBU-27, the bomb hit a target barrel and split it in half, testimony to bombing accuracy and a memento which has been kept by the 'Skunk Works'.

One report has said that F-117s carried 500-lb GBU-12 bombs (Mk 82 bombs with Paveway II kits) in attacks on the fire trench system along the Kuwaiti border during Operation Desert Storm.

Boosted bomb

In 1992, Lockheed proposed a Boosted Penetrator conventional bomb to be carried by the F-117. Like the current GBU family, the bomb would glide to its target after release (although from greater range, introducing a stand-off capability). Just before impact it would be boosted by a rocket motor to increase its velocity and kill power. Lockheed indicated that it had completed preliminary work on the booster, the warhead, the fuse and the tail airfoil group. The weapon was said to have been inspired by the GBU-

Below left: Although initial training on the F-117 could be undertaken in daylight, the aircraft was always envisaged as a nocturnal predator, and night flying continued. Throughout the 1980s there were several proposals to use the F-117 in surgical strikes, targets in Lebanon, Grenada, Libya and Nicaragua being discussed but all being rejected as a waste of the years of security.

Below: With the need for a cover story removed, the A-7 companion trainers were replaced by Northrop AT-38Bs in September 1989. These offered better economy and reliability. The base ops buildings, flightline and aircraft barns formed the inner sanctum of the Tonopah base, and the entire area was encircled by a double cordon of fencing protected by constantly-manned security posts and sturdy gates at access points. Aircraft had to taxi through these gates to gain access to the runway.

Lockheed F-117A

This five-view illustration depicts an aircraft marked for the commander of the 49th Fighter Wing, complete with non-standard fin legend and coloured wing badge on the intakes. It is shown carrying a standard GBU-10 bomb in the port weapons bay and a GBU-24A in the starboard.

Stealth features

Apart from the flat facets making up its exterior, the F-117 exhibits many other features for a low radar cross-section, notably in the front hemisphere. The straight line running from nose to wingtip (swept at 67.5°) and similar sharp sweep-back on the fins is a major dissipator of radar energy away from its source. Every door or surface excrescence has diagonal patterns on the fore and aft edges, while the whole surface is sprayed with radar-absorbent material. The glazed panels are coated with gold to conduct radar energy into the airframe. Necessary holes in the overall shape for the engine intakes and two IRADS sensors are covered with a grille. This has a fine mesh much smaller than the wavelengths of detection radars, and consequently would appear as another facetted surface.

Fin alignment

The fins were carefully positioned to keep radar reflections to a minimum, and also to help shield the engine exhausts from infra-red sensors, especially those carried by a chasing fighter.

RAM

Radar-absorbent material was originally applied to the aircraft surface in sheets, but is now available as a spray. Operational alert aircraft are regularly kept in full stealth status with regular visits to the RAM spray facility to maintain the coating in top condition.

Lockheed F-117A

Powerplant: two General Electric F404-GE-F1D2 non-afterburning turbofans, each rated in the class of 10,800 lb (48 kN) thrust
Wing span: 43 ft 4 in (13.20 m)
Length: 65 ft 11 in (20.08 m)
Height: 12 ft 5 in (3.78 m)
Wing area: 1,140 sq ft (105.9 m²)
Empty weight: approx 30,000 lb (13608 kg)
Maximum take-off weight: 52,500 lb (23814 kg)
Internal weapon load: 5,000 lb (2268 kg)
Maximum speed: 561 kt (646 mph; 1040 km/h)
Normal operating Mach number: 0.9
Take-off speed at normal combat weight: 165 kt (190 mph; 306 km/h)
Landing speed: 150 kt (172 mph; 227 km/h)
Unrefuelled combat radius with 5,000-lb (2268-kg) load: 600 nm (690 miles; 1112 km)
g limits: +6

Cockpit

The original cockpit features Texas Instruments monochrome displays surrounded by standard off-the-shelf flight instruments from other aircraft, notably the F/A-18. In the centre of the dashboard is a large TV screen which displays imagery from the IRADS, with two smaller multi-function displays on either side for aircraft information. Above the dashboard is a Kaiser head-up display based on the AVQ-18. The new OCIP cockpit replaces the TI displays with Honeywell full-colour screens, and adds a large colour moving map for improving situational awareness. The pilot sits on a McDonnell Douglas ACES II ejection seat under a heavy-framed canopy with five flat glazed panes made by Sierracin/Sylmar Corporation.

Visibility

The pilot sits high in the cockpit, and has a good view forwards, sideways and downwards across the sharply sloping nose. However, the view to the rear is virtually non-existent due to the broad fuselage and engine trunks.

IRADS

The infra-red acquisition and designation system consists of the forward-looking infra-red (FLIR) in front of the cockpit, and the downward-looking infra-red (DLIR) mounted to the starboard side of the nosewheel bay. Both are mounted in swivelling turrets, which can rotate to the rear when not in use to protect the delicate optics. The IR sensors employ a wide-angle function for initial search and target acquisition, followed by closer target designation using a zoom function. Both turrets also incorporate a laser designator.

Undercarriage

The F-117 has a Menasco tricycle undercarriage, all units retracting forward into bays covered with sawtooth doors. Loral steel brakes were originally fitted but have been replaced by carbon-carbon brakes, which improve cross-wind capability and may allow the deletion of the Pioneer Aerospace brake chute which deploys from between the fins. An emergency airfield arrestor hook is located under the rear fuselage, covered by an explosively-jettisoned cover.

Flight control system

Designing an aircraft with true stealth properties and relaxed stability was deemed virtually impossible, so the F-117 uses a fly-by-wire system to maintain stability. This is almost certainly based on the GEC Astronics quadruplex unit employed very successfully in the F-16. Providing precise air data for the system posed Lockheed designers with a problem in maintaining stealth properties. The result is a group of four air data probes projecting from the nose, each being facetted to defeat radars and with multiple ports for taking differential pressure readings. They are heated to prevent ice fouling the ports. Comparison of the readings from each probe gives adequate data for the flight control system.

Aerodynamically the F-117 relies on many vortices created by the sharp surfaces to form a lifting airflow pattern. The wing forms a simple airfoil by having three flat sections above and two below. The underwing flat surfaces blend into the underfuselage surfaces to create a whole lifting surface below the aircraft. Contrary to some press opinion, which gave rise to the 'Wobblin' Goblin' nickname, the F-117 has more than adequate handling characteristics and considerable agility for an aircraft of its size and power, although landing speeds are high.

The F-117 has just six moveable control surfaces, consisting of four trailing-edge elevons which provide both pitch and roll control, and two ruddervators which work in opposition for yaw control and in unison for pitch control. Like the rest of the aircraft, the control surfaces are made up of flat facets, the ruddervators exhibiting a flattened diamond cross-section. An unusual feature of the control surfaces, also seen on the F/A-22, are small flat-sided cut-outs along the gaps between the surfaces and the main structure. The gaps are obviously a great source of radar reflection, especially when the control surfaces are deflected. The notches reduce this to a great extent.

OCIP I and II

Since 1984 the F-117 has been the subject of an Offensive Capability Improvement Program (OCIP) which further eases the pilot's workload while improving the aircraft's ability to undertake pinpoint strikes. The first phase of the OCIP involved the replacement of the original three Delco M362F mission computers with the IBM/Loral AP-102, a repackaged version of the Shuttle computer offering 1 million instructions per second capability. The second phase, also known as Offensive Combat Improvement Program, completely revised the cockpit layout, adding Honeywell multi-function displays and a large Harris Corporation moving-map display. A 'four-dimensional' flight management system controls an autothrottle, in addition to the autopilot, and is designed to put the F-117 at a desired location with +/- 1 second time tolerance. Another feature of the second phase is the Pilot-Activated Automatic Recovery System (PAARS), which rights the aircraft to straight and level flight from any attitude with a flick of a switch, a useful aid for an aircraft which flies its operational missions mostly in darkness. The first OCIP II aircraft flew on 1 December 1988, with service redeliveries commencing in November 1990.

Weapons bay

The bomb bays are located side-by-side, with one-piece doors opening inwards from a hinge on the centreline. Each bay is 15 ft 5in (4.7 m) long and contains a trapeze for stores carriage. Bay doors and weapon arming is accomplished on a control panel immediately below the left-hand multi-function display.

Lockheed F-117

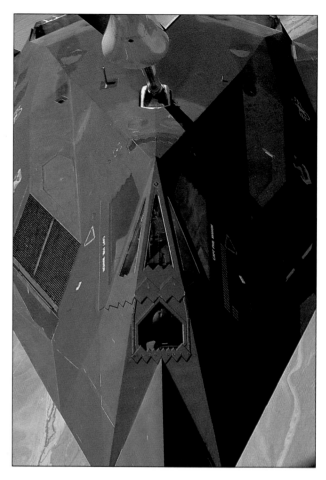

Above and right: Two views of F-117s refuelling highlights the facetted shape of the aircraft and the rotating refuelling receptacle. Radio-silent refuellings are regularly practised, and at night the only illumination comes from the small light above the cockpit and a floodlight on the tanker's tail. Noticeable on the aircraft are small blade antennas which serve the communications suite. On operational missions these are retracted to maintain full stealthiness.

28, a 4,700-lb (2133-kg) gravity bomb with BLU-113 warhead that was fabricated quickly during Desert Storm and rushed into use aboard the F-111F in the final days of the war in an apparent attempt to reach Iraqi command bunkers and, perhaps, Saddam Hussein. Nothing further has been disclosed about a Boosted Penetrator bomb for the F-117, but development may be proceeding quietly.

Although it is called a fighter, the F-117 has no capability for air-to-air combat. The aircraft has no gun and is not known to have ever carried air-to-air missiles. In fact, the 'Cockroach' carries no external weapons at all, and has very little flexibility with its internal bomb load – all of which eased, to some extent, the demands on aerodynamicists who initially conceived the F-117. Although warfighters wanted the aircraft to 'decapitate' an enemy's C3I assets (command, control, communications and intelligence), no-one ever expected the F-117 to carry nuclear weapons, making it perhaps the only tactical warplane designed without this capability. Without nuclear capability, the F-117 was never part of the SIOP (single integrated operations plan) for the initial phase of a nuclear war with the Soviet Union and its Warsaw Pact allies.

The F-117 is theoretically capable of employing air-to-air missiles such as the AIM-9 Sidewinder or air-to-ground types such as the AGM-65 Maverick, but only with its weapon-bearing hoists (trapezes) extended, again defeating the purpose of stealth. It is not clear whether the F-117 has ever been 'wired' for these weapons.

The USAF intended the F-117 to be readily deployed to trouble spots. When details about the aircraft were still 'in the black', rumours persisted that C-5A/B Galaxy airlifters were hauling the stealth fighters to various locations around the world, where they were flying clandestine night missions. Most or all of this hearsay proved to be inaccurate. The F-117 can be carried on board a Galaxy with its wings removed, but the process is not effective as a rapid response to a crisis because of the time consumed by disassembling, spraying joints, packaging and reassembling. Maintenance of the F-117 can be performed out of vans which can be moved overseas aboard C-130, C-141B or C-5A/B transports. In real life, self-deployment works faster and easier, and if indoor facilities are available at the other end, so much the better.

Propulsion

The F-117 is powered by two 10,800-lb (48.05-kN) thrust General Electric F404-GE-F1D2 engines without afterburners. After flight icing trials, the engine installation team had to resort to a wiper system to keep the F404 inlet grids free from ice; designers had rejected a plea from the airframe development team which had said it would "welcome any change of shape as it could only make [the aircraft] better." Regarded as responsive, reliable and with more than adequate thrust for the Nighthawk's high-subsonic speed regime (Mach 0.8), these engines give the aircraft a low noise signature and produce no visible exhaust. In later years, plans to retrofit the General Electric F412 engine developed for the defunct A-12 Avenger 2, or to install the newer F414 which delivers 37 per cent more thrust, were bogged down by financial constraints. Plans for

the latter engine are still being put forth by the manufacturer, in a non-afterburning form.

Only recently were full details of the F-117's stealthy exhaust tailpipe revealed. ASTECH/MCI Manufacturing of Santa Ana, California, achieved a method of reducing infrared signature without reducing thrust, by transitioning the F404 exhaust from a circular pattern to a flattened-out, louvre-type duct. A honeycomb sandwich of nickel alloy reshapes the flow of exhaust gases and absorbs much of the heat and pressure of the design.

The F-117 has "a very special nozzle" in the back, as described by Lockheed's Jack Gordon. "It uses a Coanda effect to turn the flow back into the axial direction, but

from the waterline of the trailing edge of the aeroplane and below, you cannot look up into the nozzle and into the engines, so it helps very much in controlling the signature."

Pilots describe the F-117 as pleasurable and smooth to fly, if not entirely forgiving. Its characteristics are not unlike those of other deltas, like the F-106. Landing and take-off speeds are quite high (a parachute is always used on landing) and the aircraft flies nose-high at low speeds and decelerates rapidly in a sharp turn. The thrust-to-weight ratio at maximum take-off weight is 0.4:1, which is not generous, especially in hot climates.

When the F-117 was still in the 'black', refuelling operations were carried out primarily by KC-135 crews from

A 37th TFW F-117 manoeuvres over the Nevada desert. The aircraft picked up its nickname in the early days so that crews could easily distinguish between the 'camo jets' (A-7s) and 'black jets' (F-117s) without having to use the classified designation. Later the AT-38s became the 'gray jets'.

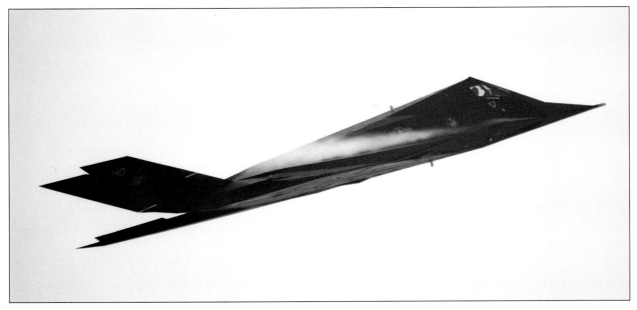

Vortices stream from the leading edge as a 49th FW F-117 pulls up sharply (note the deflection of the elevons). Despite reports to the contrary, the F-117 handles well at all speeds, although exhibiting the normal disadvantages associated with a delta. These include high landing speed and swiftly-bleeding energy in a tight turn. The low thrust/weight ratio precludes traditional fighter-style flying, but the aircraft is surprisingly agile considering its size.

At Tonopah each aircraft was housed in a separate barn, where all pre-flight checks were undertaken to hide the aircraft from passing satellites. Until the F-117 went public, the barn could not be opened until one hour after sunset, and had to be shut one hour before sunrise. On the taxiway (with the barns and double security fence in the background) is Aircraft 803, alias 'Unexpected Guest', wearing its mission marks from Desert Storm.

With end-of-runway checks complete, a pair of 37th TFW F-117s moves to the Tonopah runway. Each aircraft carries a small radar reflector in a prominent fairing just aft of the 'star-and-bar'. This is highly necessary in peacetime to allow the aircraft to show up on air traffic control radar screens.

Beale AFB, California, known as the 'Beale Bandits'. The USAF's hard-working boom operators reportedly were nervous about 'gassing up' the 'Black Jet', fearful that the flying boom would damage RAM material on the aircraft exterior. The F-117 is apparently no more or less stable when being refuelled than any other warplane, and the early skittishness seems to have gone away.

4450th TG progress

On 15 April 1984, Colonel Howell M. Estes III became the third commander of the 4450th Tactical Group. Estes led the group through its first ORI (operational readiness inspection), which was deemed a success. During his tenure, weapons delivery tactics for the Senior Trend aircraft were standardised.

In 1984, the Lockheed F-117 was still 'in the closet' and reporters and aircraft spotters were still wondering what kind of mysterious apparition was cavorting about in Nevada skies. A tragic fluke in May 1984 stirred conjecture about the Senior Trend stealth programme for the wrong reason. Lieutenant General Robert M. ('Bobbie') Bond, vice commander of Air Force Systems Command and a decorated Vietnam-era A-7D pilot, was killed attempting to eject from an aircraft while flying in the Nellis area. A joyride, some said. Outside the inner sanctum, it was mistakenly thought that Bond was flying the mysterious stealth fighter. Only much later has it become clear that the general was piloting a Soviet-built MiG-23, a Russian warplane employed in unrelated 'black' programmes at Groom Lake.

The secrecy of the F-117 programme actually helped the manufacturer to deliver on time, at cost. Later, however, Congress was to ask whether the USAF concealed teething troubles. USAF acquisition chief John Welch was to acknowledge some technical problems which delayed the

programme by nearly two years. Welch identified problems with correlating the upper and lower FLIR systems, as well as fuel leaks and exhaust gas leaks.

Potential debut over Libya

Secretly but vigorously, the 4450th Tactical Group continued to thrive in the America of the mid-1980s, when a free-spending Reagan presidency created many secrets, and many weapons, and plunged the nation into crippling debt to pay for them. At the White House, advisor Marine Lieutenant Colonel Oliver North cooked up schemes for American intervention in Lebanon and Nicaragua. Twice, North recommended using the F-117 against high-value assets. By 1986, Reagan, North and others were focusing on Libya's Colonel Muamar Khadaffi, hardly the world's worst terrorist but surely its most convenient. Almost everything, from the bombing of a discotheque to the trade deficit, could be blamed on Khadaffi, who had no defenders in the American press.

In early 1986, commanded now by Colonel Michael W. Harris (who took the helm on 6 December 1985), the 4450th TG was alerted for a secret mission to 'decapitate' Khadaffi. A grave question arose. Khadaffi was small stuff – had the Americans really been hell-bent on punishing terrorists, they would have gone after Syria's Haffez Assad – but the F-117 was big time, a crucial 'hold card' in a war with the Soviet Union. Was it worth unwrapping the secret of stealth, merely to bomb, or even to kill, Khadaffi? One officer warned, "We've worked too hard on stealth and laser-guided bombs to use them to blow up a pile of camel shit." What's more, one necessity for a successful F-117 operation – good target information – may have been lacking. The attack on Libya's capital, Tripoli, by the F-117 was called off. Instead, US forces carried out Operations Prairie Fire and Eldorado Canyon, using carrier-based warplanes and Britain-based F-111 'Aardvarks'.

Handling a loss

The F-117 fighter remained unknown to the outside world. The US Air Force was not fully comfortable keeping it that way, but decision-makers in the Reagan and Bush administrations wanted the lid to remain clamped. Plans were readied to deal with the unexpected, one of the worst scenarios being: what would happen to the secret if one of the stealth fighters crashed?

The first loss of an operational aircraft occurred at 2:00 a.m. on 11 July 1986 on a hillside along the Kern River near Bakersfield, California, killing pilot Major Ross E. Mulhare. Mulhare was flying aircraft 81-10792, callsign ARIEL 31. There is evidence that fatigue – which was chronic among the stealth pilots, who flew only at night – caused him to become disorientated and plunge into the slope. A fire started by the crash burned about 150 acres of dry grass and brush and was not extinguished for 16 hours. The immediate crash site was cordoned off by battle-garbed Security Police toting M16 rifles, and fire-fighters were not allowed within that area. London's Sunday Times reported that US officials had thrown a "ring of steel" around the "crashed bomber". Air traffic controllers were told that Mulhare's aircraft was an A-7D. Only reluctantly was the pilot's affiliation with the 4450th Test Group made public.

Model furore

That same month, legislators in Washington were up in arms when Testor Corp. of Rockford, Illinois released a $9.95 plastic kit model of the F-19 'Stealth Fighter'. Congressman Ron Wyden complained that, "What I, as a member of Congress, am not even allowed to see is now ending up in model packages." Editorials warned that 'foreign spies' might grab up the hobby kit and exploit its enclosed F-19 'Stealth Fighter' Profile. The biggest nonsense in all this was a report that Russian agents had scarfed up cartons of the new model and shipped them to Moscow via diplomatic pouch.

None of this uproar took into account the incompetence of Testors, which seemed to know less than anyone else speculating about the secret of stealth. The model-maker was completely wrong in every detail, as it has been consistently, before and since. In fact, the inability of the model-maker to come up with anything remotely like the real aircraft (or like its real designation) probably helped keep the real thing secret. The kit model was a smooth, sleek aircraft having nothing whatever in common with the faceted shape of the Senior Trend.

Others with keener minds were striving, hard, to unlock the secret of the hush-hush aeroplane flying over the Nevada desert. On 23 August 1986, in a landmark news story triggered by the Bakersfield crash the month before, the Washington Post's George Wilson peeled away layers of secrecy, disclosing that "several combat-ready squadrons of stealth fighters are reportedly hidden in hangars in the Nevada desert near Tonopah, south-east of Reno," to avoid detection. Wilson said that the new aircraft was known as the Covert Survivable In-Weather Reconnais-

A swirl of tyre smoke signals the safe return of a Tonopah 'Black Jet' after a training mission. The lack of a two-seat trainer version (proposed but turned down) has put great demands on the simulator for initial training. Once fully proficient in the sim, the new F-117 pilot takes his first ride accompanied by an experienced pilot flying chase in a T-38.

Above: With gear locked down, the 49th FW commander's aircraft turns over the snow-dusted New Mexico countryside for landing at Holloman. The landing gear retracts forward, this arrangement having the benefit of allowing the gear to fall under gravity and then be forced back to lock by aerodynamic pressure should power be lost.

Right: The 'Black Jet' is by operational nature a solitary beast, but the 410th Test Squadron put up this rare formation of three for the 1993 Edwards air show.

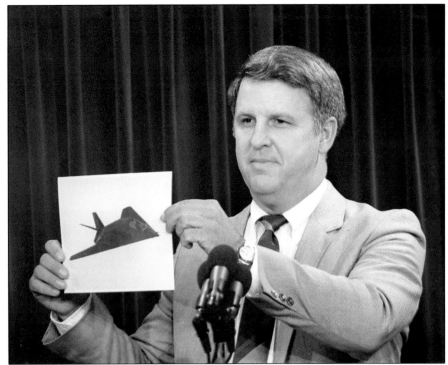

sance Strike (COSIRS) and also as the F-19. Wilson also said that "the fighter bears a top-secret, two-word code-name that replaced Have Blue, which was an umbrella term for early stealth prototypes." He meant Senior Trend.

On 14 October 1987 at a gunnery range at Nellis, another crash occurred, in which Major Michael C. Stewart died. Stewart was 40 minutes into a mission when his 'Black Jet' (85-01815, callsign BURNR 54) crashed into the gentle, sloping high desert 65 miles (105 km) east of Alamo, Nevada. The aircraft struck the earth at a steep angle, digging a hole into the powdery sand. As with Mulhare's crash the year before, insiders speculated on fatigue – an ever-present companion to men flying at night, their mental time clocks out of sequence – and resulting spatial disorientation. Again, Security Police cordoned off the crash site and covered everything beneath a cloak of secrecy.

When Colonel Michael C. Short became the fourth commander of Tonopah's 4450th Tactical Group on 3 April 1987, there was still talk about using the F-117 in

This was how the Department of Defense finally revealed the F-117 to the world, Assistant Secretary of Defense J. Daniel Howard holding a Pentagon press conference on 10 November 1988 at which this one photograph was released. The illustration was deliberately grainy to hide the details of the aircraft's facets, and taken from an intentionally misleading angle to make it look much shorter and wider than is the case.

'Black Jet' and 'Gray Jet' during initial training at Holloman. The Talon sticks close to the F-117, with experienced pilots calling out instructions and monitoring the performance of the trainee 'Bandit'. The AT-38 wears markings for the 417th Fighter Squadron, which undertook the training mission for several years. In 1993 the three F-117 squadrons eventually took up the numbers of the 49th Fighter Wing's traditional units (long after the move to Holloman), the 417th FS becoming the 7th FS 'Bunyaps' in December.

Lockheed F-117

Over 17 months elapsed from the first Pentagon press briefing to the final public unveiling, which took place on 21 April 1990. Two aircraft, one marked for the 37th TFW commander and one carrying 415th and 416th Squadron markings on either side of the fin, flew in to Nellis from Tonopah for the occasion, which was attended by thousands.

Opposite page: F-117s trail behind a KC-135 prior to refueling.

The final F-117 was delivered to the Air Force in a ceremony at Palmdale on 12 July 1990. Adhering to true 'Skunk Works' philosophy, Lockheed delivered the 59 aircraft on time and within a surprisingly low budget for such a sophisticated aircraft.

Nicaragua. Those with a compartmentalised clearance known as Veil (pertaining to US covert operations in Central America) knew of a plan to use the F-117 to attack specific buildings in Managua to take out the Sandinistas' leadership. A contingency plan called for basing Senior Trend warplanes temporarily in Honduras for this purpose. The plan was never activated.

A-7D accident

On 20 October 1987, attention was abruptly focused on the 4450th TG when one of the group's Vought A-7D aircraft lost engine power and crashed into the Ramada Inn hotel near the Indianapolis, Indiana, airport. Pilot Major Bruce L. Teagarden ejected safely but the A-7D struck the hotel and erupted in flames, killing nine people. Judged blameless in the mishap, Teagarden was publicly acknowledged as a member of the 4450th TG; the mainstream press never picked up on his connection with a mystery plane flying in Nevada.

The F-117 nose-dived into election politics again in 1988. In a move certain to boost George Bush's campaign against Michael Dukakis, the Pentagon scheduled what the Boston Globe called a "coming out party" for the as-yet unacknowledged stealth fighter for 9 October 1988, a month before American voters were to choose their next president. Press and public still thought the mystery debutante was called the F-19, and the Reagan administration

said nothing to the contrary. Some Congressmen were infuriated by the timing of this very first release of any information. The release, including the first, fuzzy photograph (of "a black bat," said George Wilson), was delayed until 10 November 1988, one week after voters had picked Bush.

New companions

In September 1989, the Vought A-7D 'companion' aircraft operated by the 4450th TG were replaced by Northrop T-38 Talons; the former were no longer needed for cover purposes and the latter were far more economical to operate. The A-7D had some commonality with the F-117 in terms of size and handling characteristics, but was no longer employed elsewhere in the active-duty inventory and was increasingly costly to maintain and operate. The T-38A (followed, in due course, by a few armed AT-38Bs) was more than adequate for training. The A-7D aeroplanes had worn a unique 'LV' tailcode, for Las Vegas, which never had been painted on the F-117 itself. The T-38s adopted the stealth fighter's 'TR' tailcode, for Tonopah Range.

The 'coming out' of the Lockheed F-117 was welcomed by Air Staff officers and others, eager to strip away the barriers which prevented them from including the aircraft in everyday operations. No longer was it necessary for the F-117 unit to shield its purpose behind an ambiguous name. In October 1989, the 4450th Tactical Group was redesignated 37th Tactical Fighter Wing. Colonel Anthony J. 'Tony' Tolin (who had taken over from Short on 10 August 1988) was commander of the 4450th-cum-37th during its most difficult period, namely its emergence from the closet, its introduction to combat, and (later) the first few days of Operation Desert Shield.

Another year was to pass, together with a war in Panama, before any further details of the hush-hush F-117 would come out.

December 1989 saw US forces deployed for Operation Just Cause, the combined arms assault on Panama aimed at ousting strongman Manuel Noriega, who had made the mistake of tweaking American noses. These were always combined arms exercises because every branch of service and every kind of military unit had to be given a role; inefficient as this was, Congress would have it no other way. With the F-117 public knowledge now, the Pentagon's Joint Staff could no longer deny a 'silver bullet' opportunity to the Tonopah-based stealth fighter. On the night of 19-20 December 1989, two F-117s were launched to support a never-disclosed Special Operations 'snatch' of Noriega, which was called off only as they approached Panamanian airspace. Two other F-117s were back-ups, and two flew a bombing mission intended to 'stun, disorient and confuse' Panamanian Defense Forces (PDF) at Rio Hato. As unlikely as it sounds, their target was a large, open field alongside a barracks housing 200 elite PDF troops, and not the barracks itself.

Just Cause mission

The six F-117s flew from Tonopah and refuelled five times during the round trip to Panama. The two Rio Hato F-117s dropped two 2,000-lb (907-kg) GBU-27A/B bombs with BLU-109B/I-2000 warheads, both of which exploded several hundred feet away from their intended target. Lead pilot for this attack was Major Greg Feest, who later dropped the first bomb on Baghdad. Four of the six F-117s returned to Tonopah with their bombs on board.

In Congress, a critic argued that the mission "could have been flown with an Aero Commander," a twin-engined, propeller-driven business aircraft. Time magazine asserted that the USAF "unleashed its F-117s not to scare Manuel Noriega, but to build a case that high-tech aircraft have a role even in a low-tech war." At the time the press was referring to the F-117 as the 'Wobbly Goblin', a term

Lockheed F-117

never used by those who worked on and flew the aircraft. It was the worst time that the US Air Force could have chosen to reveal that it would be seeking 132 Northrop B-2 stealth bombers.

On 21 April 1990, thousands witnessed a public unveiling of the F-117 stealth fighter at Nellis AFB, Nevada. That month, Colonel Ber Reiter, who had been the USAF's F-117 programme director since July 1987, acknowledged that F-117s were being upgraded with graphite thermoplastic fins. Reiter said that Lockheed and the USAF had "recently produced and flown" an F-117 vertical fin made of the composite material and that the fin was "the first primary structural component" made of "this exceptionally strong, light, damage-tolerant material." Reiter confirmed that the F-117 fleet would be upgraded with the new fins, and this apparently happened over the following two to three years.

On 12 July 1990, three weeks before an Iraqi invasion of Kuwait, the US Air Force took delivery of its 59th and last F-117 aircraft (87-0843) in a ceremony presided over by chief of staff General Michael Dugan.

Desert build-up

Almost immediately after Saddam Hussein invaded Kuwait and the military build-up known as Operation Desert Storm was launched in August 1990, the 37th Tactical Fighter Wing dispatched its 'Black Jets' on a journey halfway around the world, to King Khalid air base at Khamis Mushait in mountainous south-west Saudi Arabia near the Red Sea, 1,000 miles (1610 km) from Baghdad. It was the first overseas deployment for the Nighthawk. The journey was made via a stop at Langley AFB, Virginia, where observers were treated to the spectacular sight of 22 F-117s lined up along a flight line in broad daylight. The trip from Langley to Khamis involved 14 to 16 hours in the cockpit, and four to six aerial refuellings en route.

'Tonopah East'

The Saudi air base, elevation 6,776 ft (2065 m), quickly became known as Tonopah East. At the start of the deployment, Colonel Alton C. ('Al') Whitley, Jr (who in the distant past had been the first operational pilot to fly the F-117) took command from Tolin.

Within the 37th TFW, weaponeering and targeting officers began plotting how the F-117 would be used against Iraq if diplomacy failed and war came. Although it took

three air refuellings per sortie and inflicted much pilot discomfort – almost every 'Black Jet' pilot had a Sony Walkman rigged to his helmet earphones to listen to his music of choice while in the cruise mode – the F-117 could fly 1,000 miles (1610 km) and deliver a 2,000-lb (907-kg) laser-guided bomb with pinpoint accuracy. This accuracy was important. In the 1990s, with the merciless eye of television shining on Operation Desert Shield, American planners no longer lived in a world where 'collateral' civilian deaths and injuries were acceptable.

On 12 September 1990, the well-liked chief of staff, General Dugan, visited Khamis, where the F-117 force was now on alert. A week later, Dugan described exactly what coalition air power would do to Saddam Hussein if necessary, and was fired for doing so. Dugan said that "the cutting edge" of an air campaign "would be in downtown

Above and below: Accommodation at King Khalid AB was superb, with hardened shelters each housing two aircraft. In addition to reinforced concrete, the shelters were protected and disguised with a top cover of rocks.

Baghdad." Dugan was sacked for predicting exactly what occurred months later.

Computer war

In a command facility named the 'Black Hole' at Riyadh, Lieutenant General Charles Horner's air staff worked out all the details of a possible air campaign against Iraq, such as refuelling tracks, jamming, countermeasures and air rescue, at a time when almost nobody believed there would really be a war. On 3 October 1990, Colonel Whitley began a series of 'mirror image' combat rehearsals, named Sneaky Sultan, in which strikes on Iraq were practised, and in which computer modelling saw numerous 'Black Jets' shot down without reaching their targets. Still, everyone felt the situation would be resolved through negotiation. One day in October 1990, intelligence officer Michael P. Curphey sat in on a meeting where Horner and others confirmed that 'downtown' (Baghdad) would be set aside exclusively for unmanned cruise missiles and the 'Black Jet'. Curphey emerged shaking his head. "You know," he said, "that goddamned crazy man Saddam Hussein isn't going to back down."

The decision to set aside HVAs in Baghdad for the F-117 was reinforced as preparations continued. Even after experts reduced their estimate of Iraq's air defence network, a Studies and Analysis Agency team came up with computer models which projected extremely high losses if non-stealthy warplanes struck the capital. Baghdad belonged to the 'Black Jet'.

Eve of war

Whitley found himself in charge of the deployed version of his outfit, now known as the 37th TFW (Provisional). The designation was applied on 20 December 1990. Whitley's deployed wing included most of the 415th TFS 'Nightstalkers' under Lieutenant Colonel Ralph Getchell plus the 416th TFS 'Ghostriders', as well as a few members of the training squadron, the 417th TFTS under Lieutenant

Colonel Robert Maher.

On the evening of 16 January 1991, after a United Nations ultimatum to Saddam Hussein passed without result, the men of the 37th TFW (P) finally realised that they were going to war. Leatherman, Kerdavid and Mahar were among the pilots who flew those first missions. Each, later, admitted to the fear which gripped Mahar: each man was certain he would be the only member of the 37th TFW to live through the gauntlet of flak around Baghdad, and would be stuck with explaining to the widows and children of his buddies why he alone had survived.

Combat glitches

That eventuality was not realised, but problems arose throughout the campaign. It had been planned that follow-up F-117s striking the same target would arrive at one-minute intervals, to allow time for surface winds to push dust and smoke away from the aim points. This tactic did not work. It took at least 10 minutes for AAA (anti-aircraft artillery) gunfire to die down once the gunners had been 'excited' by the arrival of a 'Black Jet'. A second 'Black Jet' needed to arrive as much as 15 minutes after the first. The revised sequencing went into effect from the second night and may have saved some pilots' lives.

The first night, it was deemed a mistake when EF-111 Raven electronic warfare aircraft stirred up Iraqi gunners, seemingly making them more ready for the arrival of the F-117. After a second look at the tactic, it was determined that forcing the Iraqis to fire prematurely heated-up gun barrels had made the anti-aircraft batteries less accurate by the time the F-117s arrived.

Many F-117 strikes were postponed or cancelled because of the awful weather which plagued the air campaign. A adverse-weather situation highlights the lack of a radar on board the F-117, which essentially relies upon a clear air mass to carry out its mission.

As Desert Storm unfolded, F-117 pilots returned with undropped bombs because conditions would not permit the

Brothers in arms: a 'Black Jet' returns from a mission behind an F-15D of the Royal Saudi Air Force. No. 42 Squadron flew the Eagles from King Kahlid.

Infra-red film gives some idea of the eerie sensation experienced by KC-135 boomers as the F-117 loomed out of the dark as it approached the boom. During missions into Iraq the F-117 topped off its tanks just short of the Saudi/Iraq border before proceeding alone into hostile airspace.

standard of accuracy they were charged with meeting. At its best, the F-117 gave precision delivery of munitions, as when 'Black Jets' struck the main Baghdad telephone exchange without harming the Mustashfa Faydi hospital located just across a wide boulevard. Targets were taken out with surgical precision. A bomb from an F-117 destroyed an Iraqi Adnan-2, a Soviet-built Ilyushin Il-76 transport converted into an early warning aircraft with the addition of French-designed Tiger-G radars. Another, according to one report never confirmed, destroyed three of eight Tupolev Tu-16 bombers being readied at Al-Taqaddum for a chemical bombing raid. Strikes were mounted against surface-to-air missile sites containing American-made Hawk batteries, seized by Iraq during its invasion of Kuwait. As the campaign wore on, the F-117 force ran out of strategic targets; the Air Force's 'silver bullet' found itself being used much like any other fighter-bomber, taking part in the interdiction campaign against bridges and aircraft shelters.

Desert Storm statistics

The US Air Force later concluded that the F-117 represented only 2.5 per cent of the shooters in-theatre on the first day of the war, yet credited it with hitting over 31 per cent of the targets. During the war, 45 F-117s and about 60 pilots flew 1,271 combat sorties, dropped over 2,000 tons (1814 tonnes) of bombs, flew over 6,900 hours, and (said its supporters), "demonstrated accuracy unmatched in the history of air warfare." During the conflict, the F-117 had a mission-capable rate of 85.8 per cent, which was four per cent higher than in peacetime. GBU-10 and GBU-27

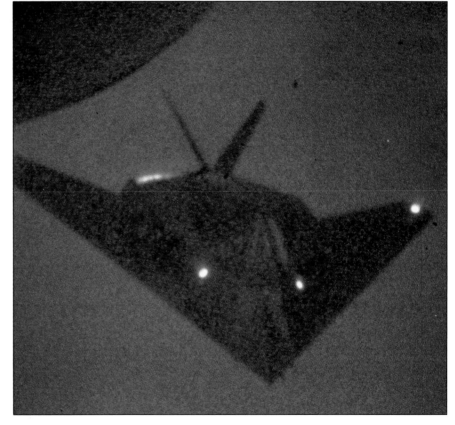

On 1 April 1991 Colonel Al Whitley led back the first F-117s from Saudi Arabia to Nellis AFB, where a tumultuous welcome from a crowd of 25,000 awaited the crews. Over the next three months the force at Khamis Mushait dwindled to a handful of aircraft, which have been maintained there ever since as a rotational deployment from the CONUS Nighthawk unit. Crew swap-overs are undertaken every three months.

Lockheed F-117A Nighthawk
49th Fighter Wing
Holloman AFB, New Mexico

Along with the B-2 bomber, the Nighthawk is the USAF's prime attack weapon, the F-117 force being able to exert an influence on an air campaign that far outweighs its meagre size. As was seen during Desert Storm, the F-117's primary role is to attack high-value command, control and communication targets to, in effect, 'decapitate' the enemy's ability to control its forces. Such targets include leadership bunkers, command posts, and air defence and communications centres. Most of these types of targets are well-defended, usually hardened against normal attacks and often in down-town areas. Many may have only one or two small weak spots, such as air shafts, where a bomb will do any damage at all. The need to deliver a high-energy penetration weapon with the least-possible collateral damage requires the utmost accuracy and high survivability. By using stealth, the F-117 can cruise into the target area unmolested, relying on its extensive low-observables properties for protection and putting the aircraft into the optimum position for an accurate attack. Whereas the crew of a conventional aircraft has to fly low and fast while dodging defences to penetrate the target area, leaving them little time to concentrate on accuracy, the F-117 pilot can take his time to use the sophisticated weapons system to ensure a pinpoint strike. If the strategic targets run out, the F-117 is a valuable weapon in a standard interdiction role, being able to hit bridges, railroad depots, airfields and industrial complexes with ease.

Having started life in a 'black' world of nocturnal flying and a secret base, the Nighthawk force has now completed its move into the public glare, although many key technological areas remain under wraps. Following the public unveiling at Nellis AFB, NV, in April 1990, the F-117 began a round of air show appearances throughout the United States, and occasional appearances in Europe, including the 1991 Paris air show. The move from Tonopah Test Range to Holloman AFB was accomplished from May 1992 with a change in wing designation from 37th TFW to 49th FW. The three old squadrons of the 37th TFW renumbered in mid-1993 as the 7th, 8th and 9th Fighter Squadrons. Of these, the 8th and 9th were the operational units with an authorised strength of 18 aircraft each, the 7th being a training squadron (ex-417th FS) operating about 16 F-117As and a handful of T-38s. Today the unit only has T-38s. Since the end of the Gulf War, a detachment of F-117s was maintained in Saudi Arabia as a deterrent to further Iraqi aggression. The test and trials fleet consists of one F-117A alongside three FSD YF-117As with the 410th Test Squadron, 412th Test Wing. Although wearing 'ED' codes, the 410th TS actually operates from the Lockheed/AF plant at Palmdale. At least one F-117 is at Holloman for operational test and evaluation purposes with a detachment from the 53rd Wing.

Powerplant and fuel

Buried deep within the F-117's fuselage are two General Electric F404-GE-F1D2 engines, each rated at approximately 10,800 lb (48 kN) thrust. Developed especially for the F-117, this engine is derived from the standard F404-GE-400 used by the F/A-18 Hornet, itself a derivative of the YJ101 employed by the Northrop YF-17. The engine is a compact low-bypass ratio turbofan, with a diameter of approximately 35 in (890 mm). In the standard Hornet version, the front fan is a three-stage unit, with the outer flow diverted to the bypass duct at a ratio of 0.34. Downstream from the fan is a seven-stage high-pressure compressor with a compression ratio in the region of 25:1. Aft of the single-piece annular combustion chamber are the high-pressure and low-pressure turbines, each consisting of a single stage of blades. The engine is aspirated through the four-sided intakes which are covered with a fine mesh. At low speeds these are augmented by large suck-in doors of six-sided shape situated in the top of the intake trunk. In order to vastly reduce the infra-red signature, the F-117 has a novel slot exhaust. Jet efflux from the circular-section jetpipe is mixed with the cold bypass air to cool it, and then widened and flattened to exit the slot exhaust in a plume some 4 in (100 mm) deep and 5 ft (1.5 m) wide. The exhausts, designed by Astech/MCI, incorporate an extended lower lip to shield the main heat source from sensors below, a series of guide vanes along the slot to maintain thrust direction, and ceramic heat tiles similar to the re-entry heat shields fitted to the Space Shuttle. Large access doors between the undercarriage and weapons bay allow the engines to be easily dropped out for maintenance.

Fuel is held in large tanks situated in the main fuselage body, filling the vacant upper areas fore and aft of the weapons bay. This can be augmented by fuel tanks in the weapons bay for ferry flights. Inflight refuelling is accomplished via a receptacle aft of the fuselage apex, normally covered by a six-sided door. The receptacle and toughened slipway rotates to stand proud from the fuselage, so aiding the boom operator. At the apex of the fuselage above the cockpit is a small 'pimple' which houses a floodlight for illuminating the receptacle area.

Laser-guided bombs

Although the USAF claims that a "full range of USAF tactical fighter ordnance" can be carried, and reports abound as to the use of AGM-65 Maverick, AGM-88 HARM and AIM-9 Sidewinders, the 2,000-lb class laser-guided bomb remains the F-117's main weapon. There are five main versions, consisting of combinations of two warhead types and two seeker heads, and a GPS-aided version. Warhead options are the standard Mk 84 high-explosive (GBU-10C/D/E/F and GBU-27) and the BLU-109 penetration warhead (GBU-10G/H/J, GBU-27A and EGBU-27), which has a thick 4340 steel alloy case, low explosive/weight ratio (30 per cent) and tail-mounted FMU-143 fuse to ensure that it explodes after having punched through a hardened structure, thereby destroying the contents. A penetration of up to 6 ft (1.83 m) of reinforced concrete has been demonstrated. The seeker heads, or CCG (computer control and guidance) units, are either Paveway II (GBU-10) or Paveway III (GBU-27, EGBU-27) units. The Paveway II CCG is a gimballed seeker whereas the Paveway III has an enclosed head. The Paveway II CCG uses full-deflection guidance, moving the front fins fully to alter the bomb's path. This 'bang-bang' guidance causes the bomb to lose a great deal of energy and some accuracy as it 'bounces' from one edge of the laser 'basket' to the other. When using Paveway IIs, crews tend to leave the laser 'sparkle' to the last possible moment so that the bomb does not lose too much energy under guidance. This requires a good level of normal ballistic bombing accuracy. On the other hand, the Paveway III uses proportional guidance, with only small deflections of the fins to control the bomb. This allows the bomb to retain most of its kinetic energy, and flies it in a much straighter attitude, vastly increasing penetrative power. Another advantage is a much greater range and improved accuracy as the bomb does not 'flap' during the final phase of its trajectory. Paveway III CCGs can also be programmed to give an optimum strike angle against differing targets. However, the Paveway III seeker does come at a much greater price, and so its use is restricted to

high-value targets. The standard Paveway III bomb is the GBU-24, as used to devastating effect by the F-111 during Desert Storm. This has the full-spec features, with much larger control fins and pop-out wings for vastly increased range. However, these fins are too big to fit the confines of the F-117's bomb bay, so the short-range Paveway II wings are fitted and the front fins cropped accordingly. The EGBU-27 weapon combines the BLU-109 penetration warhead and Paveway III seeker of the GBU-27 with a GPS guidance system. This ensures that the weapon can be dropped accurately even if laser detection is lost. It was first employed in the opening attacks of Operation Iraqi Freedom in March 2003, when two F-117s dropped four EGBU-27s against a bunker where Iraqi leader Saddam Hussein was thought to be conducting a meeting.

Weapons are held on a retractable trapeze, which swings down and forward from the bomb bay. This is of inestimable value for ground crew loading the weapons, allowing easy all-round access to the bomb carriage mechanisms. With laser-guided weapons, the warhead and fin assembly is loaded using a standard trolley, which can get under the aircraft and then offer the bomb up to the shackles. The delicate CCG section is fixed with the bomb in situ, followed by the forward control fins. The trapeze, with bomb, is then slung back up into the bay for flight. Whether the trapeze is deployed for bomb release has, at the time of writing, not been ascertained, but the provision of two small perforated baffles which deploy from the front of the bay to disrupt airflow either side of the trapeze may suggest this is the case. If missiles are employed, the trapeze would certainly be lowered to put the weapons into clear air for launch. However, the opening of the bay doors and the extension of trapeze would seriously harm the low-observable properties of the aircraft while weapon is being released. It is likely that a timed mechanism opens the door, releases the bomb and then snaps the door shut in as short a time as possible.

Structure

Due to its unorthodox shape, the F-117's internal structure is considerably different to standard construction techniques. The central carapace, including the engine trunks but minus the nose section, is constructed as a skeleton of ribs and stringers with larger members running through the key load routes. To this skeleton is attached the facetted panels, separate nose section and fins. The wings are constructed separately around a two-spar box. The rear spar forms the trailing edge of the fixed wing, and therefore the attachment point for the elevons. A leading-edge member runs the full span of the wing, curving round to form the main wingtip attachment. The wing is mated to the central structure just outboard of the engine trunks, using five main bolts along the inter-spar interface, three bolts forward of the front spar and an angled attachment strut attaching the rear spar just forward of the exhaust slot. The majority of the structure is of aluminium, although nickel alloy is used in the jetpipes, and the original metal ruddervators have recently been replaced by thermoplastic graphite composite structures.

Stealth origins

Remarkably, the history of the F-117 and its revolutionary 'stealth' technology began in 19th century Britain, where Scottish physicist James Clerk Maxwell derived a set of mathematical formulae to predict the manner in which electromagnetic radiation would scatter when reflected from a given geometric shape. The equations were further refined by famed German electromagnetic scientist Arnold Johannes Sommerfeld. In the 1960s the chief scientist at the Moscow Institute of Radio Engineering, Dr Pyotr Ufimtsev, revisited the Maxwell-Sommerfeld work and simplified it to concentrate on the electromagnetic currents at the edge of geometric shapes. In Moscow Ufimtsev published a paper in 1966 titled 'Method of Edge Waves in the Physical Theory of Diffraction', but at the time this was thought to only have applications to very simple two-dimensional shapes. Nevertheless, the work was there, and along with the earlier Maxwell-Sommerfeld work, could provide the basis for a mathematical model of a stealthy aircraft. The USAF's Foreign Technology Division regularly gathered and translated foreign scientific documents, so they were available to Lockheed engineers.

In 1974 DARPA invited five aircraft companies (not including Lockheed) to study the potential for a stealthy aircraft. In early 1975 Lockheed's 'Skunk Works' heard of the studies, and sought permission to use data from the SR-71 programme to submit its own study. The Advanced Development Projects organisation had been concerned with low radar cross-section for some time, with work on shaping and radar-absorbent material. However, to produce an aircraft with a very low radar cross-section would need a quantum leap in technology. Enter Bill Schroeder, a retired Lockheed mathematician. Using Ufimtsev's simple formulae for two-dimensional shapes, Schroeder proposed that by reducing a three-dimensional body to a finite number of two-dimensional surfaces, the overall radar dissipation patterns could be forecast, and kept to a manageable number. Armed with this information, the individual surfaces could then be angled in such a way that radar energy could be reflected away from its source (and hence the receiver) from virtually any aspect. If such a shape could then be fashioned to create lift, then a stealthy aircraft could be possible, especially since the need for natural stability in an aircraft shape had been removed by computer-controlled fly-by-wire control systems. The concept of facetting was born.

With other companies also examining stealth, Lockheed could waste no time in attempting to turn Schroeder's idea into workable technology. Led by Denys Overholser, a Lockheed ADP software team worked closely with Schroeder to produce a computer programme that would accurately predict the radar scatter patterns of a facetted shape. In just five weeks the programme Echo I was produced, a remarkable achievement by Overholser and Schroeder. To validate the software a simple, idealised aircraft model was produced, nicknamed the 'Hopeless Diamond'. This was tested in an electromagnetic facility, and was found to have a much lower radar cross-section than any previous shape tested by the company. Now known as 'Have Blue', the programme moved to larger-scale tests with pole-mounted shapes, all of which exhibited extremely low cross-sections. In April 1976 DARPA declared Lockheed the winner of the competition, the Echo I programme having proven to be the key breakthrough in achieving a practical aircraft with true low-observable properties. Lockheed's technology was such an advance that the originally-unclassified DARPA project was rapidly submerged into a deep 'black' status, with very limited access. Work then began on the two XST technology demonstrators, the first of which flew in December 1977.

With the F-117 in service, Dr Ufimtsev later said that he had devised a method of detecting stealth aircraft. Basing his thoughts on the fact that "all this dissipated radar energy has to go somehwere", he proposed the use of bistatic radars, with receivers in different locations to the transmitter. These would detect the radar refelctions which were angled away by the F-117's shape. However, the time and processing power needed to accurately compute the position of the aircraft from these deflected returns is potentially so enormous as to render the scheme unfeasible. Certainly with current technology the F-117 would have long vacated the area by the time its previous position had been fixed.

Weapons system

The F-117's weapon/nav system is designed to allow the pilot to concentrate on scoring a precise hit with the weapons. The system virtually flies the aircraft to the target area without any input from the pilot, while taking the optimum route to avoid any threat areas. A moving-map display allows the pilot to monitor precisely the aircraft's path. Prior to any F-117 operational mission, the aircraft's central computer is programmed with the mission profile. A ground-based mission planning computer (known as 'Elvira') is used to plan the precise parameters of the mission, which are then downloaded on to the EDTM (electronic data transfer module). This cartridge is then plugged into the aircraft's IBM AP-102 computer. Once loaded, the computer uses the EDTM data to integrate the navigation and flight management system to allow a hands-off approach to the target area through a complicated set of turnpoints, altitude changes and airspeed adjustments. The principal en route aid is the Honeywell SPN-GEANS INS, which allows the aircraft to be positioned accurately in the target area.

Once within sensor range, the pilot resumes control of the system, using the infra-red acquisition and designation system (IRADS). This is integrated with the weapon release system and consists of the FLIR and DLIR. These two sensors are boresighted on the ground by raising the nose of the aircraft and then using each in turn to sight on the same object. Due to its look angle, the FLIR is the principal search sensor, a zoom function allowing early identification and lock-on. The target and lock-on is handed off electronically to the DLIR as the downward look angle increases. The pilot uses the image, presented on a large central cockpit TV display, to fine-tune the lock-on before initiating weapon release. The DLIR turret also contains a boresighted laser designator, which fires a coded burst of laser energy at the locked-in aim point at some point during the bomb's trajectory. The bomb then follows the 'sparkle' to a direct hit. Flying at medium altitude, the F-117's stealth properties allow the pilot to make slow and deliberate approach runs, giving him greater time for accurate attacks. However, the current FLIR/DLIR system is often hampered by cloud and smoke. The third phase of the current OCIP programme aims to improve the performance of the F-117's IRADS with a new Texas Instruments sensor.

Markings

In keeping with the covert nature of its operations, the F-117 is painted the same all-over matt black as worn by the SR-71 and U-2R, rendering the type virtually invisible at night. Tanker boom operators report that the aircraft simply appears under the boom during night refuellings, despite the use of floodlighting. Apart from the emergency canopy release triangle below the cockpit, all markings are in low-visibility grey, consisting of national insignia on wings and fuselage, tail markings representing the last three digits of the aircraft serial, Air Combat Command badge and 'HO' tailcode for Holloman AFB. The 49th Fighter Wing badge is worn on the intake sides, this comprising a winged helmet and a covered wagon separated by a lightning bolt, and the motto 'Tutor et Ultor' ('I protect and avenge') beneath.

Lockheed F-117

bombs dropped by the F-117 proved highly effective against aircraft shelters, bunkers and other strategic targets in Baghdad. Contrary to what Mahar and others expected, not a single F-117 was touched by Iraqi fire.

Proponents of other aircraft types argue that any warplane which can designate for its own laser-guided weapons can be similarly effective: the F-111F, which used hi-tech weaponry to 'plink' main battle tanks, performed well in the Gulf; the F-16 Fighting Falcon might have demonstrated a good record of precision bombing, too, if only LANTIRN targeting pods had been available at the time.

Attempt to revive production

In October 1991, there was a brief flurry of bureaucratic jousting as Washington insiders, glowing over hyped reports of the Nighthawk's success in Desert Storm, sought to revive production. Lockheed suddenly had a rare opportunity to lobby for business it had neither expected nor sought, but the US Air Force had other plans. Eager for funding for the B-2 bomber and Advanced Tactical Fighter (which turned out to be the Lockheed F-22), blue-suiters in the Air Staff made it clear that reopening the F-117 production line was an idea whose time would never come. As it did with a premature (and later cancelled) plan to retire the F-111F 'Aardvark', the Air Staff was prepared to sacrifice a proven asset (the 'Black Jet' had won the 1989 Collier Trophy for Rich and his design team, the 1989 David C. Schilling Award for the aircraft itself, and three outstanding unit citations for the men who flew it) to justify dollars for future projects.

In June 1991, General John Loh, head of Tactical Air Command, told the Senate that the F-117 had been eight times more efficient in delivering bombs against Iraq than 'non-stealth' warplanes requiring escort fighters, radar jammers and tankers. It was not true, but the success of the F-117 was becoming an embarrassment to the USAF. In 1991, the service wanted 72 more of the rather prosaic F-16 Fighting Falcons (still, at the time, manufactured by General Dynamics rather than Lockheed), and had "absolutely, positively, zero interest," as one officer puts it, in reopening the production line for the glamorous Lockheed F-117.

Congressmen were urging exactly that reopening. Senator Sam Nunn, the most knowledgeable defence figure on Capitol Hill, declared, "The Air Force already has more than 1,600 F-16s, and buying 72 more will provide only a marginal increase in capability. Buying 24 more F-117s for the same amount [as 72 F-16s] will provide a 50 per cent increase in the number of aircraft that proved to be the superstar of Desert Storm." The Senate voted to cancel the F-16s and called on the USAF to order the F-117s. Such a vote is over overtaken by some later vote and, in this case,

the F-117 purchase did not happen.

From early in the Nighthawk's history, Britain was made a partner in development of the stealth fighter, and Lockheed made proposals for an F-117 variant for the Royal Air Force. Early proposals to the RAF met with some interest from operators, but were thought to interfere with other procurement programmes that enjoyed a higher priority. Meanwhile, the F-117 community honoured a practice which has been part of the Anglo-American alliance since the 1940s, by inviting a British exchange pilot to serve as an operational member of a squadron. (In practice, Americans serving in the RAF get the better half of this exchange deal since their British hosts give them full opportunities for command and full disciplinary authority; Britons in the USAF perform the same job as their American colleagues but are treated more like guests.) The British F-117 pilot slot has been filled by Graham Wardell, Chris Topham and, later, Ian Wood. In the 1990s, Lockheed revived a plan to sell 'new-build' F-117s to Britain, but the RAF seemed to have no politically justifiable formal need and little money to spend.

Times were changing, and the revisionists were taking hold. They argued (truthfully) that the F-117 was not nearly as accurate as claimed (although extraordinarily precise when compared with any other strike aircraft). They said it was expensive to operate, which was true. They said it might stand in the way of funding for other much-wanted programmes, which was the only real concern. The party

F-117: The Black Jet

Following years of rumours concerning the aircraft's use in Europe, the F-117 made its first official deployment to the theatre in June 1993, when eight aircraft deployed to Gilze-Rijen in the Netherlands for Exercise Central Enterprise. The aircraft were housed in the unfamiliar surroundings of a Tab-Vee hardened shelter.

was over, and it became the essence of Washington politics to display a lowered regard for the F-117. Lieutenant General 'Buster' Glossom, the Gulf War strategist who had become the USAF's top lobbyist, described the F-117 as "archaic, 15-year-old technology" that was a "nightmare to maintain." Lockheed, whose F-22 had just been chosen as the USAF's Advanced Tactical Fighter (ATF), was told not to campaign for a new F-117 production contract.

Move to Holloman

The US Air Force had been ready to bring the F-117 out of the 'black' and was eager to integrate it into everyday operations. A decision was made to move from sequestered Tonopah to readily-accessible Holloman Air Force Base at Alamogordo, New Mexico.

At Holloman, the F-15 Eagle-equipped 49th Fighter Wing was scheduled to give up its aircraft, but enjoyed a proud heritage Air Staff officers wanted to preserve. Among its 43 air aces were Lieutenant Colonel Boyd D. 'Buzz' Wagner, the first American ace in the Pacific theatre, and Major Richard I. Bong, who racked up 40 aerial victories. The 37th's name was not associated with any such claim to glory. The number of tactical wings in the USAF was shrinking rapidly (from 40, the goal during the Reagan years, to 21 or fewer), so some squadron designations had to go. With the shift to Holloman, the F-117 establishment took over the 49th designation. Plans to rename the F-117 squadrons so as to align them with previous 49th associations (the 7th, 8th and 9th TFS) did not at first materialise, and were bitterly opposed by the

An F-117 lands back at Gilze-Rijen after a Central Enterprise sortie. Noteworthy are the extremely narrow exhaust slot and the reflexed trailing edge of the intake.

pilots themselves, who wanted to keep the 415th, 416th and 417th squadron identities.

After the last F-15 Eagle departed Holloman on 5 June 1992 (ending 14 years of Eagle operations at the base), the 49th acquired the 415th, 416th and 417th Fighter Squadrons and their F-117s. The F-117 move from Tonopah to Holloman was carried out between 9 May and 7 July 1992. During this same period, the US Air Force dropped the adjective 'tactical' from the names of its fighter wings and squadrons. Only subsequently did changes in squadron identity catch up with USAF tradition. On 30 July 1993, the 415th and 416th were redesignated the 9th and 8th Fighter Squadrons, respectively. During December of that year, the training unit – the 417th FS – became the 7th FS. A detachment of the Nellis-based 57th Wing, known as the 'Dragon Test Team', intermittently operated two or three F-117s at Holloman during the post-Tonopah years.

Readiness decline

The June 1992 move to Holloman was followed by a period of neglect when the US Air Force focused on other priorities and allowed F-117 readiness to slip. Some say that taking the 'Black Jet' out of its hush-hush environment and submerging it in the mainstream Air Force caused the drop in the number of war-ready F-117s from 37 (out of a fleet of 45) in 1992 to a mere 28 aircraft in 1994. Pentagon figures show that in May 1992 an average 83 per cent of the fleet was ready for wartime operations, while in March 1994 the figure was only 62 per cent.

Holloman had no hangars to protect the fighters' radar-absorbing materials from sun damage, posing a new challenge to a maintenance force that had lost 70 per cent of its key people in the move. The number was further eroded by the deployment of some members to the Middle East with those F-117s assigned to Operation Southern Watch, monitoring the former 'No-fly' zone in southern Iraq. A funding shortfall led to a shortage of parts and forced F-117 maintenance workers to delay some avionics repairs. On 4 August 1992, a nocturnal mishap claimed a third operational F-117 when Captain John B. Mills of the 416th FS ejected while on a training mission. His aircraft (82-0802) struck a storage building but no-one on the ground was injured.

Addressing shortfalls

In 1993, the USAF allocated an extra $12 million to maintenance funding, then assigned $174 million to the problem in 1994. An extra 143 maintenance personnel were put into training. Still, in mid-1994, actual flying of the 'Black Jet' had fallen to a new low. Each F-117 was flying an average of 11.3 sorties per month, about one per month fewer than in the previous year.

After being accused of neglecting the F-117 fleet for a couple of years, the US Air Force had embarked on four major modification programmes for the type by 1994. At a cost of $191 million, the first of these was the Offensive Capability Improvement Program (OCIP), which began in 1990 with the aim of simplifying cockpit operations. It included a moving-map display, an auto-throttle, a liquid crystal display used as a data entry panel to communicate with the avionics system, a flight-attitude awareness display and, beneath it, a system to automatically return a tumbling aircraft to level flight. It is claimed that the OCIP effort improved pilot situational awareness by allowing the flight management system to fit complex profiles automatically.

Because of its unstable nature, the F-117 was equipped with a PAARS (pilot-activated automatic recovery system) as part of OCIP. PAARS is operational at all attitudes and speeds, gear up or gear down. Upon pilot command, the autopilot, even if not engaged, commands the flight control system and autothrottles to fly a pre-programmed set of manoeuvres, based on entry attitude and airspeed, to

recover the F-117 to straight and level flight. The system was installed as a response to the fatal Mulhare and Stewart crashes where spatial disorientation was deemed a factor, and was the first auto recovery system installed for general use in a USAF fighter. An IRADS modification was developed to upgrade the F-117's FLIR and DLIR retractable, steerable turrets. Costing $144 million, the goal was to double the acquisition range of the IRADS and increase the range and life of the laser. The third programme, impacting the MDPS (mission data planning system), was designed to help pilots prepare for sorties in less time and execute them more easily. Its cost was $18 million. Finally, incorporation of a differential GPS (global positioning system) to replace the INS (inertial navigation system) was undertaken at a cost of $101 million. These improvements are reviewed in greater detail below.

Off-the-shelf shortcomings

To fully understand the series of improvements that have been made to the F-117 during its years in service, it is worth reviewing the programme from an operational requirements standpoint, and how those requirements drove the aircraft's shape and equipment. In all but the most obvious respect, the F-117 was a remarkably straightforward aircraft when it entered service in 1983. Apart from its stealth characteristics, it was not a particularly sophisticated warplane when it joined the fleet, being equipped with a simple electro-optical TDAS (Target Detection and Acquisition System) that incorporated a standard laser designator.

Such simplicity lay in the aircraft's timing and roots. As described earlier, the original requirement had been for a highly specialised 'silver bullet' weapon for deniable special forces-type missions like airborne Delta Force operations against terrorist camps in third-party countries or, perhaps, against the leadership of rogue nations. Originally it was thought that only a handful of aircraft would be needed; possibly just the five FSD aircraft, or five FSD machines plus 20 production aircraft according to some sources. It was even believed that these might be flown by CIA pilots. Coupled with the small fleet, reliance on a pair of small weapons was felt to be acceptable because it was thought the force could wait for the right weather conditions and targets of opportunity under most scenarios. In any event, many of the weapons which allow a similar degree of precision in foul weather only began to be available after the aircraft had been in front-line service for some 16 years.

As previously described, under the top-secret Senior Trend programme existing equipment from other aircraft types was used wherever possible to avoid attention being drawn to a programme that officially did not exist. The strategy also ensured low costs and tended to improve reliability. It has been estimated that the F-117 enjoyed 75 per cent parts commonality with other in-service platforms. Developing a new FLIR would have risked awkward questions, whereas procuring more units of the standard OV-10D TDAS looked like normal spare parts procurement and went unnoticed. However, this strategy meant the Stealth Fighter was fitted with equipment that sometimes was less than ideal. Some of it was on the verge of obsolescence even when it was selected. As a consequence, pressure to upgrade the aircraft was there from the start.

The promise demonstrated by the Have Blue technology and first Senior Trend prototype was sufficient to quickly change the entire concept of operations for the type. The importance of the airborne Delta Force-type mission diminished, and doctrine was developed that soon saw the F-117 as an adjunct to conventional strike attack aircraft; for use against the highest-value and most heavily defended targets, as demonstrated during the 1991 Gulf War.

Experience with the F-117 gave Lockheed a tremendous boost when it came to development of the F-22, the winning design in the USAF's ATF next-generation fighter competition. The YF-22 showed some design concept similarities, notably in having a limited number of alignments of surfaces and sawtooth edges for doors, but it was a far more blended aircraft, and also attended to the operational requirement aspect more closely.

An artist's impression shows the A/F-117X proposal for the Navy, with folding wings, trapezoidal tailplanes, reworked exhaust area and a more extensively glazed canopy.

The Stealth Fighter's low RCS meant it could attack key nodes of an enemy's air defence network and clear corridors through which conventional bombers could follow. Pressure on the USAF to accept a force of up to 89 F-117s at one point, envisaged two wings based at different locations. One was to be a 'grey world' unit whose existence would be acknowledged, while the second would be the Tonopah-based 'black world' wing. In the end, the number of F-117s built included just 60 production aircraft (including one replacement for a pre-delivery attrition), comprising two 18-aircraft front-line squadrons plus a nine-aircraft training unit, four inventory backups and seven attrition replacements. By 2003 the operational fleet had been reduced to 52 aircraft, with three FSD machines undertaking test duties. The Primary Aircraft Authorized number was set at 44.

Invisible versus stealthy

Over the years many have misunderstood the F-117, accepting the gross oversimplification that the aircraft is actually invisible to radar. In fact, the aircraft can be detected by radar but it does have a very low RCS. This reduces the effective range of defensive radars to such an extent that it cannot normally be detected by the enemy in sufficient time for it to make an interception or obtain a surface-to-air missile firing solution. Sometimes, the stealth technologies employed can effectively render the aircraft invisible. Invisible or theoretically detectable, the F-117 is certainly a difficult target for conventional air defences. This was illustrated dramatically during Operation Desert Storm when they were the only allied warplanes to venture over Baghdad, where they flew hundreds of missions without suffering so much as a scratch.

Quite apart from simply reducing radar range and delaying detection, the aircraft's low RCS effectively opens

F-117 Weapons

Above: 'Bombs R Us' – despite many reports of missile armament, the laser-guided bomb is the only weapon so far confirmed for the F-117.

Left: A 57th Fighter Wing F-117 at Holloman carries an SUU-20 practice bomb and rocket dispenser. The rocket option is not used, but the underside of the pod carries six BDU-33 practice bombs which simulate the ballistics of full-size weapons. Just forward of the bomb bay are the four retractable perforated baffles which improve airflow for bomb release.

Above: The standard weapon of the F-117 is the GBU-27, seen here in its penetration version with a straight-sided, thick-cased BLU-109 warhead. The bomb combines the guidance section of the Paveway III with the smaller fins of the Paveway II.

Above: An inert GBU-10 LGB carried by a 410th TS aircraft displays the rounded Mk 84 warhead profile. A good comparison is provided between the gimballed Paveway II seeker head and the fixed head of the GBU-27 Paveway III in the other bomb bay.

Below: For deployments away from home the F-117 can carry the ubiquitous MXU-648 baggage pod, an empty case of a BLU-1/27 fire-bomb provided with a door. All weapons are carried on the retractable trapeze with 30-in lug spacing.

Right: Colonel Al Whitley inspects a GBU-27A prior to a Desert Storm mission. The Paveway III uses proportional guidance rather than the 'bang-bang' guidance of earlier Paveway II bombs, conferring greater range and accuracy.

Lockheed F-117A
8th Fighter Squadron
49th Fighter Wing
Holloman AFB, New Mexico

Bearing the name *Raven Beauty*, this F-117 wears markings for the commander of the 49th Fighter Wing, which took over from the 37th TFW as the F-117 operational unit on 5 July 1992. As well as the '49th FW' tail markings, with the 'HO' code applied in small letters, it has a white fin-stripe with the badges of the 49th's three constituent squadrons – the 7th, 8th and 9th Fighter Squadrons. The tail has the Air Combat Command crest applied, while the side of the intake trunk carries the 8th Fighter Squadron badge. The 8th FS 'Black Sheep' was formerly the 416th Fighter Squadron, which had its roots in the 'Ghostriders' of the 4451st Test Squadron, or 'P-Unit'. This squadron formerly operated the A-7D aircraft which were used for daylight training and as cover for the secret operations of the F-117 force in its early days. When the 4451st TS became the 416th TFS it acquired F-117s. *Raven Beauty* was a Desert Storm veteran, having performed 30 missions while assigned to the 416th TFS.

Mark Styling

Lockheed F-117A
415th Fighter Squadron
37th Fighter Wing
Tonopah Test Range, Nevada

This F-117 wears the markings of the 37th Fighter Wing, and is depicted how it appeared between 1 October 1991 (when the 37th dropped the 'Tactical' from its unit designation), and 5 July 1992 when the wing renumbered as the 49th Fighter Wing. F-117s which participated in Desert Storm all received individual artwork and a name applied to the bomb bay door. This aircraft was *Mad Max*, a veteran of 33 combat missions during the conflict. On the cockpit rail the aircraft carries the name of Squadron Leader Graham Wardell, the first RAF exchange officer to join the F-117 wing. Although he had left the unit by the time the aircraft was deployed to Khamis Mushayt for the looming war with Iraq, the aircraft continued to bear his name on the cockpit rail throughout the conflict, and for some time after.

111

F-117: The Black Jet

Above: The bomb bay trapeze can be used to mount a standard baggage pod in which the pilot can carry personal effects during overnight deployments.

Below: Operating the F-117 exclusively at night leads to spacial disorientation problems. A PAARS system was installed to provide the pilot with an immediate 'straight and level' recovery function.

gaps between radar stations, in what would normally be a continuous belt of radar coverage. However, the F-117's stealthiness depends on a number of factors, including the frequency of the radar 'looking' for the aircraft and its aspect in relation to the radar. Informed sources agree that the aircraft enjoys its lowest RCS only at relatively shallow slant angles. In contrast, when it banks steeply, its belly can present a relatively large radar target.

There are suggestions that one of the mission planning system's primary purposes is to tailor turns and angles of bank to minimise such exposure to known radar sites. It seems likely that an opponent could work out where an F-117 might route between two air defence radars (where their normal coverage would intersect, but where an F-117

is within their reduced radar range). If a mobile SAM and radar were deployed to plug the gap, the chances of interception would increase dramatically. Some believe the F-117 lost during Operation Allied Force over Serbia was shot down after making too steep a turn, or after the Serbs had deployed just such a gap-filling radar.

Maintaining the integrity of the RAM-covered surface is crucial, and radio aerials have to be retracted to ensure safe passage through enemy airspace. Any surface damage can increase the type's RCS several-fold. Not surprisingly, maintenance of the RAM surface imposes a heavy servicing burden, and accounts for much of the aircraft's very high maintenance man-hours per flying hour (MMH/FH) ratio. At the time the F-117 entered service, the F-15A required 32.3 MMH/FH and the F-16A came in at 19.2 MMH/FH, whereas the Stealth Fighter needed an average of 150 MMH/FH. This situation continued throughout most of the 1980s and the aircraft still required 45 MMH/FH during operations in 1990. The reason was simple. Every time access was required to service the aircraft, maintenance or repair specialists (known as

'Martians') had to strip off the RAM skin and then re-apply and recheck it once the work was completed.

When the F-117 drops its bombs, the bomb bay doors bang open and then shut again very rapidly because they significantly increase the detectability of the aircraft when open. Concern has even been expressed that rain on the special RAM coating may dramatically increase its reflectivity, and that the aircraft may be more visible to look-down or bistatic radar. The latter is a radar system with separate transmitter and receiver antennas, between which the target flies.

Little can be done to further disperse the F-117's exhaust plume, and this may well be visible to some types of radar. Interestingly, the stealthy SR-71 Blackbird was reported to be an easy target for ATC radar at supersonic speeds thanks to the shock diamonds in its exhaust plumes. Great efforts have been made to reduce the F-117's infrared signature (IRS) but, at night, a glow is visible from the exhausts above and behind the aircraft. It is hard to imagine this would not present a good enough target for a nearby IRS tracking system and IR-homing missiles.

By the time the F-117 entered service, the limitations of the Paveway II LGB, with its 'bang-bang', full-up/full-down controls were already apparent. The GBU-24 Paveway III was developed for the USAF under a 'semi-black' programme and aimed to produce a more accurate weapon with proportional guidance to allow steeper trajectories, better penetration and longer range. Inevitably, the secretive Paveway III and F-117 teams did not know

what the other was doing and, when the GBU-24 emerged, it was too big to fit in the weapons bay. The GBU-XX was drawn up as an emergency solution, combining a Paveway III guidance system with the smaller Paveway II tail and a BLU-109 penetrator instead of a standard Mk 84 bomb body. This weapon was redesignated the GBU-27, and became the weapon of choice for the F-117. Drop tests began in 1986. During Operation Desert Storm, the F-117 also made use of 500-lb (227-kg) LGBs.

Evolution of the F-117

Many details surrounding operation of the F-117 remain shrouded in secrecy, as do some of the modifications made to the type. Details about some of the programmes are sketchy, even contradictory. Accordingly, the list of upgrade programmes previously discussed and presented below is not necessarily complete or comprehensive.

OCIP I – WSCS (Weapons System Computational Subsystem): Integration of the new GBU-27 was the most important element of the F-117's WSCS upgrade. It marked the first phase of the OCIP modification and was authorised on 1 April 1984. Deliveries of WSCS-modified aircraft took place between November 1987 and June 1992. The WSCS upgrade brought replacement of the original three Delco M362F mission computers (also fitted to the F-16) with a single AP-102, a re-packaged version of the computer used on NASA's space shuttle.

OCIP II: Under the second phase of OCIP, the F-117

gained a new cockpit layout. The original centrally mounted FLIR/DLIR display screen was replaced by a Harris Corporation digital moving-map display, with IR imagery now displayed on one of the two new Honeywell colour multi-function LCD screens. These replaced the original monochrome Texas Instruments MFDs on the left- and right-hand sides of the main panel. OCIP II also introduced a four-dimensional flight management system, adding an autothrottle (automatic control of the throttle to meet planned times) as well as an autopilot. The first test flight of an OCIP II aircraft was conducted on 1 December 1988 in aircraft 831, which was bailed back from the Air Force. The first modification kit was installed in April 1990, and modification of the last aircraft was completed on 8 March 1995.

OCIP III (RNIP/RNIP+): Despite the accuracy of its INS, the F-117 was extremely weather-dependent. With no ability to use ground-mapping radar or terrain-reference navigation systems, the F-117 relied on clear skies for precision navigation to its initial point (IP) and target. The main feature of the OCIP III programme thus lay in the replacement of the specially selected and calibrated B-52 Honeywell SPN-GEANS INS. Under this RNIP (Ring laser gyro Navigation Improvement Program), the original INS was replaced by a new Honeywell H-423/E laser INS. Although accurate, the SPN-GEANS took more than 40 minutes to align and was becoming increasingly difficult to support in service, whereas the new INS aligned rapidly, was more accurate and offered a much improved mean time between failures (MTBF). Subsequent integration of a Rockwell-Collins GPS with low-observable antennas brought a programme redesignation from RNIP to RNIP+, that saw further improvement in navigational accuracy and a weapons system computer upgrade.

Even before the integration of RNIP/RNIP+, the type was probably the most accurate LGB delivery platform in the inventory, regularly demonstrating a 93-98 per cent direct-hit rate in exercises. Time-on-target competitions within front-line squadrons regularly had to be decided by counting individual frames of film, since most competitors hit their targets to the second. Further improvements in accuracy were partly driven by the increased importance of avoiding collateral damage.

MIPS/MLU: A far-reaching and comprehensive mid-life upgrade for the F-117A was formally studied under the MIPS (Mid-life Improvement Study) launched in early 1995. This was to investigate further signature reduction measures (though these were trimmed from the study in the 1996 budget), together with the integration of new weapons. The F-117's much touted success in Operation Desert Storm has tended to obscure its relative lack of versatility and has also camouflaged the occasional ineffectiveness of LGBs. The F-117's hit rate from bombs actually dropped (rather than from all bombs taken into the air, including those brought home due to poor weather over the target) was initially assessed at more than 80 per cent. Even this figure compared poorly with the 90-95 per cent hit rate achieved by RAF Jaguars and Harriers over Bosnia in 1995.

The USAF's original Gulf War claims for the Stealth Fighter now seem to represent a somewhat overgenerous assessment of its success. A subsequent General Accounting Office report (that included 'no-drops') revised the estimate of hits to between 41 percent and 60 percent. Initial claims of 'one-target/one-bomb' effectiveness for LGBs was also called into question. During Desert Storm, an average of 44

tons of unguided bombs was dropped on each target destroyed, and 11 tons of PGMs. However, this was due more to the inherent limitations of LGBs than to the F-117's shortcomings.

The MIPS looked closely at integrating weapons with GPS guidance (including JDAM and JSOW) via a MIL STD-1760 digital data bus. This was a measure also proposed for the stillborn A/F-117X, one of the 'Super Stealth Fighter' projects drawn up by the Skunk Works during the 1990s. Some sources suggest that other features from these variants (including a transparent F-22-type cockpit canopy) were examined under MIPS. The MIL STD-1760 data bus was actually installed in F-117s from September 1994 onwards, and development was completed by the end of that decade. A smart weapons-integration contract was awarded to the Skunk Works in September 1998, for full integration of the JDAM and WMCD.

IADS (Integrated Acquisition and Designation System): The Stealth Fighter's original IRADS targeting system was completely reliant on clear weather, and the aircraft was subject to a high abort/DNCO rate in anything but perfect 'gin-clear' conditions. IRADS itself was the subject of a Block 1 modification (replacement of circuit boards, provision of heavier stops and the re-routing of electrical wiring) between 1986 and 1988, plus an F3 turret modification that commenced in 1993. The original FLIR and DLIR sensors were replaced by new Texas Instruments thermal imaging sensors. The F3 turret was first flown on 14 August 1992, and flight-testing was completed on 12 February of the following year. Production turrets were retrofitted between 1 October 1994 and October 1996.

Further modification followed. The second-generation

Raytheon Systems Company IADS incorporates a new video tracker and system controller in the existing F3 turret. This allows more accurate 'painting' of the target. The IADS integrates an imaging IR sensor into the system, providing high-quality imagery that can be transmitted to other aircraft or stations on the ground using a low-probability-of-intercept, encrypted datalink. This does not compromise stealth characteristics. A $10 million contract for 50 sets (43 new production units and seven refurbished development sets) was placed by the USAF Aeronautical

*Three F-117s prepare to launch on an **Operation Southern Watch** mission from Ahmed al-Jaber air base in Kuwait. At the end of the Gulf War the F-117 remained deployed in the region until 1994, although it returned again in 1996 for a series of deployments which culminated in 12 aircraft being based in Kuwait for most of 1998.*

*An 8th Fighter Squadron F-117 taxis from its 'barn' at Ahmed al-Jaber at the start of a mission over southern Iraq. Aircraft deployed to Southern Watch operations had the new **F3 IRADS** turret fitted with new infra-red sensors. They also used a rapid targeting system which aided mission planning by drawing in imagery and intelligence from the USAF's varied ISR (intelli...*

F-117: The Black Jet

Systems Center at Wright-Patterson AFB in September 1998, and installation began in December 1999.

MPS: The F-117's original Mission Planning System (MPS) lay at the very heart of the aircraft's success. Taking account of enemy radar characteristics, the mission planner worked out the best route through enemy defences and the best bank angles at particular turn points. When linked to the autopilot, the flight plan produced by the MPS allowed the entire mission to be flown 'hands off', enabling the pilot to concentrate on monitoring the system and acquiring and designating targets. A new GDE Systems MPS that began development in 1993 and evaluation in

1997 allows the F-117 planning system to interface with the AFMSS (Air Force Mission Support System), which is used USAF-wide. From 1998 onwards, an early version of the Air Force's rapid-targeting system was made available to the F-117 community, initially for operations over southern Iraq. The ground-based computer system makes use of NRO KH-series and Lacrosse-series satellite imagery, together with radar and photographic images collected by U-2s, Joint STARS, F-14 TARPS and/or unmanned aerial vehicles (UAVs). This enables rapid preparation of a target intelligence package that correlates all of the data (new, archived and real-time) to improve accuracy. The system incorporates a terrain-elevation database and can host a terrain-reference navigation system.

IRRCA (Integrated Real-Time Information into the Cockpit/Real-Time Information out of the Cockpit for Combat Aircraft): Great efforts were made during the 1990s to get more information into the cockpits of all tactical aircraft. It was becoming increasingly vital to obtain real-time information on targets, weather and threats to allow pilots to replan and retarget in what could be a rapidly changing environment. Growing use of the JTIDS was paralleled by that of less-expensive datalink systems, including an improved data modem (IDM) on aircraft like the F-16. The F-117 benefited from the IRRCA, which began in December 1997. In the first phase, which ended on 30 June 1998, real-time information was datalinked to an F-117 in flight. The second phase saw information down-linked from the type's cockpit.

Traditionally, the F-117 retracted its communications antennas to reduce its RCS before venturing over enemy airspace, and remained out of touch until the antennas were re-extended when the aircraft returned to friendly skies. Up-to-date intelligence about threats and instructions to attack a different target cannot be passed to the F-117 once it leaves friendly airspace. In effect, the limitation makes it the equivalent of a manned cruise missile. The new system is designed to allow new, updated or revised threat information (including new target photos, text messages or even video) to be transmitted to the F-117 in flight, which can be used to generate a new flight plan on board the aircraft. A new real-time, symmetric multiprocessor (handling 1.2 billion instructions per second) can produce a flight plan far more quickly than the ground-based planning system. The pilot is presented with a revised flight plan (if necessary) to avoid the threat, complete with new fuel calculations and timings. The pilot is able to accept or reject this at the touch of a button. If

A 9th Fighter Squadron F-117 is seen arriving at Aviano on 22 February at the end of the deployment from Holloman. For the next month the F-117 force prepared for the assault on Yugoslavia, in which it would take the lead alongside cruise missile-armed B-52s and B-2s flying direct from the US. On the fourth night of the war the Aviano wing lost an F-117 to an SA-3 missile. In the aftermath of this event there was considerable debate as to the reasons why an elderly 'single-digit' missile system could shoot down a stealth fighter.

accepted, the new flight plan is flown automatically.

This highly advanced and automated system allows new target details to be transmitted to the pilot in flight, together with reconnaissance imagery and new intelligence reports. IRRCA uses a secure, encrypted data link and makes use of low-observable antennas and satellite communications. The system also includes a new LCD multi-function display that shows moving-map and FLIR/IADS images, as well as display messages. However, no decision to equip the front-line F-117 force with IRRCA has yet been taken.

SCFP: The plethora of upgrades undertaken over the years, together with improvements and changes made during the course of F-117 production, left the USAF with a fleet of aircraft in many different configurations. There were at least five variations in wing leading-edge design, while 33 aircraft were covered in sheet-applied RAM whereas the rest were sprayed with RAM in liquid form. In 1980, Lockheed began experimenting with sprayed RAM but did not use it on major portions of production aircraft until 1985. Interestingly, the original F-117 RAM was once said to add 2,000 lb (907-kg) to the aircraft's empty weight, weighing in at 1 lb per square foot. The new coating is much lighter, at 0.13 lb per square foot.

As particular subsystems were replaced or modified, and as aircraft cycled through the OCIP, the situation became more extreme and, by the late 1990s, the joke was that no two F-117s were the same. It would be easy to over-emphasise the problems caused by what are relatively minor differences in configuration, and it should be remembered that the aircraft in service are still the basic variant. However, some of the differences have had an impact on maintenance and operations. The aircraft's original steel brakes have been replaced with carbon brakes (and F-15E main wheels), but both brake types were in use for some time. Before a mission, pilots had to check which brakes were fitted to their aircraft in order to work out minimum stopping and landing distances.

The Skunk Works took over responsibility for logistics support of the F-117 on 1 October 1998, under the $1.8-billion Total System Performance Responsibility Program. Under this umbrella, the SCFP (Single-Configuration Fleet Improvement Program, originally known as the RAM recoating programme and running from FY2/99 to FY5/04), saw F-117s receive the same, more durable, spray-coated and quick-curing RAM coating, and new 'zip

Ground crew at Aviano manoeuvre a GBU-27 bomb underneath an F-117. The weapon has been the F-117's primary store since Desert Storm. Only recently has a new weapon become available – the EGBU-27 which adds GPS guidance to the laser package. The addition of GPS guidance is possible thanks to the adoption of a Mil Std 1760 weapons interface as part of the MIPS upgrade.

strips' over removable panels. The new RAM cut maintenance costs by an astonishing 65 percent and reduced the number of RAM products on each aircraft by 30 percent. The aircraft have also gained a common, leading-edge configuration, as well as common avionics.

Structural modifications

Besides the changes incorporated under the many updates, some significant structural changes have been made. Wing-root modifications were incorporated from the 24th aircraft and were subsequently retrofitted to all earlier F-117s. In 1983, Stealth Fighter number 780 was fitted with an outboard leading-edge extension (incorporating a dogtooth discontinuity at about half-span) in an effort to improve low-speed handling and reduce landing speeds. It proved successful but the cost of embodying it into production aircraft was considered to be uneconomic. Aircraft number 781 lost one of its tail fins in flight on 25 September 1985, but landed safely after the incident. The cause was flutter and a programme was instituted to design a stronger unit. A new, graphite-thermoplastic-composite tail fin was authorised in August 1986 and was flown (on 784) on 18 July 1989. It was incorporated on the production line and, by 1992, retrofitted to all earlier aircraft. New composite bomb bay doors were also added to allow simultaneous drops of two weapons. This had been impossible with the original doors. Furthermore, life-limited skin panels were replaced and

webs were retrofitted in a programme scheduled to run from FY02/99 to FY02/04.

Reports suggest the F-117 fleet began receiving a new low-observable UHF communications suite utilising stealthy antennas, with RDT&E starting in Fiscal Year 2000. In 1997, the Skunk Works received a contract for an ozone-depleting chemical modification, aimed at replacing ozone-attacking Halon in the tank-pressurisation system with a more environmentally friendly inert gas. There is some doubt as to whether the modification was carried out and a suggestion that some of the funds originally allocated were used for smart weapons integration instead.

Operation Southern Watch

Alongside the ongoing upgrade programmes, there were operational commitments to maintain. Not all the F-117s returned home from Desert Storm, a small detachment being maintained in Saudi Arabia as a deterrent to any further Iraqi aggression in support of the UN policing operation over the northern and southern 'No-fly' zones. These missions were eventually formalised as Operations Northern Watch (ONW) and Southern Watch (OSW).

In December 1992/January 1993 – in the last days of the Bush (Sr) administration – Iraq mounted a series of challenges to UN flights, including the movement into sensitive areas of SAM systems, and increased fighter activity. In response, US, French and UK warplanes mounted a retaliatory strike against air defence installations on 13 January. Six F-117s were first into the fray, although their results were less than spectacular, with only two targets reportedly being hit. The raid highlighted the type's problems when operating in cloudy conditions: two aircraft lost laser lock-on in the attack, one pilot did not drop as he could not see the target, and one hit the wrong target.

On 21 January President Bill Clinton took office, and an uneasy truce returned to the area. The Khamis Mushayt detachment, initially numbering 12 aircraft, was reduced to six, and they finally returned home in January 1994. In October, however, Saddam Hussein moved thousands of troops up near the Kuwaiti border. The US response was dubbed Operation Vigilant Warrior, and 12 F-117s were notified for deployment.

Further belligerence on the part of the Iraqi regime resulted in a series of Stealth Fighter deployments to Ahmed al-Jaber Air Base in southern Kuwait beginning in 1996. In mid-November 1997, the 8th FS took six Nighthawks to the base, even though the aircraft were still undergoing the RNIP upgrade at the time. The aircraft were moved there as part of a large expeditionary force composed of several strike and support types. On 15 February, the 49th sent six more F-117s to Kuwait as diplomatic discussions were under way between UN and Iraqi officials.

While a decision was made not to move any additional equipment to the theatre as the talks continued, the 9th FS ultimately relieved the 8th FS and began flying its sister unit's aircraft. Some 230 ground personnel were present to support the flight crews, who engaged in intensive training within Kuwait's air space and remained on a war footing throughout. Such missions were typically of short duration but sufficient to practice weapon delivery techniques. They enabled pilots to fly often. In what was essentially a shared deployment between the two squadrons, part of what was called Operation Desert Thunder, a total of 1,239 Stealth Fighter missions was flown at an average 86 percent MCR (mission-capable rate). During April 1998, the 9th FS set a record for the number of missions flown in a single night. Between sunset and sunrise, the unit completed a 36-sortie surge using 11 F-117s (the twelfth was in for maintenance).

Operation Allied Force

Throughout the 1990s Iraq remained a major thorn in the side of the US, but as the decade progressed the world's focus shifted more and more to the war-torn Balkans region, where the federation of Yugoslavia was wrenching itself apart in a series of increasingly bloody civil wars, largely fought along ethnic lines. Although the USAF had been involved in limited operations over Bosnia and Herzegovina, the F-117 had not been employed. By the end of 1998 attention was firmly fixed upon the Serbian province of Kosovo, where the majority ethnic Albanian population was involved in a civil war with Serbian troops

and special police. NATO called for those forces to withdraw, and began the build-up of a sizeable force to back up its demands. Among the aircraft were 12 F-117As from the 49th FW, which arrived at Aviano Air Base in Italy on 22 February 1999.

When the alliance's ultimatum went unheeded, a full-scale aerial attack was unleashed, targeting both local targets in Kosovo, and strategic targets throughout Serbia and Montenegro. The attack began on the night of 24/25 March, and F-117s spearheaded the attacks alongside two B-2s and cruise missile-carrying B-52s. No details were released about targets, although the F-117s are thought to have tackled those in and around Belgrade, using their stealth properties to penetrate air defences that were at least as capable as those around Baghdad. In fact, Yugoslav air defence experts had reportedly worked closely with their Iraqi counterparts, and had been involved in rebuilding Iraq's air defence system.

On the evening of 27 March Serbian TV announced that its air defences had shot down a NATO aircraft. Footage of burning wreckage in a field was unmistakeably that of an F-117, several parts − including the canopy − having survived relatively intact. The unthinkable had happened − a Stealth Fighter had been shot down!

Rumour and counter-rumour abounded in the ensuing days and weeks, with claims to the cause ranging from mechanical failure to being shot down by a MiG-29. In the event, it was ascertained that the aircraft (82-806) had been downed on the night of 26/27 March by a Neva-M (SA-3) SAM launched by the 3rd battalion of the 250.rbr PVO. The pilot ejected safely and was picked up uninjured by a major Combat SAR operation. The aircraft came to earth near the village of Budjanovci in the Srem region. It had been following a similar route to the two previous nights, and it is likely that the Serb defenders were ready for it. A lack of jamming of certain radars by EA-6B Prowlers was also postulated as a contributory factor.

As the Allied Force campaign broadened, another 13 F-117s were flown out from Holloman on 4 April, 12 of which were deployed to Spangdahlem AB in Germany, and one continued to Aviano as a replacement for the aircraft which had been shot down. On 14 April the 52nd Air Expeditionary Wing was established at the German base, and the Aviano-based F-117s moved in to create a 24-aircraft force. On 9/10 April various agencies reported that a damaged F-117 had to make an emergency landing at Zagreb in Croatia, although this cannot be confirmed. On 1 May another F-117 was allegedly hit and heavily damaged, but managed to land back at Spangdahlem. Attacks against strategic targets continued throughout May − on the 25th an F-117 dropped GBU-27s against a hardened bunker supposedly used by Serbian President Slobodan Milosevic. By early June negotiations for the withdrawal of Serbian forces from Kosovo were under way, and on 11 June NATO troops entered the troubled province. Operation Allied Force had ended, and the F-117s returned home.

Operation Iraqi Freedom

Although it played no part in Operation Enduring Freedom (Afghanistan), the F-117 was to the fore in the US's next military adventure. Having endured 12 years of brinkmanship and belligerence from Saddam Hussein and his repressive regime, the US and UK elected to take action in 2003 by launching Operation Iraqi Freedom (OIF). With the initially stated aim of finding and destroying Iraq's alleged stock of nuclear/chemical/biological weapons, OIF broadened into a major regime-change campaign.

F-117s were deployed for OIF to Al Udeid air base in Qatar, close to the US Central Command headquarters. Here the 8th Expeditionary Fighter Squadron formed part of the larger 379th Aerospace Expeditionary Wing,

alongside F-15Es and F-16s. Al Udeid also hosted RAF Tornados and RAAF Hornets.

'A-Day' - the first day of the Iraqi Freedom air campaign - was planned for the night of 21 March 2003. However, intelligence reports suggested that the Iraqi leadership, including Saddam Hussein, was in a bunker in the Baghdad vicinity and that a quick 'decapitation' mission might catch him. Killing Hussein and his cronies might effectively end the war before it had started, and was too good an opportunity to miss. The attack would be carried out by two F-117s, with support provided by nearly 40 TLAMs fired from other aircraft, naval ships and submarines.

On the evening of 19 March two F-117s, crewed by Lt Col David Toomey and Major Mark Hoehn launched from Al Udeid, having had around two hours' notice of the attack. Many of the detailed plans were forged in the air, a task made more difficult when Hoehn's aircraft suffered a malfunction which hampered communications. Facing more than 50 SAM sites and 200 AAA emplacements, the pair hit their targets to the second, dropping EGBU-27 bombs into a field, beneath which was the bunker. For this mission both pilots were awarded the Distinguished Flying Cross by Lt Gen. T. Michael Moseley, commander of the air component during OIF.

This mission represented the first use of the EGBU-27 (or Enhanced Paveway III weapon). This takes the standard laser-guided GBU-27 and integrates a GPS guidance package, similar to that of the JDAM. The result is a bomb which can be guided very accurately by laser in good weather, but if the laser lock is lost or the target is obscured, can still be dropped with a high degree of accuracy using GPS signals. The weapon can switch from laser to GPS guidance in mid-trajectory. The combined use of laser (primary) and GPS (back-up) guidance is a major factor in reducing collateral damage, itself a key driver of the OIF air campaign.

During the campaign the F-117 dropped 98 EGBU-27s and a further 11 non-GPS GBU-27s in the course of 80+

An F-117 taxis in at Spangdahlem at the end of its deployment flight from the US. The second batch comprised aircraft 786, 794, 799, 809, 810, 818, 819, 821, 824, 826, 832, 842 and 843. One of these aircraft flew on to Aviano to restore the number of F-117s there to 12 following the shootdown.

Within 10 days of arriving at Spangdahlem, the F-117 force was operating under the administration of the newly formed 52nd Aerospace Expeditionary Wing. The first batch of aircraft moved from Aviano to Spangdahlem, not only to consolidate the F-117s at one base, and so ease logistics and maintenance, but also to free up airspace at Aviano, which had become very busy with the high tempo of war operations. As well as the F-117s, the 52nd AEW controlled the operations of the F-16CJ SEAD aircraft from the 22nd Fighter Squadron, to whom Spangdahlem was already home base (the 'peacetime' 52nd Wing's other squadrons were operating from Aviano).

Right: An F-117 from the 8th Fighter Squadron 'Black Sheep' lands back at Al Udeid air base in Qatar after having undertaken the first aerial mission of Iraqi Freedom on the night of 19/20 March 2003. During its time in Qatar the squadron assumed the identity of 8th Expeditionary Fighter Squadron.

Another view shows the 842 rolling out on the Al Udeid runway after its famous first-night mission. Two days away from the pre-planned 'A-day', Central Command received what it thought was reliable intelligence as to the exact whereabouts of Saddam Hussein. The intelligence was very time-critical, requiring an immediate reaction. Two F-117s were launched at short notice, supported by a defence suppression force and around 40 Tomahawk missile launches.

The 8th EFS was part of the 379th AEW at Al Udeid. Here a mission-marked F-117 taxis to the runway, followed by bombed-up F-15Es.

missions. The 12 aircraft recorded a mission-capable rate of 89.3 per cent. The force began to return home on 14 April, the first aircraft arriving back at Holloman on the 18th.

Advanced variant studies

Although the F-117 entered USAF service only in its basic form, Lockheed did produce studies for several advanced derivatives:

RF-117A: This little-known proposed conversion of the baseline F-117 was conceived for reconnaissance missions, and there were to be two configuration choices. Although some strike capability was to be retained, the first option included a bomb bay-mounted pallet with a sideways-looking EO sensor in a ventral canoe. The price apparently quoted for 24 such recce kits was $213 million. The second proposal envisaged an integral recce suite with an IRLS, a small EO camera and a datalink, and would have allowed the aircraft to retain full attack capability. At an estimated cost of $520 million, a 1992 proposal would have added 24 RF-117As to production.

F-117A+: Lockheed proposed to the USAF an ambitious upgrade with enhanced low observables, and the aircraft was to be fitted with the same undercarriage as the F-15

Eagle and an F414 engine with afterburning. The prototype conversion was projected to cost $79 million.

F-117B: The first Stealth Fighter to be designated the F-117B was conceived as a late-production configuration when the 89-aircraft fleet was seriously proposed. The aircraft was to be fitted with a GPS and LPI radar, and have AGM-88 HARM compatibility. It was to be based on the standard F-117-type airframe.

F-117B/YF-117B: The F-117B designation was subsequently applied to an aircraft with an enlarged weapons bay and an increased span of 64 ft 11 in, as well as a reduced-sweep (42° or 48°) wing and reduced-sweep V-tails. The latter were to be augmented by conventional slab tailerons.

F-117B: A subsequent F-117B variant was proposed that combined features of the F-117A+ (enhanced LO, an F-15-type undercarriage and an afterburning F414 engine) and those of the YF-117B. This aircraft would have featured a 73,260-lb (33,230-kg) MTOW, and an 8,000-lb (3,629-kg) payload comprising four 2,000-lb LGBs. It was to have had a 1,000-nm unrefuelled radius.

'F-117C': The F-117A version proposed to Britain's Royal Air Force has been referred to as the F-117C, though this designation may be erroneous. It was to be a baseline F-117, possibly fitted with un-gridded Stealth Bomber-type intakes, a clear-view canopy, British avionics, F414 or EJ200 engines, plus a number of BAe structural components or sub-assemblies. Confusingly, the proposal was also referred to as the F-117A+ and F-117B.

F-117N: This original proposal to the US Navy was for little more than an F-117 with an off-the-shelf automatic carrier landing system (ACLS) and some limited corrosion proofing. The proposal was superseded by the F-117X.

F-117N (II): Based on the YF-117B/F-117B, this variant was to have a 65,700-lb (29,801-kg) MTOW and be equipped with powered wing-folding, an arrester hook, an off-the-shelf F-14 Tomcat main undercarriage and, probably, an F/A-18-type nose gear. This proposal was also replaced by the F-117X concept, which was rejected in mid-1993 in favour of the A/F-117X.

F-117X Sea Hawk: The F-117X designation covered the proposed conversion of a single F-117 intended to serve as a technology demonstrator and naval/carrier-borne proof-of-concept aircraft for low-speed handling trials and simulated carrier landings. Lockheed hoped for a 255-aircraft order at a unit price of $70 million. The EMD cost was estimated at $3.1 billion. The idea was dropped in favour of the F-117N (II) concept.

A/F-117X: A derivative of and replacement for the F-117N, this proposed variant was submitted as a potential alternative to the joint advanced strike technology (JAST) aircraft. It was to be fitted with an afterburning F414 engine, LPI multi-mode (air-to-air and air-to-ground) radar, have AIM-120 AMRAAM compatibility, expanded bomb bays (10,000-lb internal bomb load), provision for an 8,000-lb external bomb load (for end-of-war missions after an enemy's air defences had been degraded) and three-section spoilers forward of the trailing-edge flaps. The A/F-117X was proposed for a 'silver bullet'-type strike force to augment F/A-18E/F Hornets. Lockheed hoped for procurement of between 40 and 75 aircraft.

F-117 future

None of these proposals was taken up, many of them being superseded by the Joint Strike Fighter programme. In the meantime, with no radar and the need to avoid electromagnetic emissions, the F-117 remains limited in the kind of ordnance it can deliver. Various reports attributed an anti-radiation capability to the type, although at first glance it would appear that the wings of the AGM-88 HARM missile are too large to fit into the weapons bay. It is possible that a 'compressed-carriage' variant has been developed, although there is no evidence to support this.

The F-117 is further limited by its uniquely faceted airframe, which imposes a considerable drag penalty, and a very high specific fuel consumption. This has resulted in modest payload/range and performance characteristics. Indeed, range and radius-of-action figures are significantly smaller than most estimates in unclassified documents. To a far greater extent than comparable tactical fighter platforms, the F-117 is reliant on inflight refuelling tanker support. It seems unlikely that these characteristics can be significantly improved through possible re-engining or upgrades.

Despite these disadvantages, the F-117 remains an extremely useful asset, especially for precision attacks against heavily defended targets. It is of particular value if it is able to follow unpredictable routings to the target and when prevailing weather conditions are LGB/IRADS-friendly. Production of the F-117 is long over and the USAF is unlikely to relinquish any of its small fleet while the aircraft have life remaining or until improved technology renders them obsolete. While they remain operational, however, the aircraft are likely to continue the programme of modifications and upgrades. These will aim to keep the Stealth Fighter a step ahead of enemy defences and improve its navigational and weapons delivery accuracy, efficiency and versatility.

In the long term, the USAF's roadmap envisages a new, stealthy attacker to replace both the F-117 and the F-15E.

Lockheed Martin has proposed an FB-22 version of the F/A-22 Raptor to meet this requirement. The FB-22 is stealthy, and offers long range - addressing one of the main problems of the F-117. However, a decision on this programme is not expected for some time and, in any case, the USAF may decide that a mix of JDAM-armed F/A-22s, F-35 JSFs, B-2s and proposed UCAVs is sufficient to meet its stealthy attack requirements in the future.

Robert F. Dorr, Jon Lake and David Donald

Above: An F-117 establishes a pre-contact position behind a tanker. On the cockpit rail are six mission marks for operations over Iraq. The 12 aircraft flew over 80 missions during the Iraqi Freedom campaign.

The 'homecoming' from Iraq got under way on 14 April with the dispatch of six aircraft from Al Udeid. They flew to Langley AFB, Virginia, where an aircraft is seen arriving far left. Above the pilots receive a warm welcome from personnel at Langley, which is the headquarters of Air Combat Command. Two days later, on 16 April, the F-117s and their pilots returned to their home base at Holloman, to be reunited with friends and families. This 'Black Sheep' aircraft (left) wears 16 mission markings.

Individual Aircraft Details

The following table lists the complete XST/F-117 production run. Details of aircraft which participated in Desert Storm accompany the bomb bay door artwork.

XST-1 HB 1001 Ff 1 December 1977 (Bill Park). Crashed 4 May 1978 (Bill Park), W/O.

XST-2 HB 1002 Have Blue LO test aircraft. Ff 20 July 1978 (Lt Col Ken Dyson). Crashed July 1979 (Lt Col Ken Dyson), W/O.

79-10780 'Scorpion 1', full-scale development (FSD) aircraft. First flight 18 June 1981, Hal Farley. Listed by one source as YF-117A. Lost a tail fin during a side slip in 1987 but landed safely. Now preserved on display at Nellis AFB, Nevada.

79-10781 'Scorpion 2' FSD aircraft. First flight 18 December 1981. Listed one source as YF-117A. Now preserved on display at US Air Force Museum, Dayton, Ohio.

79-10782 'Scorpion 3' FSD aircraft. Listed by one source as YF-117A. First WSCS upgrade test aircraft. Considered as first OCIP upgrade test aircraft but rejected (in favour of 85-0831) because of expected delay in modification. 410th TS/412th TW Palmdale, 'ED' tailcode.

79-10783 'Scorpion 4' FSD aircraft. Listed by one source as YF-117A. Nicknamed 'Pete's Dragon' at Groom Lake. 410th TS/412th TW Palmdale, 'ED' tailcode.

79-10784 'Scorpion 5' FSD aircraft. Second WSCS upgrade test aircraft. Displayed for Secretary of Defense Caspar Weinberger during a secret visit to Groom Lake in 1984. Listed by one source as YF-117A. 410th TS/412th TW Palmdale, 'ED' tailcode.

—— Crashed 20 April 1982 prior to US Air Force acceptance (Robert L. Riedenauer), W/O; not assigned a serial.

79-10785 Possibly 79-0785

80-0786 Second operational aircraft delivered; used initially for weapons tests until reaching 4450th TG in September 1982. Desert Storm.

80-0787 First aircraft delivered to 4450th TG, 23 August 1982.

80-0788

80-0789 Desert Storm.

80-0790 Delivered to 4450th TG in Tonopah in December 1982 after trials at Groom Lake. Used for public unveiling ceremony at Nellis AFB, April 1990. Desert Storm. Suffered the most 'serious' damage of the Gulf War when it blew a nose wheel on landing.

80-0791 Delivered to 4450th TG in Tonopah in December 1982 after trials at Groom Lake. Desert Storm.

81-10792 Delivered to 4450th TG in Tonopah in December 1982 after trials at Groom Lake. Crashed 11 July 1986 (Major Ross E. Mulhare), W/O.

81-10793 Desert Storm.

81-10794 Desert Storm.

81-10795

81-10796 Desert Storm.

81-10797 Desert Storm.

81-10798 Desert Storm.

82-0799 Delivered to 4450th TG on 28 October 1983 enabling the group to attain IOC. Desert Storm.

82-0800

82-0801 Desert Storm.

82-0802 Desert Storm. Crashed 4 August 1992 (Captain John B. Mills, 416th FS), W/O.

82-0803 Desert Storm.

82-0804 Currently assigned to Det. 1/57th Wing at Holloman AFB for operational test and evaluation purposes.

82-0805

82-0806 Desert Storm.

83-0807 Desert Storm.

83-0808

84-0809 Desert Storm.

84-0810 Desert Storm.

84-0811 Desert Storm.

84-0812 Desert Storm.

84-0824

84-0825 Desert Storm.

84-0826 Desert Storm. (Captain Rob Donaldson).

84-0827

84-0828 Used for public unveiling at Nellis, 21 April 1990 marked for Colonel Tony Tolin and carrying '37 TFW' tail markings.

85-0813 Col. Alton C. ('Al') Whitley's wing commander's aircraft during Operation Desert Storm.

85-0814 Desert Storm. (Captain John Savidge).

85-0815 Crashed 14 October 1987 (Major Michael C. Stewart), W/O.

85-0816 Desert Storm.

85-0817 Desert Storm.

85-0818 Desert Storm.

85-0819 Desert Storm.

85-0820

85-0829 Desert Storm.

85-0830 Desert Storm. Made first overseas public display at Paris air show in June 1991. First on public display in the United Kingdom as TR (37th FW) at Mildenhall Air Fete '92.

85-0831 Third aircraft with WSCS upgrade. Chosen as first OCIP upgrade aircraft (and removed from the operational fleet for developmental work). 410th TS/412th TW Palmdale, 'ED' tailcode.

85-0832 Desert Storm.

85-0833 Desert Storm.

85-0834 Desert Storm.

85-0835 Desert Storm.

85-0836 Served as 37th TFW commander's aircraft before being deemed a 'bad actor' or 'hangar queen' at Tonopah. Desert Storm.

86-0821 Desert Storm.

86-0822

86-0823

86-0837 Desert Storm. (Captain Matthew Byrd).

86-0838 Desert Storm. (Lt. Col. Gregory ('Greg') Gonyea).

86-0839 Desert Storm. (Major Joe Salada).

86-0840 Desert Storm.

88-0841 Desert Storm.

88-0842 Desert Storm. (Captain Rich Cline).

88-0843 Delivered 12 July 1990. Final F-117 aircraft. Desert Storm.

Aircraft #786 – 'War Pig'
24 combat missions – 416th TFS

Aircraft #789 – 'Black Magic'
31 combat missions – 415th TFS

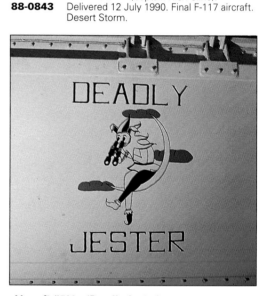

Aircraft #790 – 'Deadly Jester'
30 combat missions – 415th TFS

Aircraft #791 – 'Lazy Ace'
33 combat missions – 415th TFS

Aircraft #793 – 'Wiley E. Coyote's Tritonal Express'   33 combat missions

Aircraft #794 – 'Delta Dawn'
35 combat missions – 415th TFS

Aircraft #796 – 'Fatal Attraction'
29 combat missions – 415th TFS

Aircraft #797 – 'Spell Bound'
8 combat missions – 416th TFS

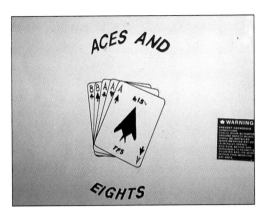

Aircraft #798 – 'Aces and Eights'
34 combat missions – 415th TFS

Aircraft #799 – 'Midnight Rider'
21 combat missions – 416th TFS

Aircraft #801 – 'Perpetrator'
38 combat missions – 415th TFS

Aircraft #802 – 'Black Magic'
19 combat missions – 416th TFS

Aircraft #803 – Unexpected Guest'
33 combat missions – 416th TFS

Aircraft #806 – 'Something Wicked'
39 combat missions – 415th TFS

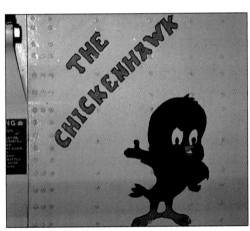

Aircraft #807 – 'The Chickenhawk'
14 combat missions – 415th TFS

Aircraft #808 – 'Thor'
37 combat missions – 415th TFS

Aircraft #810 – 'Dark Angel'
26 combat missions – 416th TFS

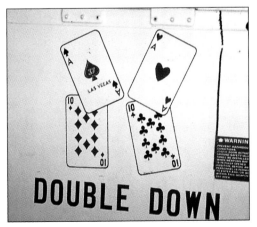

Aircraft #811 – 'Double Down'
33 combat missions – 415th TFS

Aircraft #812 – 'Axel'
42 combat missions – 415th TFS

Aircraft #813 – 'Toxic Avenger'
35 combat missions – 416th TFS

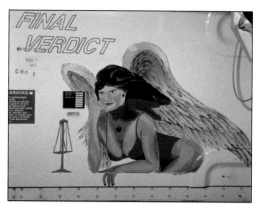

Aircraft #814 – 'Final Verdict'
34 combat missions – 416th TFS

Aircraft #816 – 'Lone Wolf'
39 combat missions – 415th TFS

Aircraft #817 – 'Shaba'
18 combat missions – 416th TFS

Aircraft #818 – 'The Overachiever'
38 combat missions – 415th TFS

Aircraft #819 – 'Raven Beauty'
30 combat missions – 416th TFS

Aircraft #821 – 'Sneak Attack'
32 combat missions – 415th TFS

Aircraft #825 – 'Mad Max'
33 combat missions – 415th TFS

Aircraft #826 – 'Nachtfalke'
29 combat missions – 415th TFS

Aircraft #829 – 'Avenging Angel'
23 combat missions – 416th TFS

Aircraft #830 – 'Black Assassin'
31 combat missions – 416th TFS

Aircraft #832 – 'Once Bitten'
30 combat missions – 416th TFS

Aircraft #833 – 'Black Devil'
30 combat missions – 416th TFS

Aircraft #834 – 'Necromancer'
34 combat missions – 416th TFS

Aircraft #835 – 'The Dragon'
26 combat missions – 416th TFS

Aircraft #836 – 'Christine'
39 combat missions – 416th TFS

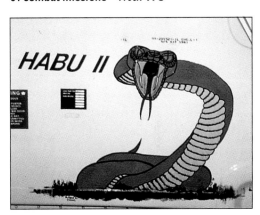

Aircraft #837 – 'Habu II'
31 combat missions – 416th TFS

Aircraft 838 – 'Magic Hammer'
36 combat missions – 416th TFS

Aircraft #839 – 'Midnight Reaper'
39 combat missions – 415th TFS

Aircraft #840 – 'Black Widow'
32 combat missions – 416th TFS

Aircraft #841 – 'Mystic Warrior'
18 combat missions – 416th TFS

Aircraft #842 – 'It's Hammertime'
33 combat missions – 416th TFS

Aircraft #843 – 'Affectionately Christine'
33 combat missions – 415th TFS

F-117 Operators

4450th Tactical Group (A-Unit)

('TR'), Tonopah Test Range, Nevada

The 4450th TG was activated on 15 October 1979 with Colonel Robert A. Jackson as commander. The four-digit number beginning with '4' signifies a 'provisional' group not entitled to permanent military lineage or heraldry. The best-kept secret of the time was the development of a strike aircraft intended to be largely invisible to radar, and the 4450th – also known as the A-Unit, one of a series of designations devised for everyday use because they conveyed no meaning – began life at Nellis AFB, Nevada, awaiting the mystery aircraft. The group began rotating pilots and maintenance personnel through the super-secret Groom Lake, Nevada, facility in 1981, although the group's home was always meant to be the Tonopah Test Range (TTR) airfield, also in Nevada.

Although Colonel Jackson never flew the Senior Trend, he had a key role in hand-picking the field-grade officers who made up the initial cadre of stealth aircraft pilots. The group's Detachment 1, alias the Q-Unit commanded by Lieutenant Colonel Alton C. Whitley, set up shop at Tonopah, initially in mobile homes once operated by a Chevron oil drilling site, and was followed by the group headquarters. The group's Detachment 2, or R-Unit, activated with the group on 15 October 1979 and was a small flight-test detachment which apparently kept a handful of test pilots at Burbank (later Palmdale) and Groom Lake.

Lieutenant Colonel Whitley's Detachment 1, with the first operational pilots who flew the Senior Trend aircraft, evolved into 4452nd Test Squadron 'Goat Suckers', still called the Q-Unit, by September 1982.

The first squadrons in the group, however, were the 4450th and 4451st Test Squadrons, activated on 11 June 1981. The 4450th Test Squadron 'Nightstalkers', or I-Unit, was first commanded by Major William C. Helper, and the 4451st Test Squadron 'Ghostriders', alias the P-Unit, by Lieutenant Colonel Jerry Fleming. The P-Unit operated the Vought A-7D aircraft stationed at Nellis AFB, Nevada, which served at first to give pilots flying time and to cover their true purpose; once Senior Trend aeroplanes began to enter service, the A-7Ds were used as chase, or 'companion', aircraft.

Colonel James S. Allen took command of the 4450th Tactical Group on 17 May 1982 and accepted the first operational Senior Trend (80-0787) at Tonopah on 23 August 1982, after the aircraft had passed initial trials at Groom Lake. The group attained IOC (initial operating capability) on 28 October 1983 with delivery of its 14th aircraft.

Colonel Howell M. Estes III became commander of the 4450th TG on 15 June 1984 and led the group through its first ORI (operational readiness inspection). The

A 4450th Tactical Group F-117 poses at Tonopah. In the early years the only unit marking was the unit badge on the intake trunk. Tail markings consisted of the last three digits of the serial and a Tactical Air Command badge.

group's third squadron, filling out its intended strength from the beginning, was the 4453rd Test and Evaluation Squadron 'Grim Reaper', or the Z-Unit, activated on 1 October 1985 under Lieutenant Colonel Roger Locher.

Colonel Michael W. Harris assumed command of the group on 6 December 1985. Colonel Michael Short became commander on 3 April 1987. Colonel Anthony J. (Tony) Tolin took command on 10 August 1988.

When the F-117 was made public, the USAF no longer needed a provisional group to operate the aircraft. Furthermore, the identity of a line fighter wing, the 37th TFW (which was then winding down F-4G Advanced 'Wild Weasel' operations at George AFB, California) was available for immediate transfer. On 5 October 1989, the USAF inactivated the 4450th TG and put the group's commander (Colonel Tolin), people and equipment under the 37th TFW banner. In practical terms, this was a change of name only, as everything stayed in place and Tonopah remained the home of the 37th Tactical Fighter Wing.

4450th Test Squadron (I-Unit) 'Nightstalkers'

The 4450th TS was one of two squadrons (with the 4451st TS) activated under the 4450th TG on 11 June 1981, some 14 months before the first operational Senior Trend aircraft was delivered. The 'Nightstalkers' were first commanded by Major William C. Helper, who did not become a Senior Trend pilot but performed interim organisational chores until replaced by pilot Lieutenant Colonel Ervin C. ('Sandy') Sharpe.

The 'Nightstalkers' flew the Senior Trend

aircraft from late 1982 onwards. The squadron came under command of Lieutenant Colonel John F. Miller (replacing Sharpe) in June 1985, and then of Lieutenant Colonel David T. Holmes on 16 January 1987 (according to one source) or in June 1987 (according to another). Lieutenant Colonel William J. Lake was the final commander of the 4450th TS and remained in place when the squadron was inactivated 5 October 1989. On that date, the squadron's people and equipment remained at Tonopah and the 'Nightstalkers' were redesignated 415th TFS.

4451st Test Squadron (P-Unit) 'Ghostriders' ('LV'), Nellis AFB, Nevada (later Tonopah)

The 4451st was activated on 11 June 1981 (together with the 4450th TS) under Lieutenant Colonel Jerry Fleming. The 'Ghostriders' operated Vought A-7D aircraft at Nellis. The A-7Ds were used as cover for the real purpose of the stealth fighter group and later as chase or 'companion' aircraft for the Senior Trend. Lieutenant Colonel Medford C. ('Med') Bowman became commander in about 1985. Lieutenant Colonel Robert E. Bruce, Jr, who was not qualified in the Senior Trend aircraft, took command in August 1986. There is no indication the 4451st was ever equipped with F-117s through the date of its inactivation, 5 October 1989. It did, however, become an F-117 squadron when, on that date, it assumed its new identity as the 416th TFS.

4452nd Test Squadron (Q-Unit) 'Goat Suckers'

4452nd Test Squadron 'Goat Suckers' (Q-Unit) began as Detachment 1 of the 4450th and was assigned to Tonopah during the brief period when group headquarters remained at Nellis; the 'Goat Suckers' took on the popular term for the American night hawk, even though Lockheed never succeeded in persuading the USAF to adopt

Nighthawk as the nickname for the Senior Trend aircraft, and were formed under Major Alton C. 'Al' Whitley in September 1982.

Major Dennis R. Larson commanded the squadron briefly after Whitley's 1985 departure and was followed by Major Robert D. Williams on 25 July 1985. Lieutenant Colonel Medford ('Med') Bowman, who had formerly commanded the P-Unit, moved to assume command of the Q-Unit in August 1986 and served briefly before being replaced on 7 January 1987 by Lieutenant Colonel Arthur P. ('Art') Weyermuller. Weyermuller was in turn replaced by Lieutenant Colonel James G. Ferguson on 14 August 1987. The squadron was inactivated on 30 May 1989, becoming the only stealth unit not to acquire a new identity as part of the 37th TFW later in the year.

4453rd Test and Evaluation Squadron (Z-Unit) 'Grim Reapers'

The 4453rd Test and Evaluation Squadron 'Grim Reaper' (Z-Unit) was activated on 1 October 1985 under Lieutenant Colonel Roger Locher to become the third Senior Trend flying squadron in the 4450th Tactical Group. In January 1989, this F-117 squadron began preparations to take charge of chase, or 'companion', aircraft with delivery of the first Northrop T-38 Talons that month; this new role became official on 30 May 1989, when the Vought A-7D unit at Nellis was inactivated.

Continuing to fly F-117s and T-38s, the 4453rd also took over the local area familiarisation function which had been an extra duty for the group's R-Unit, its small flight-test organisation, also inactivated on 30 May 1989. The final commander of the 4453rd TES was Lieutenant Colonel Richard C. Groesch. The squadron was inactivated on 5 October 1989, when its people and equipment, remaining in place at Tonopah, became the 417th Tactical Fighter Training Squadron.

37th Tactical Fighter Wing

('TR'), Tonopah Test Range, Nevada

The 37th Tactical Fighter Wing, which had operated F-4G Advanced 'Wild Weasels' at George AFB, California, took over the identity of the inactivated 4450th Tactical Group. The 37th raised its flag at Tonopah on 5 October 1989, taking over the three F-117 group's squadrons which were redesignated 415th TFS (former 4450th TS), 416th TFS (former 4451st TS) and 417th TFTS (former 4453rd TES). Colonel Anthony J. Tolin remained as commander when the change took place.

In December 1989, the wing launched six F-117s on a combat mission from Tonopah during Operation Just Cause in Panama. Two aircraft were spares, two were called off from a special operations mission aimed at Panamanian leader Manuel Noriega, and two bombed a field near the Rio Hato barracks as scheduled. Colonel Tolin continued to command the wing until 16 August 1990, at which time Operation Desert Shield was beginning.

Colonel Alton C. ('Al') Whitley, Jr, who had been the first operational pilot to fly the Senior Trend aircraft, returned to the stealth world as 37th TFW commander on 16 August 1990, and guided the wing through its deployment in Operation Desert Shield and combat in Desert Storm. The wing deployed its 415th TFS to the Middle East in August 1990 and its 416th TFS in December 1990; its third flying squadron, the 417th TFTS, remained at home at Tonopah but provided personnel and aircraft for the build-up against Iraq. As noted below, the deployed 37th TFW was designated a 'provisional' wing on 20 December 1990 to bring its nomenclature in line with other wings preparing at that time for a possible war with Iraq.

The war began on 17 January 1991 and ended just over a month later. The US Air Force later said that the 37th TFW's F-117s comprised only 2.5 per cent of the shooters on the first day of the war against Iraq, yet credited them with hitting over 31 per cent of the targets.

The unit's 'provisional' designation was dropped after the war and most of the 37th TFW returned to Tonopah, but the wing left some aircraft at Khamis Mushait as a contingency and to retain a striking potential in support of Operation Southern Watch, the coalition's enforcement of a 'No-Fly Zone' in Kurdish areas of northern Iraq. This Middle East presence has involved periodic rotation of squadrons and personnel.

The 37th TFW lost the modifier 'tactical' in its name and became the 37th Fighter Wing on 1 October 1991.

37th Tactical Fighter Wing (Provisional), King Khalid Air Base, Khamis Mushait, Saudi Arabia

The 37th TFW (P) designation, applicable to the bulk of the F-117 wing when it was deployed to Saudi Arabia, became effective on 20 December 1990. Colonel Alton C. Whitley served as commander of the wing before, during and after the war, when the 'provisional' modifier was dropped.

37th Fighter Wing ('TR'), Tonopah Test Range, Nevada

The 37th Fighter Wing accepted its designation on 1 October 1991, replacing the 37th TFW with no change in commander, personnel or equipment. When the USAF decided to move the F-117 force to Holloman AFB, New Mexico, partly to reduce operating costs now that the secrecy of Tonopah was no longer needed, a decision was taken to preserve the identity of the 49th Fighter Wing, which was then at Holloman (but giving up its F-15 Eagle fleet) and to retire the 37th designation. With the shift to Holloman, the F-117 establishment became the 49th Fighter Wing on 5 July 1992.

415th Tactical Fighter Squadron 'Nightstalkers'

The 415th Tactical Fighter Squadron came into existence on 5 October 1989 with the people and equipment of the former 4450th TS, including commander Lieutenant Colonel William J. Lake. The 415th TFS provided the six F-117s and pilots who flew the 19 December 1989 combat mission to Panama during Operation Just Cause (see main text and 37th TFW entry). Under contingency plans of the late 1980s, the squadron was considered to be the Atlantic component of the stealth fighter community, expected to 'chop' to US European Command in time of war. In fact, when war came in the Middle East, the squadron chopped to US Central Command during Operation Desert Shield.

The 'Nightstalkers' were the first of the wing's squadrons to be deployed to Khamis Mushait, Saudi Arabia, in Desert Shield, beginning 26 August 1990. The squadron bore the brunt of the difficult build-up in the Middle East, bolstered by a few personnel and aircraft from the 416th TFS (which deployed in December 1990) and 417th TFTS (which remained stateside but provided aircraft and personnel). Commanded in 1990-91 by Lieutenant Colonel Ralph Getchell, the 'Nightstalkers' fought in Operation Desert Storm from the first night, 17 January 1991, until the end on 26 February 1991. The 415th TFS had the first F-117 contingent to return from the Gulf War, eight aircraft which landed at Nellis AFB on 1 April 1991.

Final commander of the 415th TFS was Lieutenant Colonel Bruce E. Kreidler, who remained on board when the squadron's designation was changed. In keeping with USAF reorganisation, the 415th TFS became the 415th FS on 1 October 1991.

415th Fighter Squadron 'Nightstalkers,' later 'Nighthawks'

The 415th FS was the new name for the former 415th TFS, effective 1 October 1991. Lieutenant Colonel Bruce E. Kreidler was commander at the time of the name change. Another change in USAF nomenclature put an end to emblems and nicknames with satanic connotations, no matter obscure: with this change in late 1992 the 'Nightstalkers' lost their proud nickname and became, instead, the 'Nighthawks.'

When the F-117 force moved from Tonopah to Holloman AFB, New Mexico on 5 July 1992, the 37th FW became the 49th FW, but the squadron designation was not, at first changed. For a time, 416th TFS could not take on the name of the 9th Fighter Squadron because that designator was employed (from May 1992) by the F-4E Phantom unit which trains German Luftwaffe pilots; on 30 July 1993 the Phantom unit reverted to its earlier designator as the 20th FS, a move which enabled the 416th TFS, in turn, to be redesignated 9th Fighter Squadron on that date.

416th Tactical Fighter Squadron 'Ghostriders'

The 416th Tactical Fighter Squadron came into existence on 5 October 1989 with the people and equipment of the former 4451st Test Squadron, but with a new commander. On that date, Lieutenant Colonel Gerald C. Carpenter moved from the inactivated 4453rd Test Squadron to take charge of the 416th TFS. 'Ghostriders'.

The Pacific component of the 37th TFW earmarked for US Pacific Command (meaning Korea) in the event of war, the 'Ghostriders' were not at first chosen for deployment when Operation Desert Storm began in August 1990. As the build-up in the Middle East grew, the decision was made to deploy the squadron, and the long trip to Khamis Mushait, Saudi Arabia (with a stopover at Langley AFB, Virginia) began on 2 December 1990. Commanded in 1990-91 by Lieutenant Colonel Gregory ('Greg') Gonyea, the 'Ghostriders' fought in Operation Desert Storm from the first night, 17 January 1991, until the end on 26 February 1991.

In the immediate post-Desert Storm era, the 416th TFS made a deployment to Korea where it was part of contingency plans for a conflict there.

Lieutenant Colonel Gonyea was still in command when the squadron underwent its next name change, along with the other F-117 flying units. In keeping with USAF reorganisation, the 416th TFS lost its 'tactical' nomenclature and was redesignated 416th FS on 1 October 1991.

416th Fighter Squadron 'Ghostriders,' later 'Knight Riders'

The 416th Fighter Squadron was the new name for the former 416th TFS, effective 1 October 1991. Lieutenant Colonel Gregory ('Greg') Gonyea was commander at the time of the name change. When the USAF issued its ban on devilish nicknames, the 'Ghostriders' were forced to give up the nickname in which they felt considerable pride, and were renamed the 'Knight Riders'. The change is a curious one, because the taboo on satanic names followed an earlier ban on names deemed not to be 'gender neutral'; apparently no one noticed that knights, in theory at least, are male.

When the F-117 force moved from Tonopah to Holloman AFB, New Mexico, on

This pair of 37th TFW aircraft displays special markings for the wing commander (foreground), and the standard tail markings with large 'TR' code.

417th Fighter Squadron 'Bandits'

Various special markings have been applied to the F-117, this aircraft seen in 1991 wearing a revised tail marking for the 416th squadron commander.

5 July 1992, the parent 37th FW relinquished its designation in order to adopt the colours and lineage of the 49th FW. Squadron designations, however, were not changed at first. Serving as an F-117 squadron under the 49th Fighter Wing at Holloman, the 'Knight Riders' were redesignated 8th Fighter Squadron on 30 July 1993.

417th Tactical Fighter Training Squadron 'Bandits'

The 417th TFTS was formed on 5 October 1989 from the assets of the 4453rd Test and Evaluation Squadron, the 'Bandits'. The squadron served as the RTU (replacement training unit) for the F-117 and took over operation of the stealth community's Northrop T-38 Talon chase aircraft.

The 417th TFTS did not deploy during Operations Desert Shield/Storm but provided eight aircraft to stand by at Langley AFB, Virginia, as attrition replacements for

the F-117 force in the Middle East. In the event, there was no attrition and the aircraft were not needed. The 'Bandits' were commanded in 1990-91 Lieutenant Colonel Robert J. ('Bob') Maher.

In keeping with USAF reorganisation, the 417th TFTS lost the 'tactical' and 'training' adjectives in its title (although keeping its training duties) and was redesignated the 416th Fighter Squadron on 1 October 1991. Commander at the time was Lieutenant Colonel Barry Horne.

The 417th FS took on its new name on 1 October 1991 at Tonopah, retaining Lieutenant Colonel Barry Horne as commander and its mission as the RTU (replacement training unit) for the F-117.

When the F-117 force moved from Tonopah to Holloman AFB, New Mexico, on 5 July 1992, the 37th FW took over the colours and lineage of the 49th FW. Squadron designations, however, were not changed at first. In fact, the 417th FS was the last of the three F-117 squadrons to assume a new identity traditionally associated with its parent wing. Equipped with 10 F-117s and 11 AT-38B Talons, the squadron was redesignated 7th FS in December 1993.

49th Fighter Wing

('HO'), Holloman AFB, New Mexico

The 49th Fighter Wing took over the F-117 squadrons and the equipment and personnel of the dismantled 37th Fighter Wing when the move from Tonopah to Holloman AFB, New Mexico, was made on 5 July 1992. Three days later, command of the 49th FW passed to Brigadier General Lloyd W. ('Fig') Newton.

The USAF simply could not dispense with the identity of the 49th FW, which had a proud history dating to 15 January 1941 when the 49th Pursuit Group (Interceptor) trained in Seversky P-35s before moving to New Guinea. Among its 43 air aces were Lieutenant Colonel Boyd D. 'Buzz' Wagner, the first American ace in the Pacific theatre, and Major Richard I. Bong, who racked up 40 aerial victories. The 49th fought in Korea with F-80s and F-84s, flew F-4 Phantoms during the Cold War, and operated F-15 Eagles immediately prior to the change.

When it received its F-117s, the 49th FW took on the three flying squadrons, namely the 415th Fighter Squadron 'Nighthawks' (formerly 'Nightstalkers'), which was redesignated as 9th Fighter Squadron on 30 July 1993; the 416th Fighter Squadron

The 49th FW commander's aircraft displays the new 'HO' tailcodes, intake unit insignia and Air Combat Command badge.

'Knight Riders' (formerly 'Ghostriders'), redesignated 8th Fighter Squadron on 30 July 1993; and the 417th Fighter Squadron 'Bandits', redesignated 7th Fighter Squadron in December 1993. The last-named squadron change had to await the transfer of the wing's IFF (introduction to fighter fundamentals) training, performed in the AT-38B Talon, to Air Education and Training Command.

The move to Holloman brought the 'Cockroach', or 'Black Jet', out into the open, both literally and figuratively. While many aspects of F-117 operations remained classified, the warplane was no longer part of a 'black' programme; in contrast to the plush indoor facilities to which the F-117 community had become accustomed, much of the work at Holloman, today, is performed out of doors.

In addition to its three F-117 squadrons, the 49th FW operates the 20th Fighter Squadron which trains Luftwaffe pilots in German-owned F-4E Phantoms (and which

was briefly designated 9th FS from May 1992, until that designation went to an F-117 unit on 30 July 1993), the 48th Rescue Squadron with five HH-60G helicopters, and the 435th Fighter Squadron which trains Taiwanese pilots in the AT-38B Talon (to prepare them for the F-16 Fighting Falcon). In June 1993, Brigadier General Newton turned over command of the 49th FW to Brigadier General John F. Miller, Jr, who, as a lieutenant colonel, had commanded the old 4450th TS, the original 'Nightstalkers', and who also commanded the 8th TFW ('Wolf Pack') in Korea with F-16 Fighting Falcons.

7th Fighter Squadron 'Bunyaps'

The 7th Fighter Squadron 'Bunyaps' took over the F-117 operations of the former 417th FS 'Bandits' in December 1993. The 'Bunyaps' get their nickname from a mythical fanged creature in the lore of Australian Aborigines and owes their origins to the 7th Pursuit Squadron (Interceptor) formed on 20 November 1940 with Seversky P-35s. Curiously, the devil-like creature in the 'Bunyaps'' emblem

(approved in 1944) has survived the USAF's ban on satanic images even though the 'Nightstalkers' and 'Ghostriders' of the recent past did not.

The squadron's history includes combat in New Guinea and the Philippines in P-40s,

P-47s and P-38s; in Korea in F-80s and F-84s; and Cold War flying in the F-100, F-105, F-4 and F-15. Just before becoming an F-117 operator, the squadron performed IFF (introduction to fighter fundamentals) training for future F-15 Eagle pilots using the AT-38B Talon. The time consumed in winding down and transferring this function meant that the 8th and 9th FS became F-117 operators fully nine months before the 7th FS did. The 7th FS is now the RTU (replacement training unit) for the F-117 type.

8th Fighter Squadron 'Black Sheep'

The 8th Fighter Squadron 'Black Sheep' took over the F-117 operations of the former 416th FS ('Knight Riders', previously 'Ghostriders') on 30 July 1993. The squadron emblem is a silhouette of a black sheep inside a golden yellow circle bordered in black. The squadron began as the 8th

Pursuit Squadron (Interceptor) on 20 November 1940 with Seversky P-35s. The squadron's history includes combat in New Guinea and the Philippines in P-40s, P-47s and P-38s; in Korea in F-80s and F-84s; and

Cold War operations with the F-100, F-105, F-4 and F-15.

The 8th FS retains the Pacific contingency for the F-117 force and would be the first squadron deployed to Korea in event of a crisis there.

9th Fighter Squadron 'Iron Knights'

The 9th Fighter Squadron 'Iron Knights' took over the F-117 operations of the former 415th Fighter Squadron 'Nighthawks' (formerly 'Nightstalkers') 30 July 1993. The squadron emblem is a white, winged knight's helmet on a blue disk bordered in black. The squadron began as the 9th Pursuit Squadron (Interceptor) on 20 November 1940 with Seversky P-35s. The squadron's history includes combat in New Guinea and the Philippines in P-40s, P-47s and P-38s; in Korea in F-80s and F-84s; and Cold War operations with the F-100, F-105, F-4 and F-15.

The 9th FS retains the Atlantic contingency for the F-117 force and would be the first squadron deployed to Europe in event of a crisis there.

57th Fighter Weapons Wing

('WA'), Nellis AFB, Nevada

The 57th Fighter Weapons Wing at Nellis AFB, Nevada, conducted weapons, armament and tactics tests and training for the USAF's Tactical Air Command (TAC). In addition to maintaining squadrons at Nellis for various aircraft types (F-16, F-111, A-10), the 57th FWW has traditionally operated detachments at air bases in connection with less numerous types. Weaponeering with the Senior Trend aircraft was performed in the 'black' world by the 4450th Tactical Group until 5 October 1989, when (on the same day the 4450th TG became the 37th TFW) TAC activated Detachment 1, 57th FWW, at the group's base, Tonopah Test Range, Nevada. Typically, the detachment flew F-117 aircraft based at Tonopah, but carried out everyday operations, no longer constrained by 'blackness,' in better-known sectors of the Nellis reservation.

The 57th FWW detachment remained in operation on 1 October 1991 when its parent unit was redesignated 57th Fighter Wing.

57th Fighter Wing

The 57th Fighter Wing acquired its designation on 1 October 1991 and continued to operate its Detachment 1 at Tonopah.

On 12 November 1991, Brigadier General Anthony J. (Tony) Tolin, who earlier commanded the F-117 operation (10 August 1988 - 16 August 1990) took command of the 57th Fighter Wing. Tolin was in charge

of the 57th FW during the period when the F-117 force relocated from Tonopah to Holloman. His wing's Detachment 1, now known as the 'Dragon Test Team', was activated at Holloman on 1 June 1992, the date TAC became Air Combat Command (ACC), and roughly coinciding with the beginning of F-117 operations on 5 July 1992.

Typically, the 'Dragon Test Team' operates two or three F-117s at Holloman with 'WA' tailcodes but flies to Nellis for most weapon tests and training. Colonel Tolin was still in command of the 57th FW when a new change in designation took place, making it the 57th Wing, on 1 February 1993.

57th Wing

The 57th Wing at Nellis AFB, Nevada, conducts weapons, armament and tactics tests and training for the USAF's Air Combat Command, and acquired its current designation on 1 February 1993. The change was made because the wing absorbed the USAF Weapons School, which includes bombers as well as fighters. Colonel Tolin was replaced on 10 September 1993 by the current commander, Brigadier General John L. Welde, who does not come from the F-117 community.

The 57th Wing's Detachment 1, alias the 'Dragon Test Team,' continues to operate two or three F-117s at Holloman with 'WA'

Above: At least one F-117 is permanently assigned to Det 1, 57th Wing, and wears the parent unit's checkerboard fin-stripe, albeit in a toned-down version.

tailcodes and takes the aircraft to Nellis for most weapon tests and training.

The 57th Wing has an OL (operating location) at Kirtland AFB, New Mexico, where various aircraft types including the F-117 'Cockroach' have been evaluated for their vulnerability to EMP (electromagnetic pulse).

The 57th Wing is scheduled for a further major reorganisation on 1 October 1994, which is not expected to affect its F-117 element.

The 57th Wing badge highlights the weapon-testing role of the unit.

410th Flight Test Squadron

('ED'), Palmdale, California

The 410th Test Squadron acquired its designation on 1 May 1993 at the Palmdale 'Skunk Works' flight test centre. The 410th TS traces its roots, if not its formal lineage, to the 4450th Tactical Group's Detachment 2, or R-Unit, activated with the group on 15 October 1979 as a small flight test detachment which apparently kept a handful of test pilots at Burbank (later Palmdale) and Groom Lake. From the earliest days of the 'black' Senior Trend programme, the USAF maintained a detachment of test pilots at Lockheed's Burbank 'Skunk Works', where operational pilots went through an initial ground training course. An acceptance and test squadron with no name, the unit also operated at Groom Lake in early days, where the Baja scorpion was adopted as the symbol of the Lockheed-USAF development effort; the unit then moved with the rest of the F-117 community. R-Unit's last commander was Lieutenant Colonel Keat Griggers (who later commanded the 417th TFTS), and it was inactivated on 30 May 1989.

Wing) at Edwards AFB, California, the small flying unit operated without any designation from 1989 onward, and moved from Tonopah to Palmdale (rather than to Holloman, with the rest of the F-117 force) in March 1992. It was designated 410th Test Squadron on 1 May 1993 and today operates four F-117s (79-10782, 79-10783, 79-10784, and 85-0831, the first three being

According to members of the Palmdale flight test unit, which is subordinate to the 412th Test Wing (previously 6510th Test

the surviving full-scale development aircraft). Squadron commander is Lieutenant Colonel Steven Green, who recently became the first pilot to log 1,000 hours in the 'Cockroach.'

831 is the only production machine assigned to the 410th TS. There are also three FSD aircraft.

Lockheed's Blackbirds

A-12, YF-12 and SR-71

In the late 1950s the CIA had guessed that it would only be a matter of time before its high-flying yet flimsy U-2 would be shot down by the powerful Soviet SA-2 'Guideline' SAM. Accordingly, a programme was initiated to provide a follow-on which could produce overhead intelligence with vastly reduced vulnerability. The result was the Lockheed A-12, but due to the changing political climate following the forecasted U-2 loss in 1960, the aircraft never went into action over the Soviet Union. Instead, the A-12 saw only brief service over North Vietnam and North Korea. However, it was the highest-flying and fastest air-breathing aircraft ever built, breaking new technological ground in virtually every area. This experience was put to use in producing the YF-12, a Mach 3 interceptor which, although it was not chosen for production, was instrumental in developing the long-range radar and missile systems in service today. For strategic reconnaissance, the A-12 design evolved into the two-man SR-71, which for 25 years provided the United States with a unique window into the hot-spots of the world. Today, over 30 years after its first flight, the SR-71 is back in limited service, proving just how far ahead of its time it was when it was designed in the early 1960s.

Looking east across the Groom Dry Lake airfield, this line-up of Blackbirds is headed by the first A-12 built, behind which is the only A-12B two-seater. At the far end of the row are two YF-12As. Groom Lake, aka Area 51, 'the Ranch' or 'Dreamland', had been established as the flight test centre for the U-2; its proximity to the atomic weapon testing site deterred any unwanted guests, as did the security measures which were introduced. Beginning with a lakebed runway and a few shacks, the facility grew steadily in size throughout the U-2, A-12, F-117 and subsequent programmes, and now boasts a six-mile runway and a large complex of buildings.

Prior to the development which led to the A-12, the Lockheed Skunk Works was working on liquid hydrogen powered aircraft under Project Suntan. This design, designated CL-400-10, was over 160 ft (49 m) long and had two Pratt & Whitney 304 engines. The principal disadvantage of the liquid hydrogen powerplant was the lack of range, despite the fact that most of the aircraft's fuselage contained fuel.

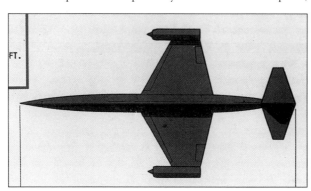

The first operational flight undertaken by Central Intelligence Agency (CIA) pilot Harvey Stockman in Lockheed U-2 article number 347, on 4 July 1956, produced a photo-take of previously denied territory, the like of which had never been seen before. At a stroke the U-2 and its associated programme, Operation Overflight, established themselves as the pre-eminent means of gathering strategic intelligence concerning the USSR and its satellites.

Despite spectacular results, informed sources were concerned about the Soviets' ability to accurately track on radar the subsonic U-2. In November 1954, CIA director Allen Dulles recruited Richard Bissell, a brilliant economist and innovator who lectured at both Yale and Massachusetts Institute of Technology (MIT), and appointed him Special Assistant for Planning and Co-ordination. Bissell, 'Kelly' Johnson (the U-2 designer) and the Killian Committee (a Department of Defense-sponsored 'think-tank' to President Eisenhower, consisting of the chairman James R. Killian, president of MIT, and 14 other eminent professionals with science and technology backgrounds) believed that the U-2 would enjoy a period of no more than two years of invulnerability from the start of Operation Overflight. Accordingly, Bissell began organising research and development of follow-on systems. In the autumn of 1957, he contacted 'Kelly' Johnson and asked if the Lockheed Skunk Works team would conduct an operations analysis into the relationship of interceptability and an aircraft's speed,

altitude and radar cross-section (RCS). Since Kelly was already immersed in related studies, he agreed to accept the project; the results concluded that supersonic speed coupled with the use of radar-attenuating materials (RAM) and radar-attenuating design greatly reduced, but not negated, chances of radar detection. Encouraged by the results, it was agreed that further exploratory work should be conducted. The CIA then focused on the possibility of operating a platform capable of flight at extremely high speeds and altitude, which also incorporated the best available radar-attenuating capabilities. During the closing months of 1957, the Agency invited Lockheed Aircraft Corporation and the Convair Division of General Dynamics to submit non-funded, non-contracted designs for a reconnaissance-gathering vehicle which adhered to the fore-mentioned performance criteria. Both companies accepted the challenge and were assured that funding would be forthcoming at the appropriate time. For the next 12 months, the Agency received designs that were developed and refined all at no expense!

High-risk programme

It was readily apparent to Bissell that developing such an advanced aircraft would be both high-risk and extremely expensive; government funding would be a prerequisite and in order to obtain this various high-ranking government officials would have to be brought into the programme and given clear, authoritative presentations on advances as they occurred. He therefore assembled a talented panel of six specialists under the chair of Dr Edwin Land. Between 1957 and 1959 the panel met on six occasions, usually in Land's Cambridge, Massachusetts office. Kelly and General Dynamics' Vincent Dolson were at times in attendance, as were the Assistant Secretaries of the Air Force and Navy, plus other select technical advisors.

Codenamed Project Gusto by the Agency, Lockheed's first submission, Archangel, proposed a Mach 3 cruise aircraft with a range of 4,000 nm (4,600 miles; 7400 km) at 90,000-95,000 ft (27430-29000 m). This, together with his Gusto Model G2A submission, were both well received by the Programme Office, as Kelly noted later. Convair, on the other hand, prepared the Mach 4-capable Super

Previous studies

Even before the U-2 of Francis Gary Powers was shot down, Lockheed (and others) was busy studying a follow-on aircraft which would be invulnerable to Soviet defences for the overflight mission. While most designs strove for greater speed and altitude, some tackled the then-novel idea of vastly reducing radar cross-section.

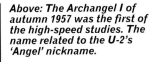

Above: During Project Gusto Lockheed produced designs from A-3 to A-12. Many, like the A-10 depicted here, featured the forward fuselage chine which was such a feature of the eventual A-12 aircraft. The A-11 was a very high-performance diamond-winged design but had a massive RCS. The A-12 attempted to combine the A-11's performance with a much lower radar cross-section.

Above: The Archangel I of autumn 1957 was the first of the high-speed studies. The name related to the U-2's 'Angel' nickname.

Left: Arrow I was another early study, with two engines mounted side-by-side in a large fairing. The design had two large vertical tail surfaces near the wingtips.

Above: Archangel II was the second of the high-speed designs (leading to the A-3/12 series). It featured a mixed powerplant of two turbojets for take-off and low-speed flight (inboard), and two large ramjets on the wingtips for high-speed flight.

Left: Dubbed Gusto 2, this large (wider span than a U-2) flying-wing design was slow but was designed to have a very low radar cross-section.

Hustler, which would be ramjet-powered when launched from a B-58 and turbojet-assisted for landing. As designs were refined and resubmitted, the Lockheed offerings' names were shortened to 'A' followed by an index number, running from A-3 to A-12. The design and designations from Convair also evolved, being known as the Kingfish. On 20 August 1959 final submissions from both companies were made to a joint DoD/Air Force/CIA selection panel. Though strikingly different, the proposed performance of both aircraft compared favourably.

	A-12	Kingfish
Speed	Mach 3.2	Mach 3.2
Range (total)	4,120 nm	4,000 nm
Range (at altitude)	3,800 nm	3,400 nm
Cruise altitudes		
Start	84,500 ft	85,000 ft
Mid-range	91,000 ft	88,000 ft
End	97,600 ft	94,000 ft
Dimensions		
Length	102 ft	79.5 ft
Span	57 ft	56 ft
Gross weight	110,000 lb	101,700 lb
Fuel weight	64,600 lb	62,000 lb
First flight	22 months	22 months

On 28 August Kelly was told by the director of the programme that Lockheed's Skunk Works had won the competition to build the U-2 follow-on. The next day Lockheed was given the official go-ahead, with initial fund-

ing of $4.5 million approved to cover the period 1 September 1959 to 1 January 1960. Project Gusto was now at an end and a new codename, Oxcart, was assigned. On 3 September the Agency authorised Lockheed to proceed with anti-radar studies into aerodynamics, structural tests and engineering designs. The small engineering team, under the supervision of Ed Martin, consisted of Dan Zuck in charge of cockpit design, Dave Robertson on fuel system requirements, Henry Combs and Dick Bochme on structures, and Dick Fuller, Burt McMaster and Kelly's protégé, Ben Rich.

Tunnel testing

The final A-12 design was arrived at after many hours of tunnel testing, across the whole spectrum of the aircraft's speed envelope. Several features, such as canard foreplanes, were tested and discarded.

Below left: This tunnel model is recognisably the A-12 in a near-definition configuration, but has triangular foreplanes added in an attempt to improve the pitch stability.

Below: This tunnel model of the A-12, by then codenamed Oxcart, dates from 1960. It has the inboard elevons and all-moving tails of the final design, conventional rudders having been tested earlier. One feature subsequently altered was the elegantly curving wing/chine join.

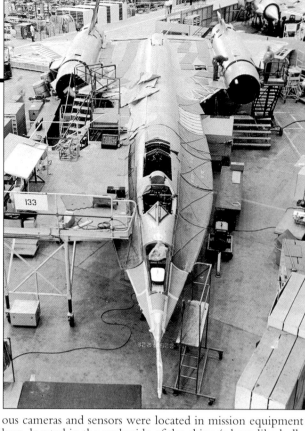

Above: Photographed in January 1962, the first A-12 (Article 121, later 60-6929) is seen virtually complete in Building 82 (final check-out) of the Burbank assembly facility. Great secrecy surrounded the A-12 programme: the aircraft was by a wide margin the most advanced anywhere in the world. It was also to be the fastest, its top speed and altitude being higher than the SR-71 which followed.

Above right: This is the last A-12, Article 133, nearing completion at Burbank. Apparent is the size of the Q-bay, which housed large downward-looking cameras behind the pilot.

An A-12 model sits atop the Groom Lake RCS pole. It has been painted with ferrous 'Iron Ball' radar-attenuating paint to test its effect. The large fairings protruding from the jetpipes were used to emulate the radar signature of the afterburner plumes from the two J58s.

The ambitious scope of performance planned for the new aircraft cannot be overstated. The best front-line fighter aircraft of the day were the early 'Century Series' jets like the F-100 Super Sabre and the F-101 Voodoo; in a single bound, the A-12 would operate at sustained speeds and altitudes treble and double, respectively, those of such contemporary fighters. The technical challenge facing the Skunk Works team was enormous, and the contracted timescale in which to achieve it was incredibly tight. Kelly later remarked that virtually everything on the aircraft had to be invented from scratch. Operating above 80,000 ft (24390 m), the atmospheric pressure was 0.4 psi (2.7 kPa) and ambient air temperature was -56° C (-69° F) – but cruising at a speed of 1 mile (1.6 km) every two seconds meant that airframe temperatures varied from 245° to 565° C (473° to 1,050° F). At a Mach 3.2 cruise, the two engines required 100,000 cu ft (2830 m³) of air per second, the equivalent of 2 million people inhaling simultaneously.

A-12 construction

How and from what was such an aircraft built? The A-12 design is characterised by an aft-body delta wing with two large engines, each located at mid-semi-span. Two all-moving vertical fins were mounted on top of each engine nacelle and canted inwards 15° from the vertical to reduce the aircraft's radar signature and to aid the control of excess offset yaw-thrust during single-engine flight. A large aft-moving inlet spike or centre-body protruded forward from each engine nacelle, which helped to regulate mass airflow to the two powerful engines at speeds above Mach 1.4. Mission equipment was housed in a large bay behind the pilot in the A-12 (this bay was occupied by a fire control officer (FCO) in the YF-12 interceptor version and a reconnaissance systems officer (RSO) in the Air Force-operated SR-71.) Weapons, a fire control system and vari-

ous cameras and sensors were located in mission equipment bays, located in the underside of the chine (a boat-like hull-form which extended along both sides of the long fuselage forebody on the YF-12 and SR-71). In all three variants, flight crews wore a full pressure suit.

Sustained operation in extreme temperatures meant lavish use of the advanced titanium alloys that account for 85 per cent of the aircraft's structural weight, the remaining 15 per cent being comprised of composite materials. The decision to use such materials was based on considerations such as titanium's ability to withstand high operating temperatures; that it weighs half as much as stainless steel but has the same tensile strength; and that conventional construction was possible using fewer parts (high-strength composites were not available in the early 1960s). The particular titanium used was B-120VCA, which can be hardened to strengths up to 200,000 psi (1.38 million kPa). Initially the ageing process required 70 hours to achieve maximum strength but, with careful processing techniques, this was reduced to 40 hours. A rigorous (and expensive) quality control programme was established wherein for every batch of 10 or more parts processed, three samples were heat-treated to the same level as those in the batch. One was then strength-tested to destruction, another tested for formability and the third held in reserve should pre-processing be required. With more than 13 million titani-

Testing the A-12

The extreme performance and exacting mission requirements of the A-12 required extensive testing of the various systems. Those tests which could not be conducted behind closed doors were

undertaken at the secret operating location at Groom Dry Lake, where radar cross-section pole tests and other visible trials could be performed in daylight and privacy. Once the first aircraft was reassembled at the base, high-speed taxi trials followed, during the course of which the aircraft took off inadvertently, on 25 April 1962.

The second A-12, Article 122, was delivered to Groom Lake on 26 June 1962, and was used initially for RCS pole tests.

Tests of the Lockheed SR-1 ejection seat were made at Groom Lake, a hired 1961 Thunderbird being used to tow the test rig across the dry lakebed.

um parts manufactured, data is available on all but a few.

Using this advanced material, it was not long before problems arose. Titanium is not compatible with chlorine, fluorine or cadmium, so for example a line drawn on sheet titanium with a Pentel pen will eat a hole through it in about 12 hours. All Pentel pens were recalled from the shop floor. Early spot-welded panels produced during the summer had a habit of failing, while those built in the winter lasted indefinitely. Diligent detective work discovered that to prevent the formation of algae in the summer, the Burbank water supply is heavily chlorinated. Subsequently, the Skunk Works washed all titanium parts in distilled water. As thermodynamic tests got underway, bolt heads began dropping from installations; this, it was discovered, was caused by tiny cadmium deposits left after cadmium-plated spanners had been used to apply torque. As the bolts were heated over 320° C (610° F) their heads dropped off. All cadmium-plated tools were removed from tool boxes.

Corrugated skin

Another test studied thermal effects on large titanium wing panels. An element 4 ft x 6 ft (1.2 m x 1.8 m) was heated to the computed heat flux expected in flight and resulted in the sample warping into a totally unacceptable shape. This problem was resolved by manufacturing chord-wise corrugations into the outer skins. At the design heat rate, the corrugations merely deepened by a few thousandths of an inch and on cooling returned to the basic shape. Kelly recalled he was accused of "trying to make a

1932 Ford Trimotor go Mach 3," but added that "the concept worked fine." To prevent this titanium outer skin from tearing when secured to heavier sub-structures, the Skunk Works developed stand-off clips, which ensured structural continuity while creating a heat shield between adjacent components.

Chosen powerplant would be the Pratt & Whitney JT11D-20 engine (designated J58 by the US military). This high bypass ratio afterburning engine was the result of two earlier, ill-fated programmes: Project Suntan, a 1956 project which envisaged a 2.7-Mach hydrogen-fuelled aircraft built by Lockheed and designated CL-400, and which was axed three years after inception: and Pratt & Whitney's JT9 single-spool high-pressure ratio turbojet, rated at 26,000 lb (115 kN) in afterburner and developed for a US Navy attack aircraft, which was also axed. Nevertheless, the engine had already completed 700 hours of full-scale engine

Above: Following the inadvertent hop on 25 April, Lou Schalk flew the A-12 on its scheduled first flight the following day. He kept the undercarriage down throughout the 30-minute sortie, during which some wing and fuselage fillets were lost. Here Schalk is seen during that first landing.

Above left: On 30 April 1962 the A-12 made its first 'official' flight in front of a small gathering of government and company officials.

Lou Schalk was subsequently joined by Lockheed test pilots Bill Park, Jim Eastham and Bob Gilliland. Here Eastham pilots the first aircraft during refuelling trials in early 1963. The short-finned modified KC-135A was based at Groom Lake for the duration of the tests.

The third A-12 arrived at the 'Ranch' in August 1962, and is seen here on a 22 December flight. At the time it was still powered by two J75 engines. The first flight-rated J58 engine had flown in the port nacelle of the prototype aircraft on 5 October 1962, and on 15 January 1963 Article 121 flew with two J58s. The remaining aircraft were either re-engined or completed from new with the intended powerplant.

For ground engine runs the A-12s were fitted with overwing tanks until the massive fuel leaks which afflicted the main tanks were fixed.

testing and results were very encouraging. As testing continued, however, it became apparent that due to the incredibly hostile thermal conditions of sustained Mach 3.2 flight, only the basic airflow size (400 lb/180 kg per second of airflow) and the compressor and turbine aerodynamics of the original Navy J58 P2 engine could be retained (even they were later modified). The stretched design criteria, associated with high Mach number and its related large airflow turn-down ratio, led to the development of a variable-cycle engine, later known as a bleed-bypass engine, a concept conceived by Pratt & Whitney's Robert Abernathy. This eliminated many airflow problems through the engine by bleeding air from the fourth stage of the nine-stage, single-spool axial-flow compressor. The excess air was passed through six low-compression-ratio bypass ducts and was reintroduced into the turbine exhaust, near the front of the afterburner, at the same static pressure as the main flow. This reduced exhaust gas temperature (EGT) and in addition produced almost as much thrust per pound of air as the main flow which had passed through the rear compressor, the burner section and the turbine. Scheduling

of the bypass bleed was achieved by the main fuel control as a function of compressor inlet temperature (CIT) and engine rpm. Bleed air injection occurred at a CIT of between 85° and 115° C (185° and 240° F) (approximately Mach 1.9).

To further minimise stalling the front stages of the rotor blades at low engine speeds, movable inlet guide vanes (IGVs) were incorporated to help guide airflow to the compressor. They changed from axial to a cambered position in response to the main fuel control, which regulated most engine functions. Set in the axial position to provide additional thrust for take-off and acceleration to intermediate supersonic speeds, the IGVs changed to the cambered position when the CIT again reached 85° to 115° C. If IGV 'lock-in' failed to occur upon reaching a CIT of 150° C (302° F), the mission would be aborted.

When operating at cruising speeds, the turbine inlet temperature (TIT) reached over 1100° C (2,012° F), which necessitated the development of a unique fuel, created jointly by Pratt & Whitney, Ashland Shell and Monsanto. It was known originally as PF-1 and latterly as JP-7. Having a

The 'Roadrunners'

Before the A-12 had flown, the CIA had begun the process of finding pilots for the programme. In all, 11 were chosen from Air Force units, all having undergone rigorous medical examinations and the CIA's own security 'sheep-dipping' process. Conversion flying carried on hand-in-hand with flight trials, the first Agency pilot flying the A-12 in the spring of 1963. The test programme reached a major milestone on 20 July, when Mach 3 was achieved for the first time. Serious intake problems were slowly overcome and by November 1965 the Oxcart team was declared operational. It was to be May 1967 before the A-12 actually went into action. In the intervening period the Oxcart pilots honed their skills, although not without the loss of four aircraft. The aircraft had been flown to Mach 3.56 and 96,200 ft (29322 m).

The CIA A-12 operation was designated the 1129th Special Activities Squadron. The roadrunner was adopted as its badge.

Early A-12 pilots christened the aircraft 'Cygnus'. Here one is seen emerging from its Groom Lake barn.

much higher ignition temperature than JP-4, standard electrical ignition systems were useless. Instead, a chemical ignition system (CIS) was developed, using a highly volatile pyrophoric fluid known as tri-ethyl borane (TEB). TEB is extremely flash-sensitive when oxidised, so the small TEB tank carried on the aircraft – to allow engine afterburner start-up both on the ground and aloft – was pressurised using gaseous nitrogen to ensure the system remained inert. Liquid nitrogen carried in three dewar flasks situated in the front nose gear well was used to provide a positive 'head' of gaseous nitrogen in the fuel tanks. This prevented the depleted tanks from crushing as the aircraft descended into the denser atmosphere to land or refuel. In addition, this inert gas reduced the risk of inadvertent vapour ignition.

Go-ahead from the CIA

Oxcart received a shot in the arm on 30 January 1960 when the Agency gave Lockheed ADP the go-ahead to manufacture and test a dozen A-12s, including one two-seat conversion trainer. With Lockheed's chief test pilot, Louis W. Schalk, onboard, work on refining the aircraft's design continued in parallel with construction work at the jet's secret test site in Nevada. Area 51, Groom Dry Lake (referred to variously as 'the Ranch' or 'the Area'), was initially built for the U-2 test programme in the mid-1950s. Located 100 miles (160 km) northwest of Las Vegas, the site offered an expansive dry lake bed, exceptional remoteness and good weather year round. Its 5,000-ft (1525-m) runway was too short, however, and all other facilities were inadequate for this new programme. A new water well was drilled and new recreation facilities were provided for the construction workers who were billeted in trailer houses. An 8,500-ft (2590-m) runway was constructed, and 18 miles (29 km) of off-base highway were resurfaced to allow 500,000 US gal (1.9 million litres) of PF-1 fuel to be trucked in every month. Three US Navy hangars together

with Navy housing units were transported to the site in readiness for the arrival of the A-12 prototype, expected in May 1961.

Difficulties in procuring and working with titanium, coupled with problems experienced by Pratt & Whitney, soon meant that the anticipated first flight date slipped. Even with completion date of the first aircraft put back to Christmas 1961 and initial test flight postponed to late February 1962, the J58 would still not be ready. Eventually, Kelly decided that J75 engines would be used in the interim to propel the A-12 to a 'halfway house' of only 50,000 ft (15245 m) and Mach 1.6.

The flight crew selection process evolved by the Pentagon's Special Activities Office representative (Colonel Houser Wilson) and the Agency's USAF liaison officer (Brigadier General Jack Ledford, succeeded by Brigadier Paul Bacalis) got under way in 1961. On completion of the final screening, the first pilots were William Skliar, Kenneth Collins, Walter Ray, Alonzo Walter, Mele Vojvodich, Jack Weeks, Jack Layton, Dennis Sullivan, David Young, Francis Murray and Russ Scott (only six of them were destined to fly operational missions). These elite pilots then began

60-6938 taxis at the 'Ranch' for an Oxcart training mission. Late in the programme the aircraft acquired an all-over 'Iron Ball' finish and national insignia. Those flying with 1129th SAS Det 1 at Kadena had no insignia and wore spurious five-digit serials (starting with '77') in red on the fin.

Bottom: The A-12B taxis for take-off at Area 51. It was never painted in the all-over black scheme, although it did receive the black edges.

Below: The 'Goose' approaches the tanker. The USAF established the 903rd ARS with KC-135Qs to support Oxcart flights.

The 'Titanium Goose'

Clarence L. 'Kelly' Johnson is seen in the rear cockpit of the A-12B, strapped in for a low-level flight. This was the only time Johnson ever flew in a member of the Blackbird family.

To aid pilot conversion the fourth aircraft (60-6927) was completed as the sole A-12B trainer, with a second, raised cockpit in the Q-bay. This aircraft retained its J75 engines throughout its career, restricting it to about Mach 1.6. It first flew in January 1963 and was based at Groom Lake until the end of the Oxcart programme in 1968. In addition to its regular use as a conversion tool, the 'Titanium Goose' was occasionally used for flight-test work where two pilots were required, although such work usually was accomplished in the simulator.

Black Shield

After many months of waiting, the 1129th SAS was finally given an operation on 17 May 1967. Three aircraft (127, 129 and 131) were dispatched to Kadena AB on Okinawa to fly missions over North Vietnam (and later Korea). The first mission was launched on 31 May, and the last on 8 May the following year. A total of 29 operational missions was flown.

The pilots of the 1129th SAS Det 1 were awarded the CIA's Star for Valor.

The 1129th SAS Det 1 Black Shield team used the large white hangars at top right. This complex was subsequently used by the SR-71s of the 9th SRW's OL-8 when they took over the Far East reconnaissance mission.

taking trips to the David Clark Company in Worcester, Massachusetts, to be outfitted with their own personal S-901 full pressure suits – just like those worn by the Mercury and Gemini astronauts.

In late 1961 Colonel Robert Holbury was appointed base commander of Groom Dry Lake; his director of Flight Operations would be Colonel Doug Nelson. In the spring of 1962 eight F-101 Voodoos to be used as companion trainers and pace/chase aircraft, two T-33s for pilot proficiency and a C-130 for cargo transportation arrived at the

remote base. A large 'restricted airspace zone' was enforced by the Federal Aviation Agency (FAA) to enhance security around 'the Area', and security measures were invoked upon North American Air Defense (NORAD) and FAA radar controllers, to ensure that fast-moving targets seen on their screens were not discussed. Planned air refuelling operations of Oxcart aircraft would be conducted by the 903rd Air Refueling Squadron at Beale AFB, California. The unit was equipped with KC-135Q tankers which possessed separate 'clean' tankage and plumbing to isolate the A-12's fuel from the tanker's JP4, plus special ARC-50 distance-ranging radios for use in precision, long-distance, high-speed join-ups with the A-12s.

With the first A-12 at last ready for final assembly, the entire fuselage, minus wings, was crated, covered with canvas and loaded on a special $100,000 trailer. At 02.30 on 26 February 1962, the slow-moving convoy left Burbank; it arrived safely at Area 51 at 13.00, two days later. By 24 April, engine test runs together with low- and medium-speed taxi tests had been successfully completed.

First flight

It was time for Lou Schalk to take to the aircraft on a high-speed taxi run that would culminate in a momentary lift-off and landing roll-out onto the dry salty lake bed. For this first 'hop' the stability augmentation system (SAS) was left uncoupled; it would be properly tested in flight. As A-12 article number 121 accelerated down the runway, Lou recalled: "I had a very light load of fuel so it sort of accelerated really fast. I was probably three or four per cent behind the aft limit centre of gravity when I lifted off the airplane, so it was unstable. Immediately after lift-off, I really didn't think I was going to be able to put the airplane back on the ground safely because of lateral, directional and longitudinal oscillations. The airplane was very difficult to handle but I finally caught up with everything that was happening, got back control enough to set it back down, and chop engine power. Touchdown was on the lake bed instead of the runway, creating a tremendous cloud of dust into which I disappeared entirely. The tower controllers were calling me to find out what was happening and I was answering, but the UHF antenna was located on the underside of the airplane (for best transmission in flight) and no one could hear me. Finally, when I slowed down and started my turn on the lake bed and re-emerged from the dust cloud, everyone breathed a sigh of relief."

Two days later Lou took the Oxcart on a full flight. A faultless 07.05 take-off was followed shortly thereafter by all the left wing fillets being shed. Constructed from RAM,

Left: This was the first picture released (in 1982) of the A-12, depicting 60-6932 which was the aircraft lost on an engine check flight just before it was due to return to the US at the end of Black Shield. The aircraft and its pilot, Jack Weeks, disappeared without trace.

Below: 60-6928 was also lost when a massive leak caused it to run out of fuel during a Groom Lake training flight. During the Black Shield deployment, training continued at Groom Lake. The final A-12 flight was conducted by Frank Murray in 60-6934 on 21 June 1968.

Tagboard

When the Powers shoot-down effectively ended US manned overflights, the idea of unmanned operations became highly attractive. Initially, the idea of a drone A-12 was discussed, before a smaller ramjet-powered vehicle was introduced. The first study authorisation was received from the CIA on 10 October 1962. The drone design drew heavily on the aerodynamics of the A-12, and used the Marquardt RJ43 engine from the Bomarc missile. Codenamed Tagboard, the drone was initially developed under the designation Q-12, later becoming the D (for Daughter) -21, while the launch vehicle, a converted A-12, became the M (for Mother) -21.

these elements were fortunately non-structural and Lou recovered the aircraft back at Groom Dry Lake without further incident.

On 30 April – nearly a year behind schedule – Lou took the A-12 on its 'official' first flight. With appropriate government representatives on hand, the 59-minute flight took the aircraft to a top speed and altitude of 340 kt (390 mph; 628 km/h) and 30,000 ft (9145 m). On 4 May the aircraft went supersonic for the first time and reached Mach 1.1. Kelly began to feel confident that the flight test programme would progress rapidly, and even recover some of the time lost during the protracted manufacturing process. Another Lockheed test pilot, Bill Park, joined the Skunk Works team to share the burden with Lou. On 26 June the second A-12 arrived at Area 51 and was immediately assigned to a three-month static RCS test programme. The third and fourth aircraft arrived during October and November. The latter was a two-seat A-12 trainer, nick-named 'the Goose' by its crews, and was powered throughout its life by two J75s. On 5 October another milestone

This series of photos shows the M-21/D-21 pair during captive carry tests from Groom Dry Lake. The M-21 arrived in August 1964 for flight trials, before being mated for the first flight with the drone on 22 December. During the trials in 1965 the D-21 was fitted with a frangible nosecone and exhaust fairing, later to be discarded. One of the problems faced was getting enough unrestricted airspace to reach the required launch speed.

*Above and right:
Without the D-21 drone,
the M-21 had the same
phenomenal
performance as a
standard A-12, but with
the extra payload
became very sluggish.
Eventually, when the
drone's intake and
exhaust covers were
discarded, the
Marquardt ramjet was
used to augment the
thrust from the M-21's
J58s. The drone engine
was started at Mach
1.24, and fuel was
transferred from the
M-21 prior to launch to
top up the D-21's tanks.*

*Below: In all-black
scheme an M-21/D-21
combination taxis for a
nosecone separation
trial.*

*Below right: One of
several methods tested
for removing the
nosecone was the use of
pyrotechnics, with this
result. It was virtually
impossible for any
system to be employed
which did not damage
the drone's airframe nor
cause debris to be
ingested.*

was achieved when the A-12 flew for the first time with a J58 (a J75 was retained in the right nacelle until 15 January 1963, when the first fully J58-powered flight took place).

National priority

On 27 October 1962, Major Rudolph Anderson's U-2 was shot down by an SA-2 while monitoring Soviet SS-N-4 medium-range ballistic missile (MRBMs) and SS-N-5 intermediate-range ballistic missiles (IRBMs) build-ups during the Cuban missile crisis. Just like the Gary Powers shoot-down two and a half years earlier, the U-2's vulnerability had been demonstrated in a spectacular fashion; regrettably, Major Anderson lost his life in the incident. The significance of this event was certainly not lost on intelligence communities involved in Oxcart, and the successful prosecution of that programme now became a matter of highest national priority.

With test pilot Jim Eastham also recruited into Oxcart, the programme was still beset with problems, which were focused around the engines and air inlet control system

(AICS). The AICS regulated massive internal airflow throughout the aircraft's vast flight envelope, controlling and supplying air to the engines at the correct velocity and pressure. This was achieved using a combination of bypass door and translating centre-body spike position. At ground idle, taxiing and take-off, the spikes were positioned in the full-forward position allowing air to flow unimpeded to the engine's compressor face. In addition, supplementary inflow air was provided through the spike exit-louvres and from six forward bypass exit-louvres.

Early tests revealed that the engine required an even greater supply of ground air when operating at low power settings, a deficiency that was overcome by installing additional bypass doors just forward of the compressor face. The size of these variable-area 'inlet ports' was regulated by an external slotted-band and could draw air through two sets of doors. The task of opening or closing the doors was manually controlled by the pilot initially, but much later was accomplished automatically when a digital automatic flight control system computer was developed. Together, the forward bypass doors and the centre-body spikes were used to control the position of the normal shockwave just aft of the inlet throat. To avoid the loss of inlet efficiency caused by an improperly positioned shockwave, the shockwave was captured and held inside the converging-

Lockheed M-21/D-21 Groom Dry Lake, Nevada 1965/66

The D-21 Tagboard programme resulted in two M-21s and 30 D-21s. There were four launches, all using the second M-21, 60-6941. The first launch was undertaken on 5 March 1966. **Although the D-21 only flew for 120 miles (195 km), the launch process had been demonstrated successfully. On 27 April the second flight reached over 1,200 nm (2220 km; 1,380 miles) while the third, on 16 June, reached about 1,600 nm (2960 km; 1,840 miles) and completed eight pre-programmed turns. The only problem was that the drone failed to eject the sensor systems package. The M-21/D-21 programme was cancelled following the disastrous fourth launch.**

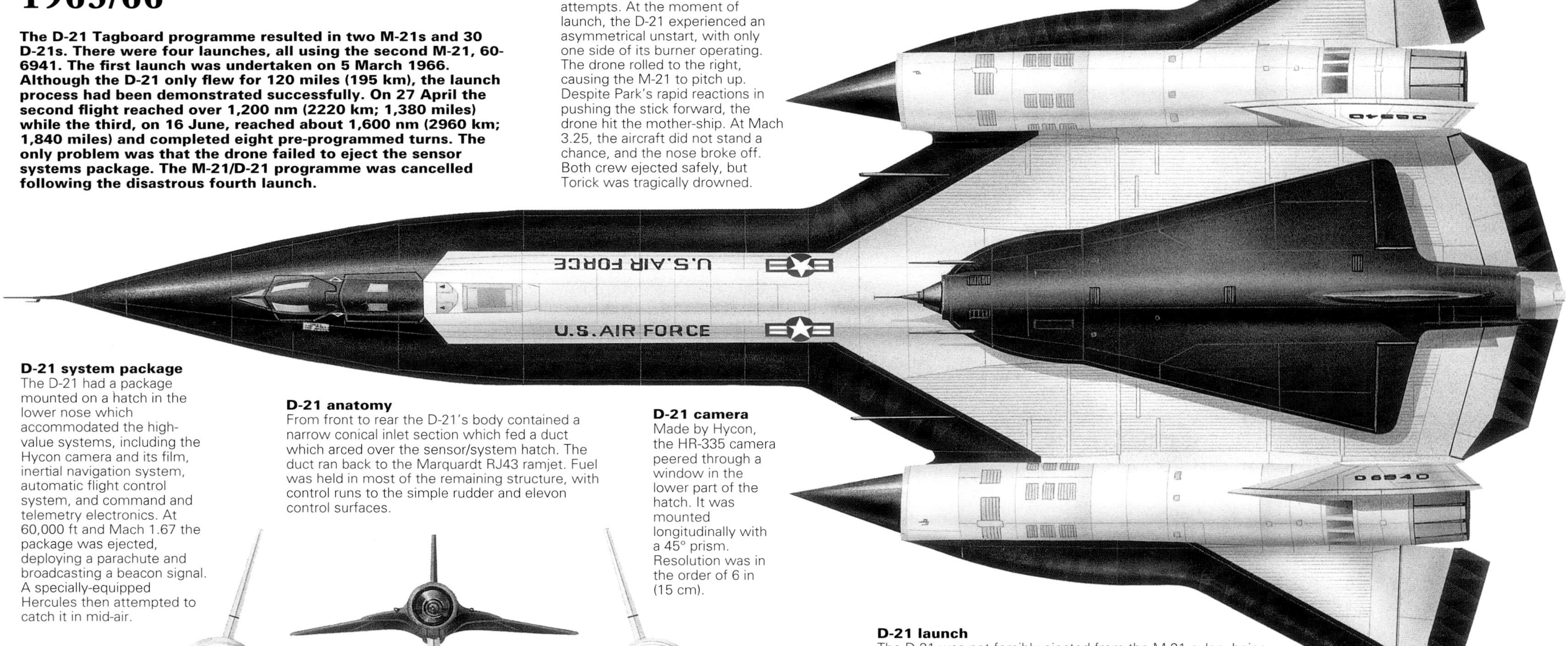

D-21 system package
The D-21 had a package mounted on a hatch in the lower nose which accommodated the high-value systems, including the Hycon camera and its film, inertial navigation system, automatic flight control system, and command and telemetry electronics. At 60,000 ft and Mach 1.67 the package was ejected, deploying a parachute and broadcasting a beacon signal. A specially-equipped Hercules then attempted to catch it in mid-air.

D-21 anatomy
From front to rear the D-21's body contained a narrow conical inlet section which fed a duct which arced over the sensor/system hatch. The duct ran back to the Marquardt RJ43 ramjet. Fuel was held in most of the remaining structure, with control runs to the simple rudder and elevon control surfaces.

D-21 camera
Made by Hycon, the HR-335 camera peered through a window in the lower part of the hatch. It was mounted longitudinally with a 45° prism. Resolution was in the order of 6 in (15 cm).

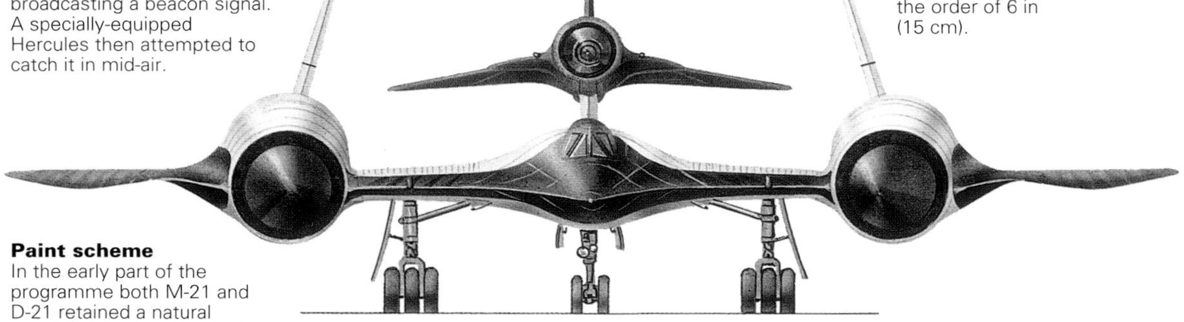

Paint scheme
In the early part of the programme both M-21 and D-21 retained a natural metal finish edged in black to cover the sections of RAM. Both later received an all-black scheme.

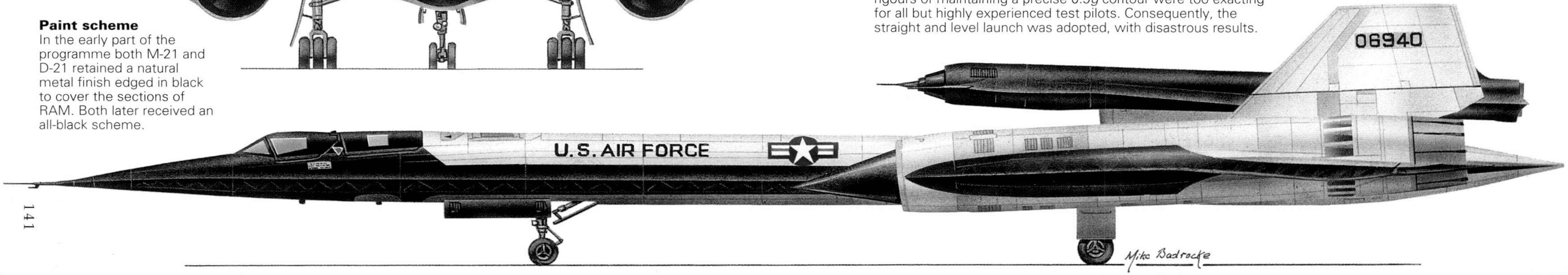

The loss of '941
On 30 June 1966 Bill Park (pilot) and Ray Torick (launch system operator) attempted the fourth D-21 launch, using a level 1 g launch instead of the slightly pitching forward 0.9 g method used in the three previous attempts. At the moment of launch, the D-21 experienced an asymmetrical unstart, with only one side of its burner operating. The drone rolled to the right, causing the M-21 to pitch up. Despite Park's rapid reactions in pushing the stick forward, the drone hit the mother-ship. At Mach 3.25, the aircraft did not stand a chance, and the nose broke off. Both crew ejected safely, but Torick was tragically drowned.

M-21 mother-ship
The M-21 differed little from the standard A-12, but incorporated a second cockpit for the launch systems operator in the Q-bay. A single dorsal pylon was provided to mount the drone, aerodynamically clean but strong enough to carry the 11,000-lb (4990-kg) D-21. The pylon included a fuel line for topping off the drone's tanks and emergency jettison equipment.

D-21 launch
The D-21 was not forcibly ejected from the M-21 pylon, being allowed to float free after engine ignition at Mach 3.25. Initially it was decided that a gentle pushover manoeuvre would be required to provide sufficient separation at launch, but after the first three successful launches it was felt that the demanding rigours of maintaining a precise 0.9g contour were too exacting for all but highly experienced test pilots. Consequently, the straight and level launch was adopted, with disastrous results.

Mike Badrocke

141

Senior Bowl

Even before the loss of the M-21, Lockheed was proposing that the B-52H would make a much safer launch platform for the D-21 drones. In order to achieve the necessary speed and altitude for launch, a booster rocket was required. The 4200th Test Wing was established at Beale to operate the Senior Bowl programme, although initial tests were flown from Groom Lake.

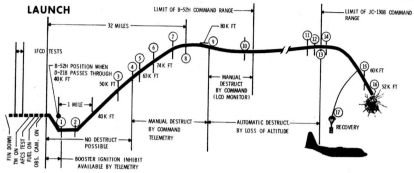

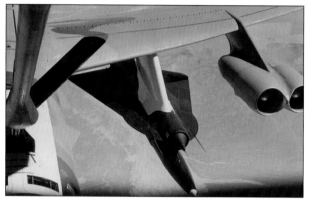

Above: A boomer's eye view of a D-21B and its booster while the B-52H carrier refuels. The test programme got off to a bad start when a drone accidentally fell from a B-52 and the booster ignited. The first scheduled launch was on 6 November 1967, the flight ending in failure. It was not until 16 June 1968 that a D-21B flew its 3,000-nm (5555-km; 3,452-mile) design range, achieving over 90,000 ft (27432 m) and ejecting its film package successfully.

D-21B Sequence of Events

BOOSTER IGNITION–	5 DESTRUCT ALTITUDE SWITCH OPEN	9 AUTOMATIC DESTRUCT CIRCUITRY ARM	14 FUEL "OFF"
5° PITCH-UP, FOLLOWED BY 1°/SEC PULL-UP	6 ENGINE IGNITION: AUTO DESTRUCT CIRCUIT COMPLETE	10 COMMAND AND T/M "OFF"	15 EJECT HATCH
TRANSITION TO FINAL CLIMB TRAJECTORY	7 APU LOAD TAKE-OVER	11 COMMAND "ON"	16 AUTOMATIC DESTRUCT
MANUAL DESTRUCT CIRCUIT COMPLETE	8 BOOSTER JETTISON, AFCS TO MACH HOLD	12 BEACONS "ON" AND T/M "ON"	17 HATCH RECOVERY
		13 DESTRUCT DISABLE	

Above left: This view shows a D-21B (as the B-52 version was known) under the specially designed carrier on a B-52H. The pylon used the Hound Dog missile attachments under the inner wings of the bomber.

diverging nozzle slightly behind the narrowest part of the 'throat', allowing the maximum pressure rise across the normal shock.

Once airborne and with landing gear retracted, the forward bypass doors would close automatically. At Mach 1.4 the doors began to modulate automatically to obtain a programmed pressure ratio between 'dynamic' pressure at the inlet cowl on one side of the 'throat' and 'static' duct pressure on the other side. At 30,000 ft (9145 m) the inlet spike unlocked and began its rearward translation at Mach 1.6, achieving its full aft translation of 26 in (66 cm) at the design speed of Mach 3.2 (the inlets' most efficient speed). Spike scheduling was determined as a function of Mach number, with a bias for abnormal angle of attack, angle of sideslip, or rate of vertical acceleration. The rearward translation of the spike gradually repositioned the oblique

Left: Only four operational D-21B launches were made, on 9 November 1969, 16 December 1970, 4 March 1971 and 20 March 1971. Two drones were lost, including one in the target area, and neither of the others managed to return the sensor packs.

Below: The solid fuel booster took the D-21 to 80,000 ft and Mach 3.2.

shockwave which extended back from the spike tip and the normal shockwave which stood at right angles to the airflow, and increased the inlet contraction ratio (the ratio between the inlet area and the 'throat' area). At Mach 3.2, with the spike fully aft, the 'capture-airstream-tube-area' had increased 112 per cent (from 8.7 to 18.5 sq ft/0.8 to 1.7 m²), while the 'throat' restriction had decreased by 46 per cent of its former size (from 7.7 to 4.16 sq ft/0.7 to 0.4 m²).

A peripheral 'shock trap' bleed slot (positioned around the inside surface of the duct, just forward of the 'throat' and set at precisely two boundary layer displacement thickness) 'shaved off' seven per cent of the stagnant inlet airflow and stabilised the terminal (normal) shock. It was then rammed across the bypass plenum through 32 shock trap tubes spaced at regular intervals around the circumference of the shock trap. As the compressed air travelled through the secondary passage, it firmly closed the suck-in doors while cooling the exterior of the engine casing before it was exhausted through the ejector nozzle. Boundary layer air was removed from the surface of the centrebody spike at the point of its maximum diameter. This potentially turbulent air was then ducted through the spike's hollow supporting struts and dumped overboard through nacelle exit louvres. The bypass system was thus able to match widely varying volumes of air entering the inlet system with an equal volume of air leaving the ejector nozzle, throughout the entire speed range of the aircraft.

Increasing the pressure differential

The aft bypass doors were opened at mid-Mach to minimise the aerodynamic drag which resulted from dumping air overboard through the forward bypass doors. The inlet system created internal pressures which reached 18 psi (124 kPa) when operating at Mach 3.2 and 80,000 ft (24390 m), where the ambient air pressure is only 0.4 psi (2.7 kPa). This extremely large pressure differential led to a forward thrust vector which resulted in the forward inlet producing 54 per cent of the total thrust. A further 29 per cent was produced by the ejector, while the J58 engine contributed only 17 per cent of the total thrust at high Mach.

Inlet airflow disturbances resulted if the delicate balance of airflow conditions that maintained the shockwave in its normal position was upset. Such disturbances were called 'unstarts'. These disruptions occurred when the normally placed supersonic shockwave was 'belched' forward from a

Above: Jim Eastham (left) made the first flight of the YF-12A on 7 August 1963. Standing with him is one of the test fire control officers, Ray Scalise.

Below: This single photograph of the prototype YF-12A was released in February 1964, the first tangible evidence of the Mach 3 aircraft programme.

AF-12 interceptor

Initially known as the AF-12, what became the YF-12A was a development of the A-12 optimised for long-range interception, utilising the Hughes AN/ASG-18 fire control system developed for the cancelled F-108 Rapier. The seventh, eighth and ninth A-12s were redirected to AF-12 development.

'Kelly' Johnson stands proudly in front of the third and final YF-12 at Groom Lake. During the early test period the aircraft had only the RAM edges painted, and carried 'FX' buzzcodes.

balanced position in the inlet throat, causing an instant drop in inlet pressure and thrust. With the engines mounted at mid-semi-span, the shockwave departure manifested itself in a vicious yaw toward the 'unstarted' inlet; sometimes they were so violent that crew members' helmets would be knocked hard against the canopy framing. To break a sustained unstart and recapture the disturbed inlet shockwave, the pilot would have to open the bypass doors on the unstarted inlet and return them to the smooth-flowing but less efficient position that they were in just prior to the disturbance. Early A-12 test flights involved increasing the aircraft's speed by increments of one-tenth of a Mach number and manually selecting the next spike position. If the inlet dynamics worked well the aircraft was decelerated and recovered back to 'the Area', where the dynamics would be further analysed and incorporated into the sched-

ule. More often, however, there would be a mismatch between spike position and inlet duct requirements and a vicious unstart would result. It took 66 flights to push the speed envelope from Mach 2.0 to Mach 3.2, and the incidence of unstarts was greatly reduced only when pneu-

Article 1001, the first YF-12A, is seen at Groom Lake. The streamlined pods under each engine nacelle contained cameras to record the launch and separation of the Hughes AIM-47 missiles. Note the folded ventral fin under the rear fuselage and the 'porthole' aft of the FCO position – painted on to confuse.

The first YF-12A touches down at the 'Ranch' after a successful maiden flight. The existence of the YF-12 was made public at an early date (although President Johnson referred to the aircraft as the 'A-11') to deflect the rumours circulating regarding the far more sensitive A-12 Oxcart programme.

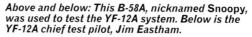

System tests

The ASG-18/AIM-47 was developed as the first pulse-Doppler long-range look-up/look-down weapon system, and after the YF-12 programme terminated was evolved into the AWG-9/AIM-54 used by the F-14. The system was thoroughly tested prior to fitment on the YF-12, including a series of tests mounted in a converted B-58. The entire system proved to be generally successful, despite its complexities.

The bulky radome covered a massive 40-in (1.02-m) diameter radome for the ASG-18. Note that both the port missile bays are open.

Above and below: This B-58A, nicknamed Snoopy, was used to test the YF-12A system. Below is the YF-12A chief test pilot, Jim Eastham.

Another aircraft used in the YF-12A test programme was this Boeing JQB-47E, which survived two AIM-47 missile shots.

Below right: Jim Eastham prepares to fly the second YF-12A on a test mission from Area 51. Note that a fairing has been fitted to hide the infra-red search and track sensors. Eastham took a YF-12A to Mach 3.23 in January 1965.

Below: Marked for the three YF-12A records, 60-0936 poses with an AIM-47 (earlier GAR-9) missile. The weapon, of which three were carried, had a 250-kT nuclear warhead.

matic pressure gauges that had been installed on the inlet systems to sense pressure variations of as little as 0.25 psi (1.72 kPa) were replaced by an electrically controlled system from aircraft number nine (60-6932).

During December 1960, a separate project group under Russ Daniell was organised in the Skunk Works, working independently of the A-12 team. From joint 715 (a point perpendicular to where the inboard wing leading edge meets the fuselage chine), the entire forward fuselage forebody of an A-12 was modified to create a Mach 3.2 interceptor. Originally designated AF-12, the aircraft would be equipped with the 1,380-lb (625-kg) Hughes AN/ASG-18 pulse-Doppler radar that had been intended for the North American F-108 Rapier, which was cancelled on 23 September 1959. DoD officials decided that development of this outstanding radar and the integrated 818-lb (371-kg) GAR-9 (later redesignated AIM-47) missile system should continue on a 'stand alone' basis. Hughes continued R&D work with both systems on a specially modified Convair B-58A Hustler (serial 55-665, nicknamed *Snoopy 1*).

AF-12 review

On 31 May 1960 the Air Force conducted a mock-up review of the AF-12, and was impressed. By June, AF-12 wind-tunnel tests revealed directional stability problems resulting from the heavily revised nose and cockpit configuration. As a result, a large folding fin was mounted under the aft fuselage, as were two shorter fixed fins beneath each nacelle. A bomber version of the A-12, designated RB-12, also reached the mock-up stage, but was still-born because

An AIM-47 is seen on its lowered rack in a YF-12A. The first powered launch was undertaken on 18 March 1965, after an earlier separation-only test. Six out of seven AIM-47 tests resulted in hits, including one launched from 75,000 ft at Mach 3.2, fired at a target approaching head-on at 1,500 ft.

A-12 cockpit

One glance inside the cockpit of the A-12 gives an impression of the kind of piloting ability required by the few candidates selected to fly the type. Not only did the pilot have to control a hugely complex machine, he also had to navigate accurately while travelling at unprecedented speeds. Furthermore, the pilot was responsible for monitoring and operating the reconnaissance systems.

The cockpit itself was dominated by the circular display for the driftsight, which allowed him to look downwards for visual checks on his progress, and to check for cloud cover in the target area. With so many instruments to cram in to a restricted dashboard area, there was little pattern to the layout, and many instruments had smaller read-outs than would otherwise be normal. The principal flight/navigation instruments were grouped to the left of centre, including radio compass, airspeed indicator, altimeter, attitude indicator and turn-and-bank indicator. Beneath these were four dials for manual control of the forward bypass doors and inlet spikes. To the right of centre was the vertical speed indicator and a strip of duplicated engine instruments.

The pilot sat on a Lockheed SR-1 ejection seat, which was fired by pulling the prominent D-ring pull.

This is the rear cockpit of the A-12B trainer. Although the instrumentation is the same as that in the front seat, the major difference is the lack of the circular driftsight.

YF-12 cockpit

Shown below is the front cockpit of the YF-12A, which is ergonomically friendly compared to the A-12. The upper circular display was a radar screen, while below that was the large attitude indicator and radio compass. To the left of these were strip displays for airspeed (in Mach and knots), while to the right were strip indicators for vertical speed and altitude. The engine instruments were again in a double column to the right, and further to the right were the fuel controls.

Below is the rear cockpit of the YF-12A, a good deal less complicated than the front. The fire control officer had large display screens for the radar and IR. On either side of these are elegant strip displays for speed (left) and altitude (right). Note that the Fire Control Officer has an early form of track-ball control on the right-hand console. The cockpit layout was subsequently altered during NASA test programmes.

Above: After the first two AIM-47 launches had been accomplished using the second YF-12, the first and third (illustrated) flew to Eglin to fire the next five. This aircraft notched up three launches, two against Q-2C drones and one against the JQB-47.

Right: A great indication of the aerodynamic effectiveness of the forward fuselage chines is provided by the amount of extra keel area needed by the YF-12A to counter the lack of nose chines. In addition to the two undernacelle fins, a large folding ventral fin was added.

Right: Immediately prior to the official announcement of the existence of the 'A-11', two YF-12As were flown into Edwards AFB and operated from there. They were finally introduced to the media on 30 September 1964 although it was to be some time further before public cameras were allowed near the type.

Below: This underview of a YF-12A shows graphically the series of auxiliary doors located along the engine nacelles.

it represented too much of a threat to the highly political North American XB-70A Valkyrie. On 7 August 1963, several weeks after being moved to Groom Dry Lake, Jim Eastham climbed aboard the interceptor prototype and took aircraft 60-6934 (the seventh A-12) for its first flight; he later modestly described it as a 'typical production test flight'.

On 24 May 1963, the programme received a temporary set-back when Agency pilot Ken Collins was forced to eject from A-12 60-6926 during a subsonic test flight. The crash occurred 14 miles (22.5 km) south of Wendover, Utah. To preserve secrecy, a media cover story referred to the aircraft as a Republic F-105 Thunderchief. An accident investigation established the cause of the incident as a pitot-static system failure due to icing.

Preparing to go public

As 1963 drew to a close, nine A-12s at Groom Dry Lake had notched up a total of 573 flights totalling 765 hours. A year later, 11 A-12s had logged over 1,214 flights amounting to 1,669 hours – only six hours 23 minutes were at Mach 3 and only 33 minutes at the design speed of Mach 3.2. As Oxcart grew in both size and cost, concern was expressed within both the Agency and Air Force about how much longer the programme could be kept a secret. It was also noted that technological data accumulated during the project would be of immense value in conjunction with 'white world' feasibility studies into supersonic transport. In November 1963, President Johnson was briefed on the programme, after which he directed that a formal announcement be prepared for release early in the new year. Kelly Johnson noted in his diary: "Plans going forward for surfacing of the AF-12 programme. I worked on the draft to be used by President Johnson and proposed the terminology 'A-11' as it was the non-anti-radar-version."

On Saturday 29 February 1964, a few hours prior to the President announcing the existence of the programme, two AF-12s – 60-6934 and 60-6935 – were flown from Groom Dry Lake to Edwards AFB by Lou Schalk and Bill Park, thereby diverting attention from Area 51 and the 'black world' A-12 programme. At Edwards, a 'buzz' had gone out to some senior staff that something special might be happening on the first morning of their weekend off. In consequence, a few dozen people witnessed the arrival of the extremely sleek aircraft, the like of which no-one outside the programme had seen before – except for desert

dwellers and the occasional incredulous sighting by airline crews. Lou Schalk remembers taxiing to their assigned hangar as eyes bulged and heads nodded in utter disbelief. Unfortunately, the arrival lost a touch of elegance when, to aid push-back into the hangar, they turned the aircraft 180° at the entrance. Lou recalls, "This turnaround sent hot engine exhaust gases flooding into the hangar, which caused the overhead fire extinguishers valves to open. These valves were big – like the flood valves on hangar decks of aircraft-carriers – and the desert had not seen so much water since Noah's embarkation!"

Air Force fighter

Now an Air Force programme, the aircraft's designation was changed to YF-12A to suit USAF nomenclature. The third YF-12A, 60-6936, soon joined the other two examples at Edwards, and Jim Eastham continued the envelope extension programme. On 16 April 1964, the first airborne AIM-47 missile separation test was conducted. Unfortunately, as onboard cameras showed, the weapon's nose-down pitch was inadequate; had rocket motor ignition also been conducted, the missile would probably have ended up in the front of the cockpit! Back at 'the Ranch', on 9 July 1964, Bill Park experienced a complete lock-up of his flight controls in aircraft 60-6939 as he descended for landing following a high-Mach flight. Despite trying to save the brand-new aircraft from rolling under while turning on to final approach, he could not stop the bank angle from increasing and was forced to eject. Punching out at 200 kt (370 mph; 600 km/h) in a 34° bank, no more than 200 ft (60 m) above the ground, Park was extremely lucky to survive unscathed.

A milestone in the programme was reached on 27 January 1965, when an A-12 flew a 2,580-mile (1170-km)

The F-12 interceptor programme officially ended on 5 January 1968, although the chances of the programme going ahead had slowly evaporated during 1967, despite the excellent results shown by the missile tests. The first aircraft was used to create the SR-71C trainer, and the remaining aircraft were loaned to NASA, albeit continuing some Air Force work. In 1970/71 the USAF used this, the third aircraft, to mimic MiG-25 'Foxbats' for air defence studies. During the course of these it was lost on landing at Edwards.

Left: The first YF-12A is seen at Edwards in full interceptor configuration, with missile bay doors open and infra-red turrets. The aircraft was grounded on 14 August 1966.

F-12B fighter

The F-12B would have been the production interceptor, based on the YF-12A design which had largely been seen as a technology demonstrator. The key change was the shoe-horning of the ASG-18 radar antenna into a slimmer, chined nose. On 14 May 1965 a development contract was received but no production decision was ever taken.

Right: This is the full-size mock-up of the proposed F-12B fighter which was displayed to USAF officials in July 1964. The return to the chined forward fuselage eliminated the need for the extra fin area employed by the YF-12A.

The YF-12A programme was very successful, thanks in part to the 'pick and shovel' work already done by Lockheed (on the A-12) and Hughes (on the ASG-18). The cancellation was resented by many in Lockheed, especially as it was accompanied by an order to cut up the jigs for the entire Blackbird programme.

sortie in one hour 40 minutes, with three-quarters of the flight time spent at Mach 3.1. On 18 March, YF-12A '935 successfully engaged a Q-2C target drone at 40,000 ft (12195 m), while the interceptor flew at Mach 2.2 and 65,000 ft (19815 m). Aware of the number of world speed and altitude records held by the USSR, the DoD informed Kelly of its desire to use the YF-12A to wrestle several of those records from the Soviets. Accordingly, on 1 May 1965 (five years to the day that Gary Powers was shot down in his U-2 by a Soviet SA-2), six records were smashed by 60-6936 (see table below for details). Fourteen days later, the Skunk Works received a contract for

$500,000 for the production version of the interceptor, designated F-12B. No production go-ahead was given with the engineering contract but considerable optimism was generated. An equivalent sum was granted on 10 November to keep alive basic F-12B design work. Similarly, Hughes received $4.5 million to continue development of the AN/ASG-18 radar and fire control system.

On 28 December Mele Vojvodich took aircraft 60-6929 for a functional check flight (FCF) following a period of deep maintenance. On applying back pressure to the stick for rotation to lift-off, the aircraft's nose yawed viciously to one side. Mele attempted to correct the yaw with rudder, but this caused the nose to pitch up. The rush of instinctive responses which followed resulted in a series of counter-movements, completely opposite to what a pilot would expect to occur. Despite all the odds, Mele managed to get the aircraft to about 100 ft (30 m), where he ejected after just six seconds of flight. Incredibly, he survived and escaped serious injury. An accident investigation discovered that the pitch stability augmentation system (SAS) had been connected to the yaw SAS actuators, and *vice versa*, when the unit was reinstalled following maintenance. Thereafter, the SAS connectors were changed to ensure incorrect wiring was impossible.

The end of the F-12

On 29 March 1966, Kelly had a long meeting with Colonel Ben Bellis, System Project Officer (SPO), Hughes Aircraft Company and various members of the F-12 test force, during which he was asked to take on the task of integrating the weapons systems. He agreed to do so, and fire control tests were continued. However, Secretary of Defense McNamara opposed production of the aircraft and, as a result, on three occasions over the next two years he denied the Air Force access to $90 million worth of funds which had been appropriated by Congress to begin F-12B production. Following a Senate Armed Services Committee hearing into the future of continental air defence, it was decided, in the light of intelligence available at the time, to downgrade Aerospace Defense Command, which in turn

YF-12 records

The USAF was eager to reclaim important world records from the Soviets and so Lockheed was instructed in August 1964 to use the YF-12A. Although Lockheed managed the attempts, which took place at Edwards, naturally it was Air Force crews flying the aircraft. The record runs did not take place for some time, but easily shattered the existing marks.

Absolute Altitude, 80,257.86 ft (24468.86 m)
1 May 1965   Pilot, Col Robert L. 'Fox' Stephens. FCO, Lt Col Daniel Andre   YF-12A 60-6936
Absolute Speed over a straight course, 2,070.101 mph (3331.41 km/h)
1 May 1965   Pilot, Col Robert L. 'Fox' Stephens. FCO, Lt Col Daniel Andre   YF-12A 60-6936
Absolute Speed over a 1000-km closed course 1,643.041 mph (2644.146 km/h)
1 May 1965   Pilot, Lt Col Walter F. Daniel. FCO, Maj. Noel T. Warner   YF-12A 60-6936

For the record attempts the YF-12s were painted with a large white cross on the undersides for tracking purposes. Six records were set, including three absolutes. The five crew involved were Colonel Robert Stephens (centre), Lt Col Daniel Andre, Major Walter Daniel, Major Noel Warner, and Captain James Cooney.

NASA and the YF-12

In 1967 a deal was struck between NASA and the USAF, whereby NASA was given access to early A-12 wind tunnel data and in exchange agreed to provide a small team of highly skilled engineers to work on the SR-71 flight test programme. Under the leadership of Gene Matranga, the team from the Flight Research Center (FRC) at Ames was engaged on various stability and control aspects of the SR-71 at Edwards. This work helped hasten the SR-71 into the inventory and led to the establishment of a close working relationship between the Air Force and NASA.

On 5 June 1969, a memorandum of understanding was signed between the Air Force and NASA, which permitted the latter access to the two remaining YF-12s in storage. NASA paid for operational expenses and ADC supplied maintenance and logistic support. After both aircraft were fully instrumented, phase one of the programme got under way when, on 11 December 1969, the first YF-12 to fly in three years climbed away from Edwards. Phase one of the programme was controlled by the Air Force, and consisted of developing procedures establishing limitations for command and control and for working out possible bomber penetration tactics against an interceptor with YF-12 capabilities. This phase of the programme was terminated on 24 June 1971, during the closing stages of the 63rd flight of 60-6936, which had been used throughout the tests by the Air Force. Lieutenant Colonel Jack Layton and systems operator Major Bill Curtis were approaching the traffic pattern before recovery back at Edwards when a fire broke out as a result of a fuel line fatigue failure. The flames quickly enveloped the entire aircraft, and while on base leg both crew members safely ejected; '963 crashed into the middle of the dry lake bed and was totally destroyed.

While the YF-12s were being readied for flight, Donald L. Mallick and Fitzhugh L. Fulton Jr, the two NASA pilots who flew most of phase two of the programme, were checked out in the SR-71B. Later, Victor Horton and Ray Young, the two NASA backseaters, were checked out by Lieutenant Colonel Bill Campbell in a YF-12, and the civilian programme began. Utilisation of the high-speed platform was extensive, since NASA engineers at Langley were interested in aerodynamic experiments and testing advanced structures. Lewis Research Establishment wanted to study

Left: Wearing photo-calibration marks, the second YF-12A is seen flying without its ventral fin on one of a series of four flights aimed at assessing directional stability.

propulsion, while Ames concentrated on inlet aerodynamics and the correlation of wind tunnel and flight data. In addition, the aircraft was used to support various specialised experimentation packages. Taken together it was hoped that problems 'worked around' during the early test programme could be designed out of any future commercial SST venture, thereby avoiding expensive mistakes.

After the 22nd flight of '6935 on 16 June 1970, the aircraft was grounded for nine months for instrumentation changes. Following an FCF on 22 March 1971, four flights were flown without the folding ventral fin, to asses directional stability up to Mach 2.8.

NASA needed more aircraft, and as a result the Air Force supplied an SR-71A (article 2002, serial 64-17951) on 16 July 1971. This aircraft had been involved in the contractor flight test programme from the beginning, but the Air Force stipulated that it should only be used for propulsion testing. The first NASA flight of this aircraft – which at the behest of the Air Force was serial 60-6937 and referred to throughout the NASA test programme as a YF-12C – occurred on 24 May 1972.

During the course of various studies, it was discovered that inlet spike movement and bypass door operations were almost as effective as elevons and rudders in influencing the aircraft's flight path at high speed. In addition, propulsion system and flight control integration was an aspect of controlled testing by NASA in an effort to improve future mixed-compression inlet design.

Honeywell and Lockheed funded the Central Airborne Performance Analyser (CAPA). It was installed and tested by NASA and proved so successful that it was later fitted to operational SR-71s. The integrated automatic support system isolated faults and recorded the performance of 170 sub-systems (relating primarily to the inlet controls), on 0.5-in (1.27-cm) magnetic tape. Pre- and post-analysis of this onboard monitoring and diagnostic system proved highly cost effective and reduced maintenance manhours.

YF-12C 60-6937 (SR-71A 64-17951) was retired from the programme and placed in storage at Palmdale after its 88th flight with NASA on 28 September 1978. YF-12A 60-6935 continued operating until the programme ceased after its 145th NASA flight, flown by Fitz Fulton and Vic Horton on 31 October 1979. A week later, Colonel Jim Sullivan and Colonel R. Uppstrom ferried the aircraft to the Air Force museum at Dayton, Ohio, where it is displayed as the sole example of the YF-12.

Above: 60-6935 bore the brunt of the NASA operations, flying from December 1969 until its 145th and last NASA flight on 31 October 1979. It then made one more journey, to the USAF Museum at Wright-Patterson AFB for display. The YF-12A offered NASA a unique research vehicle, being able to cruise at over 2,000 mph and altitudes over 80,000 ft for extended periods of time. As much of the Administration's research efforts were aimed at supersonic transport aircraft, the YF-12's abilities were particularly welcome, allowing the investigation of many areas of flight control, structure and aerodynamics. Experiments could be carried externally, although most were carried in the converted fighter's missile bays. Some sorties were lengthy affairs, requiring inflight refuelling from the 100th ARW's KC-135Q force flying from nearby Beale.

Above: NASA's Ames Research Center proposed using the YF-12As as high-speed testbeds for various propulsion tests, using externally mounted experimental installations. This wind-tunnel model is seen with a dorsal installation of an experimental high-speed ramjet. The main load-bearing pylon would have been augmented by four bracing struts.

Right: Flying with a T-38A chase aircraft, the second YF-12A is seen carrying the Coldwall experiment. This was used to acquire heat transfer data for application to a future high-speed transport. It consisted of a stainless steel tube covered by a frangible ceramic coating.

SR-71A

Development of the A-12 had led to studies for various reconnaissance and bomber derivatives, including the RB-12, RS-12 and R-12. The latter was a pure reconnaissance aircraft, with a stretched fuselage housing more fuel and a second crew member. It was ordered into production for the Air Force, initially under the RS-71 designation. This was neatly transposed to become the SR (Strategic Reconnaissance)-71.

The SR-71 wing is built on a network of ribs and spars. The area inboard of the engine nacelles forms a large fuel tank. The skin sections do not form a perfect seal at low temperatures, and the tanks are often seen leaking.

Most of the Blackbird's shape is edged in a structure incorporating radar-absorbent material in the shape of re-entrant triangles. This is an early SR-71, still labelled as an R-12. Note the upper skin corrugations.

Right: The prototype SR-71A is seen at Palmdale prior to its first flight. It has only been partially painted at this point.

Below: Article 2001, the prototype SR-71A, turns lazily over the Mojave desert. The aircraft wore unique white markings during its career. It was lost on 10 January 1967 during braking trials on a wet runway.

Five SR-71s are seen on the Burbank production line in 1965. The Senior Crown aircraft followed on the line directly from the A-12/F-12.

rendered the F-12B unnecessary. On 5 January 1968, official notification was received from the Air Force to 'close down the F-12B'; the YF-12A programme was formally ended on 1 February.

So it fell to the 'black' A-12 Oxcart programme to validate the concept of high-altitude, sustained Mach 3 plus flight in an operational environment. By late 1965, all of the Agency pilots were Mach 3 qualified and the A-12 was ready for operational testing. Despite this, political sensitivities surrounding the Gary Powers shoot-down five years earlier conspired to ensure that the aircraft would never carry out missions over the USSR – the very country it was originally built to overfly. The initial site to which to deploy this multi-million dollar national security asset was decided as Cuba. By early 1964, Project Headquarters had already begun planning contingency overflights under the programme codename Skylark. On 5 August 1965, the director of the National Security Agency, General Marshall S. Carter, directed that Skylark achieve emergency operational readiness by 5 November; this capability was achieved (albeit on a limited basis), but never deployed.

Combat debut

Instead, 'Cygnus', as Agency pilots referred to the A-12, received its baptism of fire in the skies over Southeast Asia. Moves had begun on 22 March 1965 when, following a meeting with Brigadier General Jack Ledford (the CIA/USAF liaison officer), Secretary of Defense Cyrus Vance granted $3.7 million to provide support facilities at

Kadena AB, Okinawa for a planned deployment of 'Cygnus' aircraft under a project codenamed Black Shield. On 3 June, Secretary McNamara consulted the Secretary of the Air Force about the build-up of SA-2s around Hanoi and the possibility of substituting the more vulnerable U-2s with A-12s to conduct reconnaissance flights over the North Vietnamese capital. He was informed that once adequate aircraft performance was validated, Black Shield could be cleared to go.

Four A-12s were selected for Black Shield operations, Kelly Johnson taking personal responsibility for ensuring the aircraft were completely 'sqwark-free'. On 20 November 1965 a 'Cygnus' aircraft completed a maximum endurance flight of six hours 20 minutes, during which the A-12 reached speeds above Mach 3.2 and altitudes approaching 90,000 ft (27440 m). On 2 December the highly secretive 303 Committee received the first of many proposals to deploy Oxcart to the Far East. However, the proposal was rejected, as were several other submissions made throughout 1966. On 5 January 1967 another tragedy hit the programme when A-12 60-6928 crashed 70 miles (112 km) short of Groom Dry Lake. Its pilot Walt Ray ejected but was killed when he was unable to gain seat separation.

Oxcart deployment

In May 1967, the National Security Council was briefed that North Vietnam was about to receive surface-to-surface ballistic missiles. Such a serious escalation of the conflict would certainly require hard evidence to substantiate it, and consequently President Johnson was briefed on the threat. Richard Helms of the CIA proposed that the 303 Commit-

tee authorise deployment of Oxcart, since it was ideally equipped to carry out the task, having a superior camera to that used by U-2s or pilotless drones and being 'invulnerable to shoot-downs'. President Johnson approved the plan and in mid-May an airlift was begun to establish Black Shield at Kadena AB, on Okinawa.

At 08.00 on 22 May 1967 Mele Vojvodich deployed A-12 60-6937 from Area 51 to Okinawa during a flight which lasted six hours six minutes and included three inflight refuellings. Two days later Jack Layton joined Mele in 60-6930. 60-6932 flown by Jack Weeks arrived on Okinawa on 27 May, having been forced to divert to Wake Island for a day following INS and radio problems. The detachment was declared ready for operations on 29 May.

Above: The prototype SR-71A, 64-17950, first flew from Palmdale on 22 December 1964, piloted by Bob Gilliland with the rear cockpit left vacant. The one-hour plus flight topped 1,000 mph and ended up in this low flypast for the gathered officials at the request of 'Kelly' Johnson. Flying chase in the F-104 was Jim Eastham.

Left: Robert J. Gilliland poses in the cockpit of an SR-71A. Gilliland had been the fourth pilot in the Blackbird programme, following Lou Schalk, Bill Park and Jim Eastham.

An early photograph shows the first SR-71B trainer. This aircraft is the longest serving of all the Blackbirds. Having been the first aircraft delivered to the USAF, it was still active in the late 1990s with NASA.

SR-71B

Experience with the A-12 had shown the value of the 'Goose' two-seat trainer, so two SR-71B trainers were incorporated into the Senior Crown production programme at an early stage. These were the seventh and eighth aircraft built. 64-17956 was the first SR-71 delivered to the USAF, accepted at Beale AFB by the 4200th SRW on 7 January 1966 following a first flight on 18 November 1965. The second trainer first flew exactly a month later.

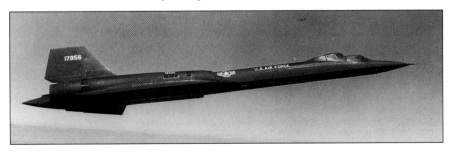

Left: The raised second cockpit of the SR-71B eroded performance slightly, although not to any drastic effect. The cockpit did reduce directional stability, requiring the addition of YF-12-style ventral fins under the engine nacelles.

YF-12C

Following the loss of one of its YF-12As, NASA requested the loan of an SR-71A to make up its test fleet. With an accepted surfeit of aircraft, the Air Force promptly loaned the second aircraft (64-17951), which received a new identity of YF-12C 06937 when it arrived at Edwards. Fitz Fulton and Victor Horton made the first NASA flight on 24 May 1972. The aircraft was used on many high-speed programmes, including Shuttle work.

Perhaps the only time different members of the Blackbird family flew together was during NASA programmes. Here the YF-12C partners the second YF-12A, the latter carrying high-speed cameras under the engine nacelles and the Coldwall high-speed heat exchange experiment.

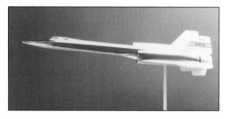

NASA proposed painting its Blackbird fleet in the house scheme of white with a blue band. This was dropped for a number of reasons: the scheme would have been difficult to keep clean, and the black paint did much to radiate heat.

Redolent of the M-21/D-21 combination, NASA proposed using the YF-12C as a launch platform for a hypersonic research drone.

SR-71A 2003 first flew on 24 March 1965, and was used heavily on the flight trial programme until it was lost on 25 January 1966. The pilot, Bill Weaver, survived, despite not using the ejection seat, but sadly the RSO, Jim Zwayer, perished.

Following weather reconnaissance flights on 30 May, it was determined that conditions were ideal for an A-12 camera run over North Vietnam, so project headquarters in Washington placed Black Shield on alert for its first operational mission. Avionics specialists checked various systems and sensors, and at 16.00 Mele Vojvodich and back-up pilot Jack Layton attended a mission alert briefing. At 22.00 (12 hours before planned take-off time) a review of the weather confirmed the mission was still on. The pilots went to bed, to ensure they received a full eight hours of 'crew rest'.

They awoke on the morning of 31 May to torrential rain – a new phenomenon to the desert-dwelling A-12s. However, meteorological conditions over 'the collection area' were good and at 08.00 Kadena received a final 'go'

Right: Refuelling became an important and regular part of SR-71 flying, and was tested at an early stage. The tankers were specially-modified KC-135Qs provided by the 9th SRW. Here the recipient is the ill-fated '952, complete with optical tracking mark just visible under the engine nacelle.

from Washington. On cue, Mele engaged both afterburners and made the first instrument-guided take-off of an A-12. A few minutes later Mele burst through cloud and flew 60-6937 up to 25,000 ft (7620 m), where he topped off the tanks from a KC-135. Disengaged from the tanker's boom, he accelerated and climbed to operational speed and altitude, after informing Kadena that aircraft systems were running as per the book and the back-up services of Jack Layton would not be required. Mele penetrated hostile airspace at Mach 3.2 and 80,000 ft (24390 m); the so-called 'front door' entry was made over Haiphong, then Hanoi, exiting North Vietnam near Dien Bien Phu. A second air refuelling took place over Thailand, followed by another climb to altitude and a second penetration of North Vietnamese airspace made near the Demilitarized Zone. Mele landed back at Kadena after three instrument approaches in driving rain.

In all, the flight had lasted three hours 40 minutes. Several SA-2s were fired at the aircraft but all detonated above and well behind their target. The photo-take was downloaded and sent by a special courier aircraft to the Eastman Kodak plant in Rochester, New York for processing. 60-6937's large camera successfully photographed 10 priority target categories, including 70 of the 190 known SAM sites. By mid-July A-12 overflights had determined with a high degree of confidence that there were no surface-to-surface missiles in North Vietnam.

SAM activity

During a sortie flown by Denny Sullivan on 28 October 1967, he had indications on his radar homing warning receiver (RHWR) of almost continuous radar activity focused on his A-12 while both inbound and outbound over North Vietnam, which also included the launch of a single SA-2. Two days later he was again flying high over North Vietnam when two SAM sites tracked him on his first pass. On his second pass, approaching Hanoi from the east, he again noted he was being tracked on radar. Over the next few minutes he counted no fewer than eight SA-2

detonations in "the general area though none were particularly close." After recovering the aircraft back at Kadena without further incident, a post-flight inspection revealed that a tiny piece of shrapnel had penetrated the lower wing fillet of his aircraft and become lodged against the support structure of the wing tank.

Pueblo missions

During 1967, a total of 41 A-12 missions was alerted, of which 22 were actually granted approval for flight. Between 1 January and 31 March 1968, 15 missions were alerted, of which six were flown, four over North Vietnam and two over North Korea. The latter two came about following seizure on the night of 23 January of the USS *Pueblo* – a US Navy signal intelligence (Sigint) vessel – by North Korea. The first sortie was attempted by Jack Weeks on 25 January, but a malfunction on the A-12 resulted in an abort shortly after take-off.

The next day, Frank Murray completed the task. "I left Kadena, topped off, then entered northern airspace over the Sea of Japan via the Korean Straits. My first pass started off near Vladivostok, then with the camera on I flew down the east coast of North Korea where we thought the boat was. As I approached Wonsan I could see the *Pueblo* through my view sight. The harbour was all iced up, except at the very entrance, and there she was, sitting off to the right of the main entrance. I continued to the border with South Korea, completed a 180° turn and flew back over North

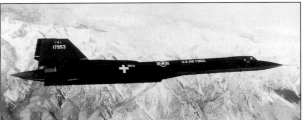

Korea. I made four passes, photographing the whole of North Korea from the DMZ to the Yahu border. As far as I know, I was undetected throughout the flight, but when I got back to Kadena some folks told me that the Chinese had detected me and told the North Koreans, but they never reacted."

Back at Kadena, the 'take' was immediately flown to Yakota AB, Japan where the 67th Reconnaissance Technical Squadron had been activated to enable the more timely exploitation of such data by theatre commanders.

On 8 May 1968 Jack Layton successfully completed a mission over North Korea, which proved to be the final operational flight of an A-12. After three years, a long-standing debate had been resolved concerning whether the A-12 or a programme known as Senior Crown should carry forward the strategic reconnaissance baton: Oxcart was vanquished. In early March 1968, SR-71s began arriving at Kadena to assume the Black Shield commitment.

Above: The first six SR-71As were used for the flight trials programme. These were followed by the two SR-71B trainers, and then the operational aircraft, which began with 2009/64-17958, which was delivered to Beale on 4 June 1966. Despite a temporary halt in deliveries, due mainly to plumbing problems, aircraft arrived quickly afterwards. This machine, the fourth operational aircraft, became something of a 'hangar queen'.

Above left: '953 was the fourth SR-71 built, and is seen here during initial flight tests, marked with a photo-calibration cross. It was lost on a test flight in December 1969.

This Lockheed drawing shows the B-71 proposal, which carried AGM-69 SRAM missiles in the chine bays and an attack radar in the recontoured nose. The aircraft was intended as an attacker of high-value targets.

B-71 bomber proposal

Despite the rejection of the RB-12 and RS-12, Lockheed continued to pursue a bomber Blackbird with the B-71. This was submitted to the Air Force following the cancellation of the XB-70 Valkyrie.

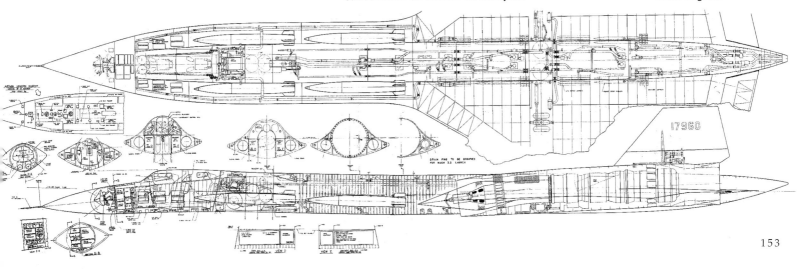

Giant Scale

Above: *SR-71s operating from Kadena were adorned with 'Habu' mission marks. This is 64-17974, which was named* Ichi Ban.

Top right: *'972 taxis in at Kadena at the end of a* Giant Scale *mission over North Vietnam. In the revetments are the special C-135s (including an RC-135M Combat Apple) of the 4252nd (later 376th) Strategic Wing.*

Far right: *An SR-71A slides away from the KC-135Q during a refuelling over the South China Sea.* Giant Scale *missions occasionally involved a 'double-header' flight with two loops through North Vietnamese airspace.*

SR-71As began arriving at Kadena AB (OL-8) in March 1968 to take over the Pacific reconnaissance role from the Black Shield A-12s, although there was an overlap of about a month between the two. The aircraft focused their attentions on North Vietnam, but were also tasked with missions against North Korea and around the coastlines of China and the Soviet Union. During the course of these missions many SAMs were fired at the 'Habu'.

Those A-12s back at 'the Area' were flown to Palmdale and placed in storage by 7 June. At Kadena, the three aircraft that had performed all the Black Shield missions were readied for a return transpacific ferry flight. On 2 June 1968 tragedy once again hit the Oxcart programme, when Jack Weeks was killed during an FCF in 60-6932. The aircraft and its pilot were lost without a trace in the Pacific Ocean. The two remaining A-12s on Okinawa – 60-6930 and 60-6937 – were ferried back to Area 51 before being flown to Palmdale, the last flight being made by Frank Murray on 21 June 1968 in aircraft '937.

Tagboard and Senior Bowl

On 10 October 1962 Kelly Johnson received authorisation from the CIA to carry out study work on a drone that would be mated with an A-12. At the root of the request was the US government's decision to discontinue manned overflights, following the Gary Powers shoot-down. Fourteen days later, Kelly, Ben Rich and Russ Daniell met representatives from Marquardt to discuss ramjet propulsion system options. Progress was rapid, and on 7 December a full-scale mock-up was completed on the craft, which within the Skunk Works was referred to as the Q-12. Still to receive mission specifications from the Agency, Kelly

worked on producing a vehicle with a range of 3,000 nm (3,450 miles; 5550 km) hauling a Hycon camera system of 425·lb (193 kg) that would be capable of a photographic resolution of 6 in (15 cm) from operating altitude. The engine to be used was the Marquardt RJ43-MA-3 Bomarc, and by October 1963 the overall configuration for the Q-12 and its launch platform – two purpose-built, modified A-12s – was nearing completion. It was codenamed Tagboard. The designation of both elements was also changed, the carrier vehicle becoming the 'M' – standing for 'Mother' – 21 and the Q-12 becoming the 'D' – for 'Daughter' – 21.

The 11,000-lb (5000-kg) D-21 was supported on the M-21 by a single, dorsally mounted pylon. Reaching launch point, the mother ship's pilot maintained Mach 3.12 and initiated a 0.9-*g* push-over. Once released by the launch control officer (LCO) who sat in what on other A-12s would be the Q-bay, the D-21 flew its sortie independently. Equipped with a Minneapolis-Honeywell inertial navigation system, the D-21 would fly a pre-programmed flight profile, executing turns and camera on/off points to produce the perfect photo-reconnaissance sortie. Having completed its camera run, the drone's INS system then sent signals to the auto-pilot system to descend to a predetermined 'feet wet' film collection point. The entire palletised unit containing INS, camera and film was then ejected at 60,000 ft (18290 m) and Mach 1.67, and parachuted towards the ocean. As the drone continued its

Above: *Although SR-71s occasionally were diverted into Udorn, the missions attempted to end at Kadena if possible. Unfortunately, this 'Habu', 64-17978, suffered irreparable damage during a landing at Kadena in a severe crosswind.*

Right: *Complete with large 'Habu' tail artwork and mission symbols behind the RSO's cockpit,* Ichi Ban *is seen shortly after its return to Beale. This aircraft was the last SR-71 to be lost.*

descent it was blown apart by a barometrically activated explosive charge. Meanwhile, the air retrieval was executed by a JC-130B Hercules. On 12 August 1964 the first M-21 was dispatched to Groom Dry Lake and on 22 December the first D-21/M-21 combination flight took place with Bill Park at the controls. Troubles dogged Tagboard and it was not until 5 March that the first successful D-21 launch was accomplished. The second launch on 27 April saw the drone reach Mach 3.3 and 90,000 ft (27440 m), and fly for 1,200 nm (1380 miles; 2220 km), holding course within 0.5 mile (0.8 km) throughout. The flight came to an end after a hydraulic pump burned out and the D-21 fell out of the sky.

Drone disaster

The Air Force remained interested in the drone and on 29 April 1966 a second batch of D-21s was ordered. On 16 June a third successful launch was made and the D-21 flew 1,600 miles (2575 km), completing all tasks on the flight card except ejecting the all-important camera pallet. The fourth and final D-21 sortie from the M-21 occurred on 30 July 1966 and ended in disaster when the drone collided with '941 moments after achieving launch separation. The impact caused the mother ship to pitch up so violently that

the fuselage forebody broke off. Both Bill Park and his LCO, Ray Torrick, successfully ejected and made a 'feet wet' landing, but unfortunately Torrick's pressure suit filled with water and he drowned before he could be rescued. Bill Park spent an hour in the ocean before he was brought aboard a US Navy vessel.

The D-21 was grounded for a year while a new launch system was developed. This new operation, codenamed Senior Bowl, involved the drone being launched from the underwing pylons of two modified B-52Hs of the 4200th Test Wing based at Beale AFB, California. Upon launch, the D-21B was accelerated to Mach 3.3 and 80,000 ft (24390 m) by a solid propellant rocket developed by Lockheed Propulsion Company of Redlands, California. When cruise speed and altitude had been achieved, the booster was jettisoned and the drone's flight continued as described earlier. The first launch attempt from a B-52 was made on 6 November 1967; it proved unsuccessful, as did three other attempts. Success was finally achieved on 16 June 1968. Between 9 November 1969 and 20 March 1971, a total of four operational flights over China was attempted. To maintain tight security, the B-52 with its unique payload departed Beale at night and lumbered westwards to the Pacific island of Guam. Just before dawn the

During the early years of the SR-71 programme the detachment at Kadena was the most important operating location, although the aircraft also began to take an interest in Cuba. Twenty-nine SR-71A aircraft were built, of which six were earmarked for test purposes. The remaining operational fleet was obviously too large for the tasks with which it was set, and many aircraft were put into storage. They were rotated with the active aircraft periodically to spread utilisation across the fleet. This practice continued throughout the career of the aircraft. At the end the USAF had 10 aircraft, of which six were active: two at Beale for training and two at each of the dets.

Three crews participated in the record flights. Shown below are Major George Morgan (left) and Captain Eldon Joersz, who captured the speed record. Above is the aircraft they used: 64-17958.

SR-71 records

Two SR-71As, '958 and '962 (illustrated), were earmarked for the record flights, each painted with a large white cross for ground tracking. The record attempts were staged out of Edwards AFB.

During early 1976 the US Air Force approved a series of record flights which would eclipse those marks set by the YF-12A. The absolute speed record still stands, although the sustained altitude record was beaten on 26 April 1995 by Roman Taskaev in a MiG-29 with a height of 90,092 ft (27460 m).

Date	Crew	Aircraft
Altitude in Horizontal Flight, 85,068.997 ft (25935.669 m)		
27/28 July 1976	Pilot, Capt. Robert C. Helt. RSO, Maj. Larry A. Elliott	SR-71A ?
Speed over a Straight Course (15/25 km), 2,193.167 mph (3529.464 km/h)		
27/28 July 1976	Pilot, Capt. Eldon W. Joersz. RSO, Maj. George T. Morgan	SR-71A 64-17958
Speed over a Closed Course (1000 km), 2,092.294 mph (3367.128 km/h)		
27/28 July 1976	Pilot, Maj. Adolphus H. Bledsoe Jr. RSO, Maj. John T. Fuller	SR-71A ?

64-17958 was the first operational aircraft delivered to the US Air Force. It is seen here during an early operation, the B-52s of the 456th Bomb Wing being visible in the background. This unit also used Beale until 1975, and was responsible for the 9th and 903rd Air Refueling Squadrons which operated the KC-135Qs. The SR-71 unit was initially the 4200th SRW, but was renumbered as the 9th SRW in June 1966. Two squadrons were established, the 1st and 99th SRS. It was intended that each unit operate eight SR-71As and one SR-71B trainer. This obviously provided far more operational capability than was needed, and so the 99th was deactivated in 1971. It was later resurrected as the U-2R squadron based in Thailand. Later, the 'Dragon Ladies' of the 100th SRW amalgamated with the SR-71 unit in 1976, having moved in from Davis-Monthan. The 100th's U-2 and drone squadron numbers (349th and 350th) were later assigned to the two tanker squadrons, which were administered by the newly formed 100th ARW. In 1982 they were subsumed by the 9th SRW upon the deactivation of the 100th ARW.

next day the flight resumed, the bomber departing Guam and heading for the launch point. Upon vehicle separation, the 'BUFF' made its way back to Guam, while the D-21 embarked upon its pre-programmed day-time reconnaissance run. Achieving only limited success, Senior Bowl was cancelled on 15 July 1971.

Senior Crown

While working on Oxcart in the early spring of 1962, Kelly had mentioned the possibility of producing a reconnaissance/strike variant for the Air Force. Lockheed was issued with a 90-day study contract wherein the various Air Force mission options were identified and defined in terms of the A-12 platform. By the end of April 1962, two different mock-ups were under construction, referred to as the R-12 and RS-12. On 18 February 1963 Lockheed received pre-contractual authority to build six aircraft with the understanding that 25 aircraft would be ordered by 1 July. Colonel Leo Geary had been the RS-12 System Program Officer (SPO), but after protracted debate it was decided that the A-12 project group under Colonel Templeton would inherit the R-12, which became designated SR-71 by the Air Force. The RS-12 and later the B-12/B-71 proposals for a strike version of the aircraft failed to win production contracts, despite Kelly having demonstrated to the Air Force the unique capabilities of such a platform. This was largely due to the far greater lobbying powers of the XB-70 and later FB-111 fraternity.

In a speech made on 24 July 1964 President Johnson revealed to the world the existence of the SR-71. Externally, the aircraft differed in shape from the A-12 by having a more elliptical nose plan. A second crew member, known as a reconnaissance systems officer (RSO), sat behind the pilot in what was the A-12's Q-bay. Sensors carried by the SR-71 also differed from its predecessors. To enhance mission flexibility, the nose section was interchangeable, variously housing a sideways-looking airborne radar (SLAR), or an optical bar camera (OBC) for horizon-to-horizon coverage, or an empty unit for routine, Stateside-training sorties. Cameras onboard the SR-71 were located on palletised units which were housed in slim bays in the underside of the chine. The physical length of the 'close-look', technical objective camera (TEOCS) was reduced by using cassegrain or 'folding optics' technology. It is ironic

that initially the resolution of these units was inferior to that produced by the large Hycon camera carried in the A-12's Q-bay. However, as technology progressed the resolution of the SR-71's camera system also improved. (Following a recent 10 per cent improvement, it is believed that today's resolution is between 1.75 and 1.5 in (4.4 to 3.8 cm) from cruising altitude. That is to say, if a series of lines 1.75 in wide were painted on the ground 1.75 in apart, a photo interpreter could count the number of lines applied.)

In August Kelly phoned Bob Murphy and asked him if he wanted to work on the SR-71 programme. At the time, Murphy was a superintendent in charge of D-21 drone production. The first drone was undergoing final check-out while nine others were at various stages of assembly. Bob accepted the offer and was immediately briefed by Kelly, who said, "I want you to go to Palmdale and get Site 2 away from Rockwell. Hire the people you need. The pieces of the SR-71 will be up to you on November 1st and I want her flying before Christmas. Oh, I also want you to move up there because I don't want you to commute." Rockwell controlled all three sites at Palmdale, using Sites 1 and 3 for B-70 production; Site 2 housed a paint shop, telephone exchange and other facilities.

New assembly location

Following a meeting with the base commander and various Rockwell representatives, 'Murph' successfully managed to gain control of Site 2 for Lockheed. The prototype SR-71A, serial 64-17950 (article number 2001), was delivered from Burbank to Site 2, Air Force Plant 42, Building 210, at Palmdale for final assembly on 29 October, by two large trailers specifically designed for the task. At that point Bob Murphy's team 'went into overdrive' in an attempt to meet the extremely tight deadline set by Kelly. Earlier that year Kelly had promoted the charismatic Robert J. Gilliland to the position of chief project pilot for the SR-71, a post for which Bob was admirably qualified, having gained a great deal of experience as a member of the F-104 and A-12 test teams. Bob worked closely with Dick Miller who led the flight test engineering effort for the entire contractor test programme, as it was Dick's responsibility to implement specific tests to be completed on individual flights.

With two J58s installed, '950 conducted its first engine

By virtue of its rarity, shape and power, the SR-71 has always been a firm favourite at air shows, despite its lack of manoeuvrability, a function of the low g stress limits. One regularly seen party piece is the asymmetric pass, performed with undercarriage down. This allows the pilot to light one 'burner to demonstrate the 'tiger tail' at low speeds. Note the nearly full deflection of the rudders to offset asymmetric thrust.

SR-71 cockpit

The front cockpit of the SR-71A (seen here with the F-1 ejection seat removed) was less complex than that of the A-12 as many of the sensor and navigation systems had been moved to the backseat.

The display was dominated by two attitude indicators at top centre (primary below and secondary right at the top), with a horizontal situation indicator below. Below that was a screen which projected a moving map image. To the left of the large primary attitude indicator was an airspeed indicator, while to the right was the altimeter. Below this was the vertical speed indicator. To the left of the HSI was the triple display indicator (TDI), which presented the key figures of Mach number, KEAS (knots, equivalent airspeed) and altitude at one glance. Below the moving map was the annunciator panel for warning.

To the right of the central instrument display were the engine instruments and at the extreme right was the fuel control panel. On the left-hand side were controls for aircraft systems, such as temperature and pressurisation for the cockpits and sensor bays, undercarriage, ejection seats and inlet/bypass system.

The left-hand console had the throttle quadrant, aft bypass door control, engine restart controls, standby oxygen and the UHF radio. The right-hand console mounted panels for the ILS, flight control system, VHF radio and intercom system. At the rear of both side consoles were banks of circuit breakers. Visible emergency handles included gear release to the right of the annunciator panel and canopy release next to the throttles.

Left: The RSO's console was dominated by a large radar display in the centre, above which was a viewsight display. Included in the other instruments is a TEOC camera look-angle indicator. The DEF (defensive electronics) were operated from the left-hand console.

Right: This is the rear (instructor's) cockpit of the SR-71B, which differs in only minor detail from the front cockpit. Note the trim thumbswitch on the top of the stick.

Lockheed's Blackbirds

Palmdale test

During the SR-71 programme the Skunk Works and AFSC/AFLC maintained one aircraft as a test vehicle for evaluating new systems and operating procedures. For much of the SR-71's career the task was handled by 64-17955.

The test aircraft usually wore the Lockheed Skunk Works badge on the fin.

The Palmdale test fleet was initially assigned the first six aircraft for testing. Four were lost in accidents and '951 was transferred to NASA, leaving just '955 (above). This flew until grounded in January 1985. 64-17972 (below) then took over the test role.

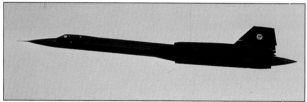

Two famous products of the Lockheed Skunk Works fly together from Palmdale. The U-2R was the ASARS-2 development aircraft. SR-71A '955 had performed the test work on ASARS-1 for the 'Habu' fleet.

64-17978 was a well-known 'Habu' thanks to its Playboy bunny tail art, which led to it being called the Rapid Rabbit. Here it is seen here over the snow-capped Sierra Nevada mountains close to the Palmdale base.

test run on 18 December 1964. Three days later, a 'non-flight' was conducted during which Gilliland accelerated the aircraft to 120 kt (138 mph; 220 km/h) before snapping the throttles back to idle and deploying the large 40-ft (12-m) drag 'chute.

SR-71 first flight

On 22 December 1964, Gilliland (using his personal call-sign DUTCH 51) got airborne from runway 25 at Palmdale in SR-71A, 64-17950. The backseat, or RSO's position, remained empty on this historic flight for safety reasons. After take-off Bob immediately retracted the landing gear, reduced afterburners to 'min', turned right and continued his climb northbound over Edwards' test range until he levelled off at 20,000 ft (6097 m) and Mach 0.9. Jim Eastham was flying chase in one of three F-104s, the other two being flown by USAF test pilots Colonel Robert 'Fox' Stephens and Lieutenant Colonel Walt Daniels. Eastham tucked his F-104 into close formation on '950's right wing, while both pilots calibrated and verified accurate pitot static derived flight data. A series of handling checks was then flown during which the aircraft's static and dynamic stability was assessed. These checks were carried out with the stability augmentation system (SAS) axes switched 'on' and 'off', both 'individually' and 'collectively'. Performance

comparisons of predicted values of speed versus thrust and fuel consumption were also recorded, followed by a climb to 30,000 ft (9145 m) where cabin pressure, oxygen flow and temperature control were checked. Having passed Mojave, he headed west before completing a 180° turn to the left and rolling out on a southerly track over the snow-covered Sierra Nevadas.

As all systems were performing well, it was time to complete a supersonic dash. So, with Jim sticking to the 'SR' like glue, Bob eased the two throttles into 'min burner', scanned the engine parameters and slid the throttles up to the 'max'. The light test-jet accelerated very rapidly to 400 kt (459 mph; 739 km/h) in level flight and then on up to supersonic speed. At Mach 1.4 Bob's attention was drawn to the flashing of the 'master caution' warning lights. A glance at the annunciator panel identified the problem as 'canopy unsafe'. Visually checking the two canopy locking hooks, Bob verified that the canopy was really 'fully locked'. The pressure-sensitive micro-switches which transmitted the electrical 'unsafe' signal had triggered due to an aerodynamic low-pressure area above the aircraft which had sucked the canopy up, against the locking hooks. In reality, the canopy remained locked, and having analysed the situation as safe Bob advanced the throttles once again, continuing his acceleration and climb while closely scanning the instruments. On reaching 50,000 ft (15245 m) and Mach 1.5, Bob eased the throttles out of 'burner into 'mil' and began a deceleration to 350 kt (402 mph; 647 km/h) indicated airspeed, whereafter he descended to 20,000 ft (6097 m) to allow the engines to cool down.

Approaching Palmdale, Bob was advised by Test Ops that Kelly had requested a subsonic flyby down the runway. Happy to comply, Bob and the accompanying '104s streaked by to highlight the successful completion of the first flight. Downwind, with the gear down and locked, he turned '950 onto a wide base leg and set up a long final approach at 185 kt (212 mph; 342 km/h). Touching down smoothly on Palmdale's runway 25, he gently lowered the nose and deployed the drag 'chute. At 50 kt (57 mph; 92 km/h) the 'chute was jettisoned. The aircraft was turned off the active runway and taxied back towards the crowd of USAF dignitaries and Lockheed engineers and technicians, who awaited Bob's debriefing.

After congratulations from Kelly and the others, Bob narrated details of his first flight chronologically from start-

up to shut-down. Clarifying questions were then fielded by some of the technicians, after which a typescript of the recorded briefing was circulated to all concerned. Further details were gathered for later dissemination from cockpit-mounted camera recordings and other 'automatic observer' panels. Aircraft '951 and '952 were added to the test fleet for contractor development of payload systems and techniques. Shortly after the Phase II, Developmental Test Program was started, four other Lockheed test pilots were brought into the project: Jim Eastham, Bill Weaver, Art Peterson and Darrell Greenamyer.

Developmental efforts within Lockheed were matched by Air Force Systems Command (AFSC) where Colonel Ben Bellis had been appointed the SR-71 SPO. His task was to structure a Development and Evaluation Program that would evaluate the new aircraft for the Air Force. This programme was undertaken by the SR-71/YF-12 Test Force at the Air Force Flight Test Center, Edwards AFB. Both Phase I Experimental and Phase II Development test flying had moved to Edwards where SR-71As '953, '954 and 955 were to be evaluated by the 'blue suiters'. On 18 November and 18 December 1965, the two SR-71B pilot trainers, '956 and '957 respectively, successfully completed their first flights, but the SR-71s were plagued by problems associated with the electrical system, tank sealing and obtaining design range.

Air Force base

While these problems were being worked on, Beale AFB, chosen home for the newcomer, had been undergoing an $8.4 million construction programme which included the installation of an army of specialised technical support facilities. The 4200th Strategic Reconnaissance Wing was activated at Beale on 1 January 1965, and three months later four support squadrons were formed. In January 1966, Colonel Doug Nelson was appointed commander of the new wing – a job for which he was eminently qualified, having been the Director of Operations for the Oxcart project. Doug began by selecting a small group of competent sub-commanders and Strategic Air Command (SAC) fliers to form the initial cadre of the SR-71 unit. Colonel Bill Hayes became the deputy commander for maintenance; Lieutenant Colonel Ray Haupt, chief instructor pilot; Colonel Walt Wright commanded the medical group; Colonel Clyde Deaniston supervised all Category III flight test planning; and the flight crews were recruited from the best SAC bomber pilots and navigators in the service. The first two of eight Northrop T-38 Talons arrived at Beale on 7 July 1965.

They were used as 'companion trainers' to maintain overall flying proficiency for the SR-71 crew at a fraction of the cost of flying the main aircraft. On 7 January 1966 Colonel Doug Nelson and his chief instructor, Lieutenant Colonel Ray Haupt, delivered the first SR-71B to Beale AFB. Five months later, on 14 April, Nelson and Major Al Pennington took delivery of Beale's first SR-71A, serial 64-17958. On 25 June 1966, the 4200th was redesignated the 9th Strategic Reconnaissance Wing (SRW), its component flying squadrons being the 1st and 99th Strategic Reconnaissance Squadrons (SRS).

Crew training and Category III operational testing

Tanker support

Fifty-six KC-135Qs were procured to support the Blackbird operations, most assigned to the 9th SRW (after 1982) but with a few allocated to the Plattsburgh-based 380th BW. The Q had a separate fuel system for the SR-71's JP-7 fuel, although it could burn the special fuel itself in an emergency. Similarly, the JP-7 tanks could also be used to house standard fuel, although they required a thorough purging afterwards. Additional communications and navaids were provided for SR-71 operations.

proceeded in earnest. Unfortunately, progress came at some cost. The first SR-71 loss occurred on 25 January 1966 when Bill Weaver and his test engineer, Jim Zwayer, took off from Edwards in SR-71A '952. The main objectives of the flight were to evaluate navigation and reconnaissance systems and to investigate procedures for improving high Mach cruise performance by reducing trim drag, thereby lowering fuel burn and increasing range. This research required that the centre of gravity (CG) be moved further aft than normal to compensate for the rearward shift of the centre of pressure at high Mach. After inflight refuelling, DUTCH 64 climbed back to cruising altitude. While in a

Seen prior to refuelling, an SR-71A glides under the KC-135Q with its refuelling receptacle open. The Q had special air-to-air TACAN equipment for radio-silent rendezvous.

Left: Most SR-71 missions, including training flights, involved at least one refuelling. Standard procedure was to launch the tanker(s) ahead of the SR-71, which followed them and topped off its tanks after take-off and a climb to around 26,000 ft. Occasionally two tankers were needed for the top-off. Here an SR-71 waits at the end of the Beale runway with its two assigned top-off tankers.

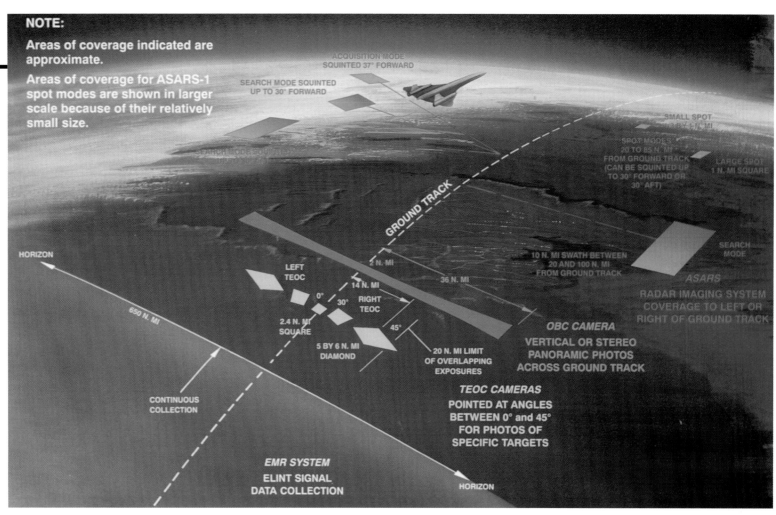

NOTE:

Areas of coverage indicated are approximate.

Areas of coverage for ASARS-1 spot modes are shown in larger scale because of their relatively small size.

ACQUISITION MODE SQUINTED 37° FORWARD

SEARCH MODE SQUINTED UP TO 30° FORWARD

GROUND TRACK

SMALL SPOT 1 BY 1 N. MI

SPOT MODES 20 TO 85 N. MI FROM GROUND TRACK (CAN BE SQUINTED UP TO 30° FORWARD OR 30° AFT)

LARGE SPOT 1 N. MI SQUARE

SEARCH MODE

HORIZON

650 N. MI

LEFT TEOC

2 N. MI

14 N. MI

0°

30°

RIGHT TEOC

36 N. MI

2.4 N. MI SQUARE

5 BY 6 N. MI DIAMOND

45°

20 N. MI LIMIT OF OVERLAPPING EXPOSURES

10 N. MI SWATH BETWEEN 20 AND 100 N. MI FROM GROUND TRACK

ASARS RADAR IMAGING SYSTEM COVERAGE TO LEFT OR RIGHT OF GROUND TRACK

OBC CAMERA
VERTICAL OR STEREO PANORAMIC PHOTOS ACROSS GROUND TRACK

TEOC CAMERAS
POINTED AT ANGLES BETWEEN 0° and 45° FOR PHOTOS OF SPECIFIC TARGETS

CONTINUOUS COLLECTION

EMR SYSTEM
ELINT SIGNAL DATA COLLECTION

HORIZON

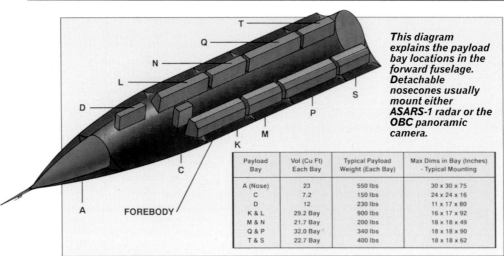

This diagram explains the payload bay locations in the forward fuselage. Detachable nosecones usually mount either ASARS-1 radar or the OBC panoramic camera.

Payload Bay	Vol (Cu Ft) Each Bay	Typical Payload Weight (Each Bay)	Max Dims in Bay (Inches) - Typical Mounting
A (Nose)	23	550 lbs	30 x 30 x 75
C	7.2	150 lbs	24 x 24 x 16
D	12	230 lbs	11 x 17 x 80
K & L	29.2 Bay	900 lbs	16 x 17 x 92
M & N	21.7 Bay	200 lbs	18 x 18 x 49
Q & P	32.0 Bay	340 lbs	18 x 18 x 90
T & S	22.7 Bay	400 lbs	18 x 18 x 62

SR-71 sensors

The SR-71's sensors fall into three groups: optical, radar and Elint. The diagram above depicts examples of the kind of coverage options available with the aircraft flying at 80,000 ft. The brown area is the continuous horizon-to-horizon Elint coverage, yellow is for the TEOC cameras, blue for the OBC panoramic and orange for the ASARS-1 radar. Electronic steering in the radar allows for a degree of forward or rearward squint, while the radar can operate in both a wide-area search mode or detailed spot mode.

Right: This diagram illustrates two typical mission profiles, the red ribbon being for a short-range mission with a top-off refuelling after launch, while the blue depicts a longer mission with three refuellings.

Below: An illustration of the clarity achievable by the SR-71's cameras is provided by this view of the Seattle Dome.

Above: '967 is seen with the Q-bay open. This usually housed the palletised TEOC (Technical Objective Camera).

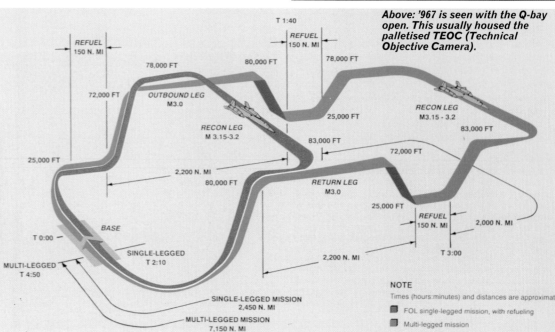

REFUEL 150 N. MI

T 1:40

REFUEL 150 N. MI

78,000 FT

80,000 FT

78,000 FT

72,000 FT

OUTBOUND LEG M3.0

RECON LEG M3.15-3.2

25,000 FT

RECON LEG M3.15 - 3.2

25,000 FT

83,000 FT

83,000 FT

72,000 FT

2,200 N. MI

80,000 FT

RETURN LEG M3.0

25,000 FT

2,200 N. MI

REFUEL 150 N. MI

2,000 N. MI

T 3:00

BASE

SINGLE-LEGGED T 2:10

T 0:00

MULTI-LEGGED T 4:50

SINGLE-LEGGED MISSION 2,450 N. MI

MULTI-LEGGED MISSION 7,150 N. MI

NOTE
Times (hours:minutes) and distances are approximate.
■ FOL single-legged mission, with refueling
■ Multi-legged mission

Lockheed SR-71A OL-8, 9th SRW, Kadena

The first operational deployment for the SR-71A was to Kadena, from where missions were flown over North Vietnam and, later, Korea, China and the Soviet Far East. This aircraft, 64-17978, was the first of three to be deployed in the initial phase, leaving Beale for Okinawa on 8 March 1968. After flying nearly 300 hours from the detachment, '978 returned to Beale in September, having gained the reputation of being a very reliable aircraft. When it returned to the detachment in 1972, it ruined its reputation by having a double generator failure over North Vietnam, causing the crew to overfly Hanoi at a perilous 41,000 ft and at only marginally supersonic speed, well within SAM range. Soon after this mission, its SAS failed while travelling at Mach 3.17 in a 30° bank, causing the crew some anxious moments and leaving them with a long subsonic slog back to Kadena. '978's luck finally ran out on 20 July 1972, when the crew attempted to land in a fierce crosswind. Having used the brake chute on a first attempt at landing, Major Denny Bush had no such luxury on the second attempt. The cross-wind was too strong, and Bush could not keep the SR-71 straight. It ran off the runway and was damaged beyond repair, although thankfully the crew emerged unscathed. While at the Kadena detachment the aircraft acquired the then-popular 'Playboy' bunny logo on its vertical fins, and became known as the 'Rapid Rabbit'.

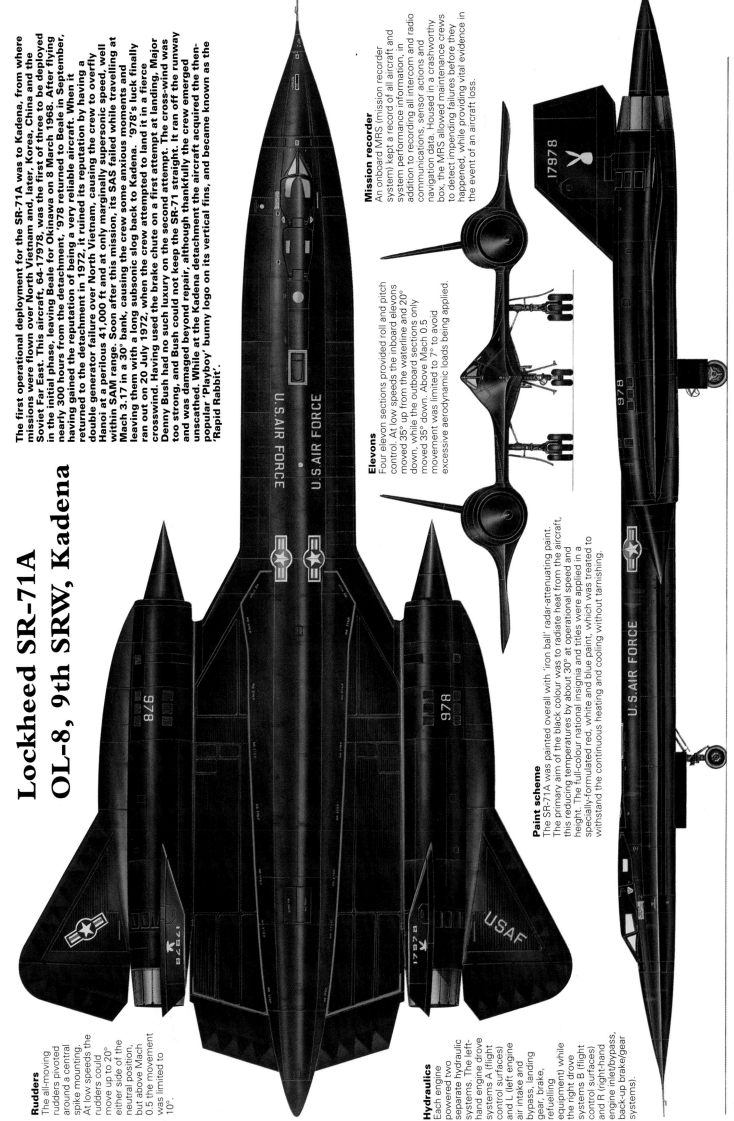

Rudders
The all-moving rudders pivoted around a central spike mounting. At low speeds the rudders could move up to 20° either side of the neutral position, but above Mach 0.5 the movement was limited to 10°.

Hydraulics
Each engine powered two separate hydraulic systems. The left-hand engine drove systems A (flight control surfaces) and L (left engine air intake and bypass, landing gear, brake, refuelling equipment) while the right drove systems B (flight control surfaces) and R (right-hand engine inlet/bypass, back-up brake/gear systems).

Mission recorder
An onboard MRS (mission recorder system) kept a record of all aircraft and system performance information, in addition to recording all intercom and radio communications, sensor actions and navigation data. Housed in a crashworthy box, the MRS allowed maintenance crews to detect impending failures before they happened, while providing vital evidence in the event of an aircraft loss.

Elevons
Four elevon sections provided roll and pitch control. At low speeds the inboard elevons moved 35° up from the waterline and 20° down, while the outboard sections only moved 35° down. Above Mach 0.5 movement was limited to 7° to avoid excessive aerodynamic loads being applied.

Paint scheme
The SR-71A was painted overall with 'iron ball' radar-attenuating paint. The primary aim of the black colour was to radiate heat from the aircraft, this reducing temperatures by about 30° at operational speed and height. The full-colour national insignia and titles were applied in a specially-formulated red, white and blue paint, which was treated to withstand the continuous heating and cooling without tarnishing.

During and immediately after the Yom Kippur War of 1973, two SR-71s flew nine missions to the war zone from East Coast bases. Four sorties were launched from Griffiss AFB and five from Seymour Johnson AFB, the last on 6 April 1974. At nearly 11 hours, and with six refuellings, the flights were gruelling affairs.

Above: Seen wheeling high over Beale, '964 was one of the two aircraft involved in the marathon flights into the Middle East war zone in late 1973. The flights not only covered the Suez theatre, but also the Israeli front with Syria.

Above right: '979 and '964 are seen in the hangar at Griffiss AFB during late 1973. '979 flew six of the nine long round-trips to the Middle East. The T-38 Talon, callsign TOXON 01, was at Griffiss to act as chase-plane to test SR-71 '955, which was conveniently at the New York base for a series of trials, thereby providing a ready-made cover for the operational missions.

64-17964 floats across the western end of the Beale runway. The SR-71A handled much like any other delta at low speed, its large wing area providing a measure of air cushioning at the high landing speeds, making touchdowns benign.

35° right back turn, manually controlling the right forward bypass doors at Mach 3.17 and between 77,000 and 78,000 ft (23470 and 23775 m), Weaver experienced a right inlet unstart. Bank angle immediately increased from 35° to 60° and the aircraft entered a pitch-up that exceeded the restorative authority of the flight controls and SAS. The aircraft disintegrated, but miraculously Weaver survived; unfortunately, Jim Zwayer was killed in the incident. The problem of excessive trim drag was solved by Kelly, who designed a 'wedge' which was inserted between the aircraft's forward fuselage and its detachable nose section. This moved the centre of lift forward, thus reducing static margin and trim drag. The visual result was a distinctive 2° nose-up tilt.

Early losses

The SR-71 prototype was written off on 10 January 1967 during an anti-skid brake system evaluation at Edwards AFB. Lockheed's test pilot Art Peterson escaped with a cracked disc in his back. Three months later, on 13 April, Beale lost SR-71A '966 following a night air refuelling. It was Captain Earle Boones's ninth training sortie and he was flying with Captain 'Butch' Sheffield because it had been discovered during the pre-flight medical that his regular RSO had a cold which prevented him from equalising his middle ear pressure. Leaving the tanker, Earle turned to avoid thunderstorms which straddled his planned acceleration-to-climb track. As he climbed prior to performing a 'dipsy doodle' manoeuvre to hasten fuel-consuming transonic breakthrough, he suffered a series of engine stalls and his airspeed drifted down to 170 kt (195 mph; 314 km/h) at 37,000 ft (11280 m). The heavy jet shuddered in the stall and Earle fought hard to regain control, but '966 suddenly entered a pitch-up rotation from which there was no recovery. Both men safely ejected as '966 made its grave not far from that of Bill Weavers's aircraft, in northern New Mexico.

On the night of 25 October 1967, a black-tie dinner was being held at the Beale Officers' club with Kelly Johnson as guest of honour. At the same time, Major Roy St Martin and Captain John Carnochan were flying a night sortie in aircraft '965. As Roy eased the aircraft into the decent profile over central Nevada, the gyro-stabilised reference platform for the ANS drifted without a failure warning. This was the source of attitude reference signals to the primary flight instruments and guidance information to the autopilot, so the aircraft entered an increasing right bank; however, the flight director and the attitude director indicator instruments displayed no deviation from wing-level flight. In the autumn, at 20.25 at high altitude over Nevada, there is no visual horizon for external reference. The aircraft rolled over, the nose fell far below a safe descent angle and it plunged through 60,000 ft (18290 m). The crew sensed something was wrong when Roy glanced at the standby artificial horizon (a small instrument awkwardly positioned low in the cockpit) and was alarmed to see it indicate a "screaming dive and roll-over toward inverted flight." He attempted a "recovery from unusual positions manoeuvre," and managed to roll the wings level but, roaring through 40,000 ft (12195 m) well above the speed from which level flight could be achieved, both men had to eject. The RSO went first, full into a Mach 1.4 slipstream, and just as Roy ejected he heard the warning horn that the aircraft was now below 10,000 ft (3050 m). Aircraft '965

SR-71C – The 'Bastard'

The loss of the second SR-71B trainer, 64-17957, on 11 January 1968 caused a shortfall in pilot conversion capacity. Accordingly, Lockheed created the SR-71C, a hybrid aircraft using the rear fuselage of the first YF-12A and a static test forward fuselage. The aircraft, inevitably called the 'Bastard', was disliked and little-flown, spending much of its life in a barn at Beale. The aircraft was easily distinguishable by its short tail, inherited from its YF-12 origins.

Overseas appearances

Throughout its operational career the SR-71 remained a sensitive programme, and overseas public appearances were rare. The first major public trip was to the 1974 SBAC show at Farnborough. The 9th SRW took the opportunity to set an unmatchable time between New York and London on the way to the show, shattering the previous record which had been held by a British Phantom. After a week as the undisputed star of the static display, sitting next to a C-5 Galaxy, the aircraft used the return flight to set a new London-Los Angeles record. Further European appearances included the Paris air show, and the aircraft became a regular at selected UK air shows when Det 4 was established at Mildenhall.

Date	Crew	Distance	Time	Aircraft
Speed over a Recognised Course – New York to London				
1 September 1974	Pilot, Maj. James V. Sullivan. RSO, Maj. Noel F. Widdifield	3,490 miles (5616 km)	1 hr 54 min 56.4 sec	SR-71A 64-17972
Speed over a Recognised Course – London to Los Angeles				
13 September 1974	Pilot, Capt. Harold B Adams. RSO Capt. William C Machorek	5,645 miles (9084 km)	3 hr 47 min 35.8 sec	SR-71A 64-17972

Above: This SR-71 appeared at the Paris Salon in 1989 after having flown in from Det 4 at Mildenhall.

Above left: Major Noel Widdifield (RSO, left) and Major James Sullivan (pilot, right) pose at Beale immediately prior to the record-breaking run to Farnborough.

Left: Sullivan streams the brake 'chute as '972 arrives at a wet Farnborough at the end of its record-breaking transatlantic run. The 3,490-mile (5616-km) distance from new York to London was accomplished at an average ground speed of 1,817 mph (2924 km/h).

plunged into the ground near Lovelock, Nevada like a hypervelocity meteorite. Luckily, both men survived without permanent injuries. Following an accident board of investigation, several instrument changes were implemented on the fleet together with an amended training programme containing less night flying until crews had accumulated more daytime experience in the SR-71.

Retiring Oxcart

With Lockheed having completed its 30th SR-71 on 25 September 1967, and with the Agency operating its small fleet of Oxcart aircraft, it was inevitable that accountants would begin to ask their age old question: "is it really necessary?" Questions were mooted by the Bureau of the Budget (BoB) as far back as November 1965, and a memo from that office questioned the requirement not only for the number of such high-performance aircraft, but also the necessity for separate 'covert' CIA and 'overt' USAF operations. Since the SR-71 was not scheduled to become operational until September 1968, the SECDEF rightly declined to consider the proposal. In July 1966, BoB officials proposed that a tri-agency study be set up to again establish ways of reducing the cost of both programmes. After the study was completed, a meeting was convened on 12

December 1966 and a vote taken on available options. Three out of four votes cast were in favour of the motion to "terminate the Oxcart fleet in January 1968 (assuming an operational readiness date of September 1967 for the SR-71) and assign all missions to the SR-71 fleet." The memorandum was transmitted to President Johnson on 16 December despite protestations from the CIA's Richard Helms, who was the sole dissenting voice in the vote. Twelve days later, Johnson accepted the BoB's recommendations and directed that the Oxcart programme be terminated by 1 January 1968. In the event, the Oxcart run-down lagged, but the original decision to terminate the programme was reaffirmed on 16 May 1968 and, as seen earlier, the first Kadena-based A-12 began its flight back to

Below left: In March 1982 the SR-71B became the first aircraft to notch up 1,000 missions. It was flown on this landmark flight by Lieutenant Colonel Dave Peters and Major Jerry Glasser.

Below: The early SR-71s exhibited an almost perfect chine planview. Later the lines were distorted by the addition of radar warning receiver pimples near the nose.

Beale operations

Situated in the Sacramento Valley, California, Beale AFB was the headquarters for the SR-71 operation. The base played host to all of the training effort, employing the SR-71B and C dual-control aircraft, T-38As and some standard SR-71As for this task, in addition to ground simulators. Many operational missions were also flown from Beale aimed at Cuba (originally codenamed Giant Plate, and subsequently Clipper); they initially involved overflights but later were amended to constitute a pass along the southern and northern coasts of the island. In 1984 Beale-based SR-71s also overflew Nicaragua.

Top: The crew of '958 lowers the gear during the downwind leg at Beale. The right-hand end of the apron accommodated B-52s and KC-135s; the left-hand end housed recce aircraft. The line of small barns on the far side of the apron was the accommodation for the SR-71s, and U-2Rs inhabited the wide hangars (two at a time) on the near side.

Above right: Most SR-71 pilots took their first ride in trusty '956, seen here over the Sierra Nevada mountains.

Below: The one-off SR-71A(BT) first flew in this guise on 11 December 1974, crewed by Darryl Greenamyer and Steve Belgeau.

the US on 7 June.

As the 9th SRW approached the time for overseas deployment, much talk in the crew lounge was devoted to anti-SAM tactics. The plan was to penetrate enemy airspace at Mach 3. If fired upon, the pilot would accelerate to Mach 3.2 and climb, thereby forcing the missile's guidance system to recalculate the intercept equation. One idea was to also dump fuel so that the aircraft would become lighter, enabling a more rapid climb, but a crew ended the debate during a sortie over Montana by dumping fuel for 10 seconds to see if the afterburner would ignite the fuel trail. Instead, it turned instantly into an ice cloud in the -55°F (-48°C) stratosphere and left a 5-mile (8-km) contrail-finger pointing directly to the aircraft. The pilot reported that he could see the trail for hundreds of miles after having turned back towards the west!

Halving the trainer fleet

During this work-up period, another incident befell the 9th SRW on 11 January 1968. Lieutenant Colonel 'Gray' Sowers and 'student' Captain Dave Fruehauf, on his third training sortie, experienced a double generator failure in SR-71B '957, near Spokane, Washington. They immedi-

ately switched off all non-essential electrically powered equipment to conserve battery power and made repeated attempts to reset both generators, which would come on briefly only to fail again. With most of the bases in Washington state unsuitable for diversion, the crew hoped to make Portland, Oregon, only to discover that they were weathered out. They had little option therefore but to press on for Beale. Their long straight-in approach looked good until the 175-kt (200-mph; 323-km/h) 'final' placed the aircraft in its natural 10° nose-up angle of attack. This allowed some dry-tank fuel inlet ports to 'suck air', which in turn interrupted the gravity flow of fuel to the engine combustion chambers, because the fuel boost pumps were inoperative. This caused cavitation, both J58s flamed out, and at 3,000 ft (915 m) Gray ordered bail-out. Both crew members survived as '957 'pancaked' inverted only 7 miles (11 km) north of Beale's long runway.

OL-8

As the 1st SRS neared operational readiness, decisions were made by Colonel Bill Hayes (9th SRW commander) and Colonel Hal Confer (Director of Operations) about which crews were to be first to be deployed to Kadena AB, on the island of Okinawa. The eight crew members selected began training for the deployment, flying simulator sorties depicting the oceanic route they would fly. It was also decided that the same sequence of crew deployment to Kadena would be repeated when it became time to fly operationally over Vietnam. Three aircraft and four crews would be deployed and the crews themselves pulled straws to decide the 'batting order'; the fourth crew would be standby for the three deploying aircraft and, if their services were not needed, would arrive on Kadena by KC-135Q tanker. Command of the operating location (OL-8) would alternate between the 9th SRW's wing commander and vice commander (and later deputy chief of operations). The OL's numbered designation was arrived at sequentially after the 9th SRW's U-2 detachments. Two days before

Glowing Heat (the codename for the deployment), six KC-135Q tankers were positioned at Hickam AFB, Hawaii. Emergency radio coverage was set up on Wake Island.

On 8 March 1968, Majors Buddy Brown and his RSO Dave Jenson left Beale in '978 and became the first Senior Crown crew to deploy to Kadena. The flight involved three air refuellings. Buddy recalls, "We had taken off from Beale at 11.00 and arrived at Kadena at 09.05 – nearly two hours earlier than take-off time, but in the next day because we had crossed the international date line. We beat the sun by a good margin." Two days later Major Jerry O'Malley and Captain Ed Payne delivered '976 to the OL. They were followed on 13 March by Bob Spencer and Keith Branham in '974. Finally, three days later in late evening rain, Jim Watkins and Dave Dempster, the back-up crew, were wearily disgorged from the KC-135. The crews and their aircraft were ready for business.

Due to maintenance problems, Buddy Brown and Dave Jenson missed their chance of being the first crew to fly the

SR-71 operationally; instead, that accolade went to Major Jerry O'Malley and Captain Ed Payne in '976. The mission was flown on Thursday 21 March 1968 and their route was similar to that flown by Mele Vojvodich in his A-12, 10 months earlier. However, with its large high-definition camera in the Q-bay, the A-12 was a photographic platform only. For its first operational mission, the SR-71 carried a downward-looking vertically-mounted terrain objective camera in the centre of the fuselage, ahead of the nose gear. Behind the cockpits in the P and Q chine bays were the left and right long focal-length 'close-look' technical objective ('TEOC' or 'Tech') cameras. Behind them, in bays S and T, were two operational objective cameras ('OOCs'), but of greater significance was the Goodyear side-looking airborne radar (SLAR) located in the detachable nose section, and its associated AR-1700 radar recorder unit in the N-bay, within the right chine.

Having refuelled after their first run, Jerry climbed and accelerated on track for their final 'take' for the mission, which was to be flown over the DMZ. For this run, the

Above: 'Big Tail' refuels from a KC-135Q during its two-year test programme. This came to an end on 29 October 1976 after the USAF lost interest in the concept, following the end of the war in Southeast Asia. The programme had been successful, offering a greater level of versatility with little performance penalty, and allowing the SR-71 to carry bigger mixed Sigint/optical loads.

Left: The SR-71A(BT)'s tail is seen here in the full 8½° up position, used to provide sufficient clearance at take-off and initial touchdown. Controls in the cockpit allowed the pilot to employ the tail as a trimming device in normal flight.

Below: 64-17959 lands at Palmdale during an early test flight, the 'Big Tail' modification sporting photo-calibration marks. Immediately after touchdown the tail was deflected from the full up position to 8½° down, after the wheels had touched the runway, to avoid fouling the brake 'chute.

'Big Tail'

The 'Big Tail' conversion was initially proposed as a way of housing more defensive electronic equipment, but rapidly evolved into a means of increasing sensor-carrying space. In one configuration the SR-71A(BT) carried OBC cameras in both nose and tail so that simultaneous frames could produce stereoscopic images. The tail section provided an additional 49 cu ft (1.39 m³) of capacity.

adopted a tanker callsign for security reasons; the three-ship formation made its slow, lumbering way to Ching Chuan Kang. On arrival, the SR-71 was quickly hangared. The next day, the 'take' was downloaded and despatched for processing – the film to the 67th RTS at Yokota AB, Japan and the SLAR imagery to the 9th RTS at Beale AFB. After two nights at CCK, Jerry and Ed ferried '976 back to Kadena and a superb reception by their friends.

Post-mission intelligence results were stunning. The SLAR imagery had revealed the location of many artillery emplacements around Khe Sanh, and a huge truck park which was used to support the guns. These sites previously had eluded US sensors on other reconnaissance aircraft. Over the next few days, airstrikes were mounted against both targets, reducing their effectiveness dramatically. After a 77-day siege, Khe Sanh was at last relieved on 7 April 1968 (two weeks after '976's discovery sortie). As a result of their highly successful mission, Major Jerome F. O'Malley and Captain Edward D. Payne were each awarded the Distinguished Flying Cross. On its very first operational mission, the SR-71 had proved its value.

Early OL-8 operational sorties were typified by problems involving the SR-71's generators, which often led to the aircraft having to divert into one of the USAF bases in Thailand. Of the 168 SR-71 sorties flown by OL-8 throughout 1968, 67 were operational missions over North Vietnam, the remaining being FCFs or for crew training. In addition, the first of many aircraft change-arounds took place when, over a period of seven days in September, '980, '970 and '962 took over from '978, '976 and '974. Crew rotation also took place, with no fewer than 21 crews having taken the SR-71 into battle over the same period (Bob Spencer and his RSO Keith Branham returned for a second temporary duty (TDY) stint).

'Habu'

While operating out of Kadena, the SR-71 received its nickname of 'Habu'. The habu is a poisonous pit viper found on the Ryuku islands; though non-aggressive, it can inflict a painful bite if provoked. Although resisted by officialdom, the name 'Habu' has proved to be permanent among all associated with Senior Crown.

OL-8 lost its first 'Habu' after more than two years of Kadena operations. On 10 May 1970 Majors Willie Lawson and Gil Martinez had completed one pass over North Vietnam and had air refuelled '969 near Korat RTAFB. Initiating an afterburner climb to prepare for a transonic 'dipsy doodle', they discovered that they were surrounded by heavy thunderclouds extending up to 50,000 ft (15245 m). The aircraft needed climb distance to get above the clouds before the dip-manoeuvre which established the

Above: An SR-71A fitted with chine-mounted RWR antennas closes on the boom of a KC-135Q during a Stateside training sortie.

The SR-71's unique shape was optimised not just for speed, but also for RCS reduction.

primary sensor was the SLAR. On arrival back at Kadena Jerry and Ed were confronted with a base completely fogged in. Despite a good ground-controlled approach (GCA), Jerry never saw the runway, and climbed back to contemplate further options. The SR-71 was low on fuel, so another tanker was launched and 25,000 lb (11340 kg) of fuel was taken onboard. The crew then received a two-figure encoded number which told them to divert to Taiwan. The SR-71 flew in company with two tankers and

Mach 1 airspeed needed for a higher rate of climb. The Mach 0.9 preliminary climb was sluggish with a full fuel load, and Willie eased '969 into a slightly steeper climb, trying to clear a 30,000 ft (9145 m) saddle-back of cloud. At that moment the aircraft entered turbulent cloud and both engines flamed out. The aircraft's angle of attack increased, then suddenly the nose pitched up and recovery was impossible. Both crew members ejected safely and landed resplendent in their silver moon suits, near U-Tapao. To date, four SR-71s have been lost in pitch-up incidents.

OL-8 against the Soviets

Although the vast majority of early 'Habu' flights from Kadena were in support operations in Vietnam, this was not exclusively the case. On the night of 27 September 1971, Majors Bob Spencer and 'Butch' Sheffield completed post take-off tanking and established '980 on a northerly track. US Intelligence had obtained details of the largest-ever Soviet naval exercise to be held near Vladivostok, in the Sea of Japan. Such an event could prove a rich fishing ground for an intelligence data trawl, and the 'Habu' was an ideal vehicle for stirring up the Soviet fleet's defence systems.

National security officials were especially interested in obtaining signal details relating to the Soviets' new SA-5 SAM system. Accordingly, Major Jack Clemance, an inventive electronic warfare officer who worked in the 9th SRW's Electronic Data Processing Centre, jury-rigged one of the aircraft's Elint sensors which allowed it to receive continuous-wave signal data.

As '980 bore down on the target area, dozens of Soviet radars were switched on; just short of entering Soviet airspace, the 'Habu' rolled into a full 35° banked turn, remaining throughout in international airspace. However, on approach to the target area, Bob noted that the right engine's oil pressure was dipping. Clearing the area, Bob once again scanned the engine instruments to discover the reading had fallen to zero. He shut down the engine and was forced to descend and decelerate to subsonic speeds. Having stirred up a hornets' nest, they were now sitting ducks for any Soviet fast jets sent up to intercept the oil-starved Habu. Worse still, at lower altitude they were subjected to strong headwinds which rapidly depleted their fuel supply. 'Butch' calculated that recovery back to Kadena was impossible – instead, they would have to divert into

South Korea.

The OL commander had been monitoring '980's slow progress and as the 'Habu' neared Korea, US listening posts reported the launch of several MiGs from Pyongyang, North Korea. In response, USAF F-102s were scrambled from a base near Hon Chew, South Korea and vectored into a position between the 'Habu' and the MiGs. It was later established that the MiG launch was unconnected with the SR-71's descent. Bob recovered '980 into Taegu, South Korea, without further incident. In all, their EMR 'take' had recorded emissions from 290 different radars, but the greatest prize was 'capture' of the much sought-after SA-5 signals – a first.

On 20 July 1972, while returning to Kadena from an operational mission, Majors Denny Bush and Jimmy Fagg were caught by excessive cross winds shortly after touch-down in '978. They jettisoned the 'chute as per the book, to prevent the aircraft from 'weather-cocking' sharply into wind, but the extended roll-out caused the aircraft to roll off the end of the runway and, in a twist of fate, the aircraft hit the concrete housing the emergency crash barriers. One of the main landing gear struts was badly damaged, which in turn caused substantial additional damage. Both crew members were unhurt, but '978 was written off. It was not

Det 1 – Kadena

Kadena was the site for the first overseas operational deployment, SR-71s taking over from the CIA A-12s. Known successively as OL-8, OL-RK and OL-KA, the Kadena operation finally settled as Det 1 of the 9th SRW in August 1974, and operated as such until retirement of the aircraft in 1990. Missions from this base were flown against Vietnam, Korea, China and the Soviet Far East. Four marathon missions were also launched against Iran.

Above: In the early 1980s the SR-71 fleet began adopting low-visibility markings. The national insignia and 'US Air Force' titles were removed altogether, leaving just the cockpit emergency information, tail numbers and 'No walk' markings in low-visibility red.

Above left: For many the SR-71 cockpit was the pinnacle of any US Air Force career, and very few were lucky or able enough to achieve it. The selection processes were rigorous.

Resplendent with a red '1' chalked on the fin, an SR-71A taxis at Kadena past 'Habu Hill', a well-known vantage point. Two or three aircraft were detached to the Okinawa base for most of the SR-71's operational career, tasked with some of the most sensitive missions.

Det 4 – Mildenhall

The 9th SRW began operations from RAF Mildenhall in 1976 with sporadic single-aircraft detachments of both the U-2R and SR-71A. Det 4 was established as such in April 1979 with a single U-2R, while SR-71 deployments increased. The U-2s primarily provided Sigint coverage and the SR-71s were used for photography (later radar imagery). In 1981 the detachment was heavily committed to covering the situation in Poland, which was under threat of Soviet intervention. By late 1982, Det 4 was assigned two SR-71s on a near-permanent basis, operations being regularly conducted along the East-West German border, in the Baltic and around the North Cape. The SR-71 operation was fully formalised in 1984.

Top: With KC-135Qs trailing in the background, 64-17964 is seen wearing the name The Bodonian Express on its tail, a reference to a diversion into the Norwegian airfield at Bodø during a 1981 mission to the North Cape from Beale.

Below: David Clark S-1030 pressure suits provided full protection in the event of a cabin depressurisation at altitude. Special ports in the helmet allowed the crew to eat and drink during the flight.

until 21 April 1989 that Kadena lost another 'Habu'. On that occasion one of the engine compressor discs disintegrated during Mach 3 flight, the debris severing one hydraulic system and damaging the other. Lieutenant Colonel Dan House and Major Blair Bozek decelerated and descended '974 down to 400 kt (459 mph; 739 km/h) and 10,000 ft (3,048 m) when the remaining hydraulic system ran dry. Both men safely ejected just a few hundred yards off the coast of Luzon and were rescued by Filipino fishermen. They were later picked up by an HH-53 'Super Jolly Green Giant' and flown to Clark AFB.

OL-8 was redesignated OL-RK on 30 October 1970, became OL-KA on 26 October 1971 and finally Detachment 1 or Det 1 of the 9th SRW in August 1974, a title it retained until deactivated in 1990. During 22 years of service, the unit flew missions to Vietnam, Laos, Cambodia, Thailand, North Korea, airspace off the USSR and China, and four 11-hour return flights to the Persian Gulf during the Iran-Iraq War.

Operations from the USA

Despite four 9th SRW aircraft losses between 13 April 1967 and 10 October 1968, Category III 'Operational' Testing ended in December 1968. The wing was awarded the Presidential Unit Citation for meeting the challenges of bringing the 'most advanced' reconnaissance system of its day to operational readiness.

Rolling down Beale's runway 14 in '977, in October 1968, were new pilot/RSO team Majors Abe Kardong and Jim Kogler. Approaching V1, a wheel failed, throwing shrapnel into the fuel cells and causing a fuel fire. Abe aborted take-off at high speed, which caused the remaining tyres on that leg to burst. The brake 'chute blossomed, only to be consumed by the fire. With one wing low and the aircraft off centre to the runway, '977's sharp inlet spike knifed through the barrier cable at the end of the runway, rendering it useless. Now on the overrun, Jim ejected while Abe rode out the high-speed sleigh ride. When the dust settled, he was helped from the cockpit by the mobile control crew for that day, Willie Lawson and Gil Martinez.

On 11 April 1969 Lieutenant Colonel Bill Skliar and Major Noel Warner lined up SR-71A 64-17954 on runway 04 at Edwards and began a maximum gross weight take-off. DUTCH 69 had just rotated when one of the left main gear tyres blew. Unable to support the additional weight, the other two on that leg also went. Bill immediately aborted the take-off, but red hot shrapnel from the disintegrating wheel hubs punctured the fuel tanks and triggered a fire which engulfed the entire aircraft. Once at a standstill, Bill exited the aircraft to the right and assisted Noel from his rear cockpit. '954 never flew again. After this accident the Goodrich tyres were 'beefed up'.

The third pitch-up accident happened on 18 December 1969, when Director of the Test Force Lieutenant Colonel Joe Rogers and RSO Lieutenant Colonel Gary Heidelbaugh were accelerating and climbing '953. They heard a

loud explosion which was accompanied by a loss of power and severe control difficulties. As the aircraft decelerated, its angle of attack continued to increase, despite Joe 'fire-walling' the control stick. Ten seconds after the explosion, realising they had entered an irrecoverable corner of the flight envelope, Joe ordered, "Let's get out, Gary," and both men safely ejected. '953 crashed at the southern end of Death Valley, and the cause of the explosion remains unknown.

On 17 June 1970 the 9th lost another SR-71A, '970, following a mid-air collision with a KC-135Q shortly after taking aboard 35,000 lb (15875 kg) of fuel. The 'Habu' hit clear air turbulence (CAT) and the entire nose of the aircraft smashed into the rear of the tanker. No-one aboard the tanker was injured and Buddy Brown and Mort Jarvis were able to safely eject, although the former sustained two broken legs during the ejection.

Yom Kippur monitoring

At 14.00 on 6 October 1973, an hour-long Egyptian artillery barrage on the state of Israel was mirrored by an equally ferocious 30-minute barrage from Syria. The attack, which spelled the beginning of the Yom Kippur War, caught the Israelis off guard and the Arabs made substantial gains both in the Sinai and the Golan Heights. In view of the grave situation faced by the Israelis, the US decided to step up intelligence efforts and use the SR-71 to provide a hot-spot reconnaissance capability. CinCSAC General John Meyer ordered Colonel Pat Halloran (9th SRW commander) to prepare for missions that would be flown from Beale across the war zone and recovered into RAF Mildenhall, England. With plans in place, Pat climbed aboard a KC-135 and left for Mildenhall on 10 October. On arrival, he was informed that the Heath government had denied the SR-71 use of Mildenhall, a move that was designed to safeguard the supply of Arab oil. The KC-135 was then fuelled up and flew back to the US – undoubtedly the shortest overseas TDY in the history of the 9th SRW!

As an alternative, round-robin missions would be flown from Griffiss AFB, New York. Additional ground support would be made available via Palmdale's flight test team operating SR-71A '955, which had already been scheduled to conduct a series of evaluations on its new A-2 electronic

defence system from the East Coast base; this would also provide a convenient security cover for the operation. Accordingly, at 22.00 on 11 October 1973, Lieutenant Colonel Jim Shelton and Major Gary Coleman left Beale in '979 and headed for Griffiss. On arrival they were met by an angry base commander and three Lockheed tech reps after they had laid "a heavy late night sonic boom track" down into New York state as they descended from altitude. Jim phoned Al Joersz and John Fuller (who would fly a second SR-71 into Griffiss) and advised them to move their descent profile over the Great Lakes to minimise the effects of the boom on urban eastern states. With the amendment incorporated into their flight plan, no boom complaints accompanied the arrival of '964. Unfortunately, this second aircraft developed a hydraulic problem that forced an engine change, leaving the new detachment with one mission-ready aircraft until specialised equipment could be flown in from Beale. An hour after the arrival of '964, the first tanker from Beale touched down carrying Tom Estes (the operation officer), three mission planners and a number of the 9th's best intelligence and maintenance personnel. At 06.00 a secure teleprinter clattered out the final details of the first sortie which was to be flown just 22 hours later.

When the crews met the mission planners the former voiced concerns about diversionary fields, but no-one could offer a satisfactory answer. Later that morning, the tanker from Mildenhall arrived and technicians began preparing '979 for the longest operational sortie to date. By mid-afternoon it was suggested that the crew should get some sleep since they had been up nearly 36 hours and would soon be readying themselves for a 16-hour day. They were directed to old quarters where they discovered their rooms

Libya

Operation El Dorado Canyon, the reprisal raid on Libya, was flown on the night of 14/15 April 1986. Three post-strike photo-reconnaissance missions were flown by Det 4 SR-71s, the first departing even before the USAF's F-111 bombers had returned to their bases. So important were the missions that both aircraft were launched, one acting as an air-spare.

Below: '980 had three camel markings applied to the left nose gear door following its 15/16/17 April missions.

Above and above right: Some of the post-strike imagery was released to the press, the first time that SR-71 photographs had been made public, although the quality was reduced to hide capability. The aircraft were fitted with two TEOC cameras each, with an OBC panoramic camera for horizon-to-horizon coverage.

Although most tanker support was provided by the KC-135Q, the SR-71 could also refuel from a KC-10A. This capability was first used operationally during the 1986 Libya missions. The SR-71s returned to Libya in 1987 during another period of tension.

were hot and their beds uncomfortable. Gary Coleman recalled, "No-one could snore like Jim Shelton and I got no sleep at all, but I consoled myself with the thought that at least my pilot was getting some solid rest!"

The belligerent attitude of usually helpful allies necessitated that JP7 fuel and tanker crews be repositioned from Mildenhall and Turkey to Zaragoza in Spain, and emergency landing sites were still proving all but impossible to find. Nevertheless, Jim Shelton cranked '979's engines on cue, and lifted off from Griffiss and headed east at 02.00. Just off the East Coast he made good the first of many ARCPs (air refuelling contact points), topped off and continued east to the next cell of tankers awaiting the thirsty 'Habu', just beyond the Azores. Returning again to speed and altitude, they made a high-Mach dash through the Straits of Gibraltar and let down for a third air refuelling just east of the heel of Italy. Due to the proximity to the war zone and Libya, the US Navy provided a CAP (combat air patrol) from carrier-based aircraft on station in the Mediterranean.

The SR-71 then resumed its climb and acceleration to

coast-in over Port Said. Gary Coleman said, "There was no indication of anything launched against us, but everyone was painting us on their radars as we made our turn inbound. The DEF panel lit up like a pin-ball machine and I said to Jim, 'this should be interesting.'"

In all, '979 spent 25 minutes over 'denied territory'. Entering Egyptian airspace at 11:03 GMT, they covered the Israeli battle fronts with both Egypt and Syria before coasting out and letting down towards their fourth ARCP, which was still being CAPped by the US Navy. Their next hot leg was punctuated by a fifth refuelling, again near the Azores, before a final high-speed run across the western Atlantic towards New York. Mindful of his own fatigue, Gary was in awe of his pilot who completed a textbook sixth air refuelling, before greasing '979 back down at Griffiss after a combat sortie lasting 10 hours 18 minutes (more than five hours of which was at Mach 3 or above) and involving 11 tanking operations from the ever-dependable KC-135Qs. Their reconnaissance 'take' was of high quality and provided intelligence and defence analysts with much needed information concerning the deposition of Arab forces in the region, which was then made available to the Israelis.

Back to the war zone

Aircraft '979 paid a second successful visit to the Yom Kippur War zone on 25 October, this time crewed by Majors Al Joersz and John Fuller. A third mission was chalked up by the same aircraft eight days later. Majors Jim Wilson and Bruce Douglas took '964 on its first sortie to the Mediterranean on 11 November. The 10-hour 49-minute flight departed Griffiss and terminated as planned at Seymour Johnson AFB, North Carolina, the reason behind this detachment move being to avoid the New York winter weather.

Despite hostilities between the factions officially ending with a Soviet-backed motion in the United Nations on 24 October, fierce fighting continued to break out at regular intervals. It was to cover disengagement that the SR-71's monitoring system continued to be called upon, with five more marathon flights being flown from Seymour Johnson AFB.

In total, these nine flights represent a pinnacle of operational professionalism and serve as a tribute, not only to the dedication of the aircrews, but also to that of the staff planners, tanker crews and of course the unsung heroes, that small group of top ground technicians who maintained the SR-71s away from home. The sorties also stand as a testament of the long-reach capability of the aircraft and its ability to operate, on short notice, with impunity in a high-threat environment.

As part of the United States bicentennial celebrations,

SAC and HQ USAF agreed to reveal some of the SR-71's performance capabilities, by securing more records for the nation. Initially, the plan was to set an 'around the world at the equator' speed record. Pat Bledsoe and John Fuller were the senior crew at the time and were chosen to make the flight. Initial planning showed it could be done in 16 hours 20 minutes with fuel taken onboard from seven air refuelling tracks. The only modification for the SR-71 would have been an additional liquid dewar. Alas, the planning came to an abrupt halt when HQ USAF generals saw the cost of deploying fuel and tankers to forward bases around the world – it would involve nearly 100 KC-135 flights! Instead, a new set of world speed and altitude records were set by the 9th on 27 and 28 July 1976 (see table, page 55).

Cuba

Early in the Senior Crown programme, Cuban reconnaissance sorties became a task for the 9th SRW. They were flown from Beale and initially codenamed Giant Plate, but the designation was later changed to Clipper. Most sorties were 'stand-off' runs, flown abeam the island in international airspace. Such a mission would typically take three and a half hours to complete and was considered very routine.

Occasionally, however, the track was modified to take the aircraft directly over Cuba. When the Carter administration entered office, they suspended all overflight actively in an act of 'goodwill'. In 1978, though, a reconnaissance satellite photographed a Soviet freighter in Havana harbour surrounded by large crates that were being moved to a nearby air base where aircraft were being reassembled. It appeared that 15 MiG-23s had been supplied to Castro's air force. The MiG-23BN 'Flogger-H' was known to be capable of carrying nuclear weapons, and if it was this variant

Above: Simple barns were used to house the SR-71, with doors at either end to allow start-up inside the barn.

Above left: Due to the high flashpoint of JP7 fuel, a unique starting method was required. A ground cart or compressed air spun up the engine spool, while a TEB (tri-ethyl borane) shot provided chemical ignition, resulting in this greenish glow.

that had been exported, then the shipment violated the 1962 Soviet pledge of not deploying 'offensive' weapons to Cuba.

Two sorties were flown by SR-71s over Cuba in November 1978. They verified that the MiGs were MiG-23Ms 'Flogger-Es' optimised for air defence, evidence which substantiated Soviet claims.

UK operations

Early in the Senior Crown programme, the total number of operating SR-71s was scaled down. The two flying squadrons became one in April 1971. As the US disengaged itself from Vietnam, and with the Yom Kippur War over, the number of unit-authorised aircraft also declined. By 1977, the SR-71A primary authorised aircraft (PAA) stood at six aircraft, and funding reduced proportionately. Since the SR-71 was primarily an imagery platform, it had lost support from the National Intelligence Committee, which had become enamoured with satellite products. Having lost much of the high-level support of that powerful constituency, the SR-71 had to be funded by the Air

64-17968 sports one of the tail-art designs which appeared sporadically throughout the SR-71's career. Such artwork was applied in chalk, as this did not damage the 'iron-ball' paint, and could easily be washed off. Artworks usually appeared at the detachments, being removed when the aircraft rotated back to Beale.

Physiological Support

A key part of the SR-71 operation was the work of the PSD (Physiological Support Division), which was responsible for all aspects of the crew's well-being, including maintenance of the pressure suits and helmets, provision of food and drink, transportation to and from the aircraft, and medical support. The work was vital to ensure the safety of the crew in the event of an emergency at high altitude, where any depressurisation would result in blood 'boiling' in the veins.

Right: A front restraint strap was fitted to stop the aircrew's head being thrown back when the pressure suit inflated. The crew rode to the aircraft in a van fitted with reclining armchairs.

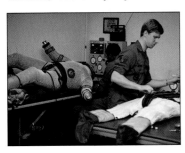

PSD technicians regularly checked the suits for leaks by inflating them. The main suit was protected by an outer orange cover.

A thorough medical preceded suiting up. The crew pre-breathed pure oxygen to purge any nitrogen from the bloodstream.

A vital check during suit-up was to ensure that the glove and helmet seals were secure. Note the helmet port for food and drink tubes.

Lockheed SR-71A 'Blackbird'
1st Strategic Reconnaissance Squadron
9th Strategic Reconnaissance Wing
Strategic Air Command, US Air Force

What became known as the SR-71A was the outcome of a series of proposals made by Lockheed to the US Air Force based on the technology of the A-12 single-seater. At the time the USAF's major programme was the North American XB-70 Valkyrie Mach 3 bomber, and any proposal that was seen to challenge it was to be avoided. However, Lockheed schemed the B-12 as a nuclear bomber which could penetrate deep into hostile airspace and clean up any targets which had not been hit in the first opening round of strikes. The proposal met with great interest, and a contract for six pre-production aircraft and 25 others was awarded on 4 June 1962. This aircraft was given the Air Force designation RS-71 (for reconnaissance-strike), and followed on in the bomber sequence from the B-70, which had been redesignated RS-70. Lockheed's refined design became known in-house as the RS-12. In the early 1960s the advent of the ICBM caused the Pentagon to radically review its thoughts, with the result that the special weapons which needed to be developed for the RS-71 were never ordered. Based on this lack of commitment, Kelly Johnson feared a cancellation of the project, and rapidly produced a pure reconnaissance version, the R-12. In May 1964 Secretary of Defense McNamara cancelled the RS-70 Valkyrie and, soon after, announced that the SR-71 (neatly transposing Reconnaissance-Strike with Strategic Reconnaissance) would be built for the USAF, a modification to the existing RS-71 contract. But for the foresight and rapid reaction of Kelly Johnson, the aircraft may never have been built.

ECS and oxygen
A complex environmental control system comprised two air cycle systems which provided heating and cooling air for the cockpits and other aircraft systems. Heating was required for various engine inlet systems, while cooler air was used for cabin pressurisation, de-icing and de-fogging. Cooling was also provided to the cockpits and the sensor bays. Air was provided to ventilate the crew's pressure suits, and to maintain an overpressure to seal the canopy. Two pressurisation schedules, one for 10,000 ft (3050 m) equivalent pressure and one for 26,000 ft (7925 m), were available. Three oxygen converters (of which one was a back-up) were provided for the crew's needs, and emergency oxygen supplies were incorporated into the ejection seat survival kit.

Powerplant
The Pratt & Whitney JT11D-20 (military designation J58) engine was the result of development work performed on the hydrogen-powered Suntan engine and the JT9 developed for the XB-70. The J58 was an 80 per cent scaled-down version of the JT9, and had been developed for a US Navy interceptor requiring a dash speed of Mach 3 for a short period. The engine showed promise for further development, and eventually emerged with continuous Mach 3 operations. The key to this capability was its bleed-bypass technology. Air was taken from the middle of the compressor stage and transported through six large bypass ducts around the remainder of the compressor and turbine sections. This eliminated the choking of high velocity air in the rear stages while maintaining the large mass flow in the forward stages. The bypass air was then reintroduced to the main flow just ahead of the afterburner, performing in much the same way as a ramjet. At low speeds no air was bypassed, allowing the engine to operate as a simple turbojet. Furthermore, the engine incorporated moveable inlet guide vanes to guide the air into the compressor face. At low speeds the IGVs were in the axial position, but as speeds and compressor inlet temperatures rose, so the IGVs moved to the cambered position. Materials proved to be a major problem for Pratt & Whitney because of the very high temperatures encountered. In the turbines a new material known as Astralloy was used, this proving to be able to withstand the high rotational loads while operating at very high temperatures.

Cameras
The A-12 carried as primary sensor either an Actron 60-in (152.4-cm) Type H or Itek KA-102A camera with a 48-in (122-cm) lens in the large Q-bay behind the cockpit. This valuable space was occupied in the SR-71A by the RSO, denying the use of such large, conventional, downward-looking sensors. In the SR-71, the only available space for camera systems was in the fuselage chine bays. Consequently, a new range of compressed-length cameras using cassegrainian optics was developed, and in the early days of the programme results were markedly inferior to those gained using the A-12.

Two types of camera were developed, the Operational Objective Camera and the Technical Objective Camera. The OOCs provided wide-area coverage, and were made by Hycon. They had a 13-in (33-cm) focal length lens, and used 9 x 9-in (23 x 23-cm) film. They were of most use for analysing large targets such as airfields or harbours, and also provided positional reference for the much greater enlargement images produced by the TEOCs. OOCs had to be switched on and off by the RSO. The programmable TEOCs were mostly made by Itek and initially provided a focal length of 36 in (91.4 cm), later improved to 48 in (122 cm). TEOCs provided a close view of the target area, and were operated automatically using signals from the aircraft's navigation system. Much of the sensor development effort was expended on the TEOCs, with the result that the OOCs were withdrawn from use in the early 1970s. By that time the development of the TEOC optics had combined with advances in film chemistry and processing to produce some superb results. Although little is known about the programme, at least two SR-71s (including the trusty test aircraft '955') carried a TEOC made by CAI, and believed to have offered a 66-in (167.6-cm) focal length.

Spelling the end for the OOC was a sensor first tested in 1968, known as the Optical Bar Camera (OBC) or Split-Scan Panoramic. This was housed in the nose of the aircraft (or in the extended tailcone of '959 'Big Tail') and provided horizon-to-horizon coverage by using a rotating optical barrel prism with an exposure slit. This swept across the film, capturing a continuous horizon-to-horizon image. It was this camera which allowed the USAF to claim that the SR-71 could photograph 100,000 sq miles (258980 km²) of territory per hour. OBC imagery could be enlarged up to 20 times, making it a very useful reconnaissance tool in its own right for both wide-area and spot coverage, while it also provided the necessary references for pinpointing TEOC imagery.

Image stabilisation, to avoid 'smearing', required a complex active stabilisation 'scan-head' on the TEOCs. This stabilised the optical axis of the camera inertially during exposure, and allowed the camera to be aimed precisely at specific targets using cues from the ANS. A forward motion compensator (FMC) eliminated the effects of flying at Mach 3 plus. Although control of the TEOCs and OBC was normally automatic, the RSO maintained the ability to control all the sensors, including camera exposure settings. Reference information for interpretation was provided by the V/H (velocity/height) system, which worked out the angular rate of motion between the aircraft and the terrain, and the sensor event/frame count system.

Autopilot
Most of the mission was flown using the autopilot, which, in AUTONAV mode, was slaved to the ANS. Prior to the sortie a pre-planned route was prepared using a series of destination points (DPs). These were loaded by tape into the ANS computer prior to take-off. Once airborne, the ANS commanded the autopilot to follow these DPs around the route of the mission. None of these DPs was ever actually flown over, as the system automatically commanded the turn before arriving at the DP so that the aircraft would cut the corner in order to roll out on the next leg precisely on track. The turn position was calculated based on the aircraft's speed and preset desired bank angle. At Mach 3.2 the maximum preset bank angle was 42°, which allowed a margin of 3° over the permissible airframe limit of 45°.

Fuel

Early problems in the Blackbird programme prompted Pratt & Whitney, Ashland Shell and Monsanto to develop a new high-flashpoint fuel. Originally known as PF-1 and later designated JP7, this fuel would only ignite at high temperatures, reducing the risk of inadvertent fires caused by the high operating temperatures encountered at high Mach numbers. For operational flights a chemical known as A-50 was added to the fuel, this reducing the frequency response of the afterburner plume, which had been shown to produce a large radar return when untreated. Other additives included fluorocarbons to improve lubricity, and toluene and mentyl isobutylketone which further reduced the fire risk. This was especially important as the fuel was used as a hydraulic fluid to operate the afterburner nozzle, which caused it to be heated to 600°F (316°C). The high-flashpoint fuel required chemical ignition by triethyl borane (TEB), which ignited on contact with the fuel.

Compared to the A/F-12, the SR-71 had a lengthened fuselage for more fuel. Whereas the internal capacity of the YF-12 was 9,785 US gal (37040 litres), that of the SR-71A was 12,219 US gal (46254 litres). There were six tanks which occupied most of the main circular fuselage structure aft of the refuelling receptacle, and the wings between the fuselage and the engine nacelles. The wing tanks were punctuated by the wheel wells. Sixteen pumps moved fuel between tanks, engines and heat-exchangers, the engines being fed by a Chandler Evans-built main fuel pump specially housed in steel to protect it from the high temperatures. The fuel itself was used as an efficient heat sink for a number of systems, including the ECS, oil systems and TEB tank. It was also used to trim the aircraft by fore/aft movements to maintain the centre of gravity within limits. Three liquid nitrogen tanks were carried which were used to pressurise the fuel tanks, preventing crushing of the tanks by aerodynamic loads. The nitrogen also served to 'inert' the tanks as a further fire precaution.

DAFICS

Between 1980 and 1985 the SR-71 fleet underwent a major modification programme which replaced the old analog flight control and inlet system with DAFICS (digital automatic flight and inlet control system). This consisted of three Honeywell HDP-5301 digital computers housed in a Faraday cage to protect them from electromagnetic pulse. Two of the computers were used as primary systems for controlling the aircraft's stability augmentation systems, autopilot and the programmed inlet control system. The third computer was a monitoring system containing BIT (built-in test) software for continuous checking for faults. Air data from the pitot system was digitised and fed into the two main computers, which then calculated and commanded appropriate actions. The monitoring computer stored the BIT data which could be downloaded by maintenance technicians upon landing for fault rectification and rescheduling of the inlet control programme if required.

Automatic inlet control was considered vital to the SR-71's mission, so critical were the parameters at high Mach and high altitude. The inlet spikes and auxiliary doors were programmed to maintain the shock wave in the correct position in the throat of the inlet, from where it could easily be expelled (an 'unstart'). The DAFICS (and earlier analog system) maintained the shock in the correct position as far as possible, and automatically recaptured the shock wave if an 'unstart' should occur. Manual control of the inlet and bypass door system was possible from the cockpit should the system fail, although this was less precise than the automatic system.

Stability augmentation

At operating speed and altitude the SR-71 was only marginally stable in pitch and yaw. During the 'accel' to high-Mach flight the centre of gravity was moved aft (by pumping fuel) to reduce trim drag and to improve elevon authority. This, combined with lift generated by the forward fuselage chine, caused stability in the pitching plane to decrease as speed increased. Yaw stability was eroded by the aerodynamic properties of the forward fuselage chine. To counter this an AFCS (automatic flight control system) was fitted, governed by the DAFICS computers. The AFCS co-ordinated the actions of the autopilots, eight rate-sensing gyros, three lateral accelerometers, a stability augmentation system (SAS) for each of the three planes (roll, pitch and yaw) and a Mach trim system. The latter provided speed stability while accelerating or decelerating through the mid-speed range, compensating for the aircraft's tendency to tuck when accelerating or pitch down when slowing down. There were two autopilots, one for pitch (giving basic attitude hold, Mach hold or KEAS hold) and one for roll (basic attitude hold or AUTONAV, slaved to either ANS or INS). The three SAS channels took signals from the gyros to detect divergence from stable flight, and applied the appropriate corrective flight surface inputs.

Radar and electronic sensors

A key feature of the SR-71 was its ability to supply 'synergistic' intelligence, combining radar imagery and signals intelligence with photographic images. The aircraft carried various Sigint sensors, most aimed at recording radar signals (Elint), as the aircraft's great speed rendered it all but useless as a Comint platform. The aircraft also played a useful part as a 'ferret', stirring up air defence systems to allow other types of aircraft (particularly the RC-135) to monitor the responses.

Radar imagery was provided by a side-looking radar in the nose, when fitted. Initially, this was the Goodyear PIP. The Loral CAPRE (pronounced 'caper') followed, replaced in the 1980s by the Loral ASARS-1 in its characteristic bulbous nose section. The ASARS-1 provided very high-resolution radar imagery by using synthetic aperture technology. The radar could operate in a search mode, providing a wide-area coverage on either side of the aircraft's track, or could be used in spot mode to provide highly detailed images of very small areas. A squint mode allowed the radar to look forward or aft from its normal central position.

This sensor is one of the key reasons for the reactivation of the SR-71 fleet in the 1990s, and the two aircraft returned to operations were fitted in 1996/97 with a Unisys datalink system just aft of the nosewheel door. This allows the downlinking in near real time of ASARS-1 imagery to a ground station for immediate interpretation.

Navigation system

One of the many key technological problems which had to be surmounted in the Blackbird programme was that of navigation. Accurate navigation was essential when flying in sensitive areas and over large distances, while the aircraft would often be far away from reliable ground stations. Consequently, the NAS-14V2 Astro-inertial Navigation System (ANS) was developed by Nortronics. The ANS combined three main reference components: a highly accurate (to five milliseconds) chronometer, an inertial platform and a star-tracker. The latter had 52 permanently visible stars logged in its memory, of which at least three were sequentially tracked at any given time by a gimbal-mounted tracker located in the top of the navigation bay aft of the RSO's cockpit. By cross-correlating the positions of the stars, an accurate position could be gained, and compared with the inertial platform.

In addition to the ANS, the SR-71 also carried a standard inertial system. This was originally the Flight Reference System (FRS), which only provided heading and attitude information, but in June 1982 was replaced by the Singer-Kearfott SKN-2417 (as used in early F-16s). This standard INS provided a useful and accurate back-up should the primary ANS fail. It was housed in the R-bay, along with other nav/comms equipment. This included an ARA-48 automatic direction finder (ADF), TACAN receiver with distance-measuring equipment, instrument landing system (ILS), and HF/VHF/UHF radios. An IFF transponder was located in the D-bay.

Drawing data from the primary ANS, the system produced a moving map strip projection in each cockpit as the main navigation display. The RSO also had a video viewsight for looking beneath the aircraft to cross-check known ground positions against ANS/INS predictions. The viewsight (with either 44° or 114° selectable fields of view) was also useful for spotting SAM launches or checking cloud cover over the target during photographic missions.

An SR-71 lopes along over the California countryside after a refuelling. When the airframe is cold the wing tanks do not seal properly, so fuel leaks from various joints on the upper surface. When the aircraft is at maximum operational altitude and speed, the airframe heats up and expands, sealing the cracks.

Companion trainer

A large fleet of Northrop T-38A Talons was assigned to the 9th Strategic Reconnaissance Wing to act as companion trainers for the SR-71 force. The Talon provided low-cost flight hours for the crews, and its landing and subsonic handling characteristics proved to be a fair mimic of the SR-71. The Talons were also used on various chase duties, and later provided co-pilot flight hours for the KC-135 fleet.

appeared to be a mortally wounded programme. Following an SR-71 briefing to intelligence officers of the Navy's Atlantic fleet, Bill Flexanher (an analyst at the Naval Intelligence Support Center at Suitland, Maryland) expressed an interest in the SR-71's sea-scanning radar capabilities to detect submarines in their home ports in the Baltic and Arctic areas. Flexenhar requested those areas to be 'SLAR-imaged' for his analysis.

A strong possibility existed that a new requirement could arise which would give Senior Crown a new lease of life. A call was made to the SAC reconnaissance centre for SR-71 missions over those areas, but at the time it was not possible. Instead, two missions were flown over the Soviet Pacific fleet near Vladivostok to test the concept. The results were impressive and another presentation was made to high-level naval and national intelligence officials.

Farnborough visit

As noted earlier, the first planned visit of an SR-71 to England was to have been 11 October 1973, during the Yom Kippur War. Instead, it was not until 9 September 1974 when Majors Jim Sullivan and Noel Widdifield in '972 established a new New York to London transatlantic speed record of less than two hours. Eighteen months later '972 returned as BURNS 31, and two aborted missions were flown in a bid to obtain SLAR imagery of the Soviet Northern Fleet. Due to abnormally warm weather conditions, fuel calculations made by the two RSOs during the missions showed that their fuel burn was so high that they would be unable to make their next ARCP. The 10-day deployment was an intelligence-gathering failure, but important lessons were learned about operating procedures in Arctic air masses.

Aircraft '962 arrived during Exercise Teamwork on 6 September 1976, and flew the very next day on a Barents Sea mission codenamed Coldfire 001. Majors Rich Graham and Don Emmons flew that and another round-robin sortie out of RAF Mildenhall, Suffolk, before returning '962 to Beale on 18 September. On 7 January 1977 SR-71A '958 arrived at Mildenhall as RING 21. It left at the end of a 10-day deployment as POWER 86. The same aircraft returned to 'the Hall' on 16 May as INDY 69, going back to Beale 15 days later as RESAY 35. The concept of using the SR-71's SLAR and camera systems 'to gather simultaneous, synoptic coverage' of the Soviet submarine fleet based on the Kolskiy Polustrov, in Murmansk and bases on the Baltic had been validated.

Force, although it was tasked by national agencies to support a variety of theatre intelligence requirements. HQ SAC was hostile to Senior Crown because it diverted funds from its bomber and tanker mission. Although part of SAC's Single Integrated Operational Plan (SIOP), the SR-71 was not capable of gathering 'long on-station' samples of Sigint like the RC-135s and U-2Rs. The loss of its SAC patronage left Senior Crown increasingly isolated and vulnerable. To survive continued budgetary raids, it was apparent that the SR-71's utility had to be improved in order to become competitive with overhead systems.

In order to compete on a level playing field with satellites and other sensor platforms, the SR-71 needed updated sensors and, most importantly, it had to be equipped with an air-to-ground datalink system which would give it a 'near real-time capability'.

A new 'marketing package' was assembled which included details of the SR-71's performance and imagery capabilities. In the mid-1970s, Senior Crown advocates embarked on a public relations campaign within the Washington intelligence community to gather support for what

To fulfil the requirement it would be necessary to permanently base two SR-71s at Mildenhall. Such a move would reduce mission response times and be much more cost effective. A permanent operating location in Europe would require permission from Britain's Prime Minister and the Ministry of Defence, and would need close co-ordination with the US State Department and Congressional Intelligence Oversight Committee. More funding would be needed for new support facilities at Mildenhall (a maintenance complex, two single-aircraft hangars, added fuel storage and an engine run-up 'hush house'). Estimated cost was $14 million, which it was believed would be far too much for the necessary approval. Cost-cutting elements were therefore incorporated into the proposal, including recycled Beale hangers, a renovated mobile processing centre (MPC) and civilian contract maintenance. Such measures brought costs down to about $10 million. Missions were planned at a rate of 10 per month – the actual requirement was greater, but this was kept from SAC HQ, which would then have insisted upon a three-aircraft complement, which in turn would have escalated costs to a point that would have jeopardised the entire proposal. After some imaginative manoeuvring, the SR-71 programme element manager (PEM) at the Pentagon finally managed to steer the programme objective memorandum (POM) through the political minefield, and the POM leapt from 450th position in the order of priorities to seventh. Concurrence came in from all parties, and Senior Crown was alive and well to fulfil its new role from Mildenhall.

On 24 October, SR-71A '976 arrived at Mildenhall for a 23-day stint of TDY, returning to Beale on 16 November. During 1978, the same SR-71 was deployed on two occasions, first on 24 April for an 18-day stay and again on 16 October for 17 days. After nearly two years of these short TDY deployments, on 31 March 1979 Detachment 4 (Det 4) of the 9th SRW was activated at RAF Mildenhall to support U-2R and SR-71 operations.

Yemen

During the early spring of 1979, tensions between Saudi Arabia and the People's Republic of Yemen were strained to the point where the US intelligence community believed that the republic was on the brink of invading its northern neighbour. As a result, on the morning of Monday 12 March, Majors Rich Graham and Don Emmons deployed '972 from Beale to Det 4 in order to furnish decision makers with the necessary intelligence information. After two early morning ground aborts due to cloud cover over the 'collection area', a mission finally got underway. 'Buzz' Carpenter and his RSO John Murphy got airborne and headed for their ARCP off Land's End. Unfortunately, 'Buzz' suffered a violent attack of diarrhoea while on the tanker boom, but despite his discomfort he

At subsonic and low-sonic speeds the inlets of the J58 engines remained in the fully forward position, and the bypass doors were open. As the aircraft accelerated past Mach 1.6 the spikes began translating to the aft position, while the bypass doors were closed.

The last SR-71 loss was that of '974, seen here being pulled from the sea off the Philippine island of Luzon in 1989. The crew had ejected successfully.

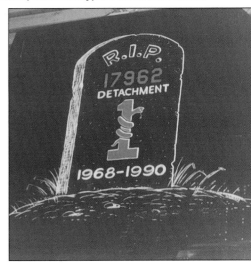

SR-71 operations came to an abrupt end in October 1989, although training continued for another month. '962 returned for the last time from Kadena wearing this tail art.

elected to continue the mission. Having convinced John that he now felt much better, they completed the full fuel off-load and accelerated due south.

Since they were unable to overfly France, it became necessary to skirt the Iberian peninsula. They therefore entered the Mediterranean Sea through the Straits of Gibraltar and completed a second refuelling before returning to high Mach flight. After overflying the Suez Canal, they descended for their third tanker rendezvous over the Red Sea. The planned double-loop coverage of the collection area was interrupted by the ANS, which tried to initiate a pre-programmed turn prior to reaching the correct

In February 1990, soon after the termination of SR-71 operations, Lockheed gathered together 11 surviving aircraft at Beale for a family photograph. At the rear of the group was the short-tailed SR-71C, which had been in storage for many years.

Above: The three SR-71s loaned to NASA pose on the Dryden facility ramp, with Rogers Dry Lake in the background. Steve Ishmael was the first NASA pilot to fly the aircraft in its second career with the Administration, and was checked out in the SR-71B on 1 July 1991 by USAF instructor pilot Rod Dyckman.

Right: Refuelling support for the NASA SR-71 operations is provided by the 412th Test Wing's fleet, in this case an NKC-135E. Beneath is the Edwards facility, the NASA complex being visible behind the ruddervators of the tanker's boom.

The SR-71B arrived at NASA Dryden on 25 July 1991 after a flight from Palmdale which completed Steve Ishmael's check-out. The next three flights allowed Ishmael to qualify Rogers Smith as the second NASA pilot. The first 19 NASA flights were accomplished using 831.

destination point (DP). Upon recognising the error, the crew flew the aeroplane manually while trying to work out what had caused the autonav 'glitch'. As a result of this miscue, they overshot the turn point but completed the rest of the route and made their way back to the tankers for another Red Sea top-up. A fifth air refuelling was completed east of Gibraltar, and an hour-and-a-half later they recovered '972 back to Mildenhall after a full 10-hour mission.

The mission had generated considerable interest within the 9th SRW as well as at SAC headquarters and in Washington. As a result, 'Buzz' and John were greeted by a large number of their colleagues as they stepped off the gantry, including Colonel Dave Young, the 9th SRW vice commander, who presented 'Buzz' with a brown SR-71 tie tack to commemorate the inflight incident when, to misquote a well known phrase, 'the world fell out of Buzz's bottom'.

When the 'take' was processed, it was of exceptional quality and the incident which had delayed their turn had yielded the most important information. That unexpected

success made additional flights to the area unnecessary. Consequently, Rich Graham and Don Emmons returned '972 to Beale on 28 March. Deployments continued to the Suffolk base throughout the early 1980s, the main 'collection areas' being the Barents and Baltic Seas in support of US Navy intelligence requirements.

On 9 July 1983, British aviation enthusiasts 'manning' the many off-base vantage points of Mildenhall noted the arrival of aircraft '962, an aircraft that had pulled TDY at the base on previous occasions. Majors Maury Rosenberg and Ed McKim had just completed a seven-hour operational flight from Beale to Mildenhall via the Barents/Baltic areas in the Palmdale flight test aircraft '955. The false serial number had been applied to ensure unwelcome attention was not drawn to the unique operational test deployment underway. In its detachable nose section, '955 was equipped with Loral's Advanced Synthetic Radar System (ASARS-1), a system that provided a quantum leap in radar resolution. With maritime data collected during the inbound flight, Majors B. C. Thomas and John Morgan conducted a 2.6-hour ASARS operational test sortie of land-based targets in East Germany nine days later. On 21 July, Maury and Ed took their turn on a four-hour mission. The final ASARS operational proving flight was conducted by B. C. and John on 30 July, when they flew '962 ('955) on a 7.3-hour flight back to Beale, again via the Baltic and Barents Seas. The series of tests was extremely successful, and following further tests back at Palmdale two production radar sets for the operational fleet were funded and deployed.

Watching the Gulf

The early 1980s also brought a resurgence of Islamic fundamentalism which was sparked off when Ayatollah Khomeini and his supporters declared Iran to be an Islamic

NASA operations

The SR-71 was retired in November 1989 amid much controversy. Six aircraft were earmarked for contingency purposes, of which three were loaned to NASA for continuing high-speed, high-altitude trials programmes, but they were theoretically available for USAF use if the need arose. The remaining three were placed in flyable storage. In the event NASA only flew two of its aircraft, using the type for a variety of experiments aimed chiefly at future supersonic airliner design and in aid of the X-30 NASP (National Aerospace Plane) programme before it was cancelled. Further trials will primarily be in support of the X-33 programme.

republic, a move that most Western intelligence sources agreed was very destabilising for the Middle East. During this period, SR-71s from Mildenhall occasionally ventured into the eastern Mediterranean to monitor the movements of various contraband supplied by sympathetic states to Islamic jihad soldiers and key terrorist leaders as their small executive support aircraft slipped from one tiny desert airstrip to another.

One such Middle Eastern SR-71 sortie took place on 27 July 1984 when, at 07.30, Majors 'Stormy' Boudreaux and Ted Ross departed Mildenhall in '979 using the callsign BOYCE 64. Due to French politicking with various Arab nations, France refused overflight transit access into the Mediterranean, which necessitated entry to the area via the Straits of Gibraltar. In addition, the flight was further complicated by inlet door and spike control problems which meant that 'Stormy' was forced to control the inlets and spikes manually. After two refuellings, and recycling all inlet switches, the 'glitch' refused to clear, but since by this time the crew had come so far, they reasoned they may as well press on. Flown in this configuration, the aircraft's emergency operating procedures dictated that performance should be limited to Mach 3 and 70,000 ft (21340 m). The mission called for a single high-speed, high-altitude pass over the target area, which the crew completed operating in the less fuel-efficient 'manual' inlet configuration.

Fuel problems

The run ended in a notably depleted fuel state. Ted urgently contacted the tankers which were orbiting near the island of Crete and asked that they head east to meet the thirsty 'Habu'. As BOYCE 64 descended, 'Stormy' caught sight of the tankers 30,000 ft (9145 m) below and

executed what he described loosely as "an extremely large variation of a barrel roll" and slid in behind the tankers "in no time flat." They stayed on the boom 12 to 15 minutes longer than normal in order to regain the pre-planned fuel disconnect point, and then cleared the tanker, accelerated and cruise-climbed back to Mildenhall. The flight, of nearly seven hours duration, produced a 'take' of exceptional quality as a result of a cold front which covered the eastern Mediterranean, the very clear air delivering 'razor sharp' photographic imagery. Det 4's commander, Colonel Jay Murphy, was especially proud of his crew's notable mission accomplishments, even though 'the book' dictated that words had to be spoken about flying a 'degraded' aircraft over a known Soviet SA-5 SAM site. However, like Jay, the National Photographic Interpretation Center (NPIC) in Washington was extremely pleased with this valuable 'take'.

Tension between the United States and much of the Arab world continued, and after a series of incidents President Reagan's patience came to an end. On 15 April 1986, Operation El Dorado Canyon was mounted, a co-ordinated strike on targets in Libya by air elements of the US Navy and 18 USAF F-111s from RAF Lakenheath. Lieutenant Colonels Jerry Glasser and Ron Tabor took off from

Above: 64-17980 is seen on the Dryden ramp shortly after its arrival. It shares the flight line with two Hornets.

Left: Four D-21 drones were recovered from Davis-Monthan AFB and delivered to NASA Dryden for possible use in a future high-speed research programme.

Below left: 844 is seen in 1996 being prepared with the LASRE (Linear Aerospike SR-71 Experiment), a dorsally mounted engine intended for the X-33 next-generation Space Shuttle.

Below: NASA's SR-71B was used to requalify Air Force pilots for the reborn 'Habu' programme.

Lockheed's Blackbirds

The last records

The last round of SR-71 records was set on 6 March 1990 by Lt Col Ed Yeilding (pilot) and Lt Col Joseph T. Vida (RSO) while delivering 64-17972 to the National Air and Space Museum's Dulles facility. The records were all established for recognised city pairs and the all-important transcontinental flight. The times and speeds were as follows:

Coast to Coast (2,086 miles/3357 km). Time 1 hr 07 min 53.69 sec, average speed 2,124.5 mph (3418.9 km/h)
Los Angeles to Washington, DC (1,998 miles/3215 km). Time 1 hr 04 min 19.89 sec, average speed 2,144.83 mph (3451.67 km/h)
St Louis to Cincinnati (311.44 miles/501.20 km). Time 8 min 31.97 sec, average speed 2,189.94 mph (3524.27 km/h)
Kansas City to Washington, DC (942.08 miles/1516.08 km). Time 25 min 58.53 sec, average speed 2,176.08 mph (3501.96 km/h)

Right and top right: '972 arrives at Washington's Dulles airport after its coast-to-coast dash in March 1990. The St Louis to Cincinnati speed was only a few miles per hour short of the overall speed record set many years before. With the rebirth of the SR-71 programme, there is some unofficial desire to recapture the sustained altitude record lost to the MiG-29.

Right: Some idea of the size of the 'Habu' can be gained from this view of NASA's SR-71B refuelling from an NKC-135E during a test hop from Edwards. A key part of the requalification process for Air Force pilots was the practising of aerial refuelling, for which the KC-135T (re-engined KC-135Q) is now used.

Below: Resplendent in the dartboard badge of Det 4, 64-17980 arrives at Edwards. It was reserialled as 844 and used by NASA as Dryden's only flying SR-71A.

Mildenhall as scheduled at 05.00 in SR-71 '980 (callsign TROMP 30). Their mission was to secure photographic imagery for post-strike bomb damage assessment. To achieve this it would be necessary to overfly those targets hit earlier, but this time in broad daylight and with the sophisticated Libyan defence network on full alert. Such was the importance of the mission that SR-71A '960 (TROMP 31), flown by Majors Brian Shul and Walt Watson, launched at 06.15 as an airborne spare in case TROMP 30 aborted with platform or sensor problems. In the event, all aircraft systems, the two chine-mounted technical objective cameras (TEOCs) for spot coverage and the nose-mounted optical bar cameras (OBC) for horizon-to-horizon coverage worked as advertised aboard the primary aircraft, and '960 was not called upon to penetrate hostile airspace. Despite launches against '980, the SR-71 again proved that it could operate with impunity against such SAM threats, and at 09.35 TROMP 30 landed safely back at 'the Hall'. The mission's 'take' was processed in the MPC located in one of Mildenhall's disused hangers. It was then transported by a KC-135 (TROUT 99) to Andrews AFB, Maryland, where national-level officials were eagerly awaiting post-strike briefings.

Two more missions over Libya were conducted on 16 and 17 April, with minor route changes and different callsigns. This intense period of reconnaissance activity scored many new 'firsts' for Det 4: the first occasion that both aircraft were airborne simultaneously; the first time KC-10s had been used to refuel SR-71s in the European theatre; the first time that photos taken by the SR-71s were released to the media (although the source was never officially admitted and the image quality was purposely severely degraded to hide the true capability). All in all, the missions were a great accomplishment and reflected well on the detachment's support personnel under the command of former SR-71 RSO, Lieutenant Colonel Barry MacKean.

Shutdown

The Senior Crown programme was 'living on borrowed time' without an electro-optical backplate for the camera system and a datalink system which would permit camera imagery and radar data from ASARS-1 to be downlinked in near real time. Eventually, funds were appropriated for the development of Senior King, a secure datalink via satellite, but its development was too late to save the SR-71.

By the late 1980s the people articulating an anti-SR-71 posture were as wide and varied as they were powerful.

Preserved aircraft

Dewain Andrews and Bob Fitch, serving on the Senate's House Permanent Select Committee on Intelligence (HPSCI), made the Senior Crown programme shutdown a personal crusade. Within the Air Force at that time, the main detractors were Chief of Staff General Larry Welch, AF/XO General Dougan, CinCSAC General John Chain, AF/Programme Requirements General Ron Fogleman, Chief of SAC Intelligence (SAC/IN) General Doyle, Colonel Tanner also of SAC/IN, and General Leo Smith of the Budget Review Board. As their assault got underway the main thrust of their argument orientated around cost and the marginal benefits of operating the SR-71 instead of satellites. In addition, the Pentagon contended that an air-breathing replacement was under development, and during a meeting on Capital Hill Welch testified (incorrectly) that the SR-71 had become vulnerable to SA-5s and SA-10s.

Stay of execution

By 1988 it looked as though the efforts of these people would be successful. But all was not quite lost: Admiral Lee Baggott, Commander in Chief, Atlantic (CinCLANT) required SR-71 coverage of the Kola peninsula because there were no other means of obtaining the quality of coverage required. He took the battle to retain the SR-71 in Europe right to the Joint Chiefs of Staff (JCS) and obtained funding for Det 4 for a another year. Meanwhile, the SR-71 PEM and his action officer were able to secure a commitment from a staffer on the Senate Appropriations Committee for $46 million to keep Kadena and Palmdale open for another year.

After that, however, the antagonists got their way. What was considered to be the final flight of an SR-71 took place on 6 March 1990, when Ed Yeilding and J. T. Vida flew '972 on a West to East Coast record-breaking flight of the United States, before landing at the Smithsonian National Aerospace Museum, Washington, DC, where the aircraft was handed over for permanent display. Thereafter, three SR-71As ('962, '967 and '968) were placed in storage at Site 2, Palmdale. Two SR-71As ('971 and '980), together with the sole surviving SR-71B ('956), were loaned to NASA. The remaining 13 aircraft (including the hybrid trainer designated SR-71C which consisted of the forward fuselage from a static specimen mated to the wing and rear section of YF-12A 60-6934) were donated to museums throughout the US, despite more than 40 members of Congress, and many other well-placed officials and senior officers, voicing their concern over the decision.

During the course of the Gulf War, two requests were made to reactivate the Senior Crown programme; both were turned down by the same SECDEF who had presided over the aircraft's shutdown – Dick Cheney. That Desert Storm was an overwhelming success for coalition forces is

At the end of the Blackbird programme in 1989/90, the surviving aircraft (including the A-12s) not assigned to NASA or Air Force storage were put up for preservation, and there were many takers. By 1997 aircraft were on display at Palmdale (A-12, SR-71A and D-21), USS *Intrepid* in New York, Huntsville, Minneapolis, San Diego, USS *Alabama* at Mobile (A-12s), Los Angeles (A-12B), Seattle (M-21/D-21), Wright-Patterson AFB (SR-71A and YF-12A), Tucson, Edwards AFB, Robins AFB, Eglin AFB, Castle AFB, Chicago, Beale AFB, Offutt AFB, Dulles Airport, March AFB, Lackland AFB (SR-71As) and Hill AFB (SR-71C).

Above: One of the best preserved aircraft is A-12 '931, which resides at Minneapolis. Thanks to the efforts of the Minnesota ANG, and Crew Chief James C. Goodall, the aircraft is in immaculate condition. It wears the all-black scheme and spurious serials it would have carried when it was part of the 1129th SAS Det 1 Black Shield operation at Kadena.

A-12 '933 is now on display outside the San Diego Aerospace Museum.

For many years the surviving A-12s were shoehorned into a hangar at Palmdale.

YF-12A '935 was delivered to the USAF Museum on 7 November 1979.

The Blackbird Air Park at Palmdale has an A-12, SR-71A and D-21 drone on display.

64-17975 is now at March AFB, where it has joined a U-2C in the museum.

Beale's SR-71A, 64-17963, is on special display below the tower.

beyond dispute. However, there were lessons to be learned from the 41-day campaign, not least of which was the lack of timely reconnaissance material available to General Schwarzkopf's field commanders.

Renaissance

It was not until March/April 1994 that events in the international arena once more took a turn. Relations between North Korea and the United States, at best always strained, reached a new low over the North's refusal to allow inspection of its nuclear sites. At this point Senator Robert Byrd took centre stage. Together with several members of the Armed Services, and various members of Congress, he contended that in 1990 the Pentagon had consistently lied about the supposed readiness of a replacement for the SR-71. The motivation behind such commitments was not the usual politicking, but one of genuine concern for the maintenance of a platform capable of broad-area synoptic coverage.

The campaigning and lobbying paid off, as noted in the Department of Defense Appropriations Bill 1995, report 103-321 dated 20 July, wherein provision was made for a modest, "three-plane SR-71 aircraft contingency reconnaissance capability," at a cost of $100 million, for FY95. Of the three SR-71As placed in deep storage at Site 2, Palmdale, only '967 was called to arms. The other A model to be recommissioned was '971, which had been loaned to NASA, renumbered 832 and regularly ground tested but never flown by its civilian caretakers. Pilot trainer SR-71B, together with the brand new flight simulator, would be shared between the Air Force and NASA, and in a further

Det 2 – Edwards

move to keep operating costs to a minimum the new detachment, designated Det 2, would, like NASA, operate its aircraft from Edwards AFB, California. Det 2's commander was a former 'Habu' RSO, Colonel Stan Gudmundson; overall command and control was still via the 9th RW at Beale AFB.

Aircraft reactivation began on 5 January 1995 with a fuel leak evaluation of '967. Seven days later, at 11.26, NASA crew Steve Ishmael and Marta Bohn-Meyer got airborne from Edwards in '971 on a 26-minute ferry flight which terminated at Lockheed Martin's Skunk Works, Plant 10 Building 602, Palmdale. Over the next three months ASARS and other sensors previously in storage at Luke AFB, Arizona, were installed. At 10.18 on 26 April, NASA crew Ed Schneider and Marta Bohn-Meyer completed a 34-minute FCF in '971. A month later Ed, and Marta's husband Bob Meyer, conducted '971's second and final FCF which lasted 2.5 hours. It took seven more FCFs to wring out all the 'glitches' in '967, the final one of which was successfully completed on 12 January 1996.

Three Air Force crews were selected to fly the aircraft: pilots Gil Luloff, Tom McCleary and Don Watkins, together with RSOs Blair Bozek, Mike Finan and Jim Greenwood. The plan was that two crews would always be qualified as mission-ready and the third crew would be mission-capable. While crew proficiency training got underway in the simulator and the B model, R&D funds were used to develop and install the long overdue datalink, the antenna for which was housed in a small radome just forward of the front undercarriage wheel well. A digital cassette recorder system (DCRsi) provided recording and playback of both Elint and ASARS data. Near real time data could be provided if the aircraft was within 300 nm (345 miles; 555 km) line-of-sight range of a receiving station; if not, the entire recorded collection could be downloaded in 10 minutes once within station range.

Budgetary battles

As qualified Air Force crews began to acquaint themselves with their operational aircraft, a long-running battle between the various factions supporting or not supporting the resurrected programme came to a head. Exploiting a complex technical loophole in the legislation concerning the deployment of funds which had been appropriated by the Senate Appropriations Committee in the FY 1996 Defense Appropriations Bill, but not authorised in two other pieces of supporting legislation, it was decided that technically it was illegal to operate the SR-71. Consequently, at 23:00 (Z) on 16 April 1996, a signal was despatched from the Pentagon suspending SR-71 operations with immediate effect. The war between various Senate committees then went into overdrive, when protagonists of the SR-71 programme serving on the Senate Appropriations Committee threatened to eliminate section 8080 of the Appropriations Act and defeat the Intelligence

Authorization Act for FY97. This would effectively ensure that all intelligence activities for FY97 would grind to a halt – one can imagine the sheer panic this action would have produced in USAF, DIA, CIA and NSA circles!

Not surprisingly, the tactic worked – at least initially. Of the $253 billion defence budget for 1997, $30 million was allocated for SR-71 operations and maintenance and another $9 million for procurement. This outlay was ratified and signed off by the President. The three flight crews were brought up to full proficiency and the ASARS-1 datalink was shown to perform extremely well. Plans were also laid for a major sensor enhancement through the development of an electro-optical backplane for the TEOC cameras. Developed by Recon Optical of Barrington, Illinois, this would have replaced film and allowed high-quality imagery to be transmitted via the datalink.

False start

Det 2 was declared operational on 1 January 1997, and for a while things looked rosy. The USAF proudly paraded its two resurrected aircraft at the service's 50th birthday 'bash' at Nellis in April 1997, but this was to be the last major act in the aircraft's long USAF career. On 14 Octo-ber President Clinton exercised his line-item veto to delete SR-71 funds from the FY98 defence budget, and on 6 March 1998 the aircraft was officially retired. The reborn SR-71 programme never got to fly a mission.

Meanwhile, NASA continued to operate one SR-71A (NASA 844) and one SR-71B (NASA 831) from Dryden, although the two-seater flew for the last time on 19 October 1997. There was, however, one last job for the SR-71A. In the LASRE (Linear Aerospike SR-71 Experiment) programme it carried a dorsal test fixture to evaluate propulsion systems for the X-33 next-generation Space Shuttle. It flew several times with the LASRE load, the last flight – and the last by any member of the 'Blackbird' family – occurring on 9 October 1999.

From the 1980s onwards, fantastic rumours circulated of hypersonic replacements for the SR-71, but nothing appeared, at least in public, and in the event it was the use of satellites and the development of UAVs which attempted to fill the intelligence-gathering gap. That the USAF lost a significant capability with the SR-71's retirement is beyond question, although the price of that capability was ultimately deemed to be too high in a budget-conscious post-Cold War world. **Paul F. Crickmore**

A-12/SR-71 details

Above: The nosewheel strut mounted a pair of landing/taxiing lamps. The housing alongside the lamps contained the steering actuator.

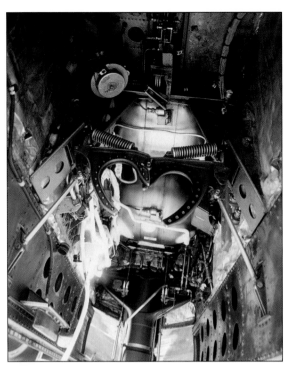

Above: This view shows the nosewheel bay, looking aft toward the strut mounting. When retracted, the strut assembly was locked in place by large callipers.

Left: This is the mainwheel bay, showing the shroud which housed the wheel when retracted. All three wheel units had these heat protection measures.

Left: The mainwheel unit was retracted by a single hydraulic jack. The wheel hub was a single titanium forging.

Right: Detail of the mainwheel shows the dual brake runs and door attachments. The strut was painted black, while the wheel hubs were usually either red or green.

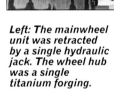

Above: The SR-1 ejection seat (later redesignated F-1) was developed by Lockheed from the C-2 seat used in early F-104 Starfighters.

Above: To test the A-12 cockpit's ability to withstand the heat experienced at operational speed and altitude, this section was tested in an oven.

Above: The tilting panel for the buried refuelling receptacle also functioned as a slipway for the boom.

Above and right: For start-up, the J58 engine was turned by a ground power cart which fed air to the compressor. The attachment for the ducts was on the underside of the nacelle.

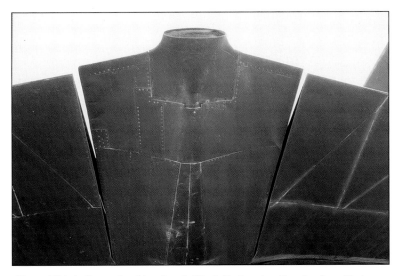

Above: This is the underside of an A-12's tail, showing the simple grilled aperture. The SR-71 had a longer fuselage, and a distinct tailcone. Note the large RAM wedges in the elevon structure.

Above: The sophisticated inlet system had a repositionable spike to correctly position the shock wave in the throat of the inlet and to increase capture area. The spike had a band of slits around it to remove boundary layer air.

Left: The SR-71 had interchangeable nose sections with four main attachment points. Note the circular fuselage structure with added chine sections.

Below: A partially disassembled aircraft displays the rib construction of the engine nacelle. The large row of attachment points along the top allowed the outer part of the nacelle, complete with outer wing panel, to be hinged up for easy access to the engine.

Above: The SR-71 mounted most of its sensors and navigation equipment in underfuselage bays. This is the E-bay, which housed electronics. On the other side of the nosewheel bay was the R-bay, which housed radios. Outboard of these bays were the chine-mounted K- and L-bays, usually used for DEF (defensive electronics) equipment.

Right: This view looking forward into the engine nacelle shows the intake spike assembly, fixed to the nacelle with four struts. The centrebody was hollow to allow the dumping of boundary layer air.

Below and right: The Nortronics astro-tracker was housed in a bay behind the cockpit, peering upwards through a small circular window in a removable spine panel.

Below: Lifted upper wing panels show the internal multi-spar construction of the wing. The internal void formed an integral fuel tank. Note the chord-wise corrugations of the upper surface.

SR-71 details

These views show the inlet spike in the full out (above) and fully retracted (below) positions, the centre-body travelling 26 in (0.66 m) between the two. The forward position is used at speeds up to Mach 1.6, above which the spike starts retracting to its full aft position achieved at Mach 3.2.

Access to the Pratt & Whitney J58 engine is by a novel folding wing/nacelle method. Most of the outer nacelle, apart from the forward section, hinges upwards along the centreline, taking the outer wing panel with it. This allows the J58 to be accessed easily for in situ maintenance or removed completely. Note the special jacked cradle which is used to lower down and then transport the removed engine.

Lockheed SR-71A cutaway

1 Pitot tube
2 Air data probe
3 Radar warning antennas
4 Nose mission equipment bay
5 Panoramic camera aperture
6 Detachable nosecone joint frame
7 Cockpit front pressure bulkhead
8 Rudder pedals
9 Control column
10 Instrument panel
11 Instrument panel shroud
12 Knife-edged windscreen panels
13 Upward-hinged cockpit canopy covers
14 Ejection seat headrest
15 Canopy actuator
16 Pilot's Lockheed F-1 'zero-zero' ejection seat
17 Engine throttle levers
18 Side console panel
19 Fuselage chine close-pitched frame construction
20 Liquid oxygen converters (2)
21 Side console panel
22 Reconnaissance Systems Officer's (RSO) instrument display
23 Cockpit rear pressure bulkhead

24 RSO's Lockheed F-1 'zero-zero' ejection seat
25 Canopy hinge point
26 SR-71B dual-control trainer variant, nose profile
27 Raised instructor's rear cockpit
28 Astro-inertial navigation star tracker
29 Navigation and communications systems electronic equipment
30 Nosewheel bay
31 Nose undercarriage pivot fixing
32 Landing and taxiing lamps
33 Twin nosewheels, forward retracting
34 Hydraulic retraction jack
35 Cockpit environmental system equipment bay
36 Air refuelling receptacle, open

37 Fuselage upper longeron
38 Forward fuselage frame construction
39 Forward fuselage integral fuel tanks
40 Palletised, interchangeable reconnaissance equipment packs
41 Fuselage chine member
42 Forward/centre fuselage joint ring frame
43 Centre fuselage integral fuel tanks; total system capacity 12,219 US gal (46254 litres)
44 Beta B.120 titanium alloy skin panelling
45 Corrugated wing skin panelling
46 Starboard main undercarriage, stowed position
47 Intake centre-body bleed air louvres
48 Bypass duct suction relief louvres

49 Starboard engine air intake
50 Moveable intake conical centre-body
51 Centre-body retracted (high-speed position)
52 Boundary layer bleed air holes
53 Automatic intake control system air data probe
54 Diffuser chamber
55 Variable inlet guide vanes
56 Hinged engine cowling/outer wing panel
57 Pratt & Whitney JT11D-20B (J58) single-spool bleed-bypass engine

61 Afterburner fuel manifold
62 Tailfin fixed root section
63 Starboard outer wing panel
64 Under-cambered leading edge
65 Outboard roll control elevon
66 All-moving starboard fin
67 Continuously operating afterburner duct

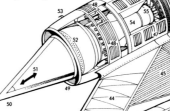

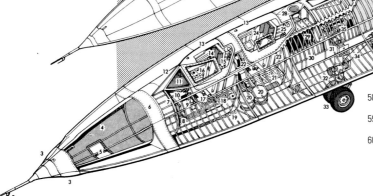

58 Engine accessory equipment
59 Bypass duct suction relief doors
60 Compressor bleed air bypass doors

68 Afterburner nozzle
69 Engine bay tertiary air flaps
70 Exhaust nozzle ejector flaps
71 Variable-area exhaust nozzle
72 Starboard wing integral fuel tank bays
73 Brake parachute doors, open

74 Ribbon parachute stowage
75 Aft fuselage integral fuel tanks
76 Skin doubler
77 Aft fuselage frame construction
78 Elevon mixer unit

Lockheed's Blackbirds

Stills from a Lockheed film show the modified Convair F-106B (left) used to test the SR-1 ejection seat, and an aerial test with an instrumented dummy (above).

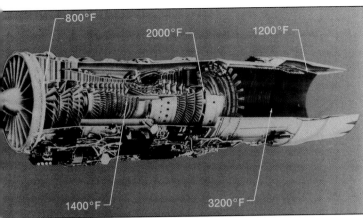

Above: This drawing shows a cutaway of the J58 engine, together with expected temperatures under normal operating conditions. In the afterburner section temperatures reached a source 3,200°F (1,760°C).

This engine is one of the YJ58 powerplants built for test purposes, and differed from production engines by having some gold-plated parts. Around 150 J58s were built for the entire Blackbird programme.

Right: Three nose sections were regularly carried: empty (for ferry or training), OBC and ASARS-1. This is the latter, easily identified by its bulged contours forward of the joint with the fuselage. Also of note is the knife-edge section mounted ahead of the windscreen.

Left: Little has been released about the SR-71's DEF (defensive electronics) system, although the aircraft has several small antennas around the airframe. This forward-facing receiver is located under the forward fuselage.

87 Ejector flaps
88 Port outboard elevon
89 Elevon titanium alloy rib construction
90 Under-cambered leading edge
91 Leading-edge diagonal rib construction
92 Outer wing panel titanium alloy construction

100 Main undercarriage wheel bay
101 Wheel bay heat shield
102 Hydraulic retraction jack
103 Main undercarriage pivot fixing
104 Mainwheel leg strut
105 Intake duct framing
106 Outer wing panel/nacelle chine
107 Three-wheel main undercarriage bogie, inward retracting
108 Port engine air intake

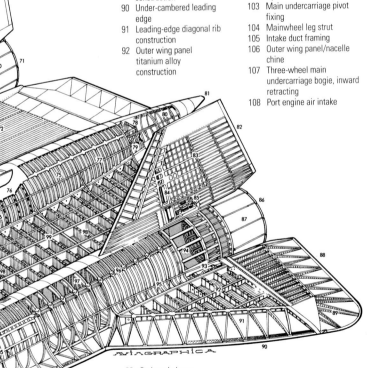

79 Inboard elevon torque control unit
80 Tailcone
81 Fuel vent
82 Port all-moving fin
83 Fin rib construction
84 Torque shaft hinge mounting
85 Fin hydraulic actuator
86 Port engine exhaust nozzle

93 Outboard elevon hydraulic actuator
94 Engine bay tertiary air flaps
95 Engine nacelle/outer wing panel integral construction
96 Engine cowling/wing panel hinge axis
97 Port nacelle ring frame construction
98 Inboard wing panel integral fuel tank bays
99 Multi-spar titanium alloy wing construction

109 Moveable conical intake centre-body
110 Centre-body frame construction
111 Inboard leading-edge diagonal rib construction
112 Inner wing panel integral fuel tank
113 Wingroot/fuselage attachment root rib
114 Close-pitched fuselage titanium alloy frames
115 Wing/fuselage chine blended fairing panels

Above: A technician runs a bench check on an OBC camera prior to installation in the nose section of an SR-71A. The camera is housed within its own environmentally controlled casing. The OBC is a horizon-to-horizon panoramic camera.

Left: Seen through the viewscope of a U-2, technicians work on a TEOC camera. This camera was mounted lengthways in the chine bays (P or Q) with the 45° prism peering downwards through a window in the rear of the bay.

A-12/SR-71 operators

Central Intelligence Agency
1129th Special Activities Squadron

This unit was established at Groom Dry Lake, Nevada, to operate the A-12 Cygnus aircraft. The base had an Air Force commander and director of flight operations, although the CIA was technically in charge of the Oxcart programme. Personnel from both government organisations, together with Skunk Works staff, worked side-by-side to bring the A-12 into operational service. In addition to the A-12 and A-12B, the Groom Lake operation also flew the McDonnell F-101 Voodoo as a trainer, T-33s, U-3s and helicopters for utility work, a C-130 as a transport and an F-104 for high-speed chase. Refuelling support was provided by the 903rd ARS of the 456th Bomb Wing, detached from Beale AFB. The Oxcart squadron was declared operational on 20 November 1965, with four aircraft ready for deployment to Kadena.

After a considerable wait, the orders to deploy came on 17 May 1967. The first aircraft flew to Kadena on 22 May, followed by two more, and all three were declared operational on 29 May. The first of 29 operational sorties was flown on 31 May 1967, and the last on 8 May 1968. The decision to end the det's Black Shield operation was reaffirmed on 16 May, and the aircraft began returning on 9 June, for storage at Palmdale. The final flight, and the end of the 1129th SAS, occurred on 21 June 1968 when aircraft 131 was ferried from Groom Lake to Palmdale.

4200th Strategic Reconnaissance Wing

The 4200th SRW was established at Beale AFB on 1 January 1965 to prepare for SR-71 operations, the first T-38A companion trainer arriving at the California base in July 1965. On 6 January 1966 the 4200th SRW received its first Blackbird in the form of the trainer '956. The first operational aircraft arrived on 4 April 1966. Soon after, on 25 June 1966, the 4200th inherited the heritage and numberplate of the 9th Bomb Wing, becoming the 9th Strategic Reconnaissance Wing.

The number was then assigned to the 4200th Test Wing, still at Beale, which became the unit responsible for testing and employing the D-21B drone, using two B-52Hs as mother ships. This programme began in late 1966. The first launch was not undertaken until 6 November 1968, at which time the 4200th TW was flying from Groom Lake. Later launches took place from Beale, and the programme was terminated on 23 July 1971.

9th Strategic Reconnaissance Wing
1st and 99th Strategic Reconnaissance Squadrons

One of the premier bomber wings in the USAF, the 9th BW had been based at Mountain Home AFB, Idaho, operating B-47s, KC-97s and controlling a Titan missile complex. Bomber/missile operations were run down during the first half of 1966 pending the numberplate being assigned to the 4200th SRW, the SR-71 unit at Beale. The formal activation of the 9th SRW occurred on 25 June 1966.

Training and tactical development occupied the wing for the first months, and it was declared fully operational in December 1968. The wing was arranged into two flying squadrons, the 1st and 99th Strategic Reconnaissance Squadrons. Both numberplates had been long associated with the 9th BW. Initially it was decreed that each squadron would have eight SR-71As and one SR-71B. The SR-71 reconnaissance effort was never as great as had originally been envisaged, and could easily be accomplished by one flying squadron. Accordingly, the 99th SRS 'Red Buffaloes' was deactivated on 1 April 1971.

Throughout the early period tanker support for the SR-71 was provided by the KC-135Qs of the 9th and 903rd ARS, 456th BW. The 456th BW was inactivated on 30 September 1975, the two tanker squadrons being then directly assigned to the 9th SRW. On 1 July 1976 Strategic Air Command formalised the consolidation of its high-altitude strategic reconnaissance assets when the U-2Rs of the 100th SRW became part of the 9th. The old U-2 wing number and two of its squadron numbers were reassigned to the KC-135Qs, which became the 349th and 350th ARS of the 100th ARW. The U-2Rs had already been using the 99th SRS number since 1972, and continued to do so after the amalgamation with the SR-71 force. Later the 9th SRW established the 4029th SRTS (renumbered 5th SRTS) as the U-2 training unit.

In addition to the ongoing training tasks, which utilised the standard SR-71As, SR-71B/C trainers and T-38s, the wing headquarters was also tasked with important reconnaissance missions as well as supporting the overseas deployments.

An SR-71A launches from Beale for a night mission. Most Beale sorties were for training, but the base was also used for operational sorties, notably those over Central America and the Caribbean.

The first major Beale-led missions were to the Middle East (using Griffiss AFB and Seymour Johnson AFB) in 1973/74. Other operational sorties launched from Beale went to Cuba, Nicaragua and occasionally to Europe.

Operational flying was ended on 1 October 1989, although training flights continued until 22 November 1989. The retirement ceremony for the SR-71 was held at Beale on 26 January 1990.

Kadena detachment (OL-8, OL-RK, OL-KA, Det 1)

Glowing Heat deployments to Kadena, Okinawa (known as the 'Rock') were first undertaken in March 1968, and for a while the SR-71 crews were co-based with their 'grey-suit' colleagues from 'the Agency'. The SR-71 detachment was known as OL (Operating Location) -8, and was declared operationally ready with three aircraft on 15 March 1968. It flew its first combat mission on 21 March 1968. In early 1970, as the need for reconnaissance grew, the detachment was enlarged to four aircraft. On 30 October 1970 it was redesignated OL-RK (for Ryukyus, the island chain in which Okinawa was situated) and on 26 October 1971 became OL-KA (for Kadena).

A high level of activity was maintained through the last months of the war in Southeast Asia, although with the end of the war the detachment was reduced in size to two aircraft. On 1 August 1974 OL-KA was redesignated as Detachment 1 of the 9th SRW. Reconnaissance missions in the post-war years were naturally aimed at the Soviet Far East, China, North Korea and Vietnam, although Det 1 was tasked with marathon flights over the Persian Gulf during the Iran/Iraq war. All operations ceased on 22 November 1989 and the two aircraft were returned to Beale.

SR-71 patches changed with rapidity at the Kadena detachment in the early 1970s. The Habu pit viper remained a constant motif.

64-17968 taxis for a mission at Kadena in the early 1970s. In the background are civil airliners used on trooping flights.

Mildenhall detachment (Det 4)

An SR-71 was first deployed to Mildenhall for operations in Europe in early 1976. The UK government stipulated that these early deployments should be no longer than 20 days and required UK permission for each sortie. However, the deployments gradually became more frequent and the aircraft stayed longer. In March 1979 Mildenhall was the operating location for a Yemen reconnaissance flight. Detachment 4 of the 9th SRW was established in April 1979 with a single U-2R employed in Europe on Senior Ruby Elint missions, and continued to support the periodic SR-71 visits. In 1981 Mildenhall was used for monitoring the situation in Poland.

By late 1982 the demands in Europe resulted in a second aircraft arriving at Mildenhall, while in July 1983 the base played host to the first operational test of an ASARS-equipped aircraft. By this time Det 4 had ceased U-2R operations, which had been transferred to the newly-established 17th Reconnaissance Wing (with TR-1As) at Alconbury. Finally, on 5 April 1984, Prime Minister Margaret Thatcher announced that Det 4 would be a permanent SR-71 detachment with two aircraft, with some UK control remaining for the more sensitive sorties.

The two-aircraft detachment ceased operations on 22 November 1989, and the last aircraft left for Beale on 18 January 1990.

Det 4 usually mounted three sorties each week, covering the German border, Baltic coastline and the Kola Peninsula. The latter was home to the Soviet Northern Fleet.

9th Reconnaissance Wing

Detachment 2

Following the retirement of the SR-71, the 9th SRW continued its U-2R operations, and in June 1991 took over the UK operations at Alconbury from the 17th RW, shortly before the wing dropped the 'Strategic' from its designation. At Beale the 5th SRTS adopted the old SR-71 squadron number (in July 1990) to become the 1st Reconnaissance Squadron (Training).

In October 1994 Congress directed the US Air Force to reactivate three SR-71s, utilising two aircraft which had been put into flyable storage at Palmdale, and one which had been loaned to NASA. The first rework was completed by Lockheed in mid-1995. Further political debates have resulted in considerable delays to the SR-71 reactivation, and a drop to two aircraft. The USAF SR-71 operation is now conducted from a location at Edwards AFB, next door to the NASA SR-71s and conveniently close to the Skunk Works facility at Palmdale. The unit is administered from Beale and is known as Detachment 2 of the 9th Reconnaissance Wing. The previous Det 2, a U-2 detachment at Osan, South Korea, was raised to squadron status (5th RS) in 1994.

Seen at Edwards in late 1996 is one of Det 2's SR-71s, alongside a black-painted T-38 used for training.

Test units

Various units have operated Blackbirds for test purposes. Test work from Edwards AFB was accomplished by the 4786th Test Squadron, which was formed on 1 June 1965. At Palmdale an Advanced Systems Project Office was established to function as an acceptance test centre. After initial manufacturer test flights, the ASPO took the aircraft and performed an exhaustive series of FCFs (functional test flights) before delivering the aircraft to Beale. Following final delivery, the ASPO became heavily involved in all forms of testing for the SR-71 fleet. Initially the first six aircraft from the line were assigned to test purposes, but following transfers and losses only one ('955) remained. This became the dedicated test aircraft until retired in 1985, being flown on joint Skunk Works/US Air Force test programmes.

On 31 December 1970 the Palmdale trials task was handed over from Air Force Systems Command to Air Force Logistics Command, which established Det 51 to perform the task. In September 1977 this unit became Det 6, 2762nd Logistics Squadron. A detachment at Norton AFB looked after the spares and logistics supply for the fleet. Det 6 operated right to the end of the SR-71 programme, using '972 as its dedicated test airframe in the late 1980s. The unit's last flying task was to fly the aircraft to Dulles on 6 March 1990, the last flight by an SR-71 before reactivation.

NASA

Operating from the Dryden Flight Research facility at Edwards AFB, NASA has enjoyed two spells operating the Blackbird. From 1969 to 1979 a single YF-12A was flown on a wide variety of high-speed trials, augmented by another YF-12A from 1969-71 and an SR-71A (rechristened YF-12C) from 1971 to 1978.

At the end of the USAF SR-71 programme, NASA elected to restart high-speed research programmes using an SR-71A and an SR-71B. A third aircraft was assigned, although it never flew with NASA and was later reactivated by the US Air Force. The NASA SR-71B proved of great value for requalifying USAF pilots, while the SR-71A is assigned to test programmes in support of the X-33 next-generation Space Shuttle.

As part of its future supersonic airliner trials programme, NASA used an F-16XL to measure sonic booms from the SR-71A 844.

Individual aircraft details

Lockheed A-12

60-6924/121
First flight 26 April 1962. Prototype A-12. Towed from Plant 42, Palmdale storage area to Blackbird Air Park display area, Palmdale

60-6925/122
Used for ground tests prior to first flight. Transported from Plant 42, Palmdale to USS *Intrepid*, New York for display. Due to vandalism the aircraft is to be repaired by Lockheed and moved for display at CIA HQ, Langley, Virginia

60-6926/123
First flight 24 May 1963. Second A-12 to fly. Lost during training/test flight after aircraft stalled due to inaccurate data being displayed to pilot. Pilot Ken Collins ejected safely

60-6927/124
Only two-seat pilot trainer. To be trucked to California Museum of Science, Los Angeles for display

60-6928/125
Last flight 5 January 1967. Lost during training/test flight. Pilot Walter L. Ray successfully ejected but was killed after he failed to separate from his ejection seat

60-6929/126
Lost seconds after take-off from Groom Dry Lake following incorrect installation of SAS. Pilot Mele Vojvodich ejected safely

60-6930/127
Deployed to Kadena from 24 May 1967 to June 1968 in support of Operation Black Shield. Was stored at Plant 42, Palmdale. Trucked to Space and Rocket Center Museum, Huntsville, Alabama for display

60-6931/128
Was stored at Plant 42, Palmdale. Transported by C-5 on 27 October 1991 to Minnesota Air National Guard, Minneapolis, for display

60-6932/129
Last flight 5 June 1968. Deployed to Kadena from 26 May 1967 in support of Operation Black Shield. Lost off the Philippines during an FCF prior to its scheduled return to the USA. Pilot Jack Weeks was killed

60-6933/130
First flight 27 November 1963. Last flight August 1965. Was stored at Plant 42, Palmdale. Trucked to San Diego Aerospace Museum, California for display

60-6937/131
Deployed to Kadena from 22 May 1967 to June 1968 in support of Operation Black Shield. Was stored at Plant 42, Palmdale. Disposition to be determined

60-6938/132
Was stored at Plant 42, Palmdale. Trucked to USS *Alabama*, located at Mobile, Alabama for display

60-6939/133
Last flight 9 July 1964. Lost while on approach to Groom Dry Lake during test flight due to complete hydraulic failure. Lockheed test pilot Bill Park ejected safely

60-6940/134
One of two A-12s converted for Project Tagboard as carrier for D-21 drones. Trucked to the Museum of Flight, Seattle, Washington for display

During the Oxcart programme all of the A-12s flew from Groom Dry Lake, the secret test location in Nevada. Twelve aircraft were completed as standard A-12s, one was diverted to be the only two-seat trainer, while the final two were completed with a second cockpit for a launch systems officer for the D-21 drone. This group is joined by two of the YF-12As at the far end.

60-6941/135
Last flight 30 July 1966. One of two A-12s converted for Project Tagboard as D-21 drone carrier. Lost during tests off the coast of California. Pilot Bill Park and launch control officer Ray Torick, both Lockheed employees, ejected safely. However, Ray Torick was tragically drowned in the subsequent feet-wet landing

Lockheed YF-12A

Above: YF-12A 60-6934 at Edwards AFB

Right: YF-12A 60-6936, flying from Edwards

60-6934/1001
First flight 8 August 1963. Last flight (as YF-12) 14 August 1966. Prototype YF-12A was used by Colonel Robert L. Stephens and his fire control officer Lieutenant Colonel Daniel Andre to establish new speed and altitude records. Due to technical problems the actual records were set by '936. Aircraft was subsequently transformed into SR-71C 64-17981

Below: YF-12A 60-6935 in NASA service

60-6935/1002
First flight 26 November 1963. Last flight 7 November 1979. After initial YF-12 test programme the aircraft was placed in storage at Edwards AFB, California. It was later made available to NASA and flew again on 11 December 1969. On completion of NASA test programme it was delivered by air to the USAF Museum at Wright-Patterson AFB, Ohio for display

60-6936/1003
First flight 13 March 1964. Last flight 24 July 1971. This aircraft was used to obtain all absolute world speed and altitude records on 1 May 1965. After a brief period of retirement the aircraft was made available to a joint Air Force/NASA/ADP test programme but was lost on 24 June 1971. Lieutenant Colonel Jack Layton and Major Billy Curtis ejected safely

Lockheed SR-71

64-17950/2001
First flight 23 December 1964. Last flight 10 January 1967. First prototype SR-71A. Lost during anti-skid brake system evaluation at Edwards AFB, California. Pilot Art Peterson survived.

64-17951/2002
First flight 5 March 1965. Last flight 22 December 1978. Operated by NASA from 16 July 1971 and known as YF-12C, serialled 60-6937. Removed from Palmdale storage and trucked to Pima Air and Space Museum, Tucson, Arizona for display

64-17952/2003
First flight 24 March 1965. Last flight 25 January 1966. Lost during test flight from Edwards AFB, California. Pilot Bill Weaver survived but RSO Jim Zwayer was killed. Incident occurred near Tucumcari, New Mexico

64-17953/2004
First flight 4 June 1965. Last flight 18 December 1969. Lost during test flight from Edwards AFB, California. Pilot Lieutenant Colonel Joe Rogers and RSO Lieutenant Colonel Gary Heidelbaugh ejected safely. Incident occurred near Shoshone, California

64-17954/2005
First flight 20 July 1965. Last flight 11 April 1969. Lost on runway at Edwards AFB, California during take-off. Pilot Lieutenant Colonel Bill Skliar and RSO Major Noel Warner escaped without injury

64-17955/2006
First flight 17 August 1965. Last flight 24 January 1985. Operated extensively by Air Force Logistics Command from Plant 42, Palmdale as the dedicated SR-71 test aircraft. This aircraft is on display at Edwards AFB, California

64-17956/2007
First flight 18 November 1965. Still flying 1997. One of two SR-71B dual-control pilot trainers. In 1997 was still on loan to NASA at the Ames Research Center, Hugh L. Dryden Research facility, Edwards AFB and used to train both NASA and USAF crews. Reserialled NASA 831

64-17957/2008
First flight 18 December 1965. Last flight 11 January 1968. One of two SR-71B dual-control pilot trainers. It was lost following fuel cavitation while on approach to Beale AFB, California. Instructor pilot Lieutenant Colonel Robert G. Sowers and student Captain David E. Fruehauf ejected safely

64-17958/2009
First flight 15 December 1965. Last flight 23 February 1990. Used on 27/28 July 1979 by Captain Eldon W. Joersz and RSO Major George T. Morgan Jr to establish speed run over 12/25-km course of 2,193.167 mph. Flown to Robins AFB, Georgia for display

64-17959/2010
First flight 19 January 1966. Last flight 29 October 1976. Underwent 'Big Tail' modification to increase and enhance sensor capacity/capability. Trucked to Air Force Armament Museum, Eglin AFB, Florida for display

64-17950, SR-71A prototype

SR-71A 64-17951 in NASA service, serialled '06937' and designated YF-12C

64-17952, wearing calibration markings

64-17953, lost on 10 January 1967

64-17954, lost on 11 April 1969

64-17955, Palmdale test aircraft

SR-71B 64-17956, later NASA 831

Wreckage of SR-71B 64-17957, 11 January 1968

64-17958 during speed/altitude record attempts

SR-71A(BT) 64-17959 'Big Tail' at Palmdale

Lockheed's Blackbirds

64-17960/2011
First flight 9 February 1966. Last flight 27 February 1990. This aircraft flew 342 operational missions, more than any other SR-71. Flown to Castle AFB Museum, California for display

64-17961/2012
First flight 13 April 1966. Last flight 2 February 1977. This aircraft was delivered to Chicago, Illinois for display

64-17962/2013
First flight 29 April 1966. Last flight 14 February 1990. Although no funds available for upkeep, this is one of two aircraft in storage at Site 2, Palmdale and still owned by the USAF

64-17963/2014
First flight 9 June 1966. Last flight 28 October 1976. Towed to current display area at Beale AFB, California

64-17964/2015
First flight 11 May 1966. Last flight 20 March 1990. Flown to Offutt AFB, Nebraska for display

64-17965/2016
First flight 10 June 1966. Last flight 25 October 1976. Lost during night training sortie following INS platform failure. Pilot St Martin and RSO Carnochan ejected safely. Incident occurred near Lovelock, Nevada

64-17966/2017
First flight 1 July 1966. Last flight 13 April 1967. Lost after night refuelling in a subsonic high-speed stall. Pilot Boone and RSO Sheffield both ejected safely. Incident occurred near Las Vegas, New Mexico

64-17967/2018
First flight 3 August 1966. Last flight 14 February 1990. Reactivated and overhauled for use by 9th RW Det 2 at Edwards AFB

64-17968/2019
First flight 3 August 1966. Still flying. Held in storage at Site 2, Palmdale after last flight 12 February 1990. Although no funds available for upkeep, this is one of two aircraft held in storage at Site 2, Palmdale, and is still owned by the USAF

64-17969/2020
First flight 18 October 1966. Last flight 10 May 1970. Lost after refuelling in subsonic high-speed stall. Pilot Lawson and RSO Martinez ejected safely. Incident occurred near Korat RTAFB, Thailand

64-17970/2021
First flight 21 October 1966. Last flight 17 June 1970. Lost following mid-air collision with KC-135Q tanker. Tanker able to limp back to Beale AFB, Pilot Buddy Brown and RSO Mort Jarvis both ejected safely. Incident occurred 20 miles east of El Paso, New Mexico

64-17960 at 1986 Mildenhall air show

64-17961, now on display in Chicago

64-17962 during speed/altitude record attempt

64-17963, now on display at Beale AFB

Below: 64-17964 marked as The Bodonian Express

64-17968, currently stored at Palmdale

64-17965 with T-33A before its loss in October 1976

64-17967, Det 4 Mildenhall. Aircraft later resurrected for use by Det 2, 9th Reconnaissance Wing at Edwards AFB

Right: 64-17969, lost on 10 May 1970 over Thailand

64-17970, on display with other Beale aircraft

64-17971/2022
First flight 17 November 1966. Still flying. One of two SR-71As loaned to NASA at Edwards AFB although the aircraft was not used. Reclaimed by USAF for service with 9th RW Det 2 at Edwards AFB

64-17972/2023
First flight 12 December 1966. Last flight 6 March 1990. Flown on 1 September 1974 by Major James Sullivan and RSO Major Noel Widdifield from New York to London in record time of 1 hour 54 minutes 56.4 seconds. Flown on 6 March 1990 by Lieutenant Colonel Ed Yielding and RSO Lieutenant Colonel Joseph T. Vida from Los Angeles to Washington, DC in 1 hour 4 minutes 20 seconds. West to East Coast record set at 1 hour 7 minutes 54 seconds. On display at Smithsonian Institute, Dulles Airport

64-17973/2024
First flight 8 February 1967. Last flight 21 July 1987. Damaged while being demonstrated at RAF Mildenhall by Major Jim Jiggens. Aircraft was placed on display at Blackbird Air Park, Palmdale

64-17974/2025
First flight 16 February 1967. Last flight 21 April 1989. One of three aircraft used on first operational deployment to Kadena AB, Okinawa. Lost in 1989 while outbound from Kadena on an operational sortie following engine explosion and complete hydraulic failure. Pilot Major Dan E. House and RSO Captain Blair L. Bozek both ejected safely

64-17975/2026
First flight 13 April 1967. Last flight 28 February 1990. Flown from Beale AFB to March AFB, California for display

64-17976/2027
First flight May 1967. Last flight 27 March 1990. One of three aircraft used on the first operational deployment to Kadena AB, Okinawa. Flown by Major Jerome F. O'Malley and RSO Captain Edwards D. Payne on 9 March 1968 on the first operational SR-71 sortie. Flown to the US Air Force Museum, Wright-Patterson AFB, Ohio for display

64-17977/2028
First flight 6 January 1967. Last flight 10 October 1968. Lost at the end of Beale runway following a wheel explosion and runway abort. Pilot Major Gabriel A. Kardong rode the aircraft to a standstill, RSO Captain James A. Kogler ejected – both survived

64-17978/2029
First flight 5 July 1967. Last flight 20 July 1972. One of three aircraft used on first operational deployment to Kadena AB, Okinawa. Lost after a landing accident at Kadena. Pilot Captain Dennis K. Bush and RSO Jimmy Fagg both escaped unhurt

64-17979/2030
First flight 10 August 1967. Last flight 6 March 1990. This aircraft flew the first three of nine sorties from the eastern seaboard of the USA to the Middle East during the 1973 Yom Kippur War. Flown to Lackland AFB, Texas for display

64-17980/2031
First flight 25 September 1967. Still flying. Following last USAF flight on 5 February 1990 was one of two SR-71As loaned to NASA and flown from the Ames Research Center, Hugh L. Dryden Research Facility at Edwards AFB. Reserialled NASA 844

64-17981/2000
First flight 14 March 1969. Last flight 11 April 1976. Designated SR-71C, this hybrid dual-control aircraft combined the wing and rear section of YF-12A 60-6934 with a static test forward fuselage. After long period in storage at Beale was trucked to Hill AFB, Utah for display

64-17971 at Det 4, Mildenhall

64-17972, Palmdale test aircraft

64-17973, now on display at Palmdale

64-17974, previously named **Ichi Ban**

64-17975 at the Alconbury air show, 1984

64-17976 with 9th SRW badge

64-17977 after a wheel explosion at Beale

64-17978, **Rapid Rabbit**

Below: 64-17981, the sole SR-71C

64-17979, about to launch from Mildenhall

Below: 64-17980 landing at Det 4, Mildenhall

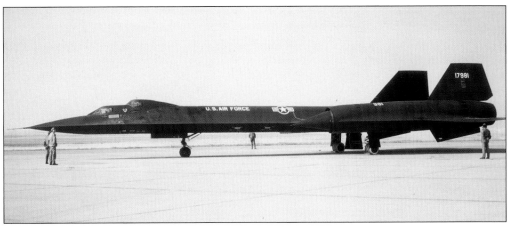

High-altitude capability, long endurance and a worthwhile sensor payload are the chief attributes of the U-2R/S. The U-2R usually operates at over 70,000 ft (21335 m), from where its sensors can peer much further into denied territory than aircraft at lower altitudes. The aircraft's ability to remain on station for many hours makes it a highly useful surveillance tool to cover ongoing operations, as opposed to a one-shot reconnaissance platform. This is especially useful during Comint (communications intelligence) missions.

TOWARD THE UNKNOWN

U-2 The Second Generation

Although public interest in the notorious U-2 waned soon after the Powers shootdown in 1960, the career of the aircraft was far from over. With one SAM attack the Soviets had made it obvious that the slender 'Angel' could no longer operate directly over well-defended territory, a fact reinforced by another shootdown over Cuba in 1962, but its sophisticated and far-reaching sensors could still provide excellent intelligence from safer airspace. With the U-2's capabilities much in demand, Lockheed undertook a complete redesign of the type in the mid-1960s to create a much bigger, better and further-ranging version: the U-2R. That aircraft was put back into production in the 1980s, and today forms the backbone of the USAF's high-altitude reconnaissance effort, having proved its worth in numerous conflicts, large and small, since its baptism of fire over Vietnam and China.

U-2 pilots are an elite crew, drawn from a variety of USAF backgrounds but with one factor in common: above-average ability. The wearing of the David Clark pressure suits is necessary on all but low-level training missions to protect the pilot in the event of a cockpit depressurisation. The main pressure suit is covered by an orange coverall containing lifevest, emergency oxygen and other paraphernalia.

Right: Article 051 takes shape in the Burbank shop, while a second U-2R forward fuselage can be seen in the background. The use of the word 'article' dated back to the earliest days of the U-2 programme, when it was employed to shield the true nature of the project. The prototype U-2R flew with the civilian registration N803X.

Conceived by a visionary group of scientists and academics, sponsored by a civilian agency with virtually no record of aerospace endeavour, and born in the now-famous Skunk Works of Lockheed's sprawling Burbank plant, the U-2 was to become one of the world's best-known aircraft. Virtually everything about the aircraft was unconventional from the very start, including its expected life span – even designer Kelly Johnson gave it no more than two years. But as the CIA's audacious and ambitious programme to photograph the Soviet Union from great altitude stretched into a third, fourth and fifth year, more roles and missions kept emerging for the jet-powered glider. The USAF bought into the programme, eventually acquiring 35 of the total 55 aircraft built from 1955 through 1958. By the time Gary Powers was shot down over Sverdlovsk in May 1960, thus putting an end to the Soviet overflights, the aircraft's versatility could not be denied.

While the world's media and some in the US government wrote off the U-2, operations were quietly resumed by both the CIA and the USAF. The aircraft's possibly finest hour came two years later, when U-2 photography confirmed US intelligence about a Soviet military build-up on Cuba, and later revealed offensive ballistic missiles pointing at the US.

By 1963, CIA U-2s had been flying over mainland China for a year in a joint project with the Nationalist government on Taiwan. Using aircraft modified with an inflight-refuelling capability, Strategic Air Command was flying Elint missions along the eastern and northern borders of the USSR, probing the defences that its bomber fleet might meet. As both superpowers continued nuclear tests in the atmosphere, SAC was also running sampling flights for weapons diagnostics. Other U-2s were proving valuable as high-altitude testbeds for a variety of sensors destined for satellites.

In March 1963, Kelly Johnson noted in his diary that the U-2 was "in great use all around the world. We haven't got nearly enough of them." Twenty-one out of the original 55 had been lost by then, mostly to accidents, and he suggested building a new batch of 25 aircraft that would cost around $1 million each. However, the USAF was by

then sponsoring the RB-57F, a bizarrely-modified B-57 which could theoretically haul a much greater payload to altitude than the U-2. It first flew in May 1963. Meanwhile, in great secrecy, the CIA was funding development of a Mach 3 successor to Kelly's 'Angel', known as the Oxcart programme. After three years of studies this had been given the go-ahead in February 1960 but the huge technical hurdles had been mounted only slowly. A first flight was made in April 1962, and the aircraft was slowly proving itself in flight tests from Groom Lake.

A larger 'Angel'

Kelly Johnson persisted. He well understood the continuing requirement for 'a good 75,000-ft airplane', despite the ongoing A-12 development. The original U-2 models were no longer capable of such altitude, having been weighed down by heavier payloads, ECM and more sophisticated navigation systems. Johnson did not think the RB-57F was a viable solution. He began drawing enlarged versions of the U-2, initially with two 30-in (76-cm) fuselage plugs. The project was given a boost by a new require-

ment from the intelligence community to evaluate Soviet satellites in orbit. Johnson proposed installing a 240-in (610-cm) focal length, upward-looking sensor in the space created by the fuselage extension. In September 1963, he formally proposed building 25 U-2L models for $1.1 million each.

In order to launch photo-reconnaissance missions against far-flung targets of interest without using foreign bases, with all the attendant political problems, the CIA had contracted Lockheed to modify some early-model U-2Cs to land and take off from aircraft-carriers. So, Johnson's new proposal was evaluated by the CIA, the USAF and the US Navy, which had by now become involved in the CIA's U-2 operations.

Rejected proposal

The days when a Skunk Works proposal would be approved and funded by a small circle of CIA and White House initiates were over. The Air Force was committed to the RB-57F; it was yet to learn that the General Dynamics project would be delayed by two years, cost much more than originally anticipated, become a maintenance nightmare, and – worst of all – never make it above 65,000 ft (19810 m). The U-2L idea was evaluated over a protracted period by the burgeoning defence intelligence bureaucracy, and eventually suffocated.

Throughout 1964 and into 1965, U-2s continued flying over China, Cuba and elsewhere. The USAF wing deployed aircraft to Vietnam for photo missions 'up north'. By May 1965, another nine U-2s had been lost, six in accidents and three to SA-2 missiles over China. Despite

the ever-more sophisticated ECM packages, the U-2 was still vulnerable to these SAMs, which had just been identified around Hanoi and Haiphong as well.

Unfortunately for the USAF, a variety of technical and political problems still prevented the A-12 from being deployed, and suddenly its interest in an improved U-2 increased. Altitude was a key concern, so Kelly Johnson gathered a design team under Merv Heal to work on a new wing. The team studied swept wings, supercritical wings and higher aspect ratios, all of which proved unpromising. They investigated recent NASA studies into high-lift wings, including a new flap designed to increase the critical Mach number. After wind tunnel tests at Burbank, Johnson rejected the NASA wing, which added extra weight and did nothing for drag.

Advanced engine

At that point, Pratt & Whitney provided new direction to the project. The engine-maker had produced a new version of the J75-P-13 turbojet which increased sea-level thrust from 15,800 to 18,500 lb (70.29 to 82.30 kN). The J75-P-13A had replaced the original J57 in the CIA's U-2 fleet in 1959, in an attempt to obtain higher altitude. This "turned the aircraft from a Cadillac into a Porsche," according to one pilot, and the resulting U-2C model was never short of power.

Top: The prototype U-2R flies with gear down during an early test flight. Compared to the earlier U-2 design, the R model offered much greater range and load-carrying capability, even though it retained the same powerplant. The prototype was fitted with an air data probe with sensitive directional vanes.

Above: Bill Park (left) flew the U-2R on its first flight, and is seen here with the programme manager Ed Baldwin (centre) and Dick Boehme, who was Kelly Johnson's assistant.

Left: Another view shows N803X during flight tests. Fluttering of the tailplanes later required the addition of external stiffeners.

Lockheed Martin U-2

Five early U-2Rs, including the unpainted prototype, are seen at Edwards North Base. This facility was the main base for the CIA U-2R operations.

Providing a good illustration of the considerable differences between the two generations of U-2, this CIA U-2R shares the North Base ramp with a U-2C. The canopy sunshade was painted white to avoid heat build-up in the cockpit but was later changed to black.

The USAF, which was still flying J57-powered U-2As, immediately ordered some higher-thrust -13Bs to re-engine its dwindling fleet. Johnson realised that this latest power increase could be the key to a better U-2, and in October 1965 he instructed Skunk Works engineer Merv Heal to start a new study on the U-2, retaining the basic principles of the original design but scaling up to take advantage of the increased power. Bob Weile led the wing redesign. Retaining the same cross-section and taper, wingspan was increased by 23 ft (7.01 m) to 103 ft (31.40 m), and overall wing area by 400 sq ft (37.16 m²) to 1,000 sq ft (92.9 m²). As a result, the wing loading was reduced to original U-2A

The first batch of U-2Rs (FY68) numbered 12 aircraft. Six of these went to the Agency, the remainder going to the Air Force, primarily for operations in Southeast Asia. CIA aircraft like this one often flew with USAF markings.

values, and the lift/drag ratio returned to 25:1. Lift coefficient was 0.6 to 0.7, and the aspect ratio 10.667.

After various studies, the empennage-design group led by Herb Nystrom opted for the all-moving tailplane which had first been employed on the Lockheed Jetstar. The so-called Kelly Johnson tail effectively distributed the pitch forces to the entire horizontal tail, and the whole slab trimmed. The design helped widen the aircraft's centre of gravity limits and eliminated the need for ballast. Ed Baldwin led a complete redesign of the fuselage, which was wider and 25 per cent longer than the earlier aircraft. Systems which once had been 'bolted-on' to the exterior U-2C as an afterthought – such as engine oil cooler, HF radio and ECM System 9 – were now accommodated within its confines. Other systems variously added to specific U-2Cs – such as ILS, TACAN and Doppler – were now included as a standard fit. There were new avionics for flight reference and flight direction. Another bonus was the longer tailpipe, which helped mask the engine's infra-red signature.

The 45 per cent increase in cockpit area allowed pilots to wear the bulkier (but much more comfortable) full pressure suit, and it was now possible to install a 'proper' zero-zero ejection seat. The characteristic driftsight was retained, but not the sextant which had provided an alternative means of navigation in the early days.

The resulting U-2R (R for Revised or Reconnaissance) was a sensor platform of superb utility. The U-2R was about one-third bigger than the original model, but some of the performance numbers increased dramatically. Ferry range was more than 7,000 nm (8,050 miles; 12950 km), 2,500 nm (2,875 miles; 4625 km) better than the U-2C and fully twice that of the RB-57F. The total fuel capacity was 2,915 US gal (11035 litres), or nearly 19,000 lb (8620 kg) – enough to keep airborne for 15 hours, which was probably beyond the pilot's endurance. Maximum altitude, achieved at the end of the cruise climb, returned to 75,000 ft (22860 m). Payload was effectively quadrupled.

Sensor carriage

In the original U-2 models, cameras, Sigint and sampling packages could be interchangeably uploaded to the Q-bay behind the cockpit, an area spanning the entire width and height of the fuselage. That modular concept was retained, and also applied to the nose of the redesigned aircraft. Payload specialist Bob Anderson kept the aircraft's equipment segregated from its payload, in the area immediately forward of the front pressure bulkhead, and in a large E-bay aft of the Q-bay. A higher-capacity AC/DC electrical system was specified to accommodate increasing sensor power requirements. At the design stage, provision had been made for more payload to be carried in pods attached

Far left: Like its predecessor, the U-2R could be rapidly dismantled for carriage in transport aircraft. Here a shrouded U-2R is loaded on to a C-141 StarLifter.

Left: Construction is modular, the main sub-assembly being the central fuselage. The tail section, wings and nosecone are all built separately.

Above: The US Navy was interested in the U-2R from an early stage, its long endurance being of interest for patrol work.

Right: Following the success of operating the first generation of U-2s from carrier decks, it was decided that the U-2R should also be tested onboard ship. This CIA aircraft, serialled N810X, flew the proving flights from USS America in 1969.

to the wings. Although these were not initially used, the provision later proved invaluable.

In January 1966, Johnson presented the U-2R study to Dr Bud Wheelon, the CIA's Deputy Director for Science and Technology. To get the programme started, Johnson offered to build the first two examples for $12.5 million. Within days, the government responded with a request for costs and schedules on 25 aircraft. It was another three months before Washington started funding the project, and then only for continuing studies. However, Johnson brought in more engineers, and put Ed Baldwin in charge of the overall project.

Production authorisation

A go-ahead to produce eight U-2Rs finally came in September, and Johnson and his assistant Dick Boehme authorised tooling, expecting a substantial follow-on order. They were to be disappointed. Another four were ordered four months later, but the Pentagon had other priorities and did not pursue its original plan to order 25 aircraft. The 12 U-2Rs that were built were shared equally between the CIA and the USAF. The Skunk Works had two customers from the outset, unlike first time round, which created a number of management problems.

Sensing the lack of customer urgency, Johnson gave his team a full year to get the new aircraft airborne. "I expected nine months at maximum," said Baldwin. Johnson wanted higher-quality tooling than on the earlier models. There was also a static test article. The mock-up review was held in late November 1966. The Air Force wanted maximum cockpit commonality with its U-2Cs, so the old-fashioned round dials were retained. Bill Park, the Skunk Works test pilot who would make the first flight, preferred the contemporary strip instruments which were going into the 'Blackbird'. Park got his way for the prototype – only.

Above: Deck crew check over the U-2R by America's island prior to take-off. Lift-off presented no problems.

Right: Bill Park takes the wire in N810X. A simple arrester hook with an aerodynamic fairing was scabbed on to the U-2R forward of the tailwheel. Other carrier modifications included sprung-steel wingtip skids and a framework guard on the port tailwheel door to stop the wheel snagging the wire.

A few problems emerged during development, including a slow rate of roll. That was solved by adding a second pair of hydraulically-actuated spoilers outboard on the wing. An inboard pair dumped lift during descent and landing, and the larger control surfaces and higher critical Mach number made the U-2R somewhat easier to control and land than the earlier models. Final assembly of the U-2R was accomplished in Building 309/310 at Burbank, with the aircraft trucked to the remote North Base at Edwards for its first flight. Bill Park took up Article 051 for the first time on 28 August 1967, in front of a crowd from CIA headquarters and the Pentagon.

Flight test

Flight testing proceeded smoothly. The bigger wing flexed as much as 4 ft (1.2 m) up or down at the tip and, for novice pilots, the aircraft was a handful to fly. The unboosted controls, worked by cables, push rods and bell cranks from a huge yoke in the cockpit, were unchanged. So was the U-2's most distinctive external feature: the bicycle landing gear and drop-out pogos. Above 60,000 ft (18290 m), the aircraft demonstrated weak static stability in all axes, requiring stability augmentation from a reliable autopilot. There was no doubt that pilots for the new U-2 would still have to be selected and trained with care.

By February 1968, the second U-2R was at North Base, which was also the location of the CIA U-2 unit. It was called Detachment G by the Agency, although for cover purposes the operation was designated the 1130th ATTG by the Air Force. Here, training of both CIA and USAF pilots soon commenced.

By December 1968 all 12 aircraft had been delivered, split equally between CIA and USAF. The military codenamed its new aircraft Senior Year, and this nomenclature survives as the overall U-2 programme name. Pilots and ground crew preferred to call it the 'Deuce' or the 'Dragon Lady'.

Carrier trials

One remaining flight test task which was not tackled until 1969 was the U-2R's carrier qualification. The new aircraft had been designed with a hinge so that the outer 6 ft (1.8 m) of wing folded back, enabling it to be moved to and from the hanger deck on the Navy's carriers. An unobtrusive arrester hook could be added forward of the tail gear, with cable deflectors attached to the tailgear doors and wingtip skids. Bill Park practised carrier landings on the lakebed at North Base before taking the navy's carrier qualification course at Pensacola. In November 1969 Park and four CIA pilots deployed to the NASA base at Wallops Island. USS *America* was waiting off the coast, but Park's first flight had to be aborted when he discovered that no-one had removed the locking pin for the tail hook.

This is one of two aircraft used for the Navy's U-2 EPX (Extended Patrol Experimental) project. This aircraft featured a shortened nose housing search radar, and sensor-equipped wing pods. Ice regularly forms under the wings during the descent to warmer lower altitudes from a long mission.

Far left: CIA U-2Rs were flown from Taoyuan AB in Taiwan, in Taiwanese markings and with RoCAF pilots.

Left: Among the many proposals for the U-2R was this aircraft, known as the Lockheed 351B. It was a two-seat derivative carrying missiles (presumably for anti-ship work) under the wings.

Below: A model of an armed U-2R is tested in a wind tunnel. The model has 14 hardpoints carrying a variety of bombs and missiles. None of the armed proposals was taken up, but decoys were launched from one aircraft during tests.

the deck of 20 kt (23 mph; 37 km/h), and the spoilers deployed, the aircraft trapped easily. Take-offs were no problem either. With the help of a naval LSO assigned to the unit, CIA pilots remained carrier-qualified for the next few years. The U-2R carrier capability was never used operationally, although it was seriously considered on one occasion. The main reason for its non-use was the disruption that U-2 operations would cause to the carrier air wing. Nevertheless, the Navy was still interested in the U-2, as an ocean surveillance aircraft operating from land bases to extend a battle group's radar horizon. The threat to the fleet from long-range cruise missiles had increased, and the new aircraft's long endurance offered the prospect of round-the-clock cover.

EPX programme

Flight tests were conducted from Edwards from February 1973, using two CIA aircraft modified for the Electronics Patrol Experimental (EPX) programme. A heavily-modified RCA X-band weather radar was mounted in a new nose section, with an RCA return beam vidicon camera and a UTL Elint receiver carried in left and right wing pods respectively. The 'take' from these sensors was downloaded via a datalink in the E-bay to the navy's surface vessels.

That mishap solved, everything else went according to Park's plan, which was to approach the deck at 72 kt (83 mph; 133 km/h) using a 45° flap setting. With a wind over

For navigation accuracy across large stretches of water, the Northrop NAS-21 astro-inertial system – similar to that carried by the SR-71 – was used (the NAS-21 became standard on the U-2R until more accurate INS, and eventually GPS systems, were developed).

The trials continued in 1975 with the more powerful Texas Instruments APS-116 radar, a purpose-built sea surveillance sensor which was developed for the S-3A Viking ASW aircraft, now rolling off the Burbank production lines. To get 360° coverage, the Skunk Works developed an air-pressure stabilised radome made from three layers of Kevlar. The radar was mounted in the Q-bay, with its antenna protruding below into this 'inflatable' radome. For access, Skunk Works engineers used a zipper taken from a U-2 pilot's partial pressure suit.

However, the advent of satellite systems that promised to provide constant, wide-ocean surveillance to the Navy's satisfaction meant that the U-2 EPX lost its appeal. Lockheed tried to keep maintain the Navy's interest by proposing the integration of Rockwell Condor AShMs, carried on mid-wing launch rails, but to no avail. The inflatable radome found a further use when the U-2R was selected as trials aircraft for the new Senior Lance side-looking reconnaissance radars.

A number of other exotic developments were also explored in the early 1970s. Briefings on other 'attack' versions of the U-2R were given to US and British officials. A scheme to launch two Beechcraft liquid-fuelled drones from the wing stations, as SAM missile decoys, reached the flight test stage. They were carried flush to the wing, and were extended on a trapeze for firing.

Camera systems

The truth was, the U-2 was best employed as a surveillance platform. A variety of camera systems were available. The original and revolutionary B-camera which had been developed for the Soviet overflights had been improved with new optics and lighter construction by the Hycon company. Redesignated HR-73B, it was still in use on the early U-2 models. The panoramic camera systems developed for the Corona satellites by Itek had been adapted for airborne use as the Intelligence Reconnaissance Imaging System (IRIS). Used on the SR-71 and later on the U-2R, these 24- and 30-in (61- and 76-cm) focal length cameras employed a folded optical path mounted on an Optical Bar Assembly (OBC). They scanned through 140° and provided good resolution across a 32-nm (37-mile; 60-km) wide swath below the aircraft. The most useful potential imaging sensor for the U-2R was the Type H, a 66-in (168-cm) folding focal length device developed by Hycon from the Type IV high-resolution camera used on the A-12. This was a LOng-Range Oblique Photographic

(LOROP) sensor which could image terrain many miles to the side of the aircraft's flight path. It was gyro-stabilised during the exposure, and employed temperature, pressure and image motion compensation. It was first introduced on the U-2C in 1965-66.

Operational deployment

As soon as the R model was finished flight testing, the CIA deployed two aircraft to Det H, the joint operation with the Republic of China air force (RoCAF). By then, overflights of mainland China had terminated, after the loss of a fifth U-2C to SAM missiles in September 1967. Using the H-camera from U-2 cruising altitudes, the 'Black Cat' squadron could fly along the mainland coast in international airspace, producing images of Chinese ports and coastal airfields, from where any preparations for aggressive moves against Taiwan would be mounted. Pilots could select photo targets ahead of the aircraft by 'eyeballing' them through the driftsight and storing them in the camera's memory.

When all worked well, the H brought back stunning imagery, actually much better than its predecessor on the A-12, partly thanks to the slower film transport past the lens required by the much slower U-2. The H was a temperamental beast, though, and had to be maintained at a constant temperature; Lockheed had to develop new air conditioners to hook up to the Q-bay during pre-flight preparation.

Above: Relieved of its duties in Southeast Asia, and bolstered by the influx of ex-CIA aircraft, the USAF U-2R fleet turned its main attention to the Cold War. Det 4 at RAF Mildenhall in England became the centre for European operations from 1976.

Above left: There have been many reports of U-2Rs changing tail numbers, mainly sparked by obvious differences in paint style between the last two digits of the serial and the first three. However, changes usually occur because the rear fuselages are interchangeable between airframes. There have been a few real incidences of spurious markings, the best-known being this aircraft which returned to Mildenhall from Akrotiri with the serial '10345'. The official serial block ran from 68-10329 to 68-10340.

The U-2Rs operating in Europe in the late 1970s were usually configured for signals intelligence gathering. This antenna suite, with a row of blades along the spine and a single paddle blade antenna under each wing, was believed to be called Senior Book.

Lockheed Martin U-2

68-10339 was used for a variety of equipment trials during the 1970s, one of the most visually striking being those concerned with the Senior Lance radar. This synthetic aperture radar was housed in an inflatable Kevlar radome under the Q-bay.

Right: Air sampling missions had figured prominently in the operations of the first generation of U-2s, and the capability was retained for the U-2R. The particulate sampler was an open-ended tube with internal filters. It was mounted on the Q-bay hatch.

Even before the Powers shootdown the gathering of signals intelligence (Sigint) was becoming an important part of the U-2's repertoire, and with the U-2R this role grew in importance. This aircraft is carrying the Senior Spear communications intelligence (Comint) suite, characterised by large farms of aerials. Senior Spear has received several updates, resulting in changing antenna configurations.

The first loss of a U-2R occurred at Det H in November. A Chinese pilot lost control after applying power during a crosswind landing at Taoyuan. The aircraft rose steeply, then rolled left and crashed at the side of the runway. The 'Black Cat' squadron continued flying missions along the Chinese coast until August 1974, when the unit was closed after Sino-US relations improved.

In the meantime, the main excitement for the CIA's American and British pilots had been the ongoing conflict between Israel and its neighbours in the Middle East. The USSR supplied a complete air defence system to Egypt in spring 1970, and Israel's dominance of the skies over the Suez Canal was challenged. Tensioned increased through the summer, culminating in a large dogfight on 30 July. The United Nations brokered a ceasefire, and Det G was tasked to fly monitoring flights along the Canal, photographing the 64-mile (103-km) strip of territory bordering both sides of the Canal, within which Egypt and Israel had promised not to make any further deployments.

The UK agreed to provide basing facilities at Akrotiri, and two aircraft arrived there in early August via RAF Upper Heyford. Flights were mounted every few days for the next three months, with the 'take' processed at Akrotiri and then scanned for datalinking to the US by satellite. Neither party to the conflict had formally agreed the flights, and the U-2's defensive systems were frequently activated as Egyptian SA-2 and SA-3 missiles, and even Israeli fighters, threatened to shoot down the aircraft.

Long-range flights

The flights were halted on 10 November, and the U-2s were flown home a month later, again via Upper Heyford. This deployment certainly demonstrated the very long range of the U-2R. The first Canal overflight was actually performed from Upper Heyford, routing all the way around France and through the Mediterranean, with a recovery into Akrotiri (both France and Italy refused to allow the U-2 through their airspace). On one of the westbound ferry flights from the UK back to Edwards, a British pilot tested pushed the endurance to its extreme by arriving over the base and orbiting until fuel finally ran low. His total flight time was 14.5 hours.

In October 1973 fighting flared up again between Israel and Egypt in what became known as the Yom Kippur War. Det G deployed a U-2R to Upper Heyford and prepared to fly a mission down the west coast of France

(which again had denied overflight rights) and into the Mediterranean, with a recovery at Akrotiri. At the same time, the USAF prepared to deploy an SR-71 to RAF Mildenhall, but the British government refused to allow the flights. The U-2R went home, and SR-71s flew round-robin missions out of Griffiss AFB, NY instead, with the aid of multiple inflight refuellings.

In April 1974 the United Nations arranged for permanent monitoring of the latest stand-off between Israel and Egypt, with the full agreement of both parties. Once again, Det H headed for the Middle East, this time with British permission to fly out of Akrotiri. Later, airborne reconnaissance of the Sinai and (from 1982) the Golan Heights was formalised in the Camp David peace agreements, with the 'take' from the U-2's cameras being shared between all parties. The Akrotiri detachment was codenamed Olive Harvest, and when the CIA U-2R unit was quietly closed down at the end of 1974, it was taken over by the USAF's 100th Strategic Reconnaissance Wing (SRW).

Cuban watch and Southeast Asia

When it first received the U-2R in late 1968, the 100th SRW was responsible for continuing photo-reconnaissance of Cuba, and a single U-2R was deployed to OL-19 at Barksdale AFB for the Cuba mission. In late August 1970, OL-19 provided imagery of new construction at the port of Cienfugos, which led to the political furore over whether the Soviet Union was about to deploy offensive missile-carrying submarines from a Cuban base. Washington ordered daily flights from mid-September, and, for the first time since 1962, the U-2s were challenged by Cuban MiGs. Despite Cuban belligerence, the USSR eventually backed down.

In 1969, the 100th SRW also deployed the U-2R to OL-20 at Bien Hoa AB, South Vietnam. Because of the SAM threat, much of the photo mission 'up north' had been assumed by the SR-71 and OL-20's own Ryan-built reconnaissance drones. The U-2 was still flying photo, Elint and communications relay sorties in more permissive environments; the SA-2 was only deemed lethal within a 30-mile (48-km) radius of its launch pad. Careful mission planning was obviously essential.

In July 1970, OL-20 moved to U-Tapao air base in Thailand, by which time a new mission beckoned for the U-2R. Lockheed was asked to integrate a Melpar Comint sensor and datalink carried by one of the latest drone variants onto the 'Dragon Lady' (the USAF's nickname for the U-2). Using typical Skunk Works ingenuity, the company improved upon the drone set-up with better antennas and a new datalink from the Sperry company. The Senior Book programme was born, and Sigint soon became

Lockheed U-2

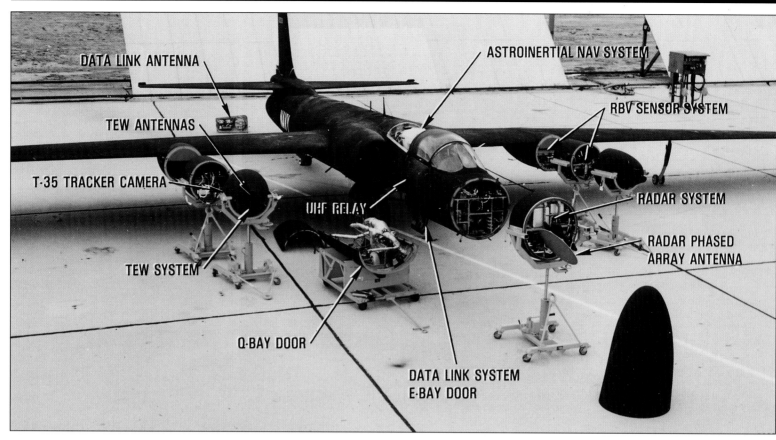

Above: This view of the **U-2EP-X** provides an example of how a reconnaissance system can be accommodated in the **U-2** airframe. Note that the **EP-X** had slipper-type wing pods rather than the full-size superpods used by later **U-2R** variants.

The most distinctive of the U-2 nose sections is that housing the **ASARS**-2 radar (left). This has a cooling air scoop on the top (right). **ASARS**-2 is undergoing an upgrade to provide full **MTI** capability.

Left: Aft of the tailwheel is this fairing for the datalink equipment.

Below: The cockpit is provided with internal mirrors either side and an external mirror to port. The latter is primarily used to check for contrails. Note the cockpit ventilation fan.

Above: Located under the cockpit are pitot/air data tubes and the glass bubble for the driftsight. The latter can be controlled from the cockpit to provide a near-hemispherical view under the aircraft.

Above: The vertical and horizontal stablisers are bolted together, so that when the horizontal surfaces are moved for trimming, the vertical fin also pivots, accounting for the small silver strip at the leading edge. U-2s are always towed tail-first.

Left: The outrigger pogo is shown in position.

U-2 DRAGON LADY

IN GOD WE TRUST, ALL OTHERS WE MONITOR

Three TR-1A/U-2Rs pose on the Beale ramp, with the SR-71 barns and a TR-1B in the background. The central aircraft is configured with the PLSS (Precision Location Strike System). Intended for service in Europe, PLSS employed three TR-1As flying along the battlefront, each linked to a central ground station. Hostile radars were detected by the system, and the central station could rapidly compute the precise location of the radar by using triangulation based on the data from the three aircraft. This in turn would allow the location to be transmitted to strike aircraft so that they could attack the radar. The system was very complex and expensive, and was terminated in favour of cheaper methods.

In the 1970s the U-2R programme attracted competition from high-altitude long-endurance drones, principally from the USAF's Compass Cope programme. Two vehicles were produced, the Boeing YQM-94A (above) and the Teledyne Ryan YQM-98A (right). Proposals for an unmanned U-2R were also put forward.

the main activity for OL-20. From racetrack orbits high above the Gulf of Tonkin (GOT), the U-2 eavesdropped on Vietnamese national and air defence communications, transmitting the data in real time to a ground station at Nakhon Phanom on the Thai border. At the same time, it provided communications relay for US aircraft, and was even tasked to 'eyeball' the SAMs fired at US bombers during the Linebacker offensive in 1972.

The GOT missions were flown mostly at night, and lasted from 10 to 12 hours. They were a test of endurance for the pilots, and also for ground crews during those periods when the operations tempo increased and round-the-clock coverage was required. In January 1973 the U-2 operation at U-Tapao (by now redesignated the 99th SRS) clocked 500 hours, a first for the 'Dragon Lady' programme, and this was topped in December 1994 with a 600-hour month.

Extended Sigint coverage

The U-2's Sigint systems were continuously improved over the next few years. Coverage was extended from HF and VHF to the UHF bands; pre-set receivers that could only monitor a few frequencies gave way to scanning receivers that could be controlled by uplink from specialists sitting in the ground station. Antennas and receivers multiplied; in the Senior Spear system, some of them migrated from the fuselage to specially-adapted pods faired into the U-2's wing. Timely analysis of the downlinked data was also addressed in the Senior Stretch programme, which

relayed Sigint data collected by the U-2 from the ground station up to satellites, and thence to the National Security Agency (NSA) in Maryland.

As the US finally withdrew from Southeast Asia, the focus of U-2 operations shifted, although the 'Dragon Lady' was finally withdrawn from Thailand only in April 1976. Three months earlier, the 100th SRW deployed U-2s to Osan air base, South Korea, where it had previously been operating the Comint drones. Despite their great contributions to intelligence gathering during the Vietnam War, drones fell out of favour as the US defence budget contracted. A virtual death sentence was passed on them when the USAF transferred their control from Strategic Air Command (SAC) to Tactical Air Command (TAC). The 100th SRW was left with only half a mission, and SAC's U-2 operation was therefore consolidated with that of the SR-71 at Beale AFB in July 1976.

NATO deployments

One month later, SAC made its first U-2R deployment to NATO, when 68-10336 arrived at RAF Mildenhall and flew during alliance exercises for the next four weeks. A longer deployment was made the following summer, and in 1978 the first aircraft to be equipped with the new E-Systems Senior Ruby Elint collection system (68-10339) was flown from Mildenhall for two months. The Ruby spiral antennas were carried at the front of new 'superpods', attached to the wing station at the same station as the Spear pods developed earlier, but they were three times larger. (Although the new pods were test-flown from Palmdale in 1975-76, it was only in the mid-1980s that the USAF ordered a full exploration of how these 24-ft/7.3-m long pods changed the flutter characteristics of the aircraft).

Western political and military leaders were worried about a growing disparity between the size of Soviet and NATO conventional forces in Europe. The Warsaw Pact now had the capability to mount an armoured Blitzkrieg, and might be able to advance several hundred miles in a surprise attack. To counter such an offensive, NATO needed to concentrate its statistically inferior fire power where it most mattered, and destroy WarPac forces as they were massing for attack. That would require effective and timely surveillance far beyond the East-West border, with the results sent quickly to the Army divisions and Air Force wings which would make the pre-emptive strikes. Spy camera satellites they could not see through cloud and were controlled by the super-secret National Reconnaissance Office (NRO) in Washington. The Sigint satellites sent all their 'take' to the NSA, which was also equally compartmented in the black world and not responsive to the needs of tactical commanders. The SR-71, now flying with production ASARS-1 radars as well as photo sensors, was a scarce and high-cost asset which was also controlled from higher headquarters.

PLSS

In Southeast Asia, the drones and the U-2 had demonstrated what might be achieved by high-altitude, long-endurance platforms equipped with real-time datalinks. Senior Lance had generated new confidence in the utility of side-looking radar for reconnaissance purposes. A development programme to identify air defence radar and communications sites for attack, by homing in on their emissions, was also underway. This was called the Precision Location Strike System (PLSS), and would also require high-flying platforms.

Although the drones had proved invaluable recce platforms in high-threat environments, the USAF hierarchy had lost faith in them. In the final analysis, it was now said, RPVs had been plagued by reliability and recovery problems. In an attempt to overcome these, the Compass Cope development programme had been funded, in which Boeing and Ryan produced all-new vehicles using the latest

Below: A U-2 floats across the Beale threshold during a training mission. For these sorties the aircraft usually fly without superpods, but with the defensive sub-systems in place. Antennas for them are located in the wingtip pods, in the fairing on the starboard wing trailing edge, and in the fin-tip. The rear-facing antenna at the top of the fin altered the fin profile, and is surmounted by the fuselage sump tank vent pipe.

Above: The **PLSS** birds featured an extended nose with slab sides for the emitter locator. The superpods featured slab sides, also for Elint antennas, while large fairings underneath housed **DME** (**D**istance **M**easuring **E**quipment).

composite materials, digital flight controls and powerplants. These RPVs were capable of reaching 70,000 ft (21335 m) and orbiting for 24 hours at a stretch. They also took off and landed conventionally, under their own power.

At Burbank, Kelly Johnson had retired from the Skunk Works in 1975 and his deputy Ben Rich had taken over. Rich began lobbying in Washington for a U-2 re-order. With the loss of a second U-2R in 1975, the fleet was already down to 10 examples. Against this background, in September 1977 the Pentagon tasked a group of USAF and US Army staff officers to urgently re-examine the services' reconnaissance resources, present and future. Headed by General Alton Slay, deputy chief of staff for R&D, they concluded that the U-2 was the best platform for PLSS and another side-looking reconnaissance radar now being developed by Hughes. They strongly recommended that control and tasking of the aircraft be vested in theatre commanders. In the past, they noted, the U-2 had been controlled by the SAC Reconnaissance Center in Omaha.

The study group's report was quickly approved by the Army and Air Force chiefs of staff. Compass Cope was cancelled, and the FY 1979 Defense Budget was altered just before publication in early 1978, to provide funds for a restart of the U-2 production line. To emphasise a break with the past, General Slay recommended that the aircraft be renamed TR-1 – for Tactical Reconnaissance. The chairman of the JCS, General David Jones, concurred. "We've got to get this spyplane label off the aircraft", he declared. As Ben Rich later noted wryly, "the Press simply called it the TR-1 spyplane instead."

TR-1 production

The FY 1979 budget signalled the intention to purchase at least 25 TR-1s, at a cost of about $550 million, including sensors and ground support equipment. Hughes Radar Systems Group in El Segundo, next to Los Angeles airport, gained further funding for ASARS-2. This much was out in the open, although the actual capabilities of ASARS-2 would be highly classified for many years. The intention to order another 10 aircraft with 'black budget' money went unreported. They would retain the U-2R designation and be used to augment the 9th SRW's small fleet engaged in Sigint and photo-reconnaissance duties in Korea, Cyprus and elsewhere.

The Skunk Works dusted off the old U-2R tooling and set up the production line again, this time at Palmdale. Under the direction of programme manager Fred Cavanaugh, some U-2 veterans were brought out of retirement to help the effort. Their experience was sorely needed; southern California's aerospace industry was booming, and Lockheed had to hire a number of unskilled workers to augment the workforce.

Only minor changes were made to the airframe. The engine was the same P&W J75, salvaged from retired F-105 and F-106 fighters and returned to P&W for overhaul and conversion into the -P-13B high-altitude version. That saved money, but the USAF procurement bureaucracy threatened to add cost. The 'old' U-2 – even the U-2R – had been procured under fast-track procedures, which accorded with the Kelly Johnson way of doing things. A new generation of Pentagon officials wanted to know why this 'new' TR-1 aircraft was not being built to MILSPECS.

The first TR-1A, 80-1066, was rolled out at Site 7 of the sprawling Palmdale airfield on 15 July 1981. This was a public occasion, unlike 1967 and 1955. The onlookers, ranging from Pentagon brass to the local Press, saw a smart black aircraft complete with the superpods. The only visible differences from the earlier U-2R were the slightly altered wingtip profile (for a new radar warning sensor) and a 'clean' horizontal tail (following some sonic vibration

The PLSS programme was developed from the ALSS trials undertaken by U-2Cs operating from RAF Wethersfield. If it had entered full-scale service, PLSS would have been a mission for the 17th RW at RAF Alconbury. That unit originally was to have been assigned an 18-aircraft fleet to provide continuous PLSS coverage in addition to its other theatre reconnaissance tasks.

A rare sight: NASA's three ER-2s cruise over the Golden Gate Bridge from their home base at Moffett, the aircraft in the foreground resplendent in the Administration's new house colours. The loaned aircraft (80-1069/NASA 708) may shortly to be returned to the USAF.

Right: The ER-2 has most of the U-2R's military systems removed. Like the Air Force aircraft, the NASA ER-2s are being re-engined with the General Electric F118 engine.

at remarkable stand-off ranges," declared General Thomas McMullen. "The combined increase in range, resolution and area coverage represents a quantum jump over currently operational systems."

Problems with PLSS

Unfortunately, the same good progress was not being made with PLSS, the other sensor intended for the TR-1. The complicated and expensive effort to produce an alternative to the Wild Weasels for SAM suppression had begun in 1972 with the Advanced Location and Strike System (ALSS). By orbiting a trio (or 'triad') of aircraft at high altitude, equipped with Elint sensors which were datalinked to a ground station, the accurate positions of threat emitters could be quickly calculated by triangulation. This overcame the problem of 'traditional' airborne Elint, where the emitter was required to stay on air long enough for the aircraft to move along track, so that the direction-finding process could be completed. The North Vietnamese had failed to co-operate in this endeavour, by quickly shutting down their transmitters. This also foiled the missiles launched at them by Wild Weasel aircraft, which homed on their radiated signals.

The ALSS ground station could not only fix a SAM site's position as soon as it came on air, it could also relay the co-ordinates to attacking aircraft, via the orbiting triad. To flight-test the new system, all seven remaining USAF U-2C aircraft had been equipped with ALSS antennas and datalinks in 1972. Development problems ensued, and it was not until 1975 that an operational test was conducted in Europe, with five U-2Cs deployed to RAF Wethersfield, UK. The results were unsatisfactory; datalinks failed, receivers and transmitters went offline, connectors failed to connect.

Undaunted, the USAF redefined and expanded the effort to a greater range of frequencies and signal types. The new PLSS contract was awarded in 1977 to Lockheed Missiles and Space Company (LMSC) as the main contractor. By the time that the TR-1 was flying, PLSS was supposed to be ready for flight test, but the first PLSS-equipped aircraft (80-1074) actually got airborne in December 1983.

Yet another nose was designed to house the E-Systems Elint antennas and receivers, while the superpods housed DME equipment. Another 18 months passed before the 9th SRW was finally able to launch a PLSS triad for weekly test missions over the China Lake weapons range. By this time, however, the Air Force top brass had lost patience, and the Wild Weasel community was openly hostile. PLSS lingered on as the Signal Location and Targeting System (SLATS) and was still being tested in a two-aircraft (dual) configuration in late 1987. There were other ways to accomplish the mission, and SLATS never did make it to Europe in 1988 as planned.

NASA's special

As noted earlier, TR-1 production was preceded by a single ER-2 version for the High-Altitude Missions Branch at NASA Ames Research Center, Moffett Field, California. NASA had been flying two U-2C models since July 1971 as Earth Resources Survey Aircraft. During that time, they had ranged across the US, using a variety of imaging systems to aid studies of the earth's surface. Some flights were tests of the sensors scheduled to be orbited on NASA's new, dedicated remote-sensing satellites (which were later named Landsat). The aircraft had proved themselves to be more than mere satellite surrogates, carrying a variety of sensors to 60,000 ft (18290 m) or higher to measure gases and particles in the atmosphere. Having started with a range of declassified imaging sensors from the CIA and USAF U-2 programmes, they were now carrying sensors which were custom-built by research scientists. The ability to fly above 95 per cent of the earth's atmosphere was good enough for many of them.

problems which threatened to cause fatigue stress, the U-2R stabilisers had been modified with stiffeners which protruded on the external surface as small ribs).

First flight

This first TR-1 had actually been preceded down the line and into the air three months earlier by a version for NASA designated ER-2 (of which, more later). Lockheed test pilot Ken Weir made the first TR-1 flight on 1 August 1981. There was no significant flight-test programme to accomplish, of course, so 80-1066 was in the customer's hands at Beale AFB by the end of the following month. By that time, the ASARS-2 radar was flying, on U-2R development aircraft 68-10336. A new, extended nose had been designed to house the long antenna, transmitter and receiver/exciter. The remaining black boxes for the radar were housed in the Q-bay, while the datalink stayed in the same place as the Sigint-equipped aircraft: in a pressurised cavity aft of the tail gear. Fibre-optic cables linked the various components. Early flight tests results confirmed the radar's promise. "It provides pictures of near-photo quality

NASA had a similar operation at Ellington Field, Houston which used three former USAF RB-57F models and, as in military service, the Ames U-2s outperformed the WB-57. When the USAF re-opened the U-2 production line with the TR-1 order, NASA opted to retire two of its WB-57s and acquire two of the new aircraft. The greater volume offered by the superpods, larger Q-bay and detachable nose was required for new experiments, while the ability to combine sensors and experiments meant that the flight costs could be shared among a number of researchers. Maximum payload would be 2,600 lb (1180 kg).

ER-2 takes to the air

Smartly painted in blue and white as N706NA, the ER-2 was first flown by Skunk Works test pilot Art Peterson on 11 May 1981. NASA project manager Marty Knutson – a veteran U-2 pilot from the earliest days of the programme – picked up the aircraft from Palmdale and flew it to Moffett on 10 June. For the next six years, it flew alongside the two U-2Cs, but when the USAF decided to retire the last of its early-model aircraft, NASA followed suit. A second purpose-built ER-2 (N709NA) was delivered in 1989, by which time NASA had also acquired the former USAF TR-1A 80-1069 on loan as N708NA. The aircraft carry their USAF serials for administrative reasons.

The earth survey flights continued with improved imaging sensors, including the same Itek IRIS II 24-in (61-cm) focal length panoramic camera as used by USAF U-2Rs. The IRIS series was derived from the CORONA reconnaissance satellites, and offered very high resolution across a wide swath. Unlike the USAF, which was slow to adopt multi-spectral imaging, the NASA installation usually used colour and 'false colour' film. Such film is sensitive to the green, red and near-IR portions of the spectrum, and can reveal features on the earth's surface which could not be detected by panchromatic film. In addition to the IRIS, NASA uses Hycon HR-732 framing cameras with 24-in

focal length lenses, but the workhorse is the Wild Heerbrug RC-10 mapping camera with 6- or 12-in (15- or 30-cm) lenses. One or more of these are flown on nearly every flight, and they can be mounted in the nose or superpods as well as the Q-bay.

High-altitude mapping

NASA's high-altitude aircraft had imaged large portions of the US (including Alaska), and an archive facility in Sioux Falls, South Dakota has over 500,000 photo frames, plus digital imagery data available. It handles hundreds of requests for the data from the remote sensing community.

The Daedalus Thematic Mapper Simulator (TMS) was introduced with the ER-2, a multi-spectral scanning radiometer recording digital data which could subsequently be computer-manipulated in ground analysis. This proved invaluable for geologists, oceanographers and agronomists in such applications as land use patterns, forestry, and disaster assessments. TMS has since been modified for many other environmental studies.

NASA flew the first-generation U-2C (above, background) on many high-altitude experiments. The larger U-2R airframe offered far greater load-carrying capability and NASA was an eager customer for the type. Two aircraft were procured as ER-2s, bolstered by a third aircraft (foreground) which was built as a TR-1A for the Air Force but subsequently operated by NASA on long-term loan.

The NASA ER-2 fleet is flown from Moffett Field. The aircraft in the foreground is configured for high-altitude atmospheric sampling.

Lockheed ER-2 details

Above: This view shows two vertical sensors mounted in the Q-bay of an ER-2. A variety of Q-bay hatches are available with various sensor windows, and are usually insulated with some quilting.

Left: The ER-2's cockpit differs in some important respects from that of the U-2R/S. The most obvious is the extended dashboard to the right of the driftsight and rearrangement of the instruments. The all-important small rectangular indicator at the top left of the dashboard announces 'Food Ready', a reference to the in-cockpit food warmer.

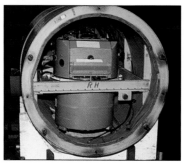

The superpods can be used for a wide variety of sensors. The fixed portion of the pod (left) is shown with digitising and recording equipment (including a tape recorder on a drop-down rack), while the removable front section of the pod (right) is shown mounting a vertical optical sensor.

Wing fold

With a 31.39-m (103-ft 0-in) span, the U-2/ER-2 presents considerable hangarage difficulties away from its normal bases. To offset this, the outer 1.78 m (5 ft 10 in) can be manually folded to reduce span.

Lockheed ER-2/TR-1A NASA Ames Moffett Field, California

For many years NASA operated a pair of U-2Cs on a variety of test programmes and earth resources monitoring work. With the reopening of the production line, the chance came to provide the Administration with new-build aircraft that were far more capable than the first-generation U-2s. The designation ER-2 was applied to reinforce the 'Earth Resources' role of the aircraft, and the first example from the reopened line was assigned to NASA. Another aircraft from further down the line was also earmarked for NASA. The first ER-2 went into service supporting the two remaining U-2Cs pending their retirement. To allow them to retire prior to the delivery of the second dedicated ER-2, the Air Force loaned this TR-1A (80-1069) to NASA, and it was redesignated ER-2. After a period of operating three ER-2s, NASA handed back this aircraft to the Air Force. The ER-2s operated from the Ames Facility at Moffett Field until they were transferred to the Dryden Flight Research Facility at Edwards AFB, California, from where the two ER-2s continue to operate.

Sensor carriage

The primary sensor locations are in the Q-bay behind the cockpit, in the detachable nose and in the superpods. In certain configurations the ER-2 has carried sensors in the rear of the superpods as well as the detachable front section. NASA aircraft have also been noted with sensors on underwing pylons in place of the superpods and with a streamlined pod carried under the rear fuselage. One ER-2 was configured to carry a Senior Span-style dorsal fairing known as Starlink.

Above: *One of the ER-2s is configured to use the STARLink (similar to Senior Spur) to transmit data across global ranges via satellite link.*

Below: *ER-2s occasionally deploy away from the Dryden Facility (Edwards AFB) to various parts of the globe as part of NASA's ongoing research. Here one is seen at Kiruna in Sweden in January 2000, as part of operations within the Arctic Circle.*

ER-2s are regularly reconfigured for various duties. The aircraft above has seven optical sensor ports, while the aircraft at right uses the superpod attachments to mount sensors on pylons.

Above: *The ER-2 can carry a sensor pod under the rear fuselage.*

Right: *This aircraft has an extended Q-bay hatch for an optical sensor.*

J75 engine

J75 engines were retrofitted to first-generation U-2s, and the powerplant was adopted as standard for the second-generation aircraft until the recent change to the F118. Designated J75-P-13B, the U-2's engine was a specially-built version of the standard J75 with a redesigned compressor stage for high-altitude operation and closer manufacturing tolerances to reduce weight. Nominal maximum thrust rating is 17,000 lb (75.65 kN) and standard cruise thrust is 15,100 lb (67.20 kN). The latter figure is rather academic as the thrust produced at operating altitudes is reduced to very low values. The engine itself is a two-spool design with coaxial shafts. The inner shaft mounts the second and third stages of the turbine, which drive the eight-stage low-pressure compressor. The hollow outer shaft connects the first stage of the turbine to the seven-stage high-pressure compressor. The compressor feeds air to the combustion chamber at a ratio of about 12:1 at take-off thrust. The eight cylindrical combustion chambers are each provided with six fuel flow nozzles, each suitably modified to handle the high-flashpoint JP-TS fuel. Ignition is initiated in chambers 4 and 5, with cross-over tubes subsequently igniting the other six burner cans.

Above: *NASA pilot James Barrilleaux climbs aboard the first ER-2, which is configured for high-altitude optical surveillance. It has a twin vertical camera installation in the Q-bay, with another vertical sensor in the nose section. The camera ports are all fitted with optically-flat glass in a flat-bottomed fairing.*

Undercarriage

The U-2/ER-2 has a bicycle undercarriage by necessity of its slender configuration. Much of the weight is supported on the mainwheel, which is forward retracting and has two wheels with tubeless tyres. The forward-retracting tailwheel has a single solid rubber tyre. It can be steered up to 6° either side. The fully-castoring wing-mounted outriggers normally fall free on take-off, but can be fixed for initial flight training.

Lockheed Martin U-2

The ER-2 was deployed abroad for the first time in spring 1985, to Mildenhall, in support of a DoD programme named HI CAMP which used a multi-wavelength infra-red sensor to obtain a database of background measurements of the earth's surface. The most significant overseas trip came two years later, when an ER-2 and NASA's DC-8 were deployed to Punta Arenas in southern Chile to investigate the hole in the ozone layer which had recently opened over the South Pole each winter. Fourteen separate sensors were carried on 12 ER-2 flights across Antarctica.

Measurements from the two-month deployment added weight to the theory that man-made chlorofluorocarbons (CFCs) were to blame. In winter 1988-89, a similar deployment was made to Stavanger, Norway to investigate ozone depletion over the North Pole. From 1991 to 1994, more flights were mounted out of Eielson AFB, Alaska, Bangor, Maine, and Christchurch, New Zealand. The NASA flights led directly to the international conventions which have mandated a phasing-out of CFCs around the world.

In a variation of this theme, the ER-2 began investigations in 1992 to determine whether a future fleet of commercial supersonic transports would also cause ozone loss. It took measurements of the known ozone depletion catalysts from 60,000 to 65,000 ft (18290 to 19810 m) in the 15-60° N latitudes where most SSTs would fly. In one 1993 sortie, the ER-2 took samples from the wake of a specially-flown Air France Concorde over New Zealand.

The ER-2 is now also participating in the SUCCESS project (SUbsonic aircraft: Contrail and Cloud Effects Special Study) to measure the effect on cirrus cloud formation of the growing world fleet of subsonic airliners. Unusually, this sometimes requires it to fly at lower levels – around 40,000 ft (12190 m).

ER-2 down under

In early 1993, an ER-2 was flown out of Townsville, Australia as part of the highly-co-ordinated TOGA COARE project to explore the formation of tropical storms over the unique 'warm pool' of water in the Pacific Ocean northeast of Papua New Guinea. This was done by measuring the heat radiating from the earth's surface, as well as with atmospheric measurement. No fewer than nine sensors were carried during the flights. The ultimate goal is to develop satellite sensors which could help predict storm formations and movement.

A laser-based system weighing 1,000 lb has recently helped improve data collection during the ER-2's atmospheric study flights. The Lidar Atmospheric Sensing Experiment (LASE) was built by NASA Langley at a cost of $20 million to operate autonomously, and flights were conducted from NASA's Wallops Island airfield in Virginia in co-ordination with other Lidars on the Space Shuttle and NASA's lower-flying Electra. The LASE will eventually go into orbit, but, like many satellite sensors before it, the high-flying capability of the U-2 has been invaluable for proving flights.

New and improved earth-imaging systems have also been introduced. The AVIRIS (Airborne Visible-InfraRed Imaging Spectrometer) is a 224-band hyper-spectral scanner developed by the Jet Propulsion Laboratory which has been flown frequently since 1991, when one of its first overseas deployments was to RAF Alconbury, UK. An Electro-Optic Camera (EOC) has been developed at Ames, to capture high-resolution (15.8 ft/4.8-m) digitised images from a solid-state video camera.

Dedicated trainer

The decision to produce dual-cockpit versions of the TR-1 from the outset was a wise one. The U-2 programme had somehow managed without conversion trainers for the first 17 years, but at the cost of numerous bangs, prangs and write-offs. In 1972 and 1975, two early-model U-2s were adapted as trainers by replacing the Q-bay with a second cockpit. In 1983, they were joined at Beale by the two TR-1Bs, all four being assigned to the 4029th Strategic Reconnaissance Training Squadron. The 4029th was later renumbered the 5th SRTS, and is now the 1st RS (T). The two U-2CTs were kept on strength until 1988, when a third new trainer arrived, bought with 'black' U-2R money (80-1091). There are now four, and they have recently been redesignated TU-2S (80-1091 is still a TU-2R at the time of writing). A cockpit procedures trainer has recently been added, but there is still no full-motion simulator for the U-2.

Pilots who wish to enter the U-2 programme must have a minimum 1,500 hours. They come to Beale for a week of interviews and tests, which include a suiting-up to ensure they are comfortable in the hermetically-sealed atmosphere of the pressure suit, and three brief flights in the trainer. After selection, they return for a six-month course which starts with a month of instrument training in the T-38 companion trainer. Pilot training is strictly one-on-one, with each course consisting of two instructors and two students. Next comes the Initial Qualification phase, consisting of one month's ground study and one month during which six sorties are flown in the trainer. The instructor usually occupies the rear cockpit, which has most of the same displays as the front cockpit, although there is no driftsight.

Solo flight

The prized solo patch is then awarded, and the student moves on to the Mission Qualification Phase. He flies 14 increasingly long and complicated sorties in the U-2R, and also learns to play the role of 'mobile'. Each U-2 flight is assigned a second pilot, who deals with many of the pre-flight preliminaries, especially those that the space-suited pilot cannot easily perform, such as the pre-flight walkaround. 'Mobile' accompanies the aircraft to the runway for take-off and remains in radio contact throughout the flight. He acts as a second brain to solve problems which might arise during the flight, and provides height-above-ground readouts during the critical landing phase.

The U-2R is somewhat easier to land than the early-model aircraft, which had to be stalled onto the runway, but the experience is still likened to riding a bicycle without any handlebars while balancing a long pole

laterally. The U-2 pilot really earns his pay when he descends from a nine-hour operational sortie, and finds fog or a crosswind at his recovery field.

Once they are qualified, new U-2 pilots spend their next 100 hours flying from Beale in the 99th SRS before they are ready to go overseas. The 99th SRS flies some interesting missions within the US, checking out new sensors or procedures, and supporting disaster relief and other environmental efforts with photography. It also flies in Red and Green Flag exercises, and launches short-notice flights to support search and rescue efforts.

The T-38 fleet at Beale numbers 12 gloss-black aircraft, which are also used by experienced U-2 pilots for standard USAF instrument check flights. They retained their standard training white colour for many years, until the 9th joined Air Combat Command where the rules dictated that their colour be changed to that of the primary wing aircraft.

When the RB-57F was retired in 1973, the U-2

Above: Normally based at Beale, the TR-1Bs occasionally deployed to RAF Alconbury while the 17th Reconnaissance Wing was resident with TR-1As to cater for mandatory check rides. A winter's evening provides a dramatic backdrop as a two-seater completes a check sortie.

Above left: After initially operating as the 4029th SRTS, the TR-1B/U-2RT squadron at Beale became the 5th SRTS. On the retirement of the SR-71 the training squadron adopted the old 'Sled' squadron number, becoming the 1st RS(T).

Below: One of the existing U-2RTs was among the first batch of three aircraft to be redelivered to Beale after re-engining with the F118. The two-seaters were redesignated U-2ST after re-engining (subsequently becoming TU-2S).

resumed the high-altitude air sampling role, a capability now also maintained by the 99th. After the Chernobyl disaster in 1986, a U-2 flew over Western Europe, configured with the specially adapted hatch and Q-bay assembly, which includes an airscoop, gas bottles and particle filters.

The standard USAF aircrew duty day is 12 hours, and a U-2 pilot scheduled for an operational mission will likely use every minute of it. The reporting, suit-up and pre-breathing phase takes about two hours, and post-flight reporting at least 30 minutes. That leaves time for a nine-hour 30-minute flight, although longer missions are technically possible with special waivers.

Climb profile

The U-2R climbs quickly to beyond 50,000 ft (15240 m), whereupon it enters a gradual cruise climb for the rest of the flight, ascending as fuel is burned off to 70,000 ft (21340 m) or above. The numbers vary depending on the mission weight, range required, outside air temperature and other factors. When it is time to return, speedbrakes and

landing gear are deployed – otherwise, the U-2 will not leave altitude until the engine quits. Contrary to popular misconception, U-2 pilots never cut the engine and glide to increase the range.

Stories of high-altitude emergencies and deadstick landings are part of U-2 lore, and could fill a book. Suffice to say, the aircraft has a safety record better than average. The 1980s were virtually accident-free, apart from three write-offs in 1984 when – for the only recorded time – a design factor was to blame in two cases. (The engine adaptor/tailpipe link failed, and had to be redesigned. Luckily, all three pilots made successful ejections).

Beale also trains mission planners, who are the hidden heroes of the U-2 community. Focusing on the targets requested by intelligence, the planners devise the ground tracks which will enable a flight to cover them. When the limitations of particular sensors, national borders, and terrain-masking factors are taken into account, this becomes a complicated process. Extreme accuracy is required; for instance, the H-camera used on some flights covers only a 2-mile (3.2-km) swath of territory when operating at nadir (e.g., looking straight down). As pilots say, it's like viewing the ground through a soda straw, and an incorrectly plotted track will miss the target completely.

Permanent European detachment

Having deployed the U-2R and the SR-71 to Mildenhall with increasing frequency in the late 1970s, the US eventually gained British permission for sustained operations. Det 4 of the 9th SRW was established at the Suffolk base in April 1979 with a single U-2R (initially 68-10338). While the Blackbird's role was still photo, the European activities of the 'Dragon Lady' were dedicated to Sigint. In the dying days of 1979, the 9th SRW deployed its first Senior Glass aircraft to Europe (68-10339). In this configuration, the Senior Ruby Elint system was combined with the Senior Spear Comint system to produce a versatile collection capability. The classically clean profile of the 'jet-powered glider' was no more. Multiple radio monitoring and direction-finding (DF) antennas protruded from the lower fuselage and the superpods, which were now asymmetric since the left pod sported a 'canoe'-type fairing housing parts of the Spear system.

The detailed capabilities of these two collection systems remain classified; they have since been updated and are still primary U-2R sensor systems. The basic capability was revealed in 1985 by the main contractor, E-Systems Melpar Division, when it gained permission to market the Airborne Remotely Controlled Electronic Support Measures System for export. Its brochure described the advantages to be gained by orbiting a small aircraft at high altitude with its sensors datalinked to a Ground Control Facility (GCF). "The critical signal processing equipment, data bases, and skilled operator/analysts with their support electronics and displays are in a safe haven," it noted. Only the antennas and receivers would be "compromised" if anything went wrong.

Sigint system

The radio monitoring system used 24 receivers in the HF, VHF and UHF bands, to detect AM, FM, CW, SSB and WBFM transmissions. Direction finding was via multi-baseline phase interferometric techniques. The radar detection system also used 'highly accurate' phase interferometer DF, and had automatic scan and reporting capability. Operators in the ground control facility could specify the search strategies. The datalink was highly directional, and provided a full-duplex HF voice or RTTY capability. The GCF itself was housed in transportable shelters, with as many as 18 consoles displaying data in full-colour graphics.

The Sigint mission was codenamed Creek Spectre by US European Command (EUCOM), and was flown by Det 4 from Mildenhall until February 1982, when the newly

activated 17th Reconnaissance Wing took it over from nearby Alconbury. The 17th was a former bomb wing which was revived to fly the TR-1s in Europe. The 95th Reconnaissance Squadron was the operating squadron, and the reporting line was ostensibly back to SAC Headquarters in Omaha. Following the principles established by the 1977 Joint Recce Study, the 17th's operational tasking came from EUCOM.

The first TR-1A for the 17th (80-1068) was flown from Beale via Patrick to an icy Alconbury on 12 February 1983. This was its second visit to the UK, having been displayed by Lockheed at the Farnborough air show in the previous September in an attempt to interest NATO nations in the aircraft's battlefield reconnaissance capability. The British government was the main potential customer, but the MoD was about to launch its own CASTOR programme and so it did not pursue the matter. (Thirteen years later, the MoD was still trying to launch the programme, by now renamed ASTOR, and the U-2 was back in contention.)

The 17th was expanded only slowly, since the ASARS-2 radar sensor was not yet ready for deployment. With its first two aircraft, the routine nine-hour Creek Spectre flights were continued. The wing's first serious mishap occurred in October 1982 when a bus containing security police was

driven into its third aircraft (80-1069). The aircraft was returned to the US inside a C-141 for repair, and subsequently redelivered. The 17th pilots and ground crews insisted that it did not fly correctly after the accident, and the USAF eventually gave up on the aircraft and leased it to NASA. The maintenance at Moffett Field was contracted to Lockheed engineers, who promptly re-rigged 069's control surfaces, and NASA pilots have flown it ever since without complaint.

ASARS arrives in Europe

In March 1985, the 17th RW received three more TR-1s and the long-awaited ASARS-2. On 9 July 1985, 95th RS commander Lieutenant Colonel John Sander flew the first operational ASARS-2 sortie. The world of airborne reconnaissance would never be the same. For the first time, tactical commanders were provided with timely results from an imaging sensor which could operate round-the-clock, with no regard to cloud cover or whether it was day or night. The U-2/TR-1 was the ideal platform for ASARS-2. It provided the highest-possible operating altitude, thus enabling the radar to see over and around terrain which would be masked from view at lower levels. By flying far above the earth's weather patterns, the aircraft

U-2 details

Cockpit instrumentation

The front cockpit of the TU-2 is essentially similar to that of the single-seat aircraft, although key operational systems such as sensor controls and RWR are removed. The rear cockpit is more austere, lacking many of the secondary controls such as circuit breakers. The side consoles are rearranged compared to the front, and the rear seat lacks the large optical scope for the driftsight.

Second cockpit

The addition of the second cockpit required only minor airframe changes as it is situated in the Q-bay sensor hatch. The floor is raised to provide adequate forward view for the instructor. The flight controls are interconnected with the front cockpit by means of push-rods and torque assemblies, mostly located in the lower fuselage beneath the raised cockpit.

Fuselage construction

The fuselage is built in three main sections. The central sub-assembly includes the cockpit, Q-bay (second cockpit in trainer version), engine intakes, wing attachment points and engine installation. The sensor-carrying nose section is attached just forward of the cockpit. There are several different nose configurations and these are routinely interchangable depending on mission requirements. The third sub-assembly attaches to the centre section aft of the wing trailing-edge, the break located at the start of the dorsal fin fairing. This section comprises the rear fuselage, tailwheel, empennage and airbrakes.

Lockheed TU-2R
1st Reconnaissance Squadron (Training)
9th Reconnaissance Wing
Beale AFB, California

Two trainer aircraft had been belatedly produced for the first-generation U-2 under the designation U2CT, and these continued in use to serve as introductory aircraft for the first U-2R batch. When the line reopened for TR-1 production, the second and third aircraft (80-1064 and 80-1065) were completed as two-seater TR-1Bs to provide a fully capable trainer for the second-generation aircraft. These were later joined by a third aircraft (80-1091) which was initially designated U-2RT to signify its assignment as a strategic (U-2R) as opposed to tactical (TR-1) trainer. A subsequent rationalisation of the fleet dispensed with the TR-1 designation altogether, all two-seaters then being known as U-2RTs. Trainer aircraft which underwent the F118 re-engining programme became U-2STs. In the first batch of three F118-powered aircraft was a single-seater (80-1071), one existing two-seater (80-1064) and another two-seater (80-1078) which was produced by conversion of a single-seater which had been badly damaged. The four trainers have since been redesignated TU-2R and TU-2S to bring them in line with standard USAF nomenclature.

Markings

The first two TR-1Bs were completed in a white scheme to signify their training status but were soon painted in the matt black of the operational aircraft. The third and fourth trainers were black from the start. Originally the markings consisted solely of a red serial on the fin made up of the last five digits of the serial (80-1091 wore 01091). When Strategic Air Command was amalgamated into Air Combat Command, the U-2 fleet acquired Tactical Air Command-style codes consisting of the fiscal year (80) in small digits and the last-three (091) in large digits. At the same time the TAC-style two-letter tailcode was applied, the 9th RW adopting 'BB'.

Fin

The tall fin is a conventional two-spar and rib aluminium construction. Trimming adjustment is accomplished on the ground by means of a simple bend tab.

Speed brakes

An electronically-controlled and hydraulically-operated airbrake is situated on either side of the rear fuselage. Maximum deflection is 60°.

The wing fold incorporates three interleaving fixtures which maintain the dynamic loads on the spars. A pin is fixed through the leaves to lock them, and a small strip then fairs over the small gap left in the skin surface.

The turned-down wingtip has abradable strips on the bottom to protect the structure on landing. The cylindrical fairing added on the end accommodates two radar warning receivers facing outwards at 45° and the wingtip navigation light.

Tail markings
In addition to the serial and tailcode, this U-2 wears the Air Combat Command badge and the 9th Reconnaissance Wing's four Maltese crosses. The latter are derived from the wing's emblem. Individual artworks are often worn on the fin, but are usually applied in chalk so as to be easily removable and to not damage the special black paint.

80-0191 was the third of the two-seaters, and the first to receive the U-2RT designation. This new designation (instead of the previous TR-1B) reflected funding channels rather than any aircraft differences.

Stall strips
At roughly mid-span on each wing leading edge is a retractable blade known as the stall strip. This is employed on landing to disrupt and destroy lift over that portion of the wing behind it. This helps cut the U-2's long float on landing.

Flaps
The U-2 has four sections of flaps, although they are arranged in pairs and appear as just two sections, one inboard and one outboard of the superpod attachment points. The flaps are interconnected to avoid any asymmetric operation. Maximum deflection is 50° down (or 35° in some configurations) and 6.25° up, the latter being the gust alleviation position for use at high speeds or in turbulent air.

Tailplane
The tailplane is built on a two-spar structure, and incorporates full-span elevators. Load trimming is accomplished by moving the entire tailplane (and the vertical fin), while inflight trimming is handled by trim tabs on each elevator, controlled by a switch on the right-hand handle of the control yoke.

Below: The pogo is a simple sprung-steel unit with solid-tyre wheels. The simple fixture allows the strut to castor freely during taxiing.

Above: A long jetpipe leads from the centrally-mounted engine to the tailpipe. This is the F118 installation in the U-2S.

Below: This frame guard was added to the port tailwheel door of the U-2R used for carrier trials. It prevented the arrester wire snagging the wheel. The carrier aircraft also had sprung-steel wingtip skids.

Fairings are mounted on the narrow fixed trailing-edge section between the flaps and the ailerons. On the starboard wing (above) is an RWR fairing, while on the port (below) is the GPS receiver. The latter is fitted on operational aircraft only.

Both undercarriage units have twin wheels. The tail unit (above) has solid tyres while the main unit (right) has tubeless 300-lb/sq in (2068-kPa) tyres.

Lockheed Martin U-2

The UK government announced its permission for the TR-1 fleet to be based at RAF Alconbury shortly before the aircraft's first flight in 1981. The first aircraft arrived with the 17th RW's 95th Reconnaissance Squadron in February 1983. This is the third production aircraft, seen configured for the photo mission with an optical Q-bay hatch.

Although the 95th RS fleet performed occasional photo missions, Sigint duties were far more important. This aircraft has a Senior Spear Comint fit. Initial plans called for the 17th RW to have 18 aircraft, 12 at the parent base at Alconbury and six detached to Wethersfield. In the event, the total was cut to 14, all at Alconbury. The force was run down with the end of the Cold War, the 17th RW being deactivated while the much-reduced 95th RS was reassigned to the 9th SRW.

provided the extreme stability which is demanded by the 'synthetic' array.

ASARS-2 operates in X-band to produce constant scale imagery in plan view, even when operating at long stand-off ranges. Ground resolution can be independent of range, by increasing the 'length' of the array in direct proportion to the area under investigation. Increased resolution can be commanded in the 'spot mode' by changing the look angle of the antenna as the aircraft moves along track, so that it repeatedly maps a smaller area of particular interest.

Like the Sigint sensors, ASARS is controlled from the ground via the wideband datalink in real time. For the European theatre, a new ground station was ordered from Ford Aerospace, which later became part of Loral (before it too was subsumed into Lockheed Martin). The TREDS (TR-1 Exploitation Demonstration System) was set up in trailers at a former missile maintenance facility near Hahn AB, Germany, codenamed Metro Tango. This interim system was scheduled to be replaced by two fully hardened underground stations named TRIGS (TR-1 Ground Stations), but the first TRIGS was never completed due to the end of the Cold War.

Operational evaluation

When ASARS flights began from Alconbury in 1985, the Cold War was still a reality. For the next three years, the system was 'wrung out' above NATO's Central European front. The process included the complicated task of integrating the operation of the Sigint systems with that of the radar. For instance, the radar's spot mode might be cued by an emission detected by the Ruby sensor. It would then image and allow identification, perhaps of vehicles belonging to a surface-to-surface missile battalion which had moved position recently.

In theory, the TR-1 could reconnoitre territory up to 350 miles (565 km) across the Warsaw Pact border. That is

the horizon for the Sigint sensors, although the radar's useful range is about 100 miles (160 km) less. The range from aircraft to ground station can be more than 300 miles (480 km) in ideal conditions.

NATO ground force commanders were excited by the new capabilities, but demanded more flexible methods of distributing the data. The US Army ordered a mobile ground station from Westinghouse known as the TRAC (Tactical RAdar Correlator). This was housed in a 40-ft (12-m) container, and could deploy to the field and operate independently from the TREDS/TRIGS. The UK and US jointly funded a programme to process and disseminate ASARS data to NATO. The TADMS (TR-1 ASARS Data Manipulation System) was built by GE and Ferranti in 1989, and manned by RAF personnel.

The 17th RW received more TR-1As directly from the production line, and was eventually assigned 12 aircraft. Although the PLSS had been cancelled, the wing needed enough aircraft for its wartime task of providing two TR-1 orbits across Central Europe on a 24-hour basis, which would mean launching six aircraft each day. Expensive new facilities were built as Alconbury, including 13 unique wide-span hardened aircraft shelters and a hardened avionics and sensor maintenance facility known as Magic Mountain. The USAF's only hyperbaric chamber in Europe was built for the 17th's Physiological Support Division.

On a typical day, seven or eight training or operational flights would be launched. There were occasional long photo sorties under SAC control codenamed Senior Look, as well as the Creek Spectre missions for EUCOM. The 17th wing grew to more than 500 personnel, and the 95th RS had an authorised strength of 18 pilots. The wing helped develop a new flight planning system running on a minicomputer, which automated much of the drudgery involved in devising flight tracks. It was the most advanced in the USAF.

Final delivery

TR-1A 80-1099, the last of the new-build aircraft, was accepted by the USAF on 3 October 1989 and reassigned to Alconbury six months later. After various changes of plan stemming mainly from the protracted development and ultimate cancellation of PLSS, a total of 37 aircraft was built at Palmdale from 1981 to 1989. They comprised 25 TR-1As, two dual-control TR-1B trainers, two ER-2s for NASA, and the 'black budget' U-2Rs – seven U-2Rs and a single dual-control U-2R (T). Three of the first five TR-1As had already been 'converted' to U-2R configuration.

The USAF professed itself well satisfied with the deal. General Mike Loh, commander of AFSC, declared that "this programme was built on partnership and trust. We kept the auditors and inspectors to the minimum. We knew that Lockheed would keep their side of the bargain, and adhere to the 14 operating rules of the Skunk Works – especially the one about not surprising the customer."

The concept of real-time reconnaissance had received a boost from the TR-1 programme, but the system which evolved in Europe had one important drawback: the aircraft remain 'tethered' to the ground station by the datalink. If a U-2 needed to roam further afield than the 220 miles (355 km) line-of-sight distance to the ground station, the sensor 'take' had to be recorded for relay when the ground station was once more within range. Moreover, political or military circumstances might not always be such that a ground station could actually be deployed.

Data uplink

Back in 1975, Skunk Works engineer Bob Anderson had devised a solution to the problem. Why not install a satellite antenna on the U-2, and uplink the data for transmission back to the US? The US military was then launching its second-generation Defense Systems Communications Satellites (DSCS) with multiple channels. Although satellites were already relaying U-2 data to the US from ground stations in the Senior Stretch programme, it was another 10 years before the USAF adopted Anderson's idea, when it approved the Senior Span development. (Anderson became U-2 programme manager when Fred Cavanaugh retired.)

Lockheed worked with E-Systems and Unisys Government Systems Group (previously named Sperry) to devise the U-2's satcom link. The three contractors had to overcome considerable technical challenges to turn the concept into reality. Unisys had provided the U-2 air-ground datalink, and now provided the buffer into which the aircraft's sensor data could flow and be configured for transmission by an airborne modem. A 30-in (76-cm) parabolic antenna was designed, steerable in both azimuth and elevation at 60° per second and capable of elevation angles up to 85°.

The challenges for the Skunk Works were to build a lightweight composite radome for the antenna and attach it

so that U-2's delicate centre of gravity was not disturbed, nor its inflight vibration increased; to provide a high-voltage power supply; and to interface the aircraft's INS system.

Aerodynamic flight tests of the Span pod began on 80-1071 in 1985. The unpressurised radome was nearly 17 ft (5.2 m) long and the whole system weighed 400 lb (180 kg). It was mounted on the upper fuselage immediately aft of the ADF antenna. Someone outside the fence at Palmdale photographed the secret new configuration from a side-on position at some distance, and sent his snap to *Janes's All The World's Aircraft*, describing it as an AWACS development of the U-2.

The programme moved slowly forward as the considerable problems were overcome, such as the requirement to constantly track the DSCS satellite through the various aircraft manoeuvres. Pointing commands of the Span antenna depended on extremely accurate positioning data being provided by the aircraft's INS (and on the satellite being in the expected location at the expected time).

Operations at Alconbury usually involved at least one mission launch each day to patrol the West/East German border. Regular training missions were also mounted, the aircraft being flown without mission equipment fitted (illustrated).

A U-2R equipped with ASARS, Spear and Ruby lands at NAS Jacksonville. Operational missions launched from the mainland United States have been aimed at Caribbean flashpoints and, especially in the 1980s, Central America.

Lockheed Martin U-2

Moreover, the whole installation had to transmit and receive through a single antenna, since the principle was preserved that the sensors could be reconfigured by ground-based operators who received and analysed the 'take'.

The first deployments with fully-configured Senior Span U-2R 68-10331 were made to Patrick AFB and Suwon AB, South Korea. In March 1989, the first deployment to Europe was made when 80-1070 arrived at Alconbury. Airborne reconnaissance had finally entered the space age.

New electro-optical sensor

When Iraq invaded Kuwait in August 1990, 80-1070 was one of the first two U-2s sent from Beale to Saudi Arabia in response. The second was also in a new configuration. It was equipped with SYERS – the Senior Year Electro-optical Relay System. SYERS had evolved from the new generation of photo reconnaissance satellites in the late 1970s, in which digitised imagery was relayed to ground stations for processing. This was made possible by replacing the traditional 'wet' film exposed by the camera lens with light-sensitive semi-conducting silicon. The silicon was arranged in arrays of charged-coupled devices (CCDs), which transformed the light energy into electrical charges, ready to be amplified and transmitted as a string of numbers.

The SYERS camera was developed for the U-2 in the mid-1980s by Itek, a division of Litton which had dominated large optics for satellite imaging. When the new concept was first presented to Lockheed, Itek assumed that

the new camera would be fitted in the Q-bay, where the U-2's existing film cameras were housed. This would have entailed designing a new Q-bay optical hatch, but Lockheed had other ideas. The company dusted off the old drawings for a rotating nose section, which had been designed to house a sensor for the tracking of re-entry vehicles. This was been one of the earliest proposed applications for the U-2R, but had fallen by the wayside. The Senior Open nose was thus fabricated, with one optical glass aperture in the first 4 ft (1.2 m) of the nose, which was rotated by a servo to 'look' left, right or below the aircraft flight path. The camera's mirror system was housed here, while its body remained fixed within the rest of the nose section.

Specifications for the SYERS camera have not been released, but after it was developed Itek was cleared to market an Electro-Optical LOROP sensor which has a 110-in (280-cm) focal length and uses a 10,240-element CCD array as the detector. This camera is 43 in (110 cm) long and weighs 490 lb (220 kg), with another 90 lb (40 kg) for the control electronics and EO processor. It provides panoramic coverage with high resolution to the horizon.

After flight tests, the first SYERS system was deployed for operational testing at the 9th SRW's Det 2 in Korea, where a hardened ground station had already been established for ASARS operations. The ground portion of SYERS is codenamed Senior Blade, and performs similar functions to the ASARS ground station: control of the sensor, processing, display and reporting of the imagery. As with ASARS, the U-2 can record SYERS imagery onboard when it flies beyond line-of-sight to the ground station.

Desert Shield

The SYERS and Span aircraft touched down at King Fahad Royal Saudi Air Base, Taif on 17 August 1990, just 15 days after the Iraqi invasion. Two days later, both aircraft mounted their first patrols of the Kuwait border, thanks to a minor miracle of logistics. Within two weeks, 160 personnel and aircraft support equipment, including a three-week supply of the U-2's special JPTS fuel, had been airlifted to the Saudi base. The Senior Blade van had been positioned nearer to the Kuwait border at Riyadh, so that the SYERS aircraft would remain 'on-tether' for most of the time.

It was quickly decided to send TR-1s from Alconbury to the new location, which had been designated Operating Location CH (for 'Camel Hump'). Although they had only begun operational testing in March, the TRAC and TADMS mobile ground stations were airlifted from

U-2 sensors

From its lofty perch the U-2 can use a range of sensors depending on mission requirements. The SYERS, H-camera and Iris are all electro-optical sensors for long-range oblique, overhead or panoramic imagery, using either daylight or infra-red. The ASARS-2 radar produces radar images of photographic quality at long oblique ranges. A comprehensive signals intelligence gathering suite can be carried, knwon as Senior Glass. This comprises the Senior Ruby Elint system (distinguished by the flat-sided forward portion of the superpods, and the Senior Spear Comint system with large antenna farm). Data can be downlinked over short distances by the antenna under the rear fuselage, but for global transfer of intelligence the data is uplinked via the Senior Span system (for Senior Glass data) or Senior Spur (for ASARS data).

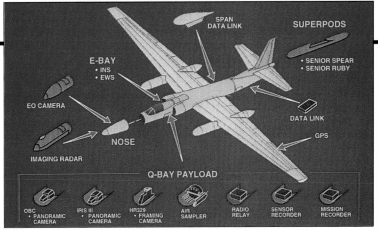

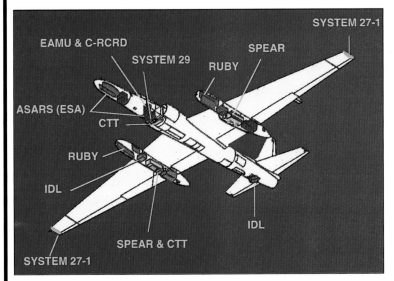

Shown above is a typical mission configuration for an ASARS/Sigint aircraft, with radar recording equipment in the Q-bay. The self-protection electronic suite (Systems 27-1 and 29) is also shown.

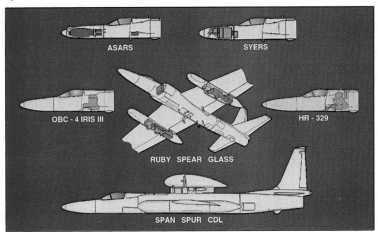

This diagram shows the main sensor-carrying areas of the U-2, with some of the different Q-bay hatches available. There are three different nose options: ASARS, SYERS (EO camera) and the standard 'slick' nose.

Above are the main payload options, comprising ASARS and SYERS, the Iris or H-cameras, Senior Ruby Elint and Senior Spear Comint systems (together known as Senior Glass), and the Senior Span/Spur datalink.

One of the most important sensors carried by the U-2R/S fleet is the Hughes ASARS-2 synthetic aperture radar, which can produce high-resolution imagery at long slant ranges on either side of the flight path. Shown at right is the first production radar being loaded into the purpose-built nose – note the two canted antenna arrays. Shown left is an example of ASARS imagery, depicting the Los Angeles International Airport area. A spot mode is available to provide far greater detail of much smaller areas. ASARS has recently received a major modification to improve its MTI (moving target indicator) capability.

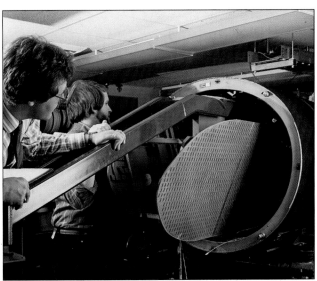

Below is H-camera imagery of another U-2 of the 9th SRW's Det 5 at McCoy AFB in Florida. Note the ground crew in appropriate formation.

The Iris III and OBC cameras provide panoramic coverage across a wide area. This oblique image shows damage after a California earthquake.

From high altitude, images like this false-colour infra-red photograph show the curvature of the earth. Here the target is San Francisco Bay.

When it was first seen by outsiders, the dorsal fairing later identified as Senior Span was thought to house a form of AEW radar. Its true purpose is to uplink data from the Sigint collection systems to satellites, which then relay the data across global distances. This allows commanders and analysts half a world away to receive data in near real-time.

Right: Groaning under the weight of the Senior Span pod and a comprehensive Senior Glass (combination of Spear and Ruby) fit, this U-2R taxis for a mission from Alconbury. Span-equipped aircraft appeared in Europe primarily in response to the crisis in former Yugoslavia.

Germany and set up next to the Blade van in the compound of the US Training Mission (USTM) at Riyadh. (They were joined there by more ground stations for the RC-135 Rivet Joint Elint aircraft and the J-STARS, which led to considerable overcrowding.)

A pair of 17th RW TR-1As arrived on 23 August, and the first ASARS mission was flown six days later. The 17th RW was tasked to support OL-CH by performing phase maintenance on the deployed aircraft, and so a steady shuttle of personnel and aircraft developed between Alconbury and Taif. OL-CH was redesignated the 1704th Reconnaissance Squadron (Provisional) when SAC established the 1700th Strategic Wing (Provisional) alongside CENTCOM's forward-deployed staff at Riyadh. Another SYERS-equipped U-2R was sent from Korea to the desert on 11 October.

By the end of November, the five aircraft at Taif had performed 204 missions, some of them lasting 11 hours. They were flown under normal peacetime rules which required that the flight tracks be no closer than 15 miles (24 km) to the Iraqi border. Even so, from 70,000 ft (21335 m) and above, the SYERS and ASARS sensors could image most of southern Iraq, while the Sigint sensors on the Span aircraft covered most of Iraq, including Baghdad. The usual routine was to fly a SYERS mission every day, an ASARS mission every night, and a Span mission every second day.

Iraq 'painted' the U-2 flights with its air defence radars, and in mid-September began launching MiG-25 fighters in response. They flew along the border, parallel to the U-2 and 5,000 ft (1525 m) below. In response, the System 20 IRCM pod which had not been regularly used on the U-2 for some years was reactivated. A direct voice link to the USAF E-3A AWACS was established for the first time – in Europe, all communications from the U-2 pilot to the outside world were channelled via Metro Tango. F-15 fighters were tasked to fly MiG-CAP in support of the U-2 flights.

Call for photos

CENTCOM commanders liked what they saw from the U-2, but those planning the air war in the 'Black Hole' at Riyadh wanted more, including hard-copy photos. (The ground stations could print ASARS and SYERS imagery, but it was a protracted process.) The call went back to Beale for camera-equipped aircraft and photo-processing vans. The 9th Reconnaissance Technical Squadron (RTS, or 'recce-tech') scrambled to bring the 15-van Mobile Intelligence Processing Element (MIPE) back into service. It had been mothballed when the SR-71 was deactivated. The MIPE deployed to Riyadh in mid-December, and the 9th deployed U-2Rs with IRIS III and H-cameras to Taif in late December and early January.

Taif was also the base for the F-111Fs of the 48th TFW

from RAF Lakenheath. Their pilots and mission planners approached the U-2 squadron directly for target information, trying to short-circuit the system. The solution was to send a 48th pilot to the ground station at Riyadh, where he could view the imagery on-screen and interpret it for his colleagues. In the last week of December, the 'Aardvark'/'Dragon Lady' alliance was cemented when an exercise confirmed the practicality of relaying target information derived from SYERS and ASARS to airborne F-111s, via the TRAC, TACC (Theatre Air Control Center), and ABCCC aircraft. Within 10 minutes of a target being imaged, its co-ordinates were in the TACC's hands.

As the United Nations' deadline for an Iraqi withdrawal approached, CENTCOM made plans to send the U-2 over Iraq if war broke out. A second Senior Blade van was requested, to be deployed closer to the border. The U-2's reconnaissance capabilities, and potential additional roles as an airborne data relay and a 'high-altitude FAC', were explored and explained to CENTCOM planners, most of whom had no knowledge of 'Dragon Lady' operations.

Desert Storm

As soon as there was enough light for SYERS on 17 January, Major Blaine Bachus flew the first U-2R mission across the border. His task was to image the fixed 'Scud' missile sites at H2 and H3 airfields, and to perform bomb damage assessment (BDA) from the initial F-117 attacks. The 'Scuds' were a high-priority target, given their potential for chemical warfare, and they soon became the major priority when Iraq began firing them at Israel.

Mission planners drew up flight tracks which ensured that Bachus and those who followed flew at least 10 miles (16 km) from known SAM sites. The exigencies of war quickly intervened, and many U-2 flights during Desert Storm were retasked when airborne, requiring pilots to replot their own tracks and make critical judgements about whether to fly near or over SAM sites. In fact, the U-2's supposed vulnerability to SAMs was did not prevent the aircraft from providing valuable intelligence about them. Some missions were specifically flown to pinpoint SAMs, such as one flown by Captain Bryan Anderson on 22 January which identified multiple SA-2, SA-3 and AAA sites in western Iraq. Lieutenant Colonel Steve Peterson (the 1704th RS commander) and Major James Milligan both flew missions which were deliberately routed within lethal range of known SAM sites. An estimated 15 fixed 'Scud' sites were identified from U-2/TR-1 imagery and eliminated during the first week of the war. Ten of them

were assessed as destroyed by one strike package which launched on the second day of the war, less than one hour after they were identified by a TR-1 flown deep into northern Iraq flown by Lieutenant Colonel James Burger.

Mobile 'Scud' sites were a more difficult proposition. The U-2 had to go 'off-tether' in order to cover the more distant parts of Iraq, although commissioning of the second Senior Blade van helped increase real-time SYERS processing. There was a time delay while the U-2 returned within range of the ground station to download its imagery. The Iraqis learned to hide their 'Scud' Transporter/Erector/Launchers (TEL) by day, and quickly move into place, fire and withdraw by night. The 'Black Hole' responded by co-ordinating the night-time patrols of a U-2R and an F-15E. When the ASARS sensor located a suspected TEL, the Strike Eagle was primed to destroy it. Several mobile 'Scud' kills were claimed with this technique, but subsequent analysis showed that the 'kills' were of decoys, shorter-range FROG missiles, or ordinary trucks.

Some of this analysis is disputed, and U-2s were certainly responsible for some TEL kills. These include the one that misfired a 'Scud' on the night of 22 February, which detonated just 3 miles (4.8 km) from a TR-1 flown by Captain Mark McDonald. (In fact, U-2 pilots observed most of the 'Scud' launches from their lofty perch.) Undoubtedly, too, the Iraqi mobile 'Scud' crews knew they were being hunted. As a result, their launch rate and accuracy declined significantly.

When Desert Storm was initiated, the 1704th had nine aircraft at Taif, and another three were quickly added. At least five missions were flown each day during the air

Top: A logical outgrowth of the Senior Span programme was Senior Spur. Whereas Span could uplink the data from the Sigint system, Spur provides a similar function for the ASARS-2 radar imagery. Shown here is Lockheed's original test aircraft for the ASARS/Spur configuration.

Above: Operational trials of the Senior Spur equipment were undertaken from Alconbury in 1992 using 68-10339, also equipped with Glass Sigint gear. The modified Skunk Works badge is noteworthy, as is the dielectric portion of the ASARS nose.

Lockheed Martin U-2

U-2Rs have remained at Taif since the end of the Gulf War, monitoring the ceasefire terms and subsequent United Nations Security Council resolutions. The unit, manned from Beale, is known as the 4402nd Reconnaissance Squadron (Provisional), and the aircraft received 'UN' tailcodes.

campaign, rising to eight on some days during the land campaign. Most lasted more than eight hours, and some were voluntarily extended by their pilots to 11 hours when the need arose.

More outfits sent pilots or artillery officers to the U-2 ground stations, from where they could convey exactly what they saw on the screens to their flight crews or gunners. On one occasion, a B-52 bombardier in the TRAC van spotted a likely bomb dump and diverted a B-52 strike inbound from Diego Garcia to hit it, with

spectacular results. Towards the end of the war, U-2 pilots became 'high-altitude FACs' by identifying tanks concentrations and relaying the co-ordinates for attack by allied artillery. On many occasions, U-2 pilots co-ordinated search and rescue attempts for downed pilots.

Assisting the ground war

When the ground forces attacked on 24 February, a TR-1 provided hour-by-hour imagery updates of precise Iraqi front-line armour and troop movements. Coalition troops advanced more quickly than expected, and another TR-1 mission the next day proved invaluable in keeping CENTCOM commanders abreast of the fluid situation, so they could cut off the Iraqi retreat.

The day after the war ended, a U-2 equipped with the IRIS camera flew back and forth across large parts of the battlefield to take a synoptic view of the carnage below. When this film was eventually analysed back in Washington, it indicated that CENTCOM had seriously overestimated the number of Iraqi weapons which had been destroyed in the air campaign. U-2 photography had been used for BDA during the war. With so many 'smart'

Below: A 9th RW U-2R cruises serenely over the California countryside near its base at Beale. On operational missions the engine is run at full power until the descent from altitude. Rated at 18,000 lb (80.10 kN) thrust at sea level, the thrust level falls off as the aircraft climbs into the thinner air at altitude.

Above: Towards the end of the 1980s the J75 engine of the U-2R was becoming increasingly difficult and costly to support, while newer engines were offering greater levels of thrust, performance and economy. Using 80-1090 as a testbed, Lockheed fitted the General Electric F101-GE-F29 engine, the aircraft flying first in 1989. This engine, a non-afterburning derivative of the Northrop B-2's powerplant, was soon redesignated F118-GE-101.

missiles and bombs flying through windows and air vents to destroy buildings, a high-resolution sensor was often needed to confirm a kill. The IRIS and especially the H-camera could do the job, but their 'wet film' take had to be flown from Taif to Riyadh on a C-21 courier aircraft for processing at the MIPE. There, it could take all day just to handle a single IRIS mission with its 10,000 ft (3050 m) of film. It all took too long.

The overall contribution made by the U-2 to Desert Storm was substantial. The 1704th RS flew 260 missions totalling over 2,000 hours, with 80 per cent of this time spent above Iraq or occupied Kuwait. The vast majority of missions took off when scheduled. The U-2 community calculated that they had supplied over 50 per cent of all imagery intelligence and 90 per cent of the Army's targeting intelligence. So much for reconnaissance satellites,

This aircraft is a U-2R in the classic clean-wing, slick-nose configuration. There are only a small number of detailed external differences between the models, including the repositioning of the external start and nitrogen panels to a position higher on the fuselage, and the deletion of the engine bleed air exhausts from the U-2S.

Pilots from the 1704th Reconnaissance Squadron (Provisional) pose in front of a U-2R at Taif. From this Saudi base the five U-2Rs maintained a vigil on Iraq throughout Desert Shield and Desert Storm, and long after. The U-2 was vital to the prosecution of the war, providing much data on Iraqi force dispositions while being used on the 'Great Scud Hunt'. The force remained alert for, but relatively untroubled by Iraqi defences, although aircraft were sometimes tracked by MiG-25s.

Inside the U-2R/S

A feature of the U-2 is the rear-view mirror. This allows the pilot to see if the aircraft is making a contrail, which may give a visual clue to defenders on the ground.

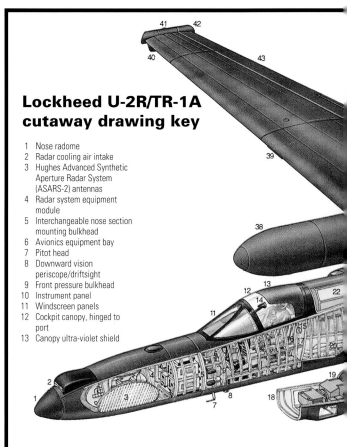

Lockheed U-2R/TR-1A cutaway drawing key

1 Nose radome
2 Radar cooling air intake
3 Hughes Advanced Synthetic Aperture Radar System (ASARS-2) antennas
4 Radar system equipment module
5 Interchangeable nose section mounting bulkhead
6 Avionics equipment bay
7 Pitot head
8 Downward vision periscope/driftsight
9 Front pressure bulkhead
10 Instrument panel
11 Windscreen panels
12 Cockpit canopy, hinged to port
13 Canopy ultra-violet shield

14 Rear view mirror
15 Canopy emergency release
16 Pilot's zero-zero ejection seat
17 Sloping rear pressure bulkhead
18 Photint system
19 Itec panoramic (horizon-to-horizon) optical bar camera
20 Equipment conditioning air ducts

21 Q-bay mission equipment compartment
22 Astro-inertial navigation system equipment package
23 Satellite antenna
24 E-bay avionics equipment compartment
25 Port engine air intake
26 Intake air spill duct
27 Mainwheel doors

28 Twin mainwhe retracting
29 Landing/taxiin
30 Main undercar bay
31 Ventral antenn Senior Spear C
32 Engine bay bul
33 Engine compre
34 Hydraulic pum

U-2R/S cockpit

These two views show the cockpits of the U-2R (above) and U-2S (right), the cockpits of both being dominated by the circular driftsight. The U-2S cockpit differs mainly by having more digital instruments and a multi-function display in place of the autopilot controls to the left of the attitude indicator. The autopilot itself is new.

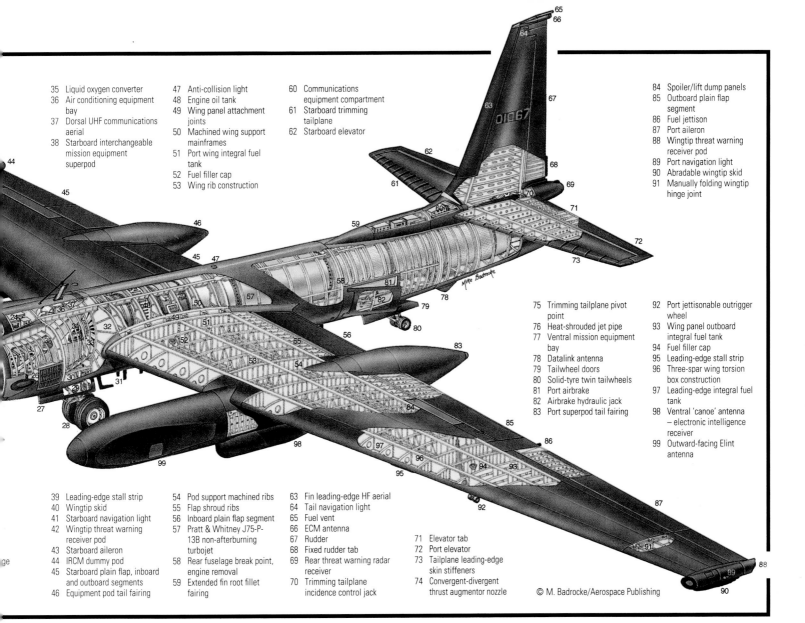

35	Liquid oxygen converter	47	Anti-collision light	60	Communications equipment compartment	
36	Air conditioning equipment bay	48	Engine oil tank	61	Starboard trimming tailplane	
37	Dorsal UHF communications aerial	49	Wing panel attachment joints	62	Starboard elevator	
38	Starboard interchangeable mission equipment superpod	50	Machined wing support mainframes			
		51	Port wing integral fuel tank			
		52	Fuel filler cap			
		53	Wing rib construction			

84	Spoiler/lift dump panels
85	Outboard plain flap segment
86	Fuel jettison
87	Port aileron
88	Wingtip threat warning receiver pod
89	Port navigation light
90	Abradable wingtip skid
91	Manually folding wingtip hinge joint

75	Trimming tailplane pivot point
76	Heat-shrouded jet pipe
77	Ventral mission equipment bay
78	Datalink antenna
79	Tailwheel doors
80	Solid-tyre twin tailwheels
81	Port airbrake
82	Airbrake hydraulic jack
83	Port superpod tail fairing

92	Port jettisonable outrigger wheel
93	Wing panel outboard integral fuel tank
94	Fuel filler cap
95	Leading-edge stall strip
96	Three-spar wing torsion box construction
97	Leading-edge integral fuel tank
98	Ventral 'canoe' antenna – electronic intelligence receiver
99	Outward-facing Elint antenna

39	Leading-edge stall strip	54	Pod support machined ribs	63	Fin leading-edge HF aerial
40	Wingtip skid	55	Flap shroud ribs	64	Tail navigation light
41	Starboard navigation light	56	Inboard plain flap segment	65	Fuel vent
42	Wingtip threat warning receiver pod	57	Pratt & Whitney J75-P-13B non-afterburning turbojet	66	ECM antenna
43	Starboard aileron	58	Rear fuselage break point, engine removal	67	Rudder
44	IRCM dummy pod	59	Extended fin root fillet fairing	68	Fixed rudder tab
45	Starboard plain flap, inboard and outboard segments			69	Rear threat warning radar receiver
46	Equipment pod tail fairing			70	Trimming tailplane incidence control jack

71	Elevator tab
72	Port elevator
73	Tailplane leading-edge skin stiffeners
74	Convergent-divergent thrust augmentor nozzle

© M. Badrocke/Aerospace Publishing

The third incarnation of the U-2R/S cockpit was introduced by the RAMP upgrade, in which virtually the entire cockpit was replaced with new instrumentation. Gone was the circular driftsight which had characterised the U-2's cockpit for so many years, and in came three large colour MFDs (multi-function displays). One is situated centrally in the head-level position, and is the primary display for aircraft flight and navigation information. In this view it is configured with a split screen, the upper portion displaying flight data such as attitude and speed, while the lower half displays bearing and other navigational data. The lower left screen is configured with a map display, while the right-hand screen has engine and aircraft system displays. Again it can be configured with various 'windows', here displaying engine, oil, cabin pressure and fuel information. Data entry for the nav/comms system is accomplished using the data entry panel and small screen above the left-hand MFD.

which were often defeated by haze, smoke or bad weather; when they did take useful images, the product was simply not available to the right people at the right time.

When it was all over, most of the plaudits went to J-STARS, the hugely expensive battlefield radar flown in two converted Boeing 707s, which was still under development. This had a Moving Target Indicator (MTI) as well as a Synthetic Aperture Radar (SAR) mode, with the data also downlinked to ground stations. Partly because the Span and SYERS sensors were still classified, the U-2 remained an unsung hero.

The end of the Cold War eliminated the TR-1's role in Central Europe, yet Desert Storm had proved that there

was no substitute for the U-2. In June 1991 the 17th RW was deactivated, but the USAF kept the squadron structure and five TR-1s at Alconbury. For a while, it seemed that some of the other TR-1s would go into storage, but continuing instability in southern Europe, the Persian Gulf, the Korean Peninsula and elsewhere forced a re-evaluation. Soon, the 'Dragon Lady' was flying over war-torn former Yugoslavia.

Force reorganisation

In October, the TR-1 designation was dropped. In June 1992, the deactivation of Strategic Air Command swept away most of the centralised control and tasking of U-2

operations, and the 9th Wing became part of Air Combat Command (ACC). Theatre commanders no longer had to go through bureaucratic hoops in Washington and Omaha to get a mission flown. The 'lessons learned' from Desert Storm were slowly being applied, as the communications architecture was improved and the U-2 slowly but surely became a reconnaissance system.

More Senior Span uplinks were procured, and the principle of transmitting the 'take' via satellite was extended to ASARS imagery. This was not a simple task, since much larger bandwidths were required. The DSCS satellites were unsuitable, so the system was adapted to use NASA's Tracking and Data Relay Satellite (TDRS) which operates in Ku-band instead of SHF. A prototype of the new Senior Spur system was deployed to Alconbury and Sigonella, Italy for operational testing in 1992-93.

CARS and CDL

On the ground, Metro Tango in Germany had been inactivated, but the equipment which had already been ordered for the TRIGS, and subsequently stored, was reconfigured as a deployable system named Contingency Airborne Reconnaissance System (CARS). The first CARS, consisting of Sigint, SYERS and ASARS modules, was put together at ACC headquarters, Langley AFB in 1992. A new Common Data Link (CDL) replaced the long-serving L51/L52 (AN/UPQ-3A) on the U-2.

The sensors were also improving. Cameras were back in vogue to some extent after Desert Storm, and after receiving rave reviews ("better resolution than the satellites"), the venerable H-camera was given solid-state electronics.

SYERS became a dual-band sensor with the addition of infra-red. Of most significance, perhaps, the USAF finally approved the addition of Moving Target Indicator (MTI) capability to ASARS.

In 1995, the 5.7-litre '95 Chevrolet Camaro began replacing 5.0-litre '87, '88 and '91 Ford Mustangs as the standard chase car. Shown below is the new car next to a line of the Mustangs. The Camaro has a top speed of more than 140 mph (225 km/h) and lightning acceleration, allowing it to catch up with the landing U-2 with ease. According to the pilots, the biggest danger is from spinning out on a wet runway.

This fine overhead view shows the enormous wing of the U-2R. A variant proposed for NASA has wingtip extensions to extract a few more thousand feet in operational altitude. The detachable superpods do little to impair performance, although they required a reconfiguration and reduction in overall area of the trailing-edge flaps. Note the open airbrakes, which can be augmented by overwing spoilers and leading-edge stall strips to help the aircraft descend.

Hughes had received a development contract to adapt the ASARS to show moving as well as fixed targets back in 1988. This entailed adding components to the receiver/exciter and processor control unit in the aircraft, and software changes in the ground station. The development was overshadowed by the J-STARS, which was first and foremost an MTI system, and one which needed large amounts of funding. It was also held up by the Gulf conflict, which interrupted operational tests of an ASARS-MTI prototype by the 17th RW in Europe.

In the ground station, the ASARS MTI shows the speed and location of moving targets in search or spot modes, against either a cartographic or synthetic aperture radar map background. While Grumman loudly proclaimed the virtues of J-STARS, Hughes quietly but firmly insisted that ASARS was "the most advanced reconnaissance radar in the world." The tests were completed in October 1991,

and the ASARS MTI finally went operational in 1995 with the U-2R in Korea.

One of the keys to the success of ASARS on the U-2 has been the navigation data interface. For years, the Litton LN-33 P2/P3 INS was used, updated periodically by the Northrop NAS-21 astro-inertial star-tracker. The advent of the Global Positioning System and its lightweight receivers allowed Lockheed to dispense with the excellent but complicated NAS-21. The GPS receiver was faired into the U-2's left wing trailing edge.

Re-engining programme

Undoubtedly the most significant upgrade to the U-2 this decade has been the re-engining programme. When the last F-106 fighter was retired, the U-2R became the sole remaining user of the P&W J75. The support costs threatened to become unaffordable. Moreover, the weight

Several Northrop T-38As are assigned to the 9th Reconnaissance Wing to provide additional flight hours for the U-2 pilots. The aircraft were first used by the SR-71 fleet, as the landing characteristics of the Talon and 'Sled' were not dissimilar.

Above: The first U-2S deliveries were made to the Air Force in 1994, with the first batch of three aircraft leaving Palmdale together. The batch comprised one single-seater, one two-seater and this aircraft (80-1078). It had entered the Lockheed Martin plant as a single-seater which had been damaged in an accident at Alconbury, and emerged as the fourth two-seater.

Left: The first three U-2S/ST aircraft taxi out to the Palmdale runway for their short redelivery flights back to Beale. All re-engining is expected to be complete by 1998.

80-1071 was the first single-seater to get the F118 engine. The new engine offers far greater operating economy in both fuel and maintenance terms, and provides a boost to altitude or range.

of new sensor and datalink systems were restricting the aircraft's operating performance. (This was history repeating itself; the same problem in the late 1950s had prompted the re-engining of the early U-2s with the J75 in the first place.) Lockheed selected the General Electric F101-GE-F29 turbofan as a potential replacement for the J75. It was a low-bypass ratio (0.8:1) unit with a three-stage low-pressure compressor and a nine-stage high-pressure compressor. It was being developed for the then still-secret B-2 'Stealth Bomber'. Rated at 18,300 lb st (81.4 kN), the GE powerplant offered equivalent thrust for the U-2R, but a significant weight reduction and improved fuel consumption. And it was a good fit.

Once again, the USAF took a long time to approve the idea. A refurbished ground test engine from the B-2 programme was eventually released to the Skunk Works in

Lockheed Martin U-2R
99th Reconnaissance Squadron
9th Reconnaissance Wing
Beale AFB, California

Known by a variety of nicknames, from the mysterious 'Dragon Lady' to the functional 'Deuce', the U-2 has been the USAF's premier high-altitude reconnaissance platform for over 30 years, proving of enormous value in both peacetime and war. Whereas the SR-71 was mainly used on occasional high-value 'snap-shot' forays against key targets, the U-2 (together with the lower-flying RC-135 Rivet Joint) provides the day-to-day continuous surveillance of regions of interest which keeps the US intelligence community in full-time work. Its ability to loiter at high altitude is the strength of the U-2, allowing it to listen in to hours of communications or watch a specific area over a long period with its Elint and radar sensors. In an era of increasing digitisation and electronics, its film-based cameras are still regularly called upon to gain high-resolution pictures in spot or swathe modes. The inherent flexibility of the airframe will allow it to carry many more types of new sensors as they are developed. A new lease of life has been given to the U-2 with the F118 re-engining programme and, despite the growing competition being offered by UAVs (unmanned

air vehicles), funding for the U-2 programme remains a high budgetary priority for the DARO (Defense Aerial Reconnaissance Office) which controls it.

Production of the second-generation U-2 has amounted to 49 aircraft, in two batches. The first batch, funded in FY (Fiscal Year) 68, comprised six aircraft for the CIA and six for the US Air Force. In late 1974, the CIA aircraft were handed over to the USAF.

A requirement for surveillance in the Central European theatre was the spur to reopen the production line with FY 80 money to produce the TR-1A. The chance was taken to also procure three dedicated TR-1B/U-2RT trainers (to replace the first-generation U-2CTs), two special mission ER-2 high-altitude experimental aircraft for NASA, and to produce extra U-2Rs for the 9th SRW, partly to make good attrition and also to expand the fleet. The aircraft was offered to the RAF as a candidate for the ASTOR battlefield radar surveillance requirement system, but the Bombardier Global Express was chosen instead.

Wing structure
The huge wings are manufactured separately and are attached directly to the fuselage either side of the engine installation. Each wing is constructed on a three-spar structure, these being located at 15 per cent, 40 per cent and 65 per cent of the wing chord. Truss and web ribs complete the shape of the wing, apart from the outboard folding section, which has no internal ribbing. The leading edge is completed as a separate assembly and attached to the front spar. Virtually the entire internal volume of the wing inboard of the wing-fold is used for integral fuel carriage, the tanks filling the inter-spar area and forward to the leading edge.

Cockpit
When compared with single-seat fighter cockpits, that of the U-2 appears roomy. However, the wearing on all but low-level training missions of a bulky pressure suit renders the cockpit quite cramped. During high-altitude cruise the pilot can collapse the rudder pedals for extra leg room. The aircraft is sluggish in roll control and a transport-style yoke is provided rather than a stick. The pilot sits on a Lockheed-designed zero-zero ejection seat. Ejection is initiated by pulling a D-ring on the front of the seat, and the sequence includes blowing off the canopy. Survival equipment is fitted in the seat bucket, and includes an emergency oxygen supply, which starts automatically on ejection. The cockpit is pressurised using an automatic schedule by bleed air from the engine compressor, which also supplies the air conditioning system. Ducted air also defogs the windscreen and canopy. The canopy itself (along with hatches for the Q-bay and E-bay, and the nose section break) is sealed using engine bleed air, with a nitrogen bottle backup system. The cockpit also has a food warmer, which heats up food contained in tubes. The tube has a pipe which can be inserted through a pressure seal into the helmet. Drinks are also consumed in this fashion.

Sensor carriage
Compared to the first generation of U-2s, the U-2R introduced a vastly increased sensor payload, although it utilises the same basic airframe locations. The principal locations are the Q-bay, E-bay, nose and superpods. The largest of these is the Q-bay, situated directly behind the cockpit. Fitted with an upper and lower hatch, the bay has a maximum load of 1,300 lb (590 kg) when the nose is empty or 750 lb (340 kg) with nose payloads, and a volume of 64.6 cu ft (1.83 m³). The upper hatch can be opened to provide access, and also for fitting a hoist which can lift heavy equipment into the bay from below. A variety of lower hatches are available, depending on the type of sensors carried. Some systems, notably ASARS-2, require the use of the Q-bay for the carriage of associated electronic equipment and recorders, precluding its use for the carriage of cameras. Behind the Q-bay in the lower fuselage, forward of the mainwheel, is the E-bay, usually used for aircraft electronic components. Some aircraft have been seen with a bulged radome on the E-bay hatch, for additional datalinks. A variety of nose sections are available, including 'slick', tracker camera, ASARS-2 and SYERS. The grossly elongated PLSS nose is no longer used. A special trolley is used to remove the nose easily, the break being located at FS (Fuselage Station) 169. The standard nose section offers 47 cu ft (1.33 m³) of capacity and is 7 ft 2 in (2.18 m) long and 3 ft 1 in (0.94 m) in diameter. The ASARS-2 nose requires additional air cooling, and a small scoop is provided on top. In some configurations the tip-mounted ADF sense antenna is displaced to a bulge on the top of the nose. The nosecone itself is removable at FS 99 to allow access to systems in the extreme tip of the nose. A further 800 lb (363 kg) of equipment can be accommodated in each of the wing superpods, which have now fully replaced the smaller 'slipper' pods used previously. These pods are attached to the underside of the wing with just four bolts, allowing their easy removal for reconfiguring the aircraft or for training sorties. Each pod offers an internal capacity of 83 cu ft (2.35 m³), and measures 23 ft 10 in (7.26 m) in length and 2 ft 8 in (0.81 m) in diameter. The pod itself has a break just forward of the wing leading-edge allowing the fitment of different nose sections (such as that containing the side-facing antennas for the Senior Ruby) system while several overall pod configurations are available, including the Senior Spear pod with a large 'canoe' on the underside of the centre section. Some equipment is held on drop-down racks for easy access. The rear of the pod is also detachable. In addition to these main locations for carrying mission equipment, the underside of the fuselage is used to mount large 'farms' of antennas for the Sigint system.

Roll control and spoilers
The U-2 has narrow-chord ailerons on the outer portions of the wings, running between the fuel dump pipe and the wingtip. Each consists of two sections either side of the wing-fold joint. Both ailerons have inboard tabs, the left-hand tab being electrically adjustable in flight by means of a control on the left-hand console in the cockpit. Control of the ailerons is achieved mechanically by cable and push-rod linkage. The ailerons are hinged from the upper surface of the wing and can travel 16.25° either side of the normal neutral position. At low speeds, where roll control authority is considerably reduced due to the sheer size of the wing, the ailerons are augmented by hydraulically operated, electrically controlled roll-assist spoilers. These are located forward of the outboard flap sections, and are activated by a switch on the aileron actuation system. When the pilot applies bank, say to the right, the left-hand aileron deflects downwards and the right-hand aileron deflects upwards, the angle being governed by the deflection of the control yoke. When the right aileron deflection reaches 13° up the spoiler switch trips, activating the right-hand spoiler. The spoiler normally deploys to full deflection. When the control deflection is eased off, the right-hand aileron returns to its neutral position. As it passes through 13° the spoiler retracts.

As part of the gust alleviation system, the neutral point of the ailerons can be shifted to a 7.5° up position, in concert with a 6.5° upwards deflection of the flaps. This downloads the wing structure during turbulence or at high speeds. The gust alleviation system is controlled from the cockpit, and overrides the flap deployment switching. It increases speed pressure limitations from 180 to 250 kt. Situated inboard of the roll-assist spoilers, straddling the two outer flap sections, are lift-dump spoilers, controlled from the cockpit. These are normally held by springs in the faired position, but can be deployed hydraulically to a 60° deflection setting to dump lift during the landing roll. The springs provide an automatic retraction function of the spoilers in case of hydraulic failure.

Senior Span

Several airframes in the U-2 fleet have been modified to carry the Senior Span pod on a hardpoint on the spine of the aircraft. The pod was first tested on TR-1A 80-1071, the rear half of the pod, together with the lower vertical tail, tailplanes and upper rear fuselage, being covered with wool tufts to visually monitor airflow. Other early aircraft modified for Senior Span carriage include 68-10329, 68-10331, 68-10339, 80-1066, 80-1070 and 80-1095. The pod itself is a simple aerodynamic fairing mounted on top of a long-chord pylon. The pylon holds an upward-facing dish antenna for a satcom link, in turn allowing the transmission of the data on a global scale in near real time. The normal downlink data transfer system has only line-of-sight range. The pod itself has a mid-section break with the front portion of the fairing sliding forward on rails to allow easy access to the satellite antenna for maintenance. The pod support pylon incorporates an airscoop to provide cooling air for the satcom equipment. The pod is almost 17 ft (5.2 m) long, and together with the pylon weighs 401 lb (182 kg). The Senior Span fit is for the transmission of data from the Sigint system only. A similar Senior Spur fit can transmit ASARS-2 radar imagery.

Nav/comms equipment

Standard communications equipment for the U-2R includes an ARC-109 and -164 UHF radios, with built-in KY-58 secure voice equipment. VHF equipment is optional, but a 718U-7 HF set is provided for long-range communications. For navigation the primary aid is the LN-33 inertial navigation system, backed up by the ARN-52 TACAN system. Recently, the U-2R fleet has been fitted with GPS (Global Positioning System) receivers in a fairing on the port wing. An ADF (Automatic Direction Finder) system is fitted which provides long-range direction-finding of transmitted signals, and can be used for voice communications in emergency. An IFF (Identification, Friend or Foe) is fitted. The U-2R has an L-201 autopilot, but this has been replaced by a new digital system in the U-2S. An air computer takes pitot-static data to provide airspeed, climb speed, ambient temperature and altitude information. The air data system is located between the nose section break and the cockpit instrument panel.

Handling characteristics

With its wide-span wings and bicycle undercarriage the U-2 is notoriously tricky to land, although the larger aircraft is much improved compared to the first generation. Even with the overwing spoilers the aircraft lacks roll control authority at low speeds, but an experienced pilot can keep the wings level even when the aircraft is stationary, in a strong enough breeze. This makes the job of fixing the pogos back in much easier for the ground crew. Another peril on landing is weathercocking, caused by the central position of the mainwheel and the tall vertical fin. Crosswind limits are therefore very restricting. At high altitude great care is paid to airspeed, for the limiting Mach number and stall speed converge, giving a band of just a few knots for safe flight.

Sigint configuration

This aircraft is depicted in the full Sigint-gathering fit, consisting of the Senior Ruby Elint system and Senior Spear Comint system. The side-facing antennas for Senior Ruby are housed in the slab-sided front portion of the superpods. These detect and classify radars at long slant ranges. The Senior Spear system is housed in the rear portion of the superpods, with its characteristic lower bulge. The large 'farm' of hook and blade antennas also serves this system, which has been considerably updated and reconfigured since it first appeared in the early 1970s. Gathered data can be datalinked by either the Senior Span system, or by a direct datalink situated under the rear fuselage. This works on line-of-sight, restricting its range. The gathered data can be recorded on board, such equipment usually being located in the Q-bay, but is generally datalinked in near real time for analysis by ground stations.

Fuel

The majority of the high-flashpoint JP-TS (thermally-stable) fuel is housed in integral wing tanks. Each wing has two tanks, the inboard tank housing 1,169 US gal (4425 litres) and the outboard tank accommodating 239 US gal (905 litres). In addition there is a fuselage sump tank (actually four tanks plumbed together) which wraps around the lower portion of the front of the engine. This houses a further 99 US gal (375 litres). The total internal capacity is 2,915 US gal (11034 litres), equating to 18,947 lb (8594 kg). Of this figure all but 35 US gal (132 litres) is usable. Fuel is fed from the wing tanks to the fuselage sump tank and then to the engine. In normal operations the outer wing tanks are drained last. Engine bleed air is used to create a positive pressure in the fuel system to aid feed to the sump tank, and there are two (primary and secondary) pumps to feed the engine. Each wing tank has a pump installed which can be used either for cross-transfer to maintain weight distribution, or to feed fuel into the sump tank as an emergency back-up to the primary feed system. A fuel dump system is installed in the wing tanks, fuel being dumped through pipes below the trailing edge of the wing between the flaps and ailerons. A small airscoop under each wing is used to provide ram air pressure to the tank in order to jettison the fuel through the dump pipe. The fuselage sump tank is vented to the outside via an outlet at the top of the vertical fin and prevents the fuel system overpressuring. For ground defuelling there are valves at the outboard end of the wing tanks so that sediment and water can be drawn off, and a similar valve is located in the bottom of the sump tank. Both the wing fuel feed lines and that from the sump to the engine have emergency shut-off valves.

Defensive systems

A variety of defensive systems has been fitted to the U-2R throughout its career. The most obvious is the System 20 aft-facing infra-red countermeasures sensor installed in a cylindrical fairing on the starboard wing trailing edge, first fitted to CIA aircraft operating out of Taiwan in the early 1970s. This equipment is no longer used, and the cylindrical housing is left empty with the tail end faired over. The early U-2Rs inherited the System 9 (air-to-air) and System 13 (surface-to-air) threat warning and jamming systems, together with the System 12 and OS (Oscar Sierra – colloquially known as 'Oh, Shit!) SAM warners. Today's more sophisticated System 27-1 radar warning installation has two receivers in each pod, facing forwards and backwards at 45° to provide complete coverage. A jammer known as System 29 is also carried, housed in the fairings on the engine intakes and in the E-bay, while System 28 was once carried, with antennas below the fuselage forward of the tail wheel.

Photographic and other configurations

For the photographic role the U-2 can carry four main sensors. The OBC and Iris III are panoramic cameras mounted in the Q-bay, peering through a bulged glazed hatch with three optically flat panes. For high-altitude framing purposes the ultra-high resolution H camera (HR-329) is used, this employing folding optics to create the equivalent of a 66-in (167.6-cm) focal length lens. This camera can be controlled by the pilot, who uses the driftsight to gauge the correct position to cover the objective. The Type H is used primarily in a LOROP (LOng-Range Oblique Photography) mode, and produces images of outstanding quality in the right atmospheric and meteorological conditions. A small T-35 tracker camera is usually carried in the tip of the nose for photographic missions to provide precise positional data. Today the most common optical sensor is the SYERS (Senior Year Extended Range System), which has dual-band (daylight and IR) capability and records digitally (allowing imagery to be datalinked to ground stations). SYERS is mounted in a special rotating nose section with an optically flat window. The camera is a long focal-length unit, and lies lengthways in the nose section, using a 45° prism to peer out through the window. The rotating nose allows the camera to face to any angle, although in practice it is usually pre-positioned. A rarely seen configuration, but one which is still an option, is the air sampling kit, which is carried in the Q-bay. The special hatch mounts a sampling tube while the Q-bay houses the recovery and storage equipment.

Lockheed Martin U-2

What had once been a wing of aircraft at Alconbury rapidly eroded to become a detachment of the 9th RW. In 1994 the OL-UK (Operating Location – United Kingdom) moved to RAF Fairford, from where its aircraft continued to monitor the war in former Yugoslavia. This aircraft is unusually configured with an ASARS-2 nose and an optical Q-bay hatch. As the ASARS radar requires some equipment to be installed in the Q-bay, this aircraft must be in a photo fit, with the non-operational ASARS nose left on from a previous mission.

1988. It was fitted to 80-1090, and made its first flight with Lockheed test pilot Ken Weir at the controls on 23 May 1989. This was four months before the B-2 first flew, incidentally. Over the next 15 months, 82 flight hours were logged. Initial flights were limited to engine-out gliding distance of Edwards AFB, because, unlike the J75 turbojet, the new turbofan could not be restarted inflight by windmilling. An emergency air-start system was then added, comprising compressed air and jet fuel which was ignited in a two-stage compressor. This was heavy, so when the re-engining programme did get the green light a hydrazine system capable of spooling up the engine to 45 per cent core rpm was developed.

Further engine trials

Before the pre-production flight tests started in late 1991, the GE powerplant was redesignated F118-GE-101, and the re-engined aircraft was designated U-2S. A host of evaluations was addressed in the next 38 flights, including some distinctly U-2-specific investigations, e.g., whether vibrations from this different engine would affect sensor or INS performance, and whether the ninth stage air bleed which provides the pilot's pressure suit cooling was satisfactory.

The flight test results showed a weight saving of 1,300 lb (590 kg) and a fuel saving of 16 per cent compared with the J75. These translate into a maximum altitude increase of 3,500 ft (1065 m), an increased payload, a 1,220-nm (1,400-mile; 2260-km) increase in range, or increased time on station. Other benefits include increased reliability and maintainability, an improved centre of gravity, and a digital engine control which provides linear thrust with stall-free operation throughout the flight envelope. Those famous U-2 flame-out incidents should now become rare events.

The first production U-2S conversion was 80-1071, flown again with the F118 on 12 August 1994. On 28 October a delivery ceremony was held at Palmdale, when the first three conversions were handed back to the USAF. (The others were two-seaters 80-1064 and 80-1078. The latter was built as a single-seater, but was damaged in a landing accident at Alconbury and rebuilt as a trainer.)

Fleet standardisation

The entire fleet is being converted as major overhaul becomes due – every 3,400 hours or five years. The last aircraft will be re-engined in 1998. At the same time, wiring and mounting provisions are being standardised, so that each aircraft can carry the entire inventory of sensors. Depot maintenance of the U-2R has always been performed by Lockheed at Palmdale Site 2, and the unique relationship between contractor and customer extends to the field, since the Skunk Works is responsible for line maintenance at some of the overseas detachments (and also at NASA Ames).

After a year or so of operations from Fairford, an otherwise successful deployment marred by a fatal crash, OL-UK became OL-FR when the U-2s moved to Istres in France. This significantly reduced the transit time to the operational area from where surveillance of Bosnia and surrounding nations was undertaken.

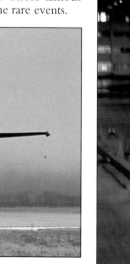

Four of the original 12 U-2R models produced in 1967-68 are still in service. Like the U-2A/H series before them, they have outlived their reputation as supposedly fragile, short-lived aircraft. In fact, the fatigue life of the U-2R was originally envisioned as 20,000 hours, but in August 1994 68-10338 became the first aircraft to pass that milestone with no problems. A new limit of 30,000 hours was set. Unfortunately, 68-10330 was destroyed in the tragic accident at RAF Fairford in August 1995, during an attempt to release a pogo which had 'hung up' on take-off.

Diverted funds

The accident was a blow to the programme, since the USAF lost the pilot, the aircraft and one of the Span systems. Such sophisticated equipment is expensive, of course, and the U-2's collection systems have been under-funded in recent years, according to some intelligence community insiders. U-2 money has been diverted to fund the accelerated development of new Unmanned Aerial Vehicles (UAVs), which it is claimed are capable of performing the U-2's mission, but a debate has raged over their utility, maturity and total cost. Observers with long memories can recall the same debate over the relative merits of Compass Cope and the U-2 in the mid-1970s.

"The performance parameters published for the UAVs and their sensors to date do not approach what the U-2

already has in many cases," notes Garfield Thomas, vice-president for reconnaissance systems at the Skunk Works. "Weather avoidance, flexibility, ground support systems and logistics support have not received a great deal of attention from the UAV proponents to date, and when they are honestly included in the trade studies, the result may shock some people."

Thomas says that the only thing the U-2 cannot do today is penetrate heavily-defended territory. "A very stealthy asset is needed to do that," he says. Lockheed is

Above and left: Much use has been made of the Senior Span equipment over Bosnia, allied to the Spear and Ruby Sigint collection system. In 1996, the Rapid Targeting System (RTS) was deployed to the theatre. Known as Gold Strike, this system relays ASARS imagery from the U-2 to a ground station at Rimini, where it is then processed and uplinked by the MOBSTR (Mobile Stretch) system back to a ground station at Beale. There the imagery is analysed and annotated before being transmitted back to the theatre, and then into the cockpits of fighter aircraft. This provides a recognition aid during the attack run for positive target identification.

The U-2Rs of OL-FR operate from a giant hangar at Istres, which provides ample comfortable accommodation. The use of Istres is not without its problems for the strong mistral wind often poses crosswind problems for the delicate U-2s.

developing the Tier 3-minus drone for this purpose, but the programme has been delayed by the crash of the prototype on its second flight.

Meanwhile, the U-2 is as busy as ever. The 9th RW is hard pushed to support the deployments, and its people undertake TDYs far beyond the call of duty. The aircraft has operated continuously out of Korea and Cyprus for more than 20 years. Unfortunately, five U-2s have been lost in accidents during the last five years, reducing the fleet to 30 operational U-2Rs, plus four trainers and the three NASA ER-2s.

Monitoring Iraq and Bosnia

U-2 flights over Iraq continue from Taif, under United Nations auspices. Using the IRIS and H-camera systems, over 300 flights since August 1991, codenamed Olive Branch, have been instrumental in identifying the weapons of mass destruction that Iraq has been hiding. The imagery is routinely used by UN officials to plan inspections, and has sometimes provided 'smoking-gun' evidence of Iraqi non-compliance with its obligations. The Iraqis do not like it, of course, and their foreign minister complained in March 1996 about the "material and psychological damage caused by the violations of its airspace by this aircraft."

At least two other U-2s have been kept in Saudi Arabia since the Gulf conflict, providing intelligence support to coalition forces. Part of the CARS-1 ground station is deployed there from Langley.

Most attention in recent years has been focused on Bosnia. On nine-hour round trips from Alconbury, the 95th RS and its successor, OL-UK, used aircraft configured

for either ASARS, Span or camera missions. When Alconbury closed, the three aircraft were moved temporarily to Fairford. In December 1995 they were moved again to Istres, France which offers a shorter transit time to the area of interest. Most of the 'take' from the Bosnia flights is processed and first analysed in the US. A new trailer-based satcom system nicknamed Mobile Stretch and located at Rimini, Italy compresses ASARS radar and other data downlinked from the U-2. It is then transmitted to the lower-bandwidth DSCS satellites and transferred to Beale AFB. A second CARS ground station was set up there in 1994-95, and can operate exactly as it would do if deployed in the field. The two-way link is maintained so that, for instance, if the Sigint sensors pick up a radar, the same U-2 could be tasked to image the location and determine if missiles are present.

The advantage is that all the ground personnel can stay at home, and the logistics burden for a U-2 deployment is much reduced. The complete CARS configuration would need seven C-5 transports to deploy, although the ground station modules are getting smaller all the time. An enhanced version of the TRAC now being manufactured for the US Army by Westinghouse can be carried in two C-130s and set up to receive the ASARS downlink in 90 minutes.

New system for NASA

The NASA operation also now benefits from 'electronic co-location'. The prototype Senior Spur system was transferred to NASA last year and has been adapted for use on one of the ER-2s as STARLink. Data from various experiments can be transmitted in near-real time via TDRS and domestic satellites to NASA's Payload Operations Control Center, and can even be further distributed via the Internet. Scientists can control their experiments inflight, and no longer need to accompany the ER-2 to remote airfields in Chile, Norway or the Australian outback.

NASA developments

In 1996 the USAF reclaimed 80-1069, the U-2R which had been loaned to NASA nine years earlier. The remaining pair received the new GE F118 powerplant, although their designation remained ER-2. The military also subsequently reclaimed the STARLink system.

NASA's Airborne Science programme moved to the Dryden Flight Research Center at Edwards AFB in 1997. From here, the ER-2s were as busy as ever, with experiments related to Earth resources, celestial observations, atmospheric chemistry and dynamics, oceanic processes, satellite calibration and data validation, and so on. By now, NASA's ER-2s and predecessor U-2Cs had flown over 4,000 missions. Some experiments were co-ordinated with NASA's DC-8, such as the 1998 deployment to Patrick AFB, Florida, when an ER-2 flew over Hurricane Bonnie at 65,000 ft (19812 m) while the DC-8 flew into the storm.

The most-flown ER-2 sensor was now the AVIRIS hyper-spectral scanner, but data derived from the wet-film RC-10 camera was still in demand. A modified multi-spectral scanner built by Daedalus Enterprises and NASA – the MODIS (Moderate Resolution Imaging Spectrometer) – was also added to the ER-2's repertoire. This records 50 channels of 16-bit data in the visible, near infrared, mid-infrared and thermal portions of the spectrum.

Back in 1987, measurements from an ER-2 deployed to Punta Arenas in southern Chile had confirmed the extent of ozone layer depletion over the South Pole. Monitoring of this serious phenomenon at both Poles had since become a key task for the aircraft. In early January 2000, NASA 809

deployed with the DC-8 to very cold, very dark Kiruna, Sweden, for more ozone layer research inside the Arctic Circle. The SOLVE (SAGE III Ozone Loss and Validation Experiment) campaign would require flights to the North Pole and, uniquely, the first flight by a U-2-type aircraft over Russia since the downing of Gary Powers 40 years earlier.

NASA pilot Dee Porter flew the first mission to the North Pole in total darkness. For navigation in this hostile

Above: Once one of the many rare jewels in the crown of Strategic Air Command, the U-2 is now firmly integrated into wider USAF operations. The 'Deuce' still retains much of the mystique which has surrounded the U-2 since its earliest days.

Right: One of the 9th RW's four 'two-headers' taxis for a training mission from Beale. It was originally built as a TR-1B, but was then redesignated U-2RT. After re-engining with the F118 engine it became a U-2ST and, following another rationalisation of fleet designations, became a TU-2S.

Left: The end of the 1991 Gulf War did not signal the end of U-2 operations over Iraq. The Taif detachment became the 4402nd RS(P), and continued to fly over Iraq to monitor compliance with UN resolutions. Here a U-2R returns to its desert base after one such Olive Branch mission in December 1993. Monitoring overflights of Iraq continued until 1998, resuming again in February 2003 just days before the US and UK launched Operation Iraqi Freedom. Having moved to Al Kharj in 1997, the U-2 detachment maintained a watch on Iraq from safe airspace throughout the break in UN overflights, becoming the 363rd Expeditionary Reconnaissance Squadron.

Six aircraft and the personnel of OL-FR pose for a group photo in 1997, as the last U-2Rs were replaced by the U-2S. At the time the Istres-based detachment was busy covering events in former Yugoslavia. Two years later the detachment had become the 99th Expeditionary Reconnaissance Squadron, and was fully employed in providing quality targeting imagery and electronic data for attack aircraft in Operation Allied Force. Wartime missions were flown from Aviano AB, or later NAS Sigonella, in Italy, which the U-2s were using as 'bolt-holes' while the Istres runway was under repair.

environment, a backup GPS/INS system named PARS – Platform Attitude Heading Reference – was added to the ER-2, supplementing the primary one which integrates GPS with the Litton LTN-92 INS. Porter was able to maintain communication with Kiruna via the commercial Iridium system, using blade antennas on the ER-2.

Porter also flew the first mission into Russia, on 27 January – a six-hour straight line southeast past Moscow to a point near the Ukraine border, and back. Russian scientists helped gain the necessary approvals, but Porter had to enter at strictly-defined waypoints. Some 17 different experiments were performed during the flight. A second, eight-hour flight on 5 February was more complicated, involving an outbound leg to Spitsbergen before turning to cross the Barents Sea and fly over northern Russia. A team of 250 scientists on the ground at Kiruna was devising new flight paths throughout the deployment, since the ozone-depletion vortex is dynamic, moving south to east. In a second series of flights during March 2000, NASA pilot Jan Nystrom also flew into Russia.

Iraqi threats

In September 1996, the southern 'No-fly' zone over Iraq, which had been established by coalition forces after the Gulf War, was extended to the 33rd parallel. Iraq objected, of course, and its air defence system stepped up harassment of US and British fighters. Despite sanctions, Iraq had managed to rebuild and refine its air defence system, including SA-2/3/6/8 SAMs and fibre-optic links between radar sites and control rooms. In Operation Desert Strike, the US launched cruise missiles against SAM sites and command bunkers.

U-2s flying from Taif were operating in the zone, helping to identify Iraqi air defence developments. They were protected by co-ordinating the sorties with RC-135 Rivet Joint aircraft, which could broadcast threats detected by their wider frequency-range ELINT and COMINT sensors. U-2s were also flying north of the zone, including over Baghdad itself, on the separate Olive Branch missions for the UNSCOM. By early 1996, some 280 such missions had been flown, each one notified to the Iraqis two days in advance in respect of entry and exit points, but not the course to be flown once inside the country. The imagery from these flights helped the UNSCOM inspectors track movements of banned weapons from suspected sites.

However, as tensions mounted over the increasingly intrusive inspections, the Iraqi regime stepped up its objections to the U-2 flights. This culminated in overt threats to shoot them down in late October 1997. During that same month, the U-2s moved to join the rest of US airpower in Saudi Arabia at Al Kharj near Riyadh, also known as Prince Sultan Air Base (PSAB). There, they eventually became part of the 363rd Expeditionary Air Wing, as the 363rd Expeditionary Reconnaissance Squadron. Despite Iraq's objections, the Olive Branch flights continued at an average weekly interval, until Iraq stopped co-operating at all with UNSCOM in August 1998. Operation Desert Fox, a four-day bombing campaign, followed in December 1998.

Operation Allied Force

Meanwhile, the tragedy of the Balkans continued to play out, and the U-2 continued to observe. In 1998, Serb paramilitary forces stepped up a campaign of repression in the semi-autonomous Yugoslav province of Kosovo. NATO countries pressured President Milosevic into accepting photo-reconnaissance flights over the province. The first U-2 mission was flown on 16 October by the 99th ERS, temporarily based at Aviano while the runway was resurfaced at Istres, France.

But the situation on the ground deteriorated, and on 24 March 1999, NATO launched Operation Allied Force to evict Serb forces from Kosovo. During the 78-day campaign, the 99th ERS flew 189 missions and provided over 1,300 hours of collection time. By flying out of NAS Sigonella, Italy, instead of Istres, the U-2s were closer to the action and could therefore increase their time-on-station within a standard nine-hour mission. With cloud covering the region often, and with much mountainous territory to be covered, images from the high-flying U-2's ASARS radar sensor proved vital in identifying targets.

While Predator UAVs and JSTARS grabbed most of the publicity, "the U-2 was the backbone of our ISR architecture," noted USAFE's Director of Operations, Major General William Hobbins, when Operation Allied Force was all over. "We never dropped a bomb on a target without having the U-2 take a look at it," he continued. Although Serbian air defences were never completely eliminated, 39 radars and 28 aircraft were destroyed after being identified by U-2 missions. Moreover, this conflict demonstrated a significant closing of the 'sensor-to-shooter' cycle, which had become a key aim in US air combat doctrine.

From the mid-1990s, Beale-based U-2s and other US reconnaissance platforms had participated in various exercises to develop the Rapid Targeting System (RTS) and Real-Time Information to the Cockpit (RTIC). By using powerful computer hardware and software, imagery and SIGINT data from multiple sources, including satellites, was matched or 'fused' to provide target locations with enough accuracy for precision attack. Selected imagery frames were annotated and transmitted via JTIDS links from the ground to an E-3 AWACS and on to an F-15E, allowing the data to cue the Strike Eagle's APG-70 radar.

During the Kosovo conflict, the U-2 provided 66 RTS packages to strike aircraft. Moreover, because it could carry SIGINT as well as imaging sensors, the U-2 proved to be a 'one-stop shop' for providing the targeting data. On one U-2 mission, the Senior Ruby ELINT sensor operator, housed thousands of miles away in the ground station at Beale AFB, detected a mobile SA-6 SAM radar. He quickly took another direction-finding 'cut', and passed the information to his colleagues nearby who were controlling the ASARS sensor. The U-2 pilot was ordered to reverse track, so that imagery could be obtained. This imagery was then passed to the CAOC in Vicenza, Italy, and from there to an F-15E which struck the radar. Total elapsed time was 42 minutes.

After the Serbs were evicted from Kosovo, the U-2 continued to monitor the Balkans from Sigonella. In June 2000, the 1000th Sentinel Torch mission was flown. Each one of them had involved the relay of sensor data all the way back to Beale for interpretation by DGS-2 (Deployable Ground Station-2).

Collier Trophy award

The U-2 has been breaking records ever since it first flew in 1955 – but mostly in secret. In late 1998, Lockheed Martin, the USAF and NASA decided to demonstrate that the aircraft was still very much alive and, indeed, rejuvenat-

ed with the new F118 engine. Unfortunately, the USAF would not agree to declassify the maximum altitude, so the three new payload-to-altitude world records set in November and December 1998 were still not a true reflection of the aircraft's performance. Still, they helped the U-2 win the 1998 Collier Trophy – the top aeronautical award in the US. At a time when the U-2 programme was still fighting for development funds against a new generation of UAVs, the publicity was useful.

In fact, although some USAF leaders had fallen in love with the Global Hawk and now described the U-2 as "a sunset system", support for new U-2 funding initiatives was growing where it really mattered. The users in CENTCOM, EUCOM and PACOM were not willing to forego the U-2's proven performance for projections of future UAV performance. The purse-holders in Congress took a similar view. By the end of the 1990s, two major upgrades to the airframe had been approved, as well as significant improvements to the U-2's three most important sensor systems.

Power-EMI upgrade

To take advantage of the increased electrical generating capability of the F118, a new 'power distribution backbone' was designed. Using new copper wiring and the latest fibre-optic cables, the new system replaced bundles of old wiring which had been dedicated to specific sensors. This saved some weight, and made it much easier to swap sensors on the airframe. The total generator power was

Above: 80-1067 is a test aircraft permanently assigned to the Warner-Robins Air Logistics Center flight test detachment at Palmdale. It wears a red Skunk Works badge on the fin. Here it is seen fitted with the ETP/Senior Spur pod. The flight test team also has another U-2 assigned – 68-10336.

Left: Another view of 80-1067 on the Palmdale ramp shows it fitted with a non-standard satcoms-type antenna on the spine. It is also fitted with an instrumented boom in the port superpod for accurate air data measurements.

increased to 45 kVA, of which about 36 kVA was available to the sensors. Moreover, electro-magnetic interference (EMI) from the aircraft's power system was much reduced through better shielding and grounding. This was of particular value to the U-2's SIGINT systems, which could now 'listen' from a much quieter airborne environment.

In a six-year effort costing $140 million, the Power-EMI upgrade would be performed as each U-2 entered depot maintenance at Palmdale. At the same time, two other improvements would be incorporated: a new single-piece windscreen with a better anti-icing system, and replacement of the wing-mounted Trimble GPS with the USAF's standard Garmin model, in a new installation behind the Q-bay. The resulting aircraft would be designated U-2S Block 10 (the original re-engined U-2S was now retrospectively designated Block 0). Conversions began in 2000, as 80-1078 and 80-1095 entered depot maintenance. The first deployment took place in September 2002, to the 5th RS in Korea.

To coincide with the Block 10 deployment, upgrades to all three U-2 sensor systems were planned. Relatively little money had been spent on the U-2's SIGINT systems during the 1990s, partly because they were supposed to be replaced by the Joint SIGINT Avionics Family (JSAF), a common ELINT and COMINT system for the RC-135, EP-3 and U-2. But JSAF proved technically difficult, and was all but abandoned by 2001. Meanwhile, black boxes were proliferating on the U-2, and the systems could not easily be adapted to new threat frequencies. Moreover, complications such as that found in the Iraqi air defence system, where Soviet missiles were netted to French and Chinese radars, could defeat the automated detection tech-

niques used by the U-2's Senior Ruby ELINT sensor.

Raytheon did some work to rationalise the Spear (RS-6B) and Ruby (RA-1/2) systems, and added fibre-optic links between the superpods, resulting in a configuration designated Remote Avionics System 1 (RAS-1), or Senior Glass. With adaptation to the satellite uplink and the addition of some digital receivers, the designation became RAS-1A. In the late 1990s a major reconfiguration with circuit cards and RF converters produced a more flexible system which could be reprogrammed remotely through software. This was designated RAS-1R.

Improved imaging

Ever since it was introduced in the early 1980s, ASARS-2 has been the leading radar reconnaissance sensor in the US inventory. Subsequent refinements included electronic scanning of the antenna (in azimuth) and the addition of a Moving Target Indicator (MTI) mode, although only enough MTI upgrades were purchased to equip the three aircraft which patrol the North Korean border from the 5th RS base at Osan.

In June 1996, work began on the ASARS-2 Improvement Program, or AIP. Using commercially-available hardware, Hughes (subsequently Raytheon) replaced the Receiver/Exciter and Controller boxes with a combined REC, and added an onboard processor for the first time (in the Q-bay). A new Asynchronous Transfer Mode (ATM) connected the radar boxes to each other and to the datalink. The pay-off is dramatic improvements in both resolution and coverage. Three-foot (1-m) resolution is now achieved in the best search mode (versus 10-ft/3-m previously), and 1-ft (0.3-m) resolution is possible in 'spot' mode. The area covered by these modes is increased by 1500 percent and 900 percent, respectively, yet thanks to the powerful new onboard processor, radar data can be produced as quickly. The improved geolocation accuracy makes precision targeting much easier. The range of ASARS is still classified, but possibly in excess of 200 miles (320 km). Flight tests of the upgraded radar were completed in late 1998, and the first AIP sensor was delivered in September 2000. This time, MTI modes will be included in all the systems.

If ASARS/AIP is the Rolls-Royce of radar systems, then SYERS-2 must be the Cadillac of cameras. SYERS was originally a dual-band system, offering visible and infrared modes and very long range, thanks to the big telescope housed in the U-2's nose. Five of them were built by Itek, which was subsequently sold to Hughes, itself later bought by Raytheon. They produced excellent imagery in good weather, but frequent cloud cover and haze over Europe and the Korean peninsula restricted the number of days on which SYERS could usefully be used there, especially if it meant replacing the ASARS.

Thought was given to redesigning SYERS so that it could fit in the Q-bay, thereby leaving the U-2 nose free for ASARS carriage, and allowing both sensors to be carried on the same mission, but there was not enough room. Instead, funding was approved for a multi-spectral upgrade, which has added five new collection wavebands, making seven (three visible, two short-wave IR and two medium-wave IR). The use of colour in the visible bands should improve the identification of targets, while short-wave IR will cut through haze and medium-wave IR will improve night-time resolution. The combination of bands will help defeat the increasingly sophisticated camouflage and concealment techniques which are out there. As with ASARS, the upgrade also offers much greater area coverage, and improved geolocation. (SYERS is now owned and supported by Goodrich, which bought Raytheon's 'high-end' EO systems business in 2001).

In order to cope with the increased data produced by these improved imaging sensors, the U-2's line-of-sight link to the MOBSTR relay station was upgraded to a capacity of nearly 300 mb/sec, and redesignated as the Interoperable Airborne Data Link II (IADL-II). A second line-of-sight system can also be carried, for communication with mobile imagery exploitation systems in the field (the Dual Data Link or DDL).

Is there any role left for traditional, wet-film cameras? Hardly, it seems. They do not provide timely data in today's fast-paced military scenarios, and the chemicals required for processing cannot so easily be disposed of under modern environmental legislation. The U-2's excellent Optical Bar Camera (OBC), a 30-in (76.2-cm) lens panoramic system, is being retained for the moment, but another panoramic camera and two framing camera systems were placed in storage as the new decade began. These were, respectively, the IRIS III, the very-high-resolution H-camera and the broad-coverage F489 for mapping. Also, the 35-mm tracker camera, which had once been used to establish 'ground truth' for both operational and training

sorties, was retired because student navigation training sorties could now be evaluated from a GPS readout.

Glass Dragon

As the high-tech sensor upgrades proceeded, the contrast with the profoundly low-tech U-2 cockpit became acute. Apart from sensor control panels, very little had changed since the U-2R first flew in 1967, and the difficulty of sourcing spares for those old-fashioned instruments was growing. In October 1998, therefore, Lockheed Martin

Above: 80-1082 cruises over the Lockheed Martin Skunk Works plant at Palmdale. The majority of U-2 upgrade work is performed here, in the facility where the U-2 line was reopened to produce the FY80 batch.

Above: The RAMP cockpit upgrade was first applied to 68-10336, a permanent test aircraft which acted as prototype. The first 'production' conversion was 80-1082, which was handed over to the Air Force in a ceremony at Palmdale in April 2002.

Left: In common with other USAF types, a block system has been introduced for the U-2S to differentiate between various upgrade states. RAMP aircraft are now known as U-2S Block 20, whereas aircraft which retain the 'legacy' cockpit are either Block 0 (basic) or Block 10 (with the Power-EMI upgrade). A Block 30 upgrade, with better EW defences, is now being defined.

was awarded a $93 million contract for the U-2 Reconnaissance Avionics Maintainability Program (RAMP) – a new 'glass cockpit'. Three 6 x 8-in (15.2 x 20.3-cm) flat-panel multi-function displays (MFDs) would dominate the new layout, plus an upfront display and control panel which would conveniently group all the vital switches together (in the old cockpit, vital controls such as radio and navigation were housed in awkward-to-reach locations in the lower side panels).

The new system would use a standard MIL1553B data-bus: a new main avionics processor would convert analogue signals from the airframe to digital. Although off-the-shelf hardware was used (the MFDs came from the C-130J upgrade, for instance), everything had to be adapted to the rigours of high-altitude flight. The touch controls were spaced so that a pilot wearing the bulky gloves of the pressure suit could easily operate them. Operational pilots from the 9th RW made significant inputs to the design of both hardware and software for the RAMP.

The result was much-improved situational awareness. Information which pilots of other aircraft took for granted was now available to U-2 drivers for the first time: ground speed and wind vector were now displayed throughout the flight; the fuel panel accurately reflected the actual system layout; flight plan tracks and waypoints could be displayed on the moving map. An angle-of-attack indicator with aural as well as visual warnings was another first – useful for those final few feet before landing on the bicycle gear, when the Dragon Lady must be persuaded to quit flying by touching down close to the stall speed.

The new cockpit design retained the familiar large control yoke, and the sunshade, and even the rear-view mirror, but another unique U-2 feature was missing. There was no room for the bulky, hooded driftsight display which used to dominate the main panel. Generations of U-2 drivers had scanned the driftsight optics to answer such vital questions as: Are there fighters below me? Am I contrailing? Is the landing gear really down and locked? Goodrich provided a small electro-optic camera which could fit in the driftsight bubble below the fuselage, with its images displayed on one of the MFDs. This neat solution has yet to be funded for production, however.

68-10336, one of two aircraft permanently assigned to U-2 Flight Test at Beale, was the RAMP prototype. The first flight was in December 2000. 80-1082 was the first production modification, and was redelivered to Beale in April 2002. The RAMP aircraft are designated U-2S Block 20.

Operation Enduring Freedom

None of the aforementioned upgrades had reached the field, however, when the U-2's next call to action came.

Less than one month after the 9-11 outrage in 2001, they were flying over Afghanistan on Operation Enduring Freedom (OEF). This time, the missions were flown from Al Dhafra air base near Abu Dhabi in the UAE, after Saudi Arabia refused the use of its bases for OEF. The two aircraft assigned to the 363rd ERS remained at PSAB, while additional U-2s were flown from the new base. This operation was designated the 9th ERS, alternatively known as Det 4. Ironically, the hangar at Al Dhafra was shared with the Global Hawk UAV, which was making its first operational deployment.

Although the new base was closer to Afghanistan, the geography of the new conflict meant that data from the U-2's sensors could not first be downlinked to a ground station (eg MOBSTR) before relay to the US by satellite for processing and analysis. Instead, the U-2 had to operate 'off-tether', using its own satellite relay system. Fortunately, after a period in the 1990s when such systems were underfunded, new versions had been procured from L-3 Communications. The original Senior Span had limited bandwidth and proved suitable only for the relay of SIGINT. Now, though, four Senior Spur systems were in service. They provided a full bandwidth link to a classified US satellite architecture, so that ASARS or SYERS imagery could be transmitted across continents. Spur is now referred to as the Extended Tether Program (ETP). An additional five ETPs are being procured.

The OEF commitment once again stretched U-2 resources to their limit: pilots, maintainers, airframes, sensors. In late 2001, the operation at Sigonella was closed in favour of consolidation with the detachment at Akrotiri, Cyprus. This RAF base has housed U-2s ever since 1974; it is now the home of the three aircraft 'belonging' to the 99th ERS, plus a maintenance operation staffed by Lockheed Martin. Here, aircraft can be inspected every 400 hours as required, without ferrying back to the US. (The periodic depot maintenance is every 3,400 hours, and is performed by Lockheed Martin at Site 2, Palmdale).

Operation Iraqi Freedom

On 17 February 2003, U-2 flights over Iraq in support of United Nations weapons inspections resumed. But the flights were short-lived, since the US – supported by the UK – lost patience with the weapons inspection process and launched Operation Iraqi Freedom less than a month later. Once again, U-2s played a vital – if unheralded – part in providing the ISR picture. No fewer than 10 aircraft were deployed to Det 4 at Al Dhafra and, surprisingly enough, the Saudis permitted the two aircraft at PSAB to participate in OIF. The three aircraft at Akrotiri were also involved. As a result, the 15 U-2s were able to provide constant coverage of Iraq, with as many as three aircraft on-task at one time. The value of a manned, high-flying aircraft for battlefield communications relay was demonstrated frequently: U-2 pilots were able to co-ordinate the rescue of seven US Army prisoners-of-war; the search for a pilot of a downed F-14; and the fire support of Special Forces which had been cornered by Iraqi forces.

At the end of this conflict the US announced that it would be withdrawing all aircraft from Saudi Arabia. Consequently, the 363rd ERS at PSAB was closed down in early May. Det 4 at Al Dhafra was expected to remain open, with about four aircraft.

Looking to the future

In 2001, the USAF announced that the 9th RW would operate the Global Hawk UAVs, which had just been approved for low-rate production. A new squadron (the 12th RS) is forming alongside the U-2 units. Over the next few years, therefore, the 9th RW will be actively seeking answers to the big question: can the Global Hawk replace the U-2?

There is no hurry to answer that question, however.

There is plenty of life left in the U-2 airframe, although a fatal crash in Korea in January 2003 reduced the operational fleet to 30 aircraft (it was the first write-off for seven years). In 1999 and again in 2001, Lockheed Martin pitched new U-2 production at the Pentagon, including a new U-2U unmanned version. No contract was awarded, but the fact remains that over $1.4 billion has been spent on U-2 upgrades since 1990. Moreover, there are plenty more improvements from which the Dragon Lady could benefit.

The potential of the improved ASARS radar has yet to be fully exploited: the quality of radar data now streaming from the U-2 allows for advanced manipulation techniques such as coherent change detection and automatic target recognition/cueing. More wavebands could be added to SYERS. A long-mooted hyperspectral sensor could also be added. Some of these developments would make the U-2 even more useful in supporting counter-narcotics or special forces operations.

The aircraft's defensive electronic warfare systems need more attention. Considering just how often U-2 pilots have been sent in harm's way in recent years, it is surprising that EW upgrades have lagged other developments. In July 2001, an aircraft flying over southern Iraq apparently came close to being shot down, when an SA-2 exploded below and behind.

The first task will be to upgrade the current Systems 29F for warning and 56-1 for jamming with a high-speed signal processor for quicker identification of threat radars, and to integrate the EW system displays into the RAMP. This will form part of the Block 30 upgrade. Then, a long-standing plan to fit the ITT ALQ-211 system, which was developed for the US Army's AH-64D helicopters, could be implemented. The BAE Systems (ex-Lockheed Martin/Sanders) ALE-55 fibre-optic towed decoy (FOTD) could then be added. (The FOTD has already been test-flown, mounted in the GPS housing on the right wing).

The logistics tail and expense associated with the U-2's unique JP-TS (Thermally Stabilized) fuel could be elimi-

nated by modifying the aircraft's fuel system. Heat would be transferred from the engine oil circuit to the outboard fuel tanks (always the coldest) so that standard JP-8 could be used instead. Alternatively, additives could reduce the freezing-point of JP-8.

L-3 Communications is now funded for a significant upgrade to the U-2's datalinks. A common airborne modem assembly will replace the single-purpose boxes that were dedicated to IADL, DDL and ETP. New nine-inch antennas will be fitted in the Q-bay and tail. In the near future, this new system, designated DDL II, will provide multiple communications options: two line-of-sight (LOS) links; or one LOS plus one ETP (eg SATCOM) link; or one LOS plus an air-to-air (ATA) link; or the ETP plus the ATA.

This kind of flexibility is the key to the future of the U-2. It is not yet clear whether UAVs can match the operational utility of this evergreen reconnaissance system. Having outlasted its supposed replacement – the SR-71 Blackbird – who is to say that the Dragon Lady will not pull the same trick again?

Chris Pocock

Above: A 363rd ERS U-2S launches from Al Kharj at the start of an Operation Iraqi Freedom mission on 11 April 2003. It is configured with ASARS-2 nose and the RAS-1A (formerly known as Senior Glass) Sigint suite, which combines Elint and Comint functions.

Left: This 'family portrait' from April 2003 shows the 363rd ERS at its Al Kharj (PSAB) base). U-2Ss also operated from Al Dhafra during the conflicts in Afghanistan and Iraq, the UAE base also hosting the RQ-4 Global Hawk detachment. U-2s from Akrotiri in Cyprus also flew missions over Iraq under the mission name Olive Harvest.

80-1086 (with ASARS-2 and RAS-1A) of the 363rd ERS rests at Al Kharj, Saudi Arabia, between Operation Iraqi Freedom missions on 11 April 2003. At that time the U-2 fleet stood at 31 aircraft, with 29 in the Primary Aircraft Inventory (plus four TU-2s). Four aircraft survive from the original FY68 batch.

Individual aircraft details

The following table lists all U-2R, TR-1 and ER-2 production. The first number is the Lockheed 'Article Number' (e.g. construction number) followed by the USAF serial. The first batch manufactured in 1967-68 comprised Articles 051 to 062, which were all U-2R models. The second batch from 1981 to 1989 comprised Articles 063 to 099, which were a mix of U-2R, TR-1 and ER-2 models. USAF serial numbers were allocated to coincide with the Article Numbers in the second batch only.

The prototype U-2R and some subsequent aircraft sometimes carried 'civilian' registrations when serving with the CIA units (such as N803X, N810X, N812X, and N8032X). The CIA units used the 'correct' USAF serial numbers on other occasions, and RoCAF numbers (such as 3925) when deployed to Det H. In the mid-1970s, some USAF aircraft were repainted with false serials such as 10342 and 10345. These came from a batch of serials (68-10341 through 10353) which had been allocated for additional U-2R production, but not taken up.

The remaining TR-1s were redesignated U-2R in October 1991. All remaining U-2R aircraft are being converted to U-2S standard with the new engine. For ease of reference, neither redesignation is noted in the tables below (except for the first U-2S conversions).

051/68-10329: First flight 28 August 1967 as N803X, unpainted. Subsequently reworked to production standard and repainted as 10329 for use by Det G/H. Reallocated to flight test in 1975 and was first aircraft to carry superpods. To 9th SRW by 1981.
052/68-10330: Delivered to 100th SRW by late 1968. Returned to flight test around 1970 for US Navy EPX trials. 100th SRW again by early 1972. To 9th SRW in 1976. Written off by OL-OH at Akrotiri on 7 December 1977 (Capt Robert Henderson killed).
053/68-10331: Delivered to Det G. To 100th SRW in early 1975. To 9th SRW in 1976.
054/68-10332: Delivered to Det G. To 100th SRW in early 1975. To 9th SRW in 1976. Written off by Det 2 off Korean coast on 15 January 1992 (Capt Marty McGregor killed).
055/68-10333: Delivered to Det G. To 100th SRW in early 1975. To 9th SRW in 1976. Damaged by OL-OH at Akrotiri on 24 April 1980. Written off by Det 2 at Osan on 22 May 1984 (Capt David Bonsi survived).
056/68-10334: Delivered to 100th SRW. Written off by 99th SRS in Gulf of Thailand on 15 August 1975 (Capt Jon Little killed).
057/68-10335: Delivered to Det G. Written off by Det H/35th Sqn at Taoyuan on 24 November 1970 (Maj Denny Huang killed).
058/68-10336: Delivered to 100th SRW. To 9th SRW in 1976. Returned to flight test: first ASARS aircraft (1981), first Senior Spur aircraft? Still with flight test.
059/68-10337: Delivered to 100th SRW. Damaged by 99th SRS at U-Tapao on 16 May 1975. To 9th SRW in 1976. Damaged by Det 5 at Patrick on 24 May 1988.
060/68-10338: Delivered to 100th SRW. To 9th SRW in 1976. First aircraft to reach 20,000 hours, on 11 August 1994. Written off by OL-UK at Fairford on 29 August 1995.
061/68-10339: Retained for US Navy EPX trials. Delivered to 100th SRW by early 1972. To 9th SRW in 1976. Written off at Beale on 13 December 1993 (Capt Rich Snyder killed).
062/68-10340: Delivered to 100th SRW. To 9th SRW 1976. Written off by Det 2 in Korea on 5 October 1980 (Capt Cleve Wallace survived).
063/80-1063/N706NA: First new-batch aircraft to fly, on 1 May 1981. Delivered as ER-2 to NASA in June 1981.
064/80-1064: Delivered as TR-1B to 9th SRW in March 1983. Converted to TU-2S and redelivered in ceremony on 28 October 1994.
065/80-1065: Delivered as TR-1B to 9th SRW on May 1983.
066/80-1066: Second new-batch aircraft to fly, on 1 August 1981. Delivered as TR-1A to 9th SRW in September 1981.
067/80-1067: Delivered as TR-1A to 9th SRW in July 1982. Returned to flight test in 1989.
068/80-1068: Delivered as TR-1A to 9th SRW in July 1982. First aircraft to enter service with 17th RW in February 1983. To 9th SRW in April 1987.
069/80-1069/N708NA: Delivered as TR-1A to 9th SRW in July 1982. To 17th RW in July 1983. Damaged by vehicle collision at Alconbury in October 1983. To Lockheed in March 1987, converted to ER-2 and loaned to NASA.
070/80-1070: Delivered as TR-1A to 9th SRW in October 1982. To 17th RW in February 1983. To 9th SRW in May 1988.
071/80-1071: Delivered as U-2R to 9th SRW in November 1993. Returned to flight test as first Senior Span aircraft in 1985. Returned to 9th SRW by late 1988. First U-2S production conversion, redelivered in ceremony on 28 October 1994. Damaged at Beale in February 1996.
072/80-1072: Delivered as TR-1A to 17th RW in November 1993. To 9th SRW in March

1984. Written off at Beale on 18 July 1984 (Capt Tom Hubbard survived).
073/80-1073: Delivered as TR-1A to 9th SRW in February 1984. To 17th RW in January 1991. To 9th Wg in September 1992.
074/80-1074: Delivered as TR-1A to 9th SRW in February 1984. PLSS configuration 1984-85. To 17th RW in December 1990. To 9th SRW in October 1992.
075/80-1075: Delivered as U-2R to 9th RW in 1984. Written off by Det 2 in Korea on 8 October 1984 (Capt Tom Dettmer survived).
076/80-1076: Delivered as U-2R to 9th SRW in 1984/85.
077/80-1077: Delivered as TR-1A to 17th RW in March 1985. To 9th SRW in November 1989.
078/80-1078: Delivered as TR-1A to 17th RW in March 1985. Damaged at Alconbury on 24 April 1990 and returned to Lockheed for storage. Converted to TU-2S and delivered in ceremony on 28 October 1994.
079/80-1079: Delivered as TR-1A to 17th RW on March 1985. To 9th SRW in January 1991.
080/80-1080: Delivered as TR-1A to 9th SRW in May 1985. Damaged at Beale on 25 May 1988.
081/80-1081: Delivered as TR-1A to 17th RW in October 1985. To 9th SRW in August 1991.
082/80-1082: Delivered as TR-1A to 9th SRW in November 1985.
083/80-1083: Delivered as TR-1A to 17th RW in March 1986. To 9th Wg in December 1991.
084/80-1084: Delivered as TR-1A to 17th RW in April 1986. Damaged by vehicle collision at Alconbury in December 1987. To 9th SRW in 1988/89.
085/80-1085: Delivered as TR-1A to 17th RW in August 1986. To 9th SRW in February 1991.
086/80-1086: Delivered as TR-1A to 9th SRW in 1986/87. To 17th RW in April 1987. To 9th SRW in August 1991.
087/80-1087: Delivered as TR-1A to 9th SRW by May 1987.
088/80-1088: Delivered as TR-1A to 17th RW in December 1987. To 9th SRW in August 1991. Written off near Beale on 7 August 1996 (Capt Randy Roby killed).
089/80-1089: Delivered as U-2R to 9th SRW in 1988.
090/80-1090: Built as TR-1A in 1988 and retained by flight test at Palmdale. Prototype U-2S re-engined aircraft, f/f on 23 May 1989.
091/80-1091: Delivered as U-2R(T) to 9th SRW in March 1988.
092/80-1092: Delivered as TR-1A to 17th RW in April 1988. To 9th Wg in December 1991.
093/80-1093: Delivered as TR-1A to 17th RW in June 1988. To 9th Wg in April 1992.
094/80-1094: Delivered as TR-1B to 17th RW in September 1988. To 9th Wg in December 1991.
095/80-1095: Delivered as U-2R to 9th SRW by April 1989.
096/80-1096: Delivered as U-2R to 9th SRW by April 1989.
097/80-1097/N709NA: Delivered as ER-2 to NASA in 1989.
098/80-1098: Delivered as U-2R to 9th SRW in 1989. Written off by Det 2 at Osan in August 1994 (Capt Chuck Espinoza survived).
099/80-1099: Delivered as TR-1A to 9th SRW in final delivery ceremony on 3 October 1989. To 17th RW in March 1990. To 9th Wg in December 1991.

U-2 tail artwork

U-2R/TR-1 Operators

Central Intelligence Agency

Detachment G, Edwards North Base, California

This was the base for the CIA's U-2 operations, where training, development and maintenance activities took place. The unit was named the Fourth Weather Reconnaissance Squadron (Provisional) (WRSP-4) for cover purposes until mid-1969, when it was redesignated the 1130th Air Technical Training Group (ATTG). It was manned by a mix of CIA and USAF personnel, with maintenance provided by Lockheed. As part of the overall UK-USA intelligence co-operation agreement, two RAF pilots were always attached to the unit.

Det G received its first U-2R in February 1968, when Colonel 'Curly' Schambers was unit commander. Det G supported the Taiwanese U-2 operation (see below), and also conducted its own reconnaissance operations when directed by Project Headquarters in Washington, DC. These included annual deployments to the UK to demonstrate the aircraft's capabilities to senior British personnel. From August to December 1970, Det G deployed to RAF Akrotiri, Cyprus and flew reconnaissance missions along the Suez Canal ceasefire zone. Colonel Roger Cooper took command of the unit in 1971.

In April 1974 a permanent detachment was established at Akrotiri, to monitor the peace agreement between Israel and Egypt arranged by the United Nations. In December 1974, the CIA ended 14 years of U-2 operations. The USAF's 100th SRW took over the Akrotiri detachment as OL-OH, while North Base was closed.

Detachment H/35th Squadron, RoCAF, Taoyuan AB, Taiwan

The operation to conduct reconnaissance operations against mainland China was established at Taoyuan AB near Taipei in 1961. The CIA provided the aircraft and training, while the Republic of China air force provided the pilots. Lockheed maintained the aircraft, and other contractors provided sensor support. Both countries contributed intelligence and logistics support. As a cover story, the US announced the 'sale' of two U-2s to the Republic of China air force, but, in reality, the two aircraft remained the property of the US government, and were regularly rotated with others from the Edwards-based CIA fleet. At Taoyuan, the aircraft usually wore RoCAF insignia.

The unit was nicknamed 'The Black Cat Squadron' and was jointly commanded by a RoCAF and a USAF officer (the latter on a 360-day TDY). When the U-2R arrived in mid-1968, Colonel Yang Shi Chuen was the RoCAF commander, subsequently succeeded by Colonels Wang Shi Chuen, Tom Hwang and Wong Tao.

Following the improvement in Sino-US relations, the unit closed in August 1974.

The U-2Rs of Det H wore RoCAF serials and carried the Taiwanese star national insignia.

United States Air Force

100th Strategic Reconnaissance Wing

The 100th SRW had been created at Davis-Monthan AFB, Arizona in June 1966 by a renumbering of the previous USAF U-2 operating wing, the 4080th SRW. It reported to SAC headquarters through the 15th Air Force. In addition to the Davis-Monthan-based U-2 squadron (see below), the 100th controlled the 350th SRS which operated RPVs and the associated DC-130 launch and CH-3 recovery vehicles.

Although training was conducted at Davis-Monthan, most operational missions were conducted from deployments which were designated Operating Locations (OLs – see below).

When the U-2R arrived at Davis-Monthan in 1968, the wing was commanded by Colonel Marion 'Hack' Mixson. He was succeeded by Colonel Ray Haupt (August 1970), Colonel Don White (June 1972), and Colonel Chuck Stratton (May 1974).

On 1 July 1976, SAC decided to consolidate U-2 operations with that of the SR-71, under the 9th SRW at Beale. The 100th SRW designation was also transferred to Beale, becoming the 100th Air Refueling Wing in control of the KC-135Q tanker fleet which supported SR-71 operations.

349th Strategic Reconnaissance Squadron

Created by a renumbering of the 4028th SRS in June 1966, the 349th SRS conducted training in the U-2C, U-2F and (from September 1968) U-2R models. It also flew domestic reconnaissance missions in support of various US government agencies. From 1972, it was allocated responsibility for the operational trials of the Advanced Location and Strike Systems (ALSS), and deployed five U-2C models to the UK for this purpose in 1975. When U-2 operations were moved to Beale AFB in July 1976, the 349th squadron number transferred with the 100th wing designation to the KC-135Q operation already there.

Operating Location 19 (OL-19)

After the Cuban Missile Crisis in 1962, the 100th SRW was tasked with regular reconnaissance missions over Cuba to monitor compliance with the informal agreement between the US and the USSR, that no offensive strategic weapons would be deployed there. In 1969, a single U-2R was deployed to OL-19, recently moved back to McCoy AFB, Florida from Barksdale AFB, Louisiana.

Operating Location 20 (OL-20) and Operating Location RU (OL-RU)

OL-20 was created at Bien Hoa AB, South Vietnam in February 1964, when the U-2 was one of the first USAF aircraft types to be deployed in Southeast Asia. In October 1964, OL-20 expanded with the arrival of the wing's reconnaissance RPVs and DC-130 launch aircraft (CH-3 recovery helicopters were based at Da Nang).

The U-2R joined OL-20 in mid-1969. In July 1970, the unit moved to U-Tapao AB, Thailand and was redesignated OL-RU. In November 1972 it gained full squadron status as the 99th SRS (see below). During 1972, the unit was awarded the Paul T. Cullen Trophy in recognition of its work in support of the war, to be followed by a host of other awards.

U-2R/TR-1 Operators

9th Reconnaissance Wing

Commanders of the 9th RW since its association with the U-2 first began in 1976 have been Colonel John Storrie (until September 1977), Colonel Lyman Kidder (until January 1979), Colonel Dale Shelton (until July 1980), Colonel Dave Young (until July 1982), Colonel Tom Pugh (until July 1983), Colonel Hector Freese (until January 1985), Colonel Dave Pinsky (until July 1987), Colonel Rich Graham (until November 1988), Colonel James Savarda (until June 1990), Colonel Thomas Keck (until November 1991), Colonel Richard Young (until June 1993), Colonel Larry Tieman (until June 1993), Brigadier General John Rutledge (until September 1995), Brigadier General Bob Behler (current).

1st Reconnaissance Squadron (Training)

Designated the 9th Strategic Reconnaissance Wing until September 1991, and then simply the 9th Wing until October 1994, the 9th RW has been based at Beale AFB, California since June 1966, when it assumed control of the newly-established SR-71 operations there. U-2 operations were consolidated with the SR-71 at Beale in July 1976, when the 99th SRS became the U-2 squadron while the 1st SRS remained the SR-71 squadron.

At that time, the wing reported to SAC through the 14th Air Division of 15th Air Force. From September 1991 it reported through 2nd Air Force. After SAC was deactivated in June 1992, the wing joined Air Combat Command, and the 'BB' tailcode began to appear on all its aircraft. The reporting line changed from 2nd AF to 12th AF in July 1993.

The wing has since also controlled at various times the 5th RS and 97th RS (see below).

Control of U-2 (and, since its comeback in 1996, SR-71) flying operations is today vested in the 9th Operations Group, which was established in September 1991. But operational control of the overseas U-2 deployments is chopped to the relevant theatre commander (EUCOM, CENTCOM, PACOM etc.). The 9th OG also controls the 9th Intelligence Squadron, which produces and stores all domestic U-2 and SR-71 imagery.

Today, the 1st RS (T) recruits and trains all U-2 pilots. After initial interviews, orientation flights and selection, the new pilot undergoes six months of training, including 20 sorties in the U-2, mostly the squadron's four U-2RT/ST two-cockpit trainers. The 1st RS (T) also flies the wing's 13 T-38 companion trainers, and trains the U-2 mission planners. It graduates about 20 pilots and two mission planners each year.

Having been 'grounded' when SR-71 operation terminated in March 1990, the 1st designation was revived in July of that year when the U-2 training squadron was redesignated from the 5th SRS (T) (see below) to the 1st SRS (T).

5th Reconnaissance Squadron

The 5th RS is based at Osan AB, South Korea, from where U-2s have been monitoring the tense situation on the Korean peninsula continuously for 20 years. The unit usually operates two aircraft, and was the first overseas location to receive the U-2S model in October 1995. The aircraft are maintained under contract by Lockheed Martin.

Until October 1994, the unit was designated Det 2 of the 9th RW (Det 2 is now the revived SR-71 operation based at Edwards AFB). U-2 operations have been conducted continuously in Korea since February 1976, when OL-AO of the 100th SRW was established. These operations soon inherited the Black Cat emblem of the RoCAF's former 35th Squadron. OL-AO became Det 2 in July 1976.

In 1986 the USAF redesignated the 4029th SRTS training squadron at Beale as the 5th Strategic Reconnaissance Squadron (Training), thereby renewing the 5th squadron's previous association with the 9th wing. The 5th SRS (T) became the 1st SRS (T) in July 1990.

99th Reconnaissance Squadron

Today, the 99th RS is the Beale-based operational U-2R squadron which supports the overseas deployments and conducts domestic reconnaissance missions for various US government and non-government agencies. These have included earthquake and flood damage assessment, and environmental change detection flights. The 99th also conducts some operational testing of newly-fielded systems.

Having been the SR-71 training squadron at Beale until deactivation in April 1971, the 99th first became a U-2 squadron in November 1972 at U-Tapao AB, Thailand (see OL-RU, above). As the US military presence in Indo-China wound down, the 99th SRS left Thailand in April 1976, and was re-established at Beale in July of that year.

Other Current Detachments and Operating Locations

Det 1 is the continuing deployment at RAF Akrotiri, from where one or two U-2R

The Beale-based 9th RW supports all U-2 operations worldwide, including pilot training and intelligence data processing.

A U-2R wheels over the Beale tower, an SR-71 being displayed outside. In addition to its U-2 operation, the 9th RW operates the two SR-71s recently brought out of retirement. These fly with Det 2 at Edwards AFB.

models have continuously monitored compliance with United Nations resolutions since mid-1974. The detachment re-equipped with U-2S models in February 1996, and uses Lockheed Martin contract maintenance.

OL-FR is the detachment at Istres AB, France which continues to monitor the Bosnian conflict. The U-2 has flown over Bosnia for the last five years, originally from the UK as the 95th RS and OL-UK (which see). It usually operates three aircraft with differing sensor fits.

4402nd RS is based at Taif in Saudi Arabia, reporting for operations to the 4404th Composite Wing at Dhahran AB. It conducts the Olive Branch photo-reconnaissance monitoring flights over Iraq on behalf of the United Nations, and has operated two or more other aircraft for coalition force reconnaissance requirements. It re-equipped with U-2S models in August 1996.

Previous Detachments, Operating Locations and Squadrons

Det 2 was the designation of the U-2 operation at Osan AB, South Korea from 1976 until 1994 (see 5th RS above).
Det 3 was a redesignation of OL-OH at RAF Akrotiri in September 1980. The operation was again redesignated, to Det 1, in 1994.
Det 4 was created in April 1979 at RAF Mildenhall, UK to fly the U-2R (and the SR-71) in the European theatre on a routine basis (previously, missions had been flown on a temporary deployment basis). At most times a single U-2R aircraft was deployed. The U-2R element of Det 4 ceased operations in February 1983 when the first TR-1A reached the 17th RW at RAF Alconbury. The SR-71 operation continued until December 1988.
Det 4 was re-established at Howard AFB, Panama in 1991, but closed again in late 1993.
Det 5 was a redesignation of OL-OF at Patrick AFB in January 1983. It was closed in November 1990.
Det 8/FT was a flight test organisation created in late 1977 to work in conjunction with Lockheed's U-2 flight test and depot-level overhaul activities at Site 2, Palmdale, California. (Det 8 itself was the logistics support activity for the U-2, based at Robins

AFB, Georgia.) Control of this activity was transferred to the 412th Test Wing at nearby Edwards AFB in April 1993 as **OL-HM**. Due to the ongoing nature of sensor and equipment development for the U-2, OL-HM usually has two aircraft and two pilots assigned. They share post-depot acceptance flights, and flight test sorties.
OL-OF (for Olympic Flare) was established at Patrick AFB, Florida in January 1982. Redesignated Det 5 in January 1983.
OL-OH (for Olive Harvest) was the operation at RAF Akrotiri in support of United Nations and other objectives, which was taken over from the CIA in mid-1974. It was redesignated Det 3 in September 1980.
OL-UK (for United Kingdom) was established in September 1993 to take over three U-2Rs from the 95th RS at RAF Alconbury. When Alconbury closed in March 1995, the unit relocated to RAF Fairford. In December 1995, it moved to Istres AB, France and was redesignated OL-FR.
OL-CH (for Camel Hump) was opened at King Fahd RSAB, Taif, Saudi Arabia in mid-August 1990, as coalition forces responded to the Iraqi invasion of Kuwait. Initially operating two U-2R aircraft, two TR-1A aircraft were added from the 17th RW after

one week. As the Desert Shield deployments mounted, SAC chopped tactical (though not operational) control of OL-CH to CENTCOM, whereupon it was redesignated on 21 September as ....
1704th RS (Provisional) reporting to the 1700th Strategic Wing (Provisional). Another U-2R was added from Det 2 in October 1990, and when Desert Storm was mounted on 16 January the squadron had nine aircraft and had already accomplished 325 sorties. Eventually, squadron strength reached 12 aircraft (six U-2Rs and six TR-1As), allowing another 195 sorties to be performed during the war. After the war, the squadron remained at Taif in slimmed-down form, until it was redesignated 4402nd RS (P).

4029th Strategic Reconnaissance Training Squadron

The 4029th SRTS was activated at Beale in August 1981 to train all U-2 and TR-1 pilots. Until then, training had been conducted by the 99th SRS, but the arrival of the TR-1 and the consequent greater demand for new

pilots mandated the creation of a separate training outfit. The 4029th SRTS received the first two-seat TR-1B trainer in March 1983. (In earlier times, this squadron number had been assigned to the 4080th SRW, the original USAF U-2 wing.) Redesignated 5th SRTS in 1986.

17th Reconnaissance Wing

The 17th RW was reactivated in October 1982 at RAF Alconbury, UK to operate the TR-1 in Europe. It reported to SAC through the 7th Air Division and 8th Air Force, but operational tasking came from USAFE and NATO (via US European Command). In 1990-91, the wing supported Desert Shield/Desert Storm by deploying aircraft and personnel to the 1704th RS (P) in Saudi

A 95th RS TR-1A returns from a mission along the German border. The original plans for the 17th RW involved basing 12 aircraft at Alconbury and six at Wethersfield. In the event the 17th only had 11 aircraft at most.

Arabia. Following the end of Desert Storm and the Cold War, the wing was deactivated in June 1991.

Colonel George Freese was the first commander of the 17th RW at Alconbury (until July 1983), followed by Colonel Tom Lesan (until August 1985), Colonel James Wrenn, Colonel Art Saboski, Colonel John Sander, and Colonel Doug Cole.

95th Reconnaissance Squadron

The 95th RS was reactivated alongside the 17th RW in October 1982 at Alconbury, and

received an initial two TR-1A models to continue the Det 4 Sigint mission. More aircraft were steadily added, particularly from 1985 when the ASARS sensor was deployed. By early 1989, the 95th RS operated 11 TR-1As. The 95th RS survived the deactivation of the 17th RW in June 1991, remaining at Alconbury under the control of the 9th Wing at Beale. However, it was reduced in size, and eventually deactivated in September 1993, when Alconbury became a TDY location as OL-UK.

The badge of the 95th RS was the famous 'Kicking Mule' insignia first used in World War I.

Appendix A: Lockheed D-21 drone

Following the loss of Gary Powers's U-2 on 1 May 1960, many meetings with senior Central Intelligence Agency and key Air Force personnel were held to discuss the loss and to brainstorm possible alternatives. Kelly Johnson of Lockheed came up with the winning concept, which was an unmanned extension of the existing A-12 Oxcart programme. On 10 October 1962, Lockheed was authorised to make a study, which eventually spawned the Tagboard programme. Johnson was also given the go-ahead from the CIA to begin a formal study regarding the development of what culminated in the D-21. The initial meeting with Marquardt was held on 24 October 1962, at which Johnson, Ben Rich and Rus Daniel discussed engine requirements.

Lockheed had extensive experience with the ramjet-powered X-7A-1, X-7A-2 and X-7A-3 test vehicle series, and a close working relationship with Marquardt, a neighbouring company in the San Fernando Valley. Together, they determined that the unmanned drone could be powered by a highly-modified Marquardt RJ43-MA-11 ramjet engine, formerly used on the retired USAF/Boeing Bomarc IM-99B air defence weapon.

The D-21 engine is properly identified as an XRJ43-MA20S-4. The Bomarc A used Marquardt RJ43-MA-3 ramjet engines, and the Bomarc B used two externally-mounted RJ43-MA-11s. The MA20S-4 engine employed in the D-21 used many MA-11 components but was modified to operate at lower pressures and higher temperatures. The S-4 was immersed in the body of the D-21 and had no inlet structures of its own, instead using the D-21's inlet system. The engine's centre body and main structure remained to house the fuel control, fuel pump, fuel injector nozzles and flame-holder assemblies. The flame-holder system was redesigned to allow stable combustion at extreme high-altitude, high-temperature and low-pressure situations. Ignition was by TEB (Tri Ethyl Boron) to enable re-ignition in the event of flame-out. The combustion chamber/exit nozzle was redesigned to provide for the much greater expansion ratio required for high-altitude cruising. The design also incorporated an ejector system for engine structure cooling. Of interest is that, until the advent of the D-21, no ramjet had ever powered any craft for more than a few minutes. The D-21's XRJ-MA20S-4 would be powered up during its entire flight of over 1.5 hours.

By November 1962, the drone's design was beginning to take shape. Kelly Johnson outlined the basic requirements for the overall system. The design speed would be Mach 3.3 to 3.5 with an operational altitude over target between 87,000 and 95,000 ft (26517 and 28956 m). The D-21 would be designed with a very small radar cross-section and a photographic resolution capability of less than 6 in (15 cm). It would have a combat range of at least 3,000 nm (5556 km) and a recoverable payload bay (with camera) weighing approximately 425 lb (193 kg).

With these requirements laid down, Kelly Johnson's smallest Blackbird began development under the capable guidance of the Skunk Works chief of manufacturing, Bob Murphy.

By 7 December 1962, Lockheed had completed a full-scale mock-up including RCS (Radar Cross Section) simulation; the D-21 was then sent to the test site for further evaluation. Meanwhile, Marquardt had a very successful run of the Bomarc engine in its wind tunnel, simulating high-speed flight conditions. A large number of Skunk Works D-21 crew members, together with Marquardt staff, were in attendance at this event, and all were amazed that the engine could be shut off for as long as 45 seconds and still restart. This feat was possible because of the hot engine parts.

On 20 March 1963, Lockheed was given an official CIA letter of contract for the D-21. (At this early date, the D-21 was still referred to as the Q-12; that designation was later changed.) The contract gave Lockheed responsibility for the navigation systems, the ramjet and the airframe. The programme reached another milestone in September 1963, when Marquardt demonstrated a very good engine run to the highest temperatures required. The company also appeared to be proceeding well in the development of the MA20S-4 variant.

Tagboard project

The D-21 was the heart of this programme and was designed as an extremely high-speed, high-altitude reconnaissance vehicle – in a sense, a much smaller, unmanned version of the A-12, with similar capabilities. It was considered to be a 'one-way aircraft', meaning that each D-21 would make one flight only and then self-destruct. While still in the design stages, two A-12s were modified to carry the D-21 on a dorsal pylon located on the rear centreline between the engines and the vertical stabilisers. A second cockpit was installed for the D-21 launch control officer (LCO) in the area of the A-12's 'Q' bay. The 'Q' bay was already pressurised and refrigerated, making the modification relatively easy.

The A-12 became known as the M-21, the letter M indicating that it was the Mother aircraft; the D in D-21 designated it as the Daughter aircraft. The 21 designation was an intentional reversal of the number 12, intended to reduce the possibility of Skunk Works personnel confusing the A-12 with the M-21 in documentation or security issues.

At this point, the Tagboard programme overall was progressing rather slowly. By mid-May 1965, the M/D-21 had achieved Mach 2.6, but not launch speeds. Problems had arisen from using the Hamilton Standard inlet control system in conjunction with Pratt & Whitney J58s. Between May and 21 October 1965, Kelly Johnson decided to put the newer 34,000-lb (151.21-kN) thrust J58 engines into M-21 number 135, and also converted from the Hamilton Standard inlet control system to one designed by Johnson's crew.

On 5 March 1966, a D-12 finally launched from the back of a Mother aircraft. The launch itself was a great success, but the D-21 was lost about 120 nm (222 km) from the launch point; nonetheless, the exercise demonstrated that Lockheed had developed a successful launch technique. Kelly Johnson was quoted as saying, "This was the most dangerous manoeuvre we have ever been involved in, in any airplane I have ever worked on." In this groundbreaking mission, Bill Park was at the helm and Keith Beswick was the LCO.

Following that very successful first launch, Kelly Johnson (accompanied by Dick Boehme) went to Point Mugu, California, to witness the second launch of a D-21, number 506. Once again, Johnson was delighted with the launch. The D-21 flew over 1,200 nm (2222 km) while holding course to within 0.5 mile (0.8 km) for the entire flight, reaching 90,000 ft (27432 m) and a speed of Mach 3.3. It came to an abrupt halt and fell out of the sky, however,

In its first guise (Tagboard), the D-21 drone was launched at Mach 3 from the back of an M-21 (a converted A-12). The D-21 was not forcibly ejected, but was released to float free, The first three launches were undertaken with the M-21 in a shallow bunt to aid this process: the fourth was made in straight and level flight, with fatal consequences. These two views are from captive flights of the 'Mother/Daughter' combination, undertaken from Area 51, the first of which was accomplished on 22 December 1964. The drone was initially fitted with aerodynamic fairings over the intake and nozzle to reduce drag, as here, but the problems of jettisoning them safely proved insurmountable.

D-21 no. 501 is about to be lifted on to the back of M-21 60-6940/134 in preparation for the first captive flight. The location is Hangar 1 at Area 51 (Groom Dry Lake, Nevada). Even at this top-secret location, security around the Tagboard programme was very tight, as evidenced by the plywood security wall behind.

when a hydraulic pump overheated and failed. The failure was due to running the pump unpressurised several times during checkout.

At this point in the programme, Johnson proposed substituting a B-52H as a new launch platform, with the D-21 being propelled to speed and altitude by a solid rocket booster. Johnson's goal was to get the greatest benefit from the programme at the lowest cost.

On 16 June 1966, Lockheed staged the third and most successful D-21 launch from an M-21. It flew almost 1,600 nm (2963 km), making eight programmed turns (in order to stay within a line of sight from the tracking ship). Everything went as planned except the ejection of the package due to an electronic failure. To quote Johnson, "It was a very successful go."

On 30 July 1966, on the fourth and final launch from the M-21, D-21 number 504 suffered an asymmetrical unstart and crashed back into the Mother aircraft. The collision resulted in the death of one of the crew members aboard the M-21: Ray Torick, the LCO, survived the mid-air collision and successfully ejected from the stricken aircraft, but drowned in the Pacific Ocean. Bill Park, the Lockheed test pilot at the controls of the M-21, survived and went on to become the senior test pilot for Lockheed's Skunk Works.

This was the Blackbird programme's first fatality and it proved to be the demise of the Tagboard programme. The follow-on programme relied on a more conventional launch platform – the tried and proven Boeing B-52H Stratofortress.

Overview of the B-52H/D-21B

In conjunction with the CIA and senior Air Force staffers (under the direction of Kelly Johnson), plans were advanced for Lockheed to modify the D-21 to be launched from an Air Force/Boeing B-52H Stratofortress. The B-52 had already proved its success with NASA, launching hundreds of craft up to and including the North American X-15A-2, so it was accepted as being potentially safer than the previous Tagboard scheme. This programme eventually evolved into Project Senior Bowl (initially designated as 'A' Flight and later as the

4200th Support Squadron at Beale AFB, California). The 4200th, although designated as a squadron, was actually a wing-level unit with direct and primary responsibility to Strategic Air Command (SAC) headquarters. Administrative functions were through the 14th Air Division at Beale, while operational functions were handled through SAC and other still-classified hierarchy.

Configuring the drop of the drone was the easier part of the transition, as similar operations had already met with success. Of greater difficulty were the challenges of it achieving a speed of Mach 3 at 80,000 ft (24384 m), and ensuring a safe separation of the booster without damage to the 'Tag', as it was called throughout the entire programme. Much work also needed to be done on fine-tuning the remote engine start-up, and on all aspects of the D-21's navigational system.

On 12 December 1966, the Air Force delivered the programme's first Boeing B-52H (assigned Air Force serial number 61-0021) to the Lockheed Palmdale facility at Air Force Plant 42, Site 2. A few months later, it was joined by number 60-0036. Both B-52H aircraft had undergone extensive modifications to enable them to carry and launch the D-21B.

In its proposed configuration, the Senior Bowl B-52H/D-21B combination, with the D-21's combat radius of over 3,000 nm (5556 km), could conceivably cover any location, anywhere in the world, with its global reach

capabilities. Its operational altitude rendered it relatively safe from interception.

Senior Bowl aircraft modifications

Senior Bowl called for the modified D-21 to be carried on an underwing pylon, similar to that used for launching the X-15 from the NASA/Boeing NB-52B. Due to the change in launch aircraft and the subsequent modifications to the D-21, the programme warranted a new designation. In the absence of mock-ups, models or working drawings of the D-21A (although some casual sketches may well have been made), the programme's progression officially went straight from D-21 to D-21B.

The major modifications to the two B-52H Senior Bowl aircraft encompassed the elimination of the electronic countermeasures operator and tail gunner's panels at the upper-rear crew station, and the installation of identical launch control panels for the D-21Bs on the right and/or left pylons. Two camera-mounting stations were installed in the B-52H's left and right forward wheel wells, holding a set of 35-mm very-high-speed cameras used to record the launch of the D-21B from the B-52H. The cameras were aimed at the D-21B from different angles and with a variety of lenses to capture the D-21B as it dropped from the pylon. The addition of special pylons, telemetry gear and communications systems, together with the associated wiring and instrumentation, completed the modification of the aircraft.

Inside the D-21B

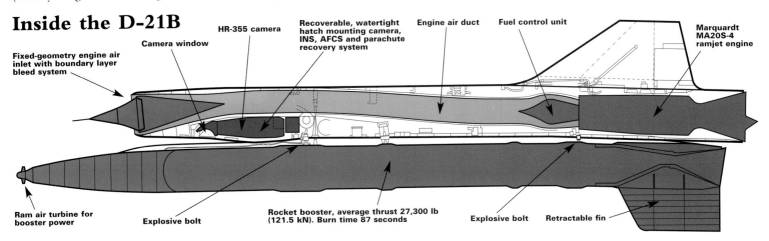

- Fixed-geometry engine air inlet with boundary layer bleed system
- Camera window
- HR-355 camera
- Recoverable, watertight hatch mounting camera, INS, AFCS and parachute recovery system
- Engine air duct
- Fuel control unit
- Marquardt MA20S-4 ramjet engine
- Ram air turbine for booster power
- Explosive bolt
- Rocket booster, average thrust 27,300 lb (121.5 kN). Burn time 87 seconds
- Explosive bolt
- Retractable fin

Appendix A: Lockheed D-21 drone

D-21 drones from the Tagboard programme were modified by the Skunk Works to D-21B status for launching from B-52s. The ventral points which had originally been designed to attach the drone to the M-21 were the natural points from which to hang the rocket booster.

All D-21B vehicles launched by 'A' Flight/ 4200th Support Squadron B-52Hs were from the starboard pylon only, and the port pylon station was never used during operational launches. A number of publications have shown pictures of the D-21B hanging from both pylons; most likely, these photographs were of sorties flown by the Skunk Works.

The Marquardt RJ43-MA20S-4 ramjet engine powered both the D-21 and the B-52-launched D-21B. When released from the pylon of the subsonic B-52H, the D-21B needed a rocket booster capable of propelling it to above Mach 1.5, at which speed the ramjet would light. The nosecone of the booster was fitted with a Marquardt B-4 supersonic ram air turbine to provide the electrical and hydraulic power necessary during the drop and boost phase. Lockheed's Missile and Space Division in Sunnyvale, California, developed this unique propulsion system.

In late 1968, the Senior Bowl unit gained operational status and the 'A' Flight designation was changed to the 4200th Support Squadron. While the team had been stationed at the test site, civilian contractors had been busy remodelling the nose dock at Beale (located near the current site of the fuel cell and phase hangars) as the home for the new 4200th Support Squadron. In December 1969, the unit moved permanently to the remodelled quarters at Beale. The two Senior Bowl B-52Hs (serial numbers 61-0021 and 60-0036) were parked at the farthest point of the northern end of the ramp, near the alert facility.

There were three land-based locations where the team would most likely be sent TDY: Andersen AFB, Guam; Kadena AFB, Okinawa (as a backup to Andersen); or Hickam AFB, Hawaii. An assortment of Navy ships also served as destination points.

The first location, Andersen AFB, Guam, would receive and deploy the B-52H/D-21B aircraft as scheduled, and from there the B-52H/D-21B would depart on its mission. On a few occasions, however, the missions commenced directly from Beale, in which case Andersen AFB personnel would recover the B-52 following launch of the D-21B. If weather conditions prevented missions from Andersen, then Kadena AFB, Okinawa, would be considered the alternative launch site. Once the D-21B had completed its mission, the hatch would be brought to location number two, Hickam AFB, Hawaii, for equipment recovery operations.

The third location, a 'floating TDY' (usually a Liberty Ship or Navy destroyer), could perform secondary recovery operations of the hatch in the event the 'Cat's Whiskers' (a JC-130B Hercules equipped with a nose-mounted fork) was unable to snag the hatch.

Mission profile

Once the D-21B was installed on the B-52's pylon, the rocket booster was mounted to under the D-21B using the original connecting points where the D-21 had formerly been attached to the back of the M-21.

The B-52H, with its D-21B and booster mounted on the right pylon, was then ready to take off for a sortie. At a precise, pre-planned time and geographic location, the LCO onboard the B-52H would start the sequence of operations by first dropping the D-21B from the pylon. Following separation from the pylon, the booster would ignite and then propel the D-21B to a speed in excess of Mach 3.0, at or above 75,000 ft (22860 m). After a burn time of about 90 seconds, the booster would separate from the D-21B via explosive bolts, and the D-21B would begin its programmed solo sortie.

As the D-21B/booster dropped, automatic sequencing within the D-21B kicked in instantaneously. Approximately one to three seconds following the drop, the booster would ignite and the AFCS, INS, ADC and other systems inside the D-21B would follow their sequencing to start up the ramjet and propel the D-21B into proper trajectory. The AFCS had a very simple pitch programme, putting the D-21B into a steep climb and levelling off at the end of booster burn. At the end of the 90-second burn, the booster would be jettisoned, the programmed operations from the onboard computer would commence, and the D-21B would be on its way. Now all that could be done (other than a few actions remaining under control of the LCO) was to wait and hope. The most vital command the LCO could order was a signal for the destruc-tion of the D-21B, sent if conditions demanded instant destruction of the drone for safety and/or security reasons. The mission track was programmed into the INS, which provided steering commands to the roll channel of the AFCS. The ADC was pre-set to keep the D-21B flying at a fixed Mach number.

Once en route and over target, the payload/ camera equipment would begin operating and would continue functioning until the computer shut it down. The D-21B would then be vectored on to its final return leg. At an exact spot determined by the INS, the Marquardt engine would shut down and the vehicle would decelerate and enter a controlled descent to a lower altitude of about 60,000 ft (18288 m). At a pre-determined point, explosive bolts would fire and the hatch would be ejected. The hatch-less vehicle would then tumble on its way until an explosive charge went off, destroying the entire D-21B and leaving behind only a meaningless residue of ashes and debris.

After ejection, the hatch would drop to an altitude of about 15,000 ft (4572 m), when the drogue and main chute (attached to the inside of the hatch) would engage, trailing the hatch via cable a few hundred feet below the chute.

One of the Senior Bowl B-52Hs cruises with two D-21B 'Tags' aboard. This must have been a captive-carry test flight from Area 51: all cases of D-21 launches involved the carriage of a drone from the starboard pylon only.

There were calculated markings on the cable that the JC-130B would hopefully engage. The hatch would then be taken into the aircraft and delivered to location number two for recovery operations by 'A' Flight/4200th Support Squadron personnel.

If the JC-130B missed its target, the ship (location number three) would attempt recovery operations, performed by 'A' Flight/4200th Support Squadron staff members already on board. In the case of a successful recovery, the ship would return to port and the camera pallet would be sent to the photo analysis centre at Hickam AFB, Hawaii. Not once did the Navy successfully recover a hatch; it was always either recovered by the JC-130B or lost completely.

Operational launches

It is believed that all four operational launches targeted the People's Republic of China nuclear weapons test facility in remote west-central China, near Lop Nor.

The first operational launch (D-21B number 517, launched on 9 November 1969) did not successfully institute the return manoeuvre to take it back to the recovery area. Instead, the D-21B continued on a straight course and crashed somewhere in the wilderness of the former Soviet Union. The cause for this loss was later determined by Honeywell to have been an error build-up in the computation of sine/cosine routines in the nav system.

After the fall of the Soviet Union, Ben R. Rich (then retired president of Lockheed's Skunk Works) finally had an opportunity to tour Russia. While in Moscow, the KGB presented Rich with a gift of what it thought was the remains of a stealth fighter that had crashed in their territory. As it turned out, the wreckage was actually pieces of the lost D-21B.

The second operational mission was launched on 16 December 1970, flown by D-21B number 523. It completed its 2,648-nm (4904-km) trip only to lose its payload at sea, this time due to a partially failed parachute.

The third operational launch of a Senior Bowl D-21B occurred on 4 March 1971. D-21B number 526 flew the complete mission profile of 2,935 nm (5436 km), the JC-130B missed the aerial recovery due to damaged parachute lines, and the payload landed safely in the Pacific. Once in the water, it was the Navy's task to recover the package.

The Navy recovery ship failed to pick up the package on the first pass, so a Navy SEAL team was put into the water. The SEALs could not cut through the parachute cables, which had been reinforced with stainless steel wire. In standard Navy fashion, the recovery manoeuvre procedure was to approach the pallet from the windward side and drift towards the package. The problem was that the parachute (still attached) acted like a sea anchor, and when the recovery ship came beside the pallet, it drifted right over it. The result was that the only recoverable camera images from an operational mission were sunk at sea.

D-21B number 527 was launched on 20 March 1971 as the fourth and final mission. Experts at the 4200th Support Squadron and the Skunk Works concluded that number 527 must have malfunctioned; it was thought to have been shot down near Lop Nor.

James C. Goodall and Nora D. Goodall

Tagboard and Senior Bowl launches – D-21 flight log summary

Serial number	Launch date	Launch vehicle	Distance flown (nm/km)
Functional fit/captive flights			
501	19 June 1964	M-21/134	0
First fit check in building 309/310; no launch			
501	22 December 1964	M-21/134	0
First mated flight of M/D-21; no launch			
Tagboard launches			
502	5 March 1966	M-21/135	150/278
Crew – Park/Beswick			
506	27 April 1966	M-21/135	1,120/2074
Crew – Park/Torick			
505	16 June 1966	M-21/135	1,550/2870
Crew – Park/Beswick			
504	30 July 1966	M-21/135	0
Crew – Park/Torick. M-21/D-21 mid-air collision; Ray Torick lost his life; aircraft/drone lost; Tagboard programme cancelled			
Senior Bowl launches			
501	28 September 1967	B-52H	0
Drone fell off the B-52H pylon en route from the test site because of poor workmanship in trying to retap a stripped nut in the right forward attachment to the pylon; the booster fired			
507	6 November 1967	B-52H	134/248
The booster took the drone to altitude but the drone nosed over and dived in after a relatively short flight			
509	2 December 1967	B-52H	500/926
Drone flew only 500 nm, at a too-low altitude and too-slow speed; quit flying when it ran out of hydraulic fluid			
508	19 January 1968	B-52H	280/518
After a few minutes, number 508 went out of control and was lost			
511	10 April 1968	B-52H	0
An unsuccessful launch; the engine did not light			
512	16 June 1968	B-52H	2,850/5278
Very good launch; reached an altitude of over 90,000 ft (27432 m) and the hatch and camera were recovered; the engine blew out in turns but re-ignited in climb-back			
514	1 July 1968	B-52H	80/148
Engine did not light; nosed over and was lost			
516	28 August 1968	B-52H	78/144
Carried two drones from 'the area' to Kauai, HI; D-21 number 516 was put into a perfect launch position, but the Marquardt MA20S-4 did not light and it was lost			
515	15 December 1968	B-52H	2,953/5469
Hatch and camera recovered; photos okay			
518	11 February 1969	B-52H	751/1389
Loss thought to have been caused by water contamination in the autopilot			
519	10 May 1969	B-52H	2,753/5098
Hatch and camera recovered; photos fair			
520	10 July 1969	B-52H	2,937/5439
Drone flew the Captain Hook route extremely well; hatch and camera recovered; photos good (The programme had now met all of the design requirements and objectives to the point where the Air Force deemed the programme successful and completed up to the operational phase.)			
517	9 November 1969	B-52H	unknown
First operational mission; crashed in the former USSR; subsequently, Lockheed changed the navigation system programming to enable the drone to miss one destination checkpoint but still continue to the following one			
521	20 February 1970	B-52H	2,909/5387
Ran another Captain Hook mission with the new navigation programming; the D-21 performed superbly, reaching an altitude of over 95,000 ft (28956 m) and meeting all of its checkpoints within 2-3 nm (3.7-5.5 km); hatch and camera recovered; photos good			
523	16 December 1970	B-52H	2,648/4904
Second operational mission; hatch lost due to parachute failure			
526	4 March 1971	B-52H	2,935/5435
Third operational mission; drone returned after a fine flight. The parachute was damaged during descent with the hatch, however, and it fell slowly into the water. The hatch floated and the Navy arrived with the recovery ship. During the recovery operation, the hatch was run over by the Navy recovery ship and damaged to the point where it sank. Another Navy ship found the D-21 afloat but was unable to get cables around it before it also sank			
527	20 March 1971	B-52H	unknown
Fourth operational mission; aircraft shot down three-quarters of the way through its mission to overfly the Chinese nuclear test facility near Lop Nor			

Appendix B: Preserved aircraft

Northrop Tacit Blue

The only example of Northrop's stealth demonstrator for the BSAX battlefield surveillance concept is on display at the USAF Museum, where it arrived on 22 May 1996.

Tacit Blue	–	USAF Museum, Wright-Patterson AFB, Dayton, Ohio

Lockheed Martin F-117

Of the first five F-117s built for full-scale development testing, two have been retired and placed on display, including one on a pole at the south end of Nellis AFB.

F-117A/FSD	79-10780	Nellis AFB, Nevada
F-117A/FSD	79-10781	USAF Museum, Wright-Patterson AFB, Dayton, Ohio

Lockheed A-12 series

After retirement and replacement by the SR-71, the surviving A-12s were gathered together at Palmdale, where they were stored in a hangar for many years. With the ending of the SR-71 programme they were put up for museum display. An exception was the sole surviving YF-12A, which had arrived at the USAF Museum on 7 November 1979 following its retirement from NASA use, and for many years had been the only 'Blackbird' on museum display.

A-12	60-6924	Blackbird Air Park, Palmdale, California (AFFTC Museum)
A-12	60-6925	USS Intrepid Sea-Air-Space Museum, New York
A-12B	60-6927	California Museum of Science, Los Angeles, California
A-12	60-6930	Space and Rocket Center Museum, Huntsville, Alabama
A-12	60-6931	Minnesota ANG Museum, Minneapolis-St Paul, Minnesota
A-12	60-6933	San Diego Aerospace Museum, California
YF-12A	60-6935	USAF Museum, Wright-Patterson AFB, Dayton, Ohio
A-12	60-6937	Southern Museum of Flight, Birmingham, Alabama
A-12	60-6938	USS Alabama Battleship Museum, Mobile, Alabama
M-21	60-6940	Museum of Flight, Seattle, Washington

Lockheed SR-71

Although a small number of SR-71s were held back for potential NASA/USAF use, the majority were disposed of to museums after the 1990 retirement. Only one was sent overseas, to the Imperial War Museum's US aircraft collection at Duxford – close to the SR-71's regular operating location at Mildenhall. The aircraft which were retained for service were also put up for preservation later. NASA's two-seater (64-17956) was transferred to the Kalamazoo Air Zoo as recently as April 2003.

SR-71A	64-17951	Pima Air and Space Museum, Tucson, Arizona
SR-71A	64-17955	AFFTC Museum, Edwards AFB, California
SR-71B	64-17956/831	Kalamazoo Air Zoo, Kalamazoo, Michigan
SR-71A	64-17958	Museum of Aviation, Robins AFB, Georgia
SR-71A	64-17959	USAF Armament Museum, Eglin AFB, Florida
SR-71A	64-17960	Castle Air Museum, Castle Field, Merced, California
SR-71A	64-17961	Kansas Cosmosphere and Space Center, Hutchinson, Kansas
SR-71A	64-17962	American Air Museum, Duxford, England
SR-71A	64-17963	Beale AFB, California
SR-71A	64-17964	Strategic Air and Space Museum, Ashland, Nebraska
SR-71A	64-17967	NASA Dryden, Edwards AFB, California (in store, for 8th Air Force Museum, Barksdale, Louisiana)
SR-71A	64-17968	Virginia Aviation Museum, Richmond, Virginia
SR-71A	64-17971	Evergreen Aviation Museum, McMinnville, Oregon
SR-71A	64-17972	Steven F. Udvar-Hazy Center, National Air and Space Museum, Dulles Airport, Maryland
SR-71A	64-17973	Blackbird Air Park, Palmdale, California (USAF)
SR-71A	64-17975	March Field Museum, March ARB, Riverside, California
SR-71A	64-17976	USAF Museum, Wright-Patterson AFB, Dayton, Ohio
SR-71A	64-17979	USAF History and Tradition Museum, Lackland AFB, Florida
SR-71A	64-17980/844	NASA Dryden, Edwards AFB, California (on display)
SR-71C	64-17981	Hill Aerospace Museum, Hill AFB, Utah

Lockheed U-2

As all surviving second-generation U-2s remain in use, the museum population consists entirely of early aircraft. In the 1960s the Chinese pieced together the remains of no fewer than four U-2s shot down over their territory and placed them on display in Beijing. Only one of these remains today.

U-2C	56-6680	National Air and Space Museum, Washington, DC
U-2C	56-6681	Moffett Field Museum, California
U-2C	56-6682	Museum of Aviation, Robins AFB, Georgia
U-2C	56-6691	PRC Military Museum, Beijing (wreckage)
U-2CT	56-6692	American Air Museum, Duxford, England
U-2C	56-6701	Strategic Air and Space Museum, Ashland, Nebraska
U-2C	56-6707	Laughlin AFB, Texas
U-2C	56-6714	Beale AFB, California
U-2C	56-6716	Davis-Monthan AFB, Tucson, Arizona (on gate)
U-2D	56-6721	AFFTC, Edwards AFB, California
U-2D	56-6722	USAF Museum, Wright-Patterson AFB, Dayton, Ohio
U-2CT	56-6953	Bodø, Norway

NASA's last 'Blackbirds'

Above: NASA 844 (67-17980) was the last flying aircraft in the 'Blackbird' series, surviving on NASA experiments until grounded in 1999. It was subsequently placed on display outside the NASA Dryden Flight Research Facility at Edwards AFB. The last major task of the aircraft was to be the vehicle for the LASRE (Linear Aerospike SR-71 Experiment) programme, which mounted a 20 percent, half-span model of a lifting body shape for the X-33, which was intended to be the follow-on to the Space Shuttle until it was cancelled in March 2001. The LASRE test model included eight thrust cells of a linear aerospike engine. The first two test flights verified the aerodynamic behaviour of the 14,300-lb (6486-kg), 41-ft (12.5-m) assembly before experiments got under way. The two 'cold-flow' flights were used to check the propulsive system's plumbing by cycling gaseous helium and liquid nitrogen through the system. In the photo above water is dumped after the first 'cold-flow' flight on 4 March 1998. Three further flights were conducted in which the intended liquid oxygen fuel was cycled through the aerospike engine. Two 'hot' engine runs were completed on the ground, but the eighth flight – with a 'hot' engine firing inflight – was cancelled and the aircraft was grounded.

Left: Another view of 844 from its last year of operations (1999) shows the aircraft with an experimental test fixture mounted dorsally.

Right: 'Blackbird' on the move: the front fuselage section of NASA's SR-71B 831 (64-17956) prepares to leave the Dryden ramp on 24 March 2003 for the long cross-country haul to its new home at the Kalamazoo Air Zoo. This move virtually completed the disposition of the entire 'Blackbird' fleet: only '967 remained at Edwards in early 2003, awaiting the funds for its move to Barksdale AFB. NASA 831 had not flown since October 1997. Prior to its grounding it had been jointly used by the Administration and the USAF, and had been employed in the effort to retrain USAF crews following the decision to return the SR-71 to service in 1996.

INDEX

Picture acknowledgments

The publishers would like to thank the following individuals and organisations for their kind assistance in supplying photographs for this book.

6: Bill Sweetman. **7:** USAF. **8:** Northrop Grumman. **9:** Ted Carlson/Fotodynamics, Northrop Grumman. **11:** USAF/Tim Garrison, USAF, Northrop Grumman. **12:** Northrop Grumman (two), Bill Sweetman, USAF. **13:** USAF, Anthony D. Chong (two). **14:** Northrop Grumman, USAF/Bill Krause. **15:** Northrop Grumman. **16:** USAF, Northrop Grumman. **17-18:** Northrop Grumman. **19:** USAF/Dave Strong, Northrop Grumman. **22:** Northrop Grumman, TSgt Gary Howard/163ARW via Ted Carlson/Fotodynamics. **23:** Northrop Grumman. **24:** USAF (two). **25:** USAF. **26:** Bill Sweetman, James Benson. **27:** USAF, Northrop Grumman. **28:** Northrop Grumman. **29:** Northrop Grumman. **32:** USAF/SSgt Hamilton, USAF, USAF/Dave Strong. **33:** USAF, USAF/Davin Russell. **34-35:** USAF/Davin Russell. **36:** Robert Hewson, Dirk Geerts, USAF. **37:** USAF/Bill Krause, USAF/Davin Russell (two). **38:** Northrop Grumman. **39:** USAF, USAF/Davin Russell. **40:** via Robert F. Dorr, Robert Hewson (two), Northrop Grumman. **42:** USAF (three). **43:** USAF, USAF/Bill Krause (two). **44:** Randy Jolly (two), Geoff Stockle. **45:** Ted Carlson/Fotodynamics, Northrop Grumman. **46:** Northrop Grumman. **47:** Anthony D. Chong, Randy Jolly, Northrop Grumman. **48:** Northrop Grumman, Anthony D. Chong. **49:** USAF, Northrop Grumman. **50:** Anthony D. Chong (two). **51:** Warren Thompson (eleven), Northrop Grumman, Robert Hewson. **52:** USAF (three). **53:** Mark Farmer (two), USAF. **54:** USAF, Mark Farmer (two). **55:** Mark Farmer (four). **56:** Northrop Grumman, USAF. **57-59:** USAF. **60:** USAF (ten). **61:** USAF (two), Ted Carlson/Fotodynamics (two). **62-63:** Randy Jolly. **64-65:** Randy Jolly, US DoD via Randy Jolly. **66:** US DoD via Tim Ripley, US DoD. **67:** Randy Jolly, Lockheed. **68-69:** Lockheed. **71-73:** Lockheed. **74:** Lockheed (two). **75:** David Donald, Lockheed. **78:** Jim Dunn via René J. Francillon. **79:** Lockheed, Ted Carlson/Fotodynamics. **80:** Lockheed, US DoD via Randy Jolly. **81:** Lockheed. **82:** Lockheed, Randy Jolly, David Donald. **83:** Lockheed, Frederick Sutter. **84:** Lockheed (two). **85:** Lockheed, David Donald. **86:** Lockheed (two). **87:** Lockheed (two). **90:** Flightline/Chuck Lloyd, James Benson. **91:** Randy Jolly, John Gourley. **92:** Randy Jolly (two). **93:** Randy Jolly. **94:** Randy Jolly, Ted Carlson/Fotodynamics. **95:** Lockheed, Randy Jolly. **96:** Frederick Sutter, P. Martin. **97:** Flightline/Chuck Lloyd. **98-100:** US DoD via Randy Jolly. **101:** US DoD via Randy Jolly (two), US DoD. **104:** David Donald. **105:** 49FW/PA, Randy Jolly. **106:** R.A. Cooper (two). **107:** Lockheed (two). **108-109:** Randy Jolly (two), James Benson. **110:** Randy Jolly, US DoD, Bill Turner, David Donald, Ted Carlson/Fotodynamics, US DoD via Randy Jolly. **112:** Ted Carlson/Fotodynamics (two), Randy Jolly. **113:** Randy Jolly. **114:** Ted Carlson/Fotodynamics, Randy Jolly. **115-121:** US Air Force. **122-125:** Randy Jolly. **126:** Steven D. Eisner (three), René J. Francillon, Lockheed. **127:** René J. Francillon (three), Randy Jolly. **128:** Randy Jolly (two), René J. Francillon, John Gourley. **129:** Randy Jolly (two), Chris Lofting. **130-131:** Lockheed, Paul F. Crickmore. **132:** Paul F. Crickmore (two). **133:** Lockheed via Jay Miller via Paul F. Crickmore (five), James C. Goodall Collection (two). **134:** Lockheed via Jay Miller via Paul F. Crickmore, James C. Goodall Collection (four). **135:** Paul F. Crickmore, James C. Goodall Collection (two). **136:** Lockheed via Jay Miller via Paul F. Crickmore, James C. Goodall Collection, Paul F. Crickmore (three). **137:** James C. Goodall Collection (two), Lockheed, Paul F. Crickmore. **138:** Paul F. Crickmore (two), USAF via James C. Goodall, Lockheed. **139:** Lockheed via Paul F. Crickmore (four). **140:** Lockheed via Paul F. Crickmore (three), Lockheed via Jay Miller via Paul F. Crickmore. **142:** James C. Goodall Collection (four), Lockheed via Jay Miller via Paul F. Crickmore (two). **143:** Jim Eastham via Paul F. Crickmore, Lockheed via Paul F. Crickmore, Lockheed, USAF, James C. Goodall Collection. **144:** Jim Eastham via Paul F. Crickmore, Hughes via Paul F. Crickmore, Paul F. Crickmore (two), Norm E. Taylor via Paul F. Crickmore, James C. Goodall Collection, Lockheed via Jay Miller via Paul F. Crickmore. **145:** James C. Goodall Collection (four). **146:** Lockheed (four). **147:** Lockheed, USAF, James C. Goodall Collection. **148:** Lockheed (three), James C. Goodall Collection. **149:** NASA (two), James C. Goodall Collection, NASA via Paul F. Crickmore. **150:** James C. Goodall Collection, Lockheed (four). **151:** Lockheed via Paul F. Crickmore (two), Lockheed (two). **152:** NASA via Paul F. Crickmore, James C. Goodall Collection (two), Lockheed, USAF. **153:** Lockheed, USAF, Paul F. Crickmore. **154:** B. Bailey via David Donald (three), Lockheed via Paul F. Crickmore, USAF via James C. Goodall. **155:** Lockheed (four). **156:** Lockheed, USAF. **157:** James C. Goodall Collection (two), Paul F. Crickmore. **158:** D.M. Brown via Paul F. Crickmore, Lockheed (three), David Donald. **159:** Lockheed (two), David Donald. **160:** via Paul F. Crickmore (five). **162:** USAF, Tom Pugh via Paul F. Crickmore, Lockheed, James C. Goodall Collection. **163:** USAF (two), GIFAS, Aerospace, Lockheed. **164:** Lockheed via Paul F. Crickmore, USAF, Paul F. Crickmore. **165:** James C. Goodall Collection (three). **166:** Paul F. Crickmore, USAF. **167:** Paul F. Crickmore (two), USAF via Paul F. Crickmore. **168:** Paul F. Crickmore, USAF, Lockheed. **169:** David Donald, Paul F. Crickmore, MoD via Paul F. Crickmore, via David Donald. **170:** Paul F. Crickmore, USAF (two), DoD via Paul F. Crickmore (two). **171:** Lockheed (two), USAF, Paul F. Crickmore (four). **174:** Lockheed, Paul F. Crickmore. **175:** Lockheed via Paul F. Crickmore (two), Paul F. Crickmore (two). **176:** NASA via Paul F. Crickmore, NASA (three). **177:** NASA via Paul F. Crickmore, NASA (three). **178:** Lockheed, USAF, NASA via Paul F. Crickmore (two). **179:** James C. Goodall, David Donald (two), Lockheed (two), USAF, Ted Carlson/Fotodynamics. **180:** Lockheed, David Donald (two). **181:** Don Emmons via Paul F. Crickmore (two), Lockheed (two). **182:** James C. Goodall (six), James C. Goodall Collection (three), Lockheed. **183:** David Donald, James C. Goodall (four), James C. Goodall Collection (three), Paul F. Crickmore. **184:** Paul F. Crickmore (three). **185:** Pratt & Whitney, Paul F. Crickmore (five), David Donald (two). **186:** Paul F. Crickmore (eight), Lindsay Peacock via Paul F. Crickmore. **187:** Jim Winchester (two), Paul F. Crickmore (three), Ted Carlson/Fotodynamics, NASA. **188:** Paul F. Crickmore (two), USAF, NASA. **189:** Lockheed (three), NASA, Lockheed via Paul F. Crickmore, USAF via Paul F. Crickmore, USAF (two), Marysville Appeal-Democrat via Paul F. Crickmore, James C. Goodall Collection. **190:** David Donald (two), Lockheed (three), L. Peacock via Paul F. Crickmore, USAF via Paul F. Crickmore, Paul F. Crickmore, James C. Goodall Collection (two). **191:** Chris Ryan (two), Paul F. Crickmore (two), Lockheed (two), USAF (two), Marysville Appeal-Democrat via Paul F. Crickmore, David Donald, James C. Goodall Collection. **192-193:** Lockheed Martin, via Chris Pocock. **194:** Lockheed Martin (two). **195:** Lockheed Martin (two), LADC via Chris Pocock, Lockheed Martin. **196:** via Chris Pocock, Lockheed Martin. **197:** Lockheed Martin (three). **198:** Lockheed Martin (four). **199:** Lockheed Martin, via Chris Pocock, LADC via Chris Pocock (two). **200:** 100th SRW via David Donald (two), Bruce Bailey via David Donald. **201:** Chris Pocock (two), Bob Archer via Chris Pocock. **202:** LADC via Chris Pocock, USAF, Lockheed Martin. **203:** Lockheed Martin (two), USAF. **204:** Lockheed Martin, Ted Carlson (four), Steven D. Eisner (three). **205:** Lockheed Martin via Chris Pocock (two). **206:** Lockheed Martin, NARA via Chris Pocock (two). **207:** Aerospace, Lockheed Martin, MAP. **208:** NASA via Chris Pocock, Lockheed Martin. **209:** Lockheed Martin (two). **210:** Robert E. Kling, John Gourley (three). **211:** John Gourley, Doug Youngblood (two), Robert E. Kling, Bob Burns, NASA (two). **212:** Lockheed Martin (two). **213:** Peter R. Foster, Randy Jolly, Chris Pocock. **214:** Ted Carlson/Fotodynamics, Steven D. Eisner, Randy Jolly. **215:** Lockheed Martin, Steven D. Eisner. **216:** Steven D. Eisner, Ted Carlson/Fotodynamics. **217:** Randy Jolly, Lockheed Martin (two), Ted Carlson/Fotodynamics (four), Joe Cupido. **218:** Peter R. Foster, Chris Ryan. **219:** David Donald, Robert E. Kling. **220:** Peter R. Foster, Lockheed Martin. **221:** Lockheed Martin via Chris Pocock (three), Hughes Radar Systems Group via Chris Pocock (two), via Chris Pocock, USAF via Chris Pocock, Lockheed Martin. **222:** Peter R. Foster, Richard Gennis. **223:** Lockheed Martin via Chris Pocock, Richard Gennis. **224:** via Chris Pocock, Joe Cupido, Randy Jolly. **225:** Randy Jolly, via Chris Pocock. **226:** Ted Carlson/Fotodynamics (two). **227:** Lockheed Martin. **228-229:** Ted Carlson/Fotodynamics (four). **230:** Lockheed Martin, Ted Carlson/Fotodynamics. **231:** Lockheed Martin (three). **234:** Jeremy Flack/API, Frederic Lert. **235:** Frederic Lert (three). **236:** Lockheed Martin. **237:** Ted Carlson/Fotodynamics (two). **238:** Chris Pocock (three). **239-241:** Lockheed Martin via Chris Pocock. **242:** Lockheed Martin via Chris Pocock, USAF. **243:** USAF (two), via Chris Pocock. **244:** John Gourley, Dana Bell, Robert E. Kling, Hendrik J. van Broekhuizen, Chris Wheatley via Chris Pocock, Richard Gennis, David Donald (four). **245:** via Chris Pocock, Randy Jolly (six), David Donald (two). **246:** Ted Carlson/Fotodynamics (three), Steven D. Eisner (two). **247:** Randy Jolly, Stephen Kill, via Chris Pocock (three). **248-250:** Jim Goodall Collection. **253:** NASA (three).